SOCIAL LEGITIMACY IN THE INTERNAL MARKET

This book is concerned with the social legitimacy of internal market law. What does social legitimacy entail within the multi-level 'embedded liberalism' construction of the internal market? How can the objectives of the internal market that focus on economic rights and a commitment to social diversity both be pursued without one necessarily trumping the other? These questions continue to challenge the very core of European integration. How can the diversity of Member States' 'social systems' and the varying normative infrastructure of their economies be sustainably accommodated within the internal market? This book seeks to contribute to these questions by discussing what has come to be known as the argument from transnational effects and the development of an adjudicative model for the European Court of Justice that can be termed 'socially responsive'. Drawing on the historical insights of Karl Polanyi it argues that the internal market can only be held to be socially legitimate where it supports the requirement for further market integration while still responding to social practices and values within the member states. The book presents in-depth studies of the case law of the Court in the areas of EU free movement, competition and state aid law. In so doing, this important new study aims to provide the language and tools for assessing social legitimacy in the internal market.

Volume 86 in the Series Modern Studies in European Law

Modern Studies in European Law

Recent titles in this series:

Family Reunification in the EU
Chiara Berneri

EU Liability and International Economic Law
Armin Steinbach

The EU and Nanotechnologies: A Critical Analysis
Tanja Ehnert

Human Rights Between Law and Politics:
The Margin of Appreciation in Post-National Contexts
Edited by Petr Agha

The European Union and Social Security Law
Jaan Paju

The Rule of Law in the European Union: The Internal Dimension
Theodore Konstadinides

The Division of Competences between the EU and the Member States: Reflections on the Past, the Present and the Future
Edited by Sacha Garben and Inge Govaere

Unity in Adversity: EU Citizenship, Social Justice and the Cautionary Tale of the UK
Charlotte O'Brien

The Use of Force and Article 2 of the ECHR in Light of European Conflicts
Hannah Russell

Environmental Crime in Europe
Edited by Andrew Farmer, Michael Faure and Grazia Maria Vagliasindi

Questioning EU Citizenship: Judges and the Limits of Free Movement and Solidarity in the EU
Edited by Daniel Thym

The European Union under Transnational Law: A Pluralist Appraisal
Matej Avbelj

Illegally Staying in the EU: An Analysis of Illegality in EU Migration Law
Benedita Menezes Queiroz

For the complete list of titles in this series, see 'Modern Studies in European Law' link at www.bloomsburyprofessional.com/uk/series/modern-studies-in-european-law

Social Legitimacy in the Internal Market

A Dialogue of Mutual Responsiveness

Jotte Mulder

•HART•
OXFORD • LONDON • NEW YORK • NEW DELHI • SYDNEY

HART PUBLISHING
Bloomsbury Publishing Plc
Kemp House, Chawley Park, Cumnor Hill, Oxford, OX2 9PH, UK

HART PUBLISHING, the Hart/Stag logo, BLOOMSBURY and the Diana logo are trademarks of Bloomsbury Publishing Plc

First published in Great Britain 2018

A catalogue record for this book is available from the British Library.

Library of Congress Cataloging-in-Publication Data

Names: Mulder, Jotte, 1981- author.

Title: Social legitimacy in the internal market : a dialogue of mutual responsiveness / Jotte Mulder.

Description: Oxford ; Portland. Oregon : Hart Publishing, 2018. | Series: Modern studies in European law ; volume 86 | Based on author's thesis (doctoral—European University Institute, Florence, 2016). | Includes bibliographical references and index.

Identifiers: LCCN 2017058626 (print) | LCCN 2017059589 (ebook) | ISBN 9781509914548 (Epub) | ISBN 9781509914531 (hardback : alk. paper)

Subjects: LCSH: Law—Social aspects—European Union countries.

Classification: LCC KJE947 (ebook) | LCC KJE947 .M85 2018 (print) | DDC 343.2408—dc23

LC record available at https://lccn.loc.gov/2017058626

ISBN:	HB:	978-1-50991-453-1
	ePDF:	978-1-50991-455-5
	ePub:	978-1-50991-454-8

Typeset by Compuscript Ltd, Shannon

To find out more about our authors and books visit www.hartpublishing.co.uk. Here you will find extracts, author information, details of forthcoming events and the option to sign up for our newsletters.

Foreword

CHRISTIAN JOERGES*

This is a timely book of topical importance. Both attributes relate to the highly uncomfortable state of the Union. After years of financial crisis to which Europe has reacted with ever more hectic responses, we are far from regaining a new state of normalcy. Quite to the contrary, observes Jürgen Habermas, the most prestigious and prominent among the defenders of the European project, these politics have created new asymmetries and new tensions because of their 'palpable, indeed glaring social injustice'.[1] The philosopher's wake-up call resonates strongly in recent political initiatives, most visibly in the campaign of the Commission for a 'Pillar of Social Rights'.[2] So much for the topicality of the 'social legitimacy' *problématique*. Its timeliness stems from another less clearly visible challenge, namely, the need to re-think what we were once so sure about. This crisis and its impact confront us, to turn Bruce Ackerman's seminal notion[3] upside down, with an *un-constitutional* moment: a dilemma which we have to understand as a *theoretical* moment, in which Europe has to re-invent itself.

This is, of course, a task of proportions which are beyond the potential of a one single book—and beyond the author's ambitions. And yet, what this work envisages is an important step towards a renewal of the ideational basis of the 'social legitimacy', or the lack thereof, in the dominating understanding linked to the legacy of the post-war European welfare state.[4] This legacy eroded, according to Fritz Scharpf's diagnosis, through a 'decoupling' of European market-building from the embeddedness of Europe's formerly national economies in the broad variety of national welfare regimes.[5] For a reversal of this process, we would need a response at European level. The establishment of a 'European social model' has

* Christian Joerges is Professor of Law and Society at the Hertie School of Governance in Berlin, and Co-Director of the Centre of European Law and Politics at the University of Bremen.

[1] J Habermas, 'Democracy in Europe: Why the Development of the EU into a Transnational Democracy Is Necessary and How It Is Possible', (2015) 21 *European Law Journal*, 546–547, at 551.

[2] https://ec.europa.eu/commission/priorities/deeper-and-fairer-economic-and-monetary-union/european-pillar-social-rights/european-pillar-social-rights-20-principles_en.

[3] B Ackerman, "The Storrs Lectures: Discovering the Constitution, (1984) 93 *Yale LJ* 1013–1072 (1984) and id, 'Constitutional Politics/Constitutional Law' (1989) *Faculty Scholarship Series* Paper 140. http://digitalcommons.law.yale.edu/fss_papers/140.

[4] See for just one pertinent example D Kochenov, G de Búrca and A Williams (eds), *Europe's Justice Deficit* (Oxford, Hart Publishing, 2015).

[5] FW Scharpf, 'The European Social Model: Coping with the Challenges of Diversity' (2002) 40 *Journal of Common Market Studies* 645, 646.

been advocated relentlessly for decades. The recent campaign for a 'European pillar of social rights' is nothing new in principle, nor is, *hélas*, the futility of all endeavours with comprehensive ambitions. Mulder's approach is so innovative and important here because he re-conceptualises the challenges of 'the social' in the integration project.

His re-conceptualisation departs from the foundational idea and promise of what was then the European Economic Community. Peace *and* welfare will go hand in hand, market integration will enhance the welfare of all Europeans. It will do this without the destruction of the welfare regimes which had been established after the Second World War. This was the *communis opinion* in the golden age of embedded liberalism shared by progressive economists[6] and renowned political scientists.[7] It was an ideational background and source from which the European Court of Justice, leading academics, and an influential network of experts inferred the establishment of a body of law to which they assigned constitutional validity.[8] 'Integration through law' became the trademark and the agenda of European legal studies, and it has dominated the mindset of generations of lawyers.

This success was phenomenal. But the whole legal edifice stood on shaky grounds. How could one assume that more uniformity would not only facilitate trade but also ensure normative progress? How could one disregard the disintegrative effects of the necessarily selective interventions into national legal systems?[9] How could the integration through law orthodoxy remain so attractive in a post-formalist era in which 'law and …' studies had become *en vogue* and the European University Institute asked its students to look at the law 'in its political, economic and social context'? With the benefits of hindsight, we can understand both the disregard for such objections in the formative stage of the integration project and the irritating impact that they were bound to unfold in their later stages.

This, however, is not yet the gist of the matter. The book digs much deeper. It questions the adequacy of the market/politics dichotomy on which the whole debate on the social deficit of the integration project is premised. This is a premise deeply engraved in the legal re-construction of the relations between politics and economics. 'The economic' is conceptualised as an unpolitical, more or less autonomous, sphere. The great theoretical divide is between those who believe in the stability and fairness of market processes, and those who question such harmony

[6] Most famously the 'Ohlin Report' of the International Labour Organisation, 'Social Aspects of European Economic Co-operation. Report by a Group of Experts', in (1956) *International Labour Review* 74, 99–123.

[7] JG Ruggie, 'International Regimes, Transactions and Change: Embedded Liberalism in the Postwar Economic Order', (1982) 36 *International Organization*, 375–415.

[8] A Vauchez, *L'Union par le droit. L'invention d'un programme institutionnel pour l'Europe*, (Paris, Presses de Sciences Po 2013); A Boerger and M Rasmussen, 'Transforming European Law: The Establishment of the Constitutional Discourse from 1950 to 1993', (2014) 10 *European Constitutional Law Review* 199–225.

[9] G Calabresi, *A Common Law in the Age of Statutes* (Cambridge MA, Harvard University Press, 1985).

and assume, instead, a need for the political stabilisation of economic processes and authoritative corrections of market outcomes so as to achieve social justice. Against this background, it seems but logical that the defenders of the welfare state insist on a transfer of pertinent legislative powers and regulatory capacities to the European level. The quest for the establishment of a European *Sozialstaat*, Mulder submits, is not only politically illusionary, but also conceptually flawed. The conceptual inadequacy does not come to the fore in the above-mentioned re-construction of the foundational equilibrium between national welfare regimes and the opening of the formerly national economies which prevailed in the 'golden age of embedded liberalism'. That age is gone forever for two interdependent reasons. One is the success of the 'integration-through-law' agenda, which has promoted the deepening of economic integration without providing for an equivalent social integration. The other is the deepening of Europe's socio-economic diversity. This diversity is an obvious and unavoidable implication of the enormous enlargement of the Union after the break-up of the former Soviet Union. Equally important, albeit more surprising, is the deepening of socio-economic diversity among the 'old' Member States, even and in particular those 'whose currency is the euro'.

This observation is the turning-point at which both the original complacency and the later/successive quest for a deepening of Europe's commitments to social justice through the Europeanisation of the welfare state is replaced by a theoretical re-orientation of paradigmatic dimensions. The focus of this re-orientation is the core of all European endeavours since the establishment the European Economic Community, the move from the 'common' to the 'internal' market and the consummation of all these market-building efforts with the common currency. The guidance on which Mulder relies is economic sociology in the tradition of a century-old classic, namely, Karl Polanyi's *Great Transformation*.[10] 'We are all Polanyians now', proclaimed Germany's leading authority in this discipline a decade ago.[11] He is certainly wrong as far as we the lawyers are concerned. But there are many good reasons to overcome the complacency of legal scholarship and there are signals that these reasons are by now more widely understood.[12] The most important one is explained lucidly in Mulder's introductory chapter: in Karl Polanyi's account, markets are anything but mechanically-functioning entities; instead, they represent socially-embedded institutions. There is more to this insight than a mere reference to the dependence of markets on institutional frameworks. The notion of 'social embeddedness' discredits the dominating understanding of markets as unrealistic and fictitious. The working of markets

10 K Polanyi: *The Great Transformation. The Political and Economic Origins of Our Time* [1944], 2nd edn. (Boston, MA, The Beacon Press 2001).

11 J Beckert, '*The Great Transformation of Embeddedness: Karl Polanyi and the New Economic Sociology*'. MPIfG Discussion Paper 07/1, Cologne 2007, 7.

12 Pertinent citation can be found throughout the book. I would add an enormously insightful non-lawyer: S. Frerichs, 'The Rule of the Market: Economic Constitutionalism Understood Sociologically', in P Blokker and C Thornhill (eds), *Sociological Constitutionalism* (Cambridge, CUP 2017) 241–264.

depends, to paraphrase Böckenförde's famous insight about the life of democratic constitutions, on political and cultural conditions which they, the markets, cannot create themselves.[13] The dominant understanding of the economy-society relationship is a fundamental misunderstanding:

> Ultimately that is why the control of the economic system by the market is of overwhelming consequence to the whole organization of society: it means no less than the running of society as an adjunct to the market. Instead of economy being embedded in social relations, social relations are embedded in the economic system.[14]

Polanyi's message is not just sociological. His economic sociology has normative implications. Through awareness of the cultural and sociological infrastructure, 'the economic' will (or should!) strengthen the sensitivity for the failures of legal formalism, the tensions between policy programmes and their implementation, and we will, to come back to the beginning, understand why the project of 'integration through law' with its insistence on ever more legal unity and its disregard for the societal underpinnings legal rules and institutions is so thoroughly misconceived. Long before the financial crisis taught us this lesson, Gunther Teubner had explained, in a seminal essay, 'how unifying law ends up in new differences'.[15] Again, this is not just a sociological finding. The 'integration through law' agenda with its one-size-fits-all philosophy is not only sociologically, but also normatively, flawed because of its disregard of the normative infrastructure of the economy. As Mulder rightly underlines, the normative fabric of our economic orders is a 'social *acquis*' which is, of course, subject to changes, but nonetheless deserves to be protected against willful and destructive intrusions.

This conclusion may sound simply protective, conservative, or merely 'nostalgic' as Habermas has put it in an angry response to Wolfgang Streeck.[16] With this critique, the great philosopher rephrases his plea for a transnational democracy which seeks to protect 'the social' through a deepening of European integration. Is there no alternative? Very remarkably, Polanyi has anticipated precisely such a perspective. The pertinent passage reads:

> [G]overnments will find it possible to … tolerate willingly that other nations shape their domestic institutions according to their inclinations, thus transcending the pernicious nineteenth century dogma of the necessary uniformity of domestic regimes within the orbit of world economy. Out of the ruins of the Old World, cornerstones of the New can be seen to emerge: economic collaboration of governments and the liberty to organize national life at will.[17]

[13] 'Der freiheitliche, säkularisierte Staat lebt von Voraussetzungen, die er selbst nicht garantieren kann', E-W Böckenförde, *Staat, Gesellschaft, Freiheit* (Frankfurt aM: Suhrkamp 1976) 60.

[14] Polanyi (n 10) 60.

[15] 'Legal Irritants: Good Faith in British Law or How Unifying Law Ends up in New Differences', (1998) 61 *Modern Law Review* 11–32.

[16] J Habermas, "Demokratie oder Kapitalismus? Vom Elend der nationalstaatlichen Fragmentierung ineiner kapitalistisch integrierten Weltgesellschaft", (2013) *Blätter für deutsche und internationale Politik*. 68–70.

[17] Polanyi (n 10) 253–254.

Mulder does not cite this particular passage, but he endorses its messages and develops them further. Polanyi had lived through the fascist transformation of European market societies. In 1944, he envisioned another transformation, a 'countermovement' through which societies would protect themselves against the destructive social effects of commodification and marketisation. Polanyi had obviously realised that such a defence would have to overcome what contemporary political scientists and international relations scholars criticise as 'methodological nationalism'.[18] This is to say, under conditions of Europeanisation and globalisation, it will no longer be reasonable and not even possible to treat the nation state as an autonomous unity which would function in splendid isolation. The implication of this insight is that we have to promote and defend 'the social' in a twofold perspective. We certainly have to continue to care for social justice within our respective polities, but we also have, by the same token, to take the exposure of our polities to 'the others' into account, and consider the impact of our political and economic activities beyond our borders.

It is obvious from all my preceding remarks that I see and appreciate many affinities between this book and my own work. What I appreciate most highly, however, are not these *Geistesverwandtschaften*, but the innovative move forward which Mulder undertakes with his plea for 'mutual responsiveness': this is a promising theoretical perspective for a re-construction of 'the social' in the European project. Mulder substantiates his key concept first through three 'normative standards': 'the interplay of principles of substantive efficiency, margins of discretion and good governance in free movement adjudication'. This 'interplay' contrasts more sharply with the orthodoxy of the integration through law doctrines than with my own 'reconceptualisation of European law as conflicts law'. It is a more open-ended approach but not one which invites the Euripoean judiciary to discretionary exercises, but seeks, instead, to both structure *and* discipline the evaluation of a highly specific conflicts-constellation in an 'ever more diverse' Union. Mulder does not claim that litigation and adjudication will generate a new 'system'. What he does claim and then convincingly documents is the re-constructive potential and validity of the normative standards which guide his analyses in a series of exemplary studies on free movment law and the various sub-disciplines of European competition law and policy. I refrain from commenting on the subtleties of these explorative deliberations in any detail, but note that the complex variety of complex constellations becomes as plainly visible as the need for constructive conflict mitigation. In particular, the use of the proportionality principle seems to be susceptible to such interpretations. There is encouraging evidence for the validity of re-constructions which discern the propensity of the CJEU towards 'a dialogue of mutual responsiveness'.

[18] M Zürn, 'Globalization and Global Governance', in H Enderlein, S Wälti and M Zürn (eds), *Social Science Handbook on multi-level governance* (Cheltenham, Edward Elgar, 2010) 80–99.

To come back to the beginnings of these remarks: the financial crisis and the following cascade of further threatening developments necessitate a reconceptualisation of the integration project. The alternative, simply to legalise what has happened as Europe's new normalcy, is to transform these challenges into a 'theoretical moment' and embark upon largely unchartered waters. This book provides guidance.

Acknowledgements

The foundation of this book is based on my PhD thesis. The journey towards completion was not a linear process and, perhaps necessarily not so. I have strayed away many times from the work that is eventually presented here and I suspect that I have written and then discarded another half-book. In a more favourable reading: I have decided to park a lot of ideas for potential future research. I lost about six months of working and thinking on Michel Foucault and developing a 'governmentality' approach to internal market law. Also, I still hope one day to reap the full benefits of attending additional training on critical discourse analysis. Although one might see these intellectual outings as a loss since they have not been, with the exception of a footnote here and there, included here, I would highly recommend such outings for the young academic mind because it sows benefits of a more hidden and subtle nature. They shape and 'embed' the academic mind-set, contributing to the development of a certain individualised 'voice' and will determine, I am sure, much of my future choices of academic work. Although not included here, all my intellectual straying was certainly not a 'deadweight loss'.

The principal person responsible for, eventually, nudging me to the path that has led to a manageable and measured project is my PhD-supervisor, Giorgio Monti. Supervision is a delicate process that ideally allows for some level of intellectual straying but should also put tangible limits to it. I clearly remember an eerie moment during my PhD where nearly all works I passed by in the library seemed somehow relevant to me. Luckily, the necessary limits arose fluently and quickly on the basis of Giorgio's natural aversion to the nebulous over-usage of concepts and his near *clairvoyance* to foresee the potential and limitations of a line of argumentation. These have been the crucial elements that allowed me to complete and now present this work and I owe much of what is good in this book to the dedication, professionalism, level of detail and effort that Giorgio has put in supervising my work.

There are many occasions when I have benefited enormously from comments on my work both within and outside the European University Institute. Within the EUI, in particular comments and instructions from Loïc Azoulai and Claire Kilpatrick have made a lasting impact. Outside of the EUI, I have greatly benefited from a research visit to the Copenhagen Business School, where I was able to tap from the deep theoretical insights of Poul Kjaer on 'governing and governance'. Christian Joerges has been an immense source of inspiration, both through his work, to which this book is profoundly endowed, and on the basis of his enduring positive encouragement for this project, throughout the process, from the very beginning.

The project could not have been undertaken without the financial support of the Dutch government (the grant authority Nuffic) or without the financial support of the EUI for mission funding. I have also benefited from a grant of the Hijmansbeurs at the University of Amsterdam to develop my original research ideas, with the support of Rein Wesseling. The EUI is an immensely stimulating academic environment, with excellent seminars, dedicated to creating the conditions for researchers to commit fully to developing their ideas. Specifically, the excellent library services and, not to think lightly of, the outstanding lunch made available in the canteen, have made the whole experience quite agreeable.

However, the biggest surprise and most unexpected gift I shall cherish from this adventure is not of an intellectual but more ubiquitous nature. That I have found my Noelle, my love (and my favourite proofreader) and that we have now together found Ezra has made it all worthwhile.

JM

Contents

Foreword by Christian Joerges......v
Acknowledgements......xi
Abbreviations......xvii

Introduction......1
I. Background......1
II. The Argument......8
III. Approach......13
IV. Outlook and Contribution......15

1. Social Legitimacy, the Social Sphere and Embeddedness within the Internal Market......19
I. The Normative Framework of Social Legitimacy......19
II. The Social Sphere within the Internal Market......23
A. The 'Positive' Social Sphere in the Internal Market......26
B. The Internal Market Rules as a Negative Contingent Form for the Social Sphere......29
C. The Value of Social Diversity......31
D. Social Legitimacy through Responsiveness......32
III. The Instructive Value of Embeddedness......34
A. Notes on Polanyi......35
B. The Enduring Relevance of Polanyi......38
C. Embeddedness and the Double-movement......40
D. A Rationale of Responsiveness: Moving beyond Polanyi?......42
E. Polanyi in Luxembourg?......45
IV. Transnational Effects and the Legitimacy of the Social Deficit......49
A. Joerges and Maduro......49
B. Somek's Fundamental Challenge......53
C. The Constitutional Obligation of Responsiveness......54
V. Social Legitimacy in the Context of Internal Market Adjudication......57
A. (E)valuation and the Expressive Function of Internal Market Law as a Dialogue of Mutual Responsiveness......57
VI. Outlook......63

2. Social Legitimacy in EU Free Movement Law......66
I. Introduction......66
II. Valuation, Indeterminacy and Incommensurability in Free Movement Adjudication......68

A. Organisational Principles within EU Free Movement Law 68
B. The Expedient 'Rights Inflation' Proportionality Model in EU Free Movement Adjudication 72
C. The Structure of Proportionality 81
III. The Proportionality Analysis of the Court 83
A. Substantive Efficiency Model 84
B. The Margin of Discretion Model 89
C. The Procedural Good Governance Model 91
D. Incoherence in the Application of the Different Rationales 100
IV. A Dialogue of Mutual Responsiveness 102
A. Between Managerialism, Margins of Discretion and Good Governance: A Responsive Model 102
B. *Volkswagen*: Valuing the '*Social acquis*' of a Member State within the Internal Market 103
C. *Omega*: The Importance of *Mutual* Responsiveness in the Pursuit of Legitimate Objectives 105
D. *Viking*: Recognising the Substantive Limits of the Internal Market 106
V. Conclusion 109

3. Social Legitimacy in EU Competition Law 113
I. Introduction 113
II. Valuation, Indeterminacy and Incommensurability in EU Competition Law 118
A. Economisation and Modernisation of EU Competition Law 118
B. Goals of Competition Law 121
C. Non-competition Interests within Competition Law Assessments 123
D. The Problem of Indeterminacy and the Expressive Value of Competition Law 126
E. Competition Law as a Platform for Societal Dialogue 133
F. Irreconcilable Conflicts within Competition Law 134
i. The Friesian Horse: The Legitimacy of Private-led Public Interest Objectives 136
ii. The Energy Agreement for Sustainable Growth: The Societal Relevance of the Process or the Rationality of its Outcome? 138
iii. The Chicken of Tomorrow: The Market Rules When the State Retracts? 141
G. The Consumerist Push from the Commission 144
III. Responsiveness in the Case Law of the Court 146
A. The *Albany* Building Block: Valuation of Different Social Spheres 147
B. *Poucet and Pistre* Building Block: A Rationale for the Alternative Valuation of a Non-economic Social Sphere (Part One) 149

C. *Wouters*: A Rationale for the Alternative Valuation of a Non-economic Social Sphere (Part Two) 155
D. The Requirements of *Mutual* Responsiveness in *Arduino, Cipolla* and *Mauri* 160
IV. A Dialogue of Mutual Responsiveness 163
A. A Return to the Case Studies on the Basis of Mutual Responsiveness 165
i. The Friesian Horse 165
ii. Mutual Responsiveness in the Energy Agreement for Sustainable Growth 167
iii. Mutual Responsiveness in the Chicken of Tomorrow Case 168
V. Conclusion 169

4. Social Legitimacy in EU State Aid Law 171
I. Introduction 171
II. Valuation, Indeterminacy and Incommensurability in State Aid Law 172
A. The Proceduralisation of the State Aid Rules 174
B. Modes of Valuation in State Aid: Market versus Regulation 180
C. The Expedient Nature of Market-derived Standards within State Aid Law 181
D. The Potential Expedient Scope of the Market Economy Operator Principle (Part One): The Absence of Rationale for Genuine Regulation versus the Clear Rationale of a Private Investor/Creditor 184
E. The Scope of the Market Economy Operator Principle (Part Two): Control over Economic Assets or Public Infrastructure 187
F. The Potential Crowding out Effects of the Market Operator Principle 188
G. The Conditional Pursuit of Services of General Interest on the Basis of Adversarial Relationships 192
III. Responsiveness in the Case Law of the Court 195
A. Introduction 195
B. Mutual Responsiveness: Between Regulation and the Market 197
C. The Individual Aid Measure in its Wider Context 200
D. The Connection to the Wider Regulatory Context: A Good Governance Model 202
E. Mutual Responsiveness in the Application of the *Altmark* Framework 209
IV. A Dialogue of Mutual Responsiveness 215
A. Introduction 215
B. The Dialogue of Mutual Responsiveness in State Aid 216
C. The Required *Mutuality* of the Dialogue 218
V. Conclusion 220

5. Conclusion: Social Legitimacy in the Internal Market on the Basis of a Dialogue of Mutual Responsiveness 223
I. The Argument as a Whole: Normative Claims and Results 223
II. Social Legitimacy in the Internal Market: Free Movement, Competition and State Aid 227
A. Social Legitimacy in EU Free Movement Law 227
B. Social Legitimacy in EU Competition Law 230
C. Social Legitimacy in EU State Aid Law 234
III. Some Final Remarks 237

Bibliography 239
Index 257

Abbreviations

ACM	Authority for Consumer and Market
AG	Advocate General
Art	Article
CJEU	Court of Justice of the European Union
COM	Communication
EC	European Community
ECJ	European Court of Justice
ECR	European Court Reports
EU	European Union
FSU	Finnish Seamen's Union
GC	General Court
ITF	International Transport Worker's Federation
OJ	Official Journal of the European Union
TEU	Treaty on European Union
TFEU	Treaty on the Functioning of the European Union
TGT	The Great Transformation
VoC	Varieties of Capitalism

Introduction

I. BACKGROUND

NEW ASYMMETRIC BURDENS, challenges and interests amongst the Member States of the European Union threaten its unity and pose profound challenges to the future of the integration project. Addressing these challenges reaches beyond the modest ambition of this book, which is to address a 'classic' question that continues to challenge the stability of European integration: how can the diversity of Member States' 'social systems' and the varying normative infrastructure of their economies be sustainably accommodated within the internal market?

This is not a novel question but one that represents a continuing challenge that lies at the core of European market integration. The challenge concerns in its essence a balance between unity and diversity. President of the Court of Justice of the European Union (the Court) Koen Lenaerts, describes this balance as follows:

> beyond a core nucleus of shared values where the ECJ must ensure uniformity, EU law cannot disregard the cultural, historical and social heritage that is part and parcel of national constitutional traditions. Beyond that core nucleus, the ECJ welcomes 'value diversity'.[1]

However, where exactly this dividing line is remains the subject of much contentious case law and debate. In this book I shall provide an argument with respect to how this dividing line can be approached in the context of adjudication within the internal market and thus contribute to the question just raised. A broadly shared perception is that this dividing line is becoming increasingly unclear. This has occurred, on the one hand, owing to an increasing amount of issues that are harmonised through directives, regulations and forms of soft law. On the other, a strong perception exists that the Court threatens this balance through neoliberal-tinted 'activist case law'.[2] Indeed, the Court is regularly confronted with the challenge of reconciling the social diversity of Member States with the European integration objectives and outcomes in these cases are often criticised for a trade bias that would not only be anchored in the ontology of the whole of

[1] K Lenaerts, 'The Court's Outer and Inner Selves: Exploring the External and Internal Legitimacy of the European Court of Justice' in H Clemens (ed), *Judging Europe's Judges: The Legitimacy of the Case Law of the European Court of Justice* (Oxford, Hart Publishing, 2013) 13–60, at 15.

[2] C Kaupa, 'Maybe not Activist Enough? On the Court's Alleged Neoliberal Bias in its Recent Labor Cases' in B de Witte, E Muir and M Dawson (eds), *Judicial Activism at the European Court of Justice: Causes, Responses and Solutions* (Cheltenham, Edward Elgar Publishing, 2013) 56–75.

Union law but ranks highest on the institutional agendas of the Court of Justice.[3] The argument from social critiques on the case law of the Court can be broadly summarised as follows.

As a result of a trade interest bias that is part of the legal infrastructure of internal market law there exists a structural preference in favour of deregulation that is targeted against forms of social regulation within Member States. Moreover, privatisation of public sectors is pushed through internal market legislation and the application of the competition rules, targeting sectors that were previously in public hands.[4] Unsurprisingly, according to these critiques, the internal market set-up has not resulted in a strong publicly supported European Union but rather, to a status quo where it seems that scepticism directed towards the EU is distributed unevenly among social groups: between those who have the capability to benefit from the supremacy of the free trade objectives and those who do not.[5] Negative public sentiment is shaped through the impact of case law of the Court that often appears to set aside social objectives whose impetus originates from a longstanding Member State context.[6]

This 'judicial activism' of the Court of Justice does not pass by unnoticed and it has become commonplace in political circles and mainstream media to question the agenda of the Court of Justice. Former German President and former President of the German Constitutional Court, Roman Herzog, for example, wrote in 2008 that 'the ECJ deliberately and systematically ignores fundamental principles of the Western interpretation of law' so that 'its decisions are based on

[3] Amongst an ever-increasing and daunting amount of literature the publications selected here are just a small sample: B Van Apeldoorn, J Drahokoupil and L Horn, *Contradictions and Limits of Neoliberal European Governance: from Lisbon to Lisbon* (London, Palgrave Macmillan, 2008); C Joerges, 'A Critique of the Disregard for History in European Constitutional Theory: Are Those that Forget the Past Doomed to Repeat its Mistakes?' Florence, EUI Working Paper, LAW No 2005/14; C Joerges and F Rödl, 'Informal Politics, Formalised Law and the "Social Deficit" of European Integration: Reflections after the Judgments of the ECJ in Viking and Laval' (2009) *European Law Journal* 1–19; F Scharpf, 'The Asymmetry of European Integration, or why the EU Cannot be a "Social Market Economy"' (2009) 8 *Socio-Economic Review* 211–50; F Scharpf, 'The European Social Model: Coping with Challenges of Diversity' (2002) 4 *Journal of Common Market Studies* 645–70; M Höpner and A Schäfer, 'Embeddedness and Regional Integration: Waiting for Polanyi in a Hayekian Setting' (2012) 66 *International Organization* 429; S Deakin, 'The Lisbon Treaty, the Viking and Laval Judgments and the Financial Crisis: In Search of New Foundations for Europe's Social Market Economy' in N Bruun et al, *The Lisbon Treaty and Social Europe* (Oxford, Hart Publishing, 2012) at 19.

[4] Höpner and Schäfer, 'Embeddedness and Regional Integration' (n 3) at 11.

[5] L McLaren, 'Explaining Mass-Level Euroskepticism: Identity, Interests, and Institutional Distrust' (2007) 42 *Acta Politica* 233–51; H Kriesi, *West European Politics in the Age of Globalization* (Cambridge, Cambridge University Press, 2009).

[6] Frequently referred to examples in CJEU case law are cases such as *Centros*, *Überseering* and *Inspire Art*, which allow companies to circumvent, eg, national co-determination procedures in Germany by establishing themselves in the UK (C-212/97 *Centros*; C-208/00 *Überseering*; C-167/01 *Inspire Art*) or the *Viking*, *Laval* and *Rüffert* cases (C-438/05 *Viking*; C-341/05 *Laval*; C-346/06 *Rüffert*), which frame the right to strike as a narrow exception to the free trade rules, or the *Cadbury Schweppes* and *Marks & Spencer* cases (C-196/04 *Cadbury Schweppes*; C-446/03 *Marks & Spencer*), which, similarly, allow tax-avoidance practices by companies. Further reflection on these cases is in Ch 2.

sloppy argumentation, it ignores the will of the legislator, or even turns it into its opposite'.[7] The EU-induced austerity programmes have further entrenched the view that the EU is the 'key driver in the dismantling of social rights within the Member States'.[8] This, coupled with the fact that these instances receive high levels of public attention, have been an additional cause for Euro-scepticism and what can be coined as a crisis of social legitimacy.[9] Commentators often propose that the EU internal market instils regulatory competition between Member States with the effect that the overall standard will spiral downwards.[10] This *problématique* is strengthened by the approaches of Member States to social, cultural and ecological objectives that are characterised by variety.[11] Some, most prominently Fritz Scharpf, argue that due to a structural institutional incapacity, the EU will forever be inhibited from dealing with social issues.[12] The view of many commentators therefore is that there will be a continuing institutional asymmetry between the Union's trade and social objectives, which has been coined as the 'social deficit'.[13] As Höpner and Schäfer have noted, this continued asymmetry means in practice that proponents of the social have to direct their demands mainly to the national level, while proponents of liberalisation and free trade benefit from the supremacy of free market objectives.[14] These developments have led to a plethora of critical

[7] *Frankfurter Allgemeine Zeitung* (8 September 2008). See also Editorial Comments, 'The Court in the Limelight—again' (2008) 45 *Common Market Law Review* 1571–79.

[8] D Ashiagbor, 'Unravelling the Embedded Liberal Bargain: Labour and Social Welfare Law in the Context of EU Market Integration' (2013) 19(3) *European Law Journal* 303–24, at 324.

[9] See G Davies, 'Internal Market Adjudication and the Quality of Life in Europe' (2014) EUI Working Paper 2014/07. Brexit may be an example of this *in extremis,* although clearly the arguments that have been put forward with regard to the role of the Court as part of the debate in the UK were mostly false and overstated.

[10] eg in general on the federalist competition structure in the EU, see L Hooghe and G Marks, 'The Making of a Polity: The Struggle over European Integration' in H Kitschelt et al (eds), *Continuity and Change in Contemporary Capitalism* (Cambridge, Cambridge University Press, 1999) 70–97.

[11] P Beramendi, 'Inequality and the Territorial Fragmentation of Solidarity' (2007) 4 *International Organization* 783–820. As Beramendi demonstrates, the more diverse the EU Member States are in terms of wealth, inequality and the organisation of public tasks, the less likely it is that social policies emerge at the European level, despite the fact that EU primary law sources increasingly refer to social progress.

[12] Scharpf, 'The European Social Model' (n 3).

[13] See for coining of the term Joerges and Rödl, 'Informal Politics, Formalised Law and the "Social Deficit" of European Integration' (n 3). Similar issues are explored in G de Burca, 'The Quest for Legitimacy in the European Union' (1994) 59 *Modern Law Review* 349; J Weiler, 'Fin-De-Siècle: Do the New Clothes Have an Emperor?' in *The Constitution of Europe: 'Do the New Clothes Have an Emperor?' And other Essays on European Integration* (Cambridge, Cambridge University Press, 1999) at 238; C Joerges, 'What is Left of the European Economic Constitution?' European University Institute, Working Paper Law No 2004/13. On the general democratic deficit of the Union, see S Hix and A Follesdal, 'Why There Is a Democratic Deficit in the EU: A Response to Majone and Moravscik' (2006) 44 *Common Market Studies* 533–55.

[14] Höpner and Schäfer (n 3). The conceptualisation of the supremacy of free trade objectives and the struggle for social objectives originates from the original legal infrastructure of the EU which is designed to promote competitive federalism as proposed by G Marks, L Hooghe and K Blank, 'European Integration since the 1980s: State-Centric versus Multi-Level Governance' (1996) 34 *Journal of Common Market Studies* 343–78.

analyses, which now constitute a virtual encyclopaedia of social commentary that across the board highlight how fundamental social interests such as the right to strike and collective negotiating/agreements appear to have been subordinated to the economic objectives of market integration in the European Union. These critiques narrate a 'new phase' in the case law of the Court that is based on a renewed neoclassical economic theology of free markets, which at times has been considered as a pure and unfettered neoliberalism that has sanctified 'the Freedom of Enterprise and Liberty of Contract' as fundamental (natural) European rights. It is considered within this narrative that the constitutional foundation of the European Union has converted economic power into a fundamental right and collective labour rights are today considered mostly as an obstructive power that have to be limited.[15] As such, the spontaneous functioning of the market-order has to be protected from undue interferences like collective action and more generally discretionary social policies which are policed by the Court on the basis of a strict scrutiny test. By and large, it is considered by some that this has now culminated into a near Hayekian dream of a near complete reversal of the constitutional social pacts underpinning the post-war Keynesian welfare states in Europe,[16] in which constitutionalised market access and the pursuit of economic freedom are the overarching benchmarks of access to justice in the EU market-polity.[17] Critiques within this narrative consider that interests that are promoted on the basis of market integration displace what makes the traditional values of social life in Europe worthwhile.[18] The law of the internal market within this narrative is often considered to be negatively constitutive of socio-economic life within the Member States. Repairs may necessitate 'radical' reforms, such as the possibility to transfer powers back to the Member States, or a more limited scope of the internal market freedoms and objectives.[19] Within this narrative a solution to the social deficit is also conceived in the form of a reconceptualisation between

[15] eg L Azoulai, 'The "Retained Powers" Formula in the Case Law of the European Court of Justice: EU Law as Total Law?' (2011) 4(2) *European Journal of Legal Studies* 192–219; M Everson and C Joerges, 'Reconfiguring the Politics–Law Relationship in the Integration Project through Conflicts–Law Constitutionalism' (2012) 18(5) *European Law Journal* 644–66; D Chalmers, 'The European Redistributive State and a European Law of Struggle' (2012) 18(5) *European Law Journal* 667–93; M Dani, 'Rehabilitating Social Conflicts in European Public Law' (2012) 18(5) *European Law Journal* 621–43; F De Witte, 'Transnational Solidarity and the Mediation of Conflicts of Justice in Europe' (2012) 18(5) *European Law Journal* 694–710; G Davies, 'Democracy and Legitimacy in the Shadow of Purposive Competence' (2015) 21 *European Law Journal* 2–22; G Davies, 'Subsidiarity: The Wrong Idea, in the Wrong Place, at the Wrong Time' (2006) 43 *Common Market Law Review* 63–84.

[16] eg W Streeck, 'Democratic Capitalism and its Contradictions' in A Schäfer and W Streeck (eds), *Politics in the Age of Austerity* (Cambridge, Polity Press, 2013).

[17] HW Micklitz, 'Social Justice and Access Justice in Private Law' (2011) EUI Working Paper Law 2011/02.

[18] eg G Davies, 'Internal Market Adjudication and the Quality of Life in Europe' (2014) EUI Working Paper Law 2014/07.

[19] Editorial Comments in (2015) 52 *Common Market Law Review* 881–88.

EU economic and social policy, which must be achieved by increasing the EU's legislative competence in the social field in order to remedy this asymmetry.[20]

At the time of inception of the European Economic Community (EEC) there existed some clarity with respect to the social impact that the European project would entail. Most importantly, a division was envisaged between what would later be coined in academic quarters as the Economic Constitution and nationally embedded social law and policies.[21] This conceptualisation of the Treaty of Rome originated from German ordoliberal scholars who envisaged a very specific socio-economic paradigm with normative implication for the scope of European Law.[22] Not only would the EEC be limited in terms of its competences to create social (redistributive) policy, the national social sphere would also largely be insulated from the supranational market order.[23] Thus came into existence the idea of a 'de-coupled' supranational market order that was largely separate from the national democratic social constitutions of the Member States.[24] The idea behind de-coupling the economic from the social was in part envisaged to secure the social embeddedness of market liberalisation and can be traced to a commitment to fulfil the post-war Ruggian notion of embedded liberalism.[25] In addition, the national welfare states were, at that time of their short-lived golden age, providing post-war European citizens with not only much needed financial support, but also the governing methods to strengthen and repair the fragile bonds between citizens and national institutions.[26] The paradigmatic example of this de-coupling has always been the insulation and preservation of the 'autonomy' of national

[20] eg D Schiek, 'The EU Constitution of Social Governance in an Economic Crisis in Defence of a Transnational Dimension to Social Europe' (2013) 2 *Maastricht Journal of Comparative and European Law* 185–208.

[21] M Streit and W Mussler, 'The Economic Constitution of the European Community: From Rome to Maastricht' (1994) 5 *Constitutional Political Economy* 319; MP Maduro, *We the Court. The European Court of Justice and the European Economic Constitution: a Critical Reading of Article 30 of the EC Treaty* (Oxford, Hart Publishing, 1998); W Sauter, 'The Economic Constitution of the European Union' (1998) 4 *Columbia Journal of European Law* 27; C Joerges, 'What is Left of the European Economic Constitution? A Melancholic Eulogy' (2005)30 *European Law Review* 461–89; S Giubboni, *Social Rights and Market Freedom in the European Constitution* (Cambridge, Cambridge University Press, 2006) 15–29; K Tuori and K Tuori, *The Eurozone Crisis* (Cambridge, Cambridge University Press, 2014) at 13; C Joerges, 'The European Economic Constitution and its Transformation through the Financial Crisis' ZenTra Working Papers in Transnational Studies No 47/2015; H Hofmann and K Pantazatou, 'The Transformation of the European Economic Constitution' University of Luxembourg Law Working Paper 2015-01.

[22] Further on this, see C Kaupa, *The Pluralist Character of the European Economic Constitution* (Oxford, Hart Publishing, 2016).

[23] See also M Dawson, *New Governance and the Transformation of European Law* (Cambridge, Cambridge University Press, 2011) at 39.

[24] eg Scharpf, 'The Asymmetry of European Integration, or why the EU Cannot be a "Social Market Economy"' (n 3); Joerges and Rödl (n 3) 1–19.

[25] Giubboni, *Social Rights and Market Freedom in the European Constitution* (n 21) 15–29.

[26] F Costamagna, 'The Internal Market and the Welfare State: Anything New after Lisbon? in M Trybus, and L Rubini (eds), *The Treaty of Lisbon and the Future of European Law and Policy* (Cheltenham, Edward Elgar, 2012) 381–400.

labour law.[27] Labour law was considered to provide the fundamental shielded separation of the weaker party against the more powerful capitalist owner and modes of mass production that would commodify labour within its efficiency rationales.[28]

Originally, therefore, the choice for de-coupling was made with the intention to strengthen national welfare states from supranational market forces and the economic benefits that would be derived from the establishment of an integrated market would in time provide increased financial means to ensure the maintenance of higher social standards.[29] It is pertinent to understand that what can be considered as the autonomy of the national social sphere allowed for the existence and development of insulated nationally embedded organisational rationales. These were largely based on a logic of *closure*[30] that could develop separately from the integrating European market, which logic was concomitantly being progressively interpreted by the European Court of Justice as one of *opening* up national markets. A fundamental clash was therefore always long in the making, a clash that was arguably catalysed by the revealed flaws in the design of the welfare state during the crisis of the 1970s.[31] Although the fundamental aspects of national social law and policy such as collective action and national solidarity have historically been preserved and shielded from the dynamics of the internal market, today this de-coupling is no longer maintained.

In addition to processes of globalisation, a significant challenge to the social insulation of Member States has come in the form of an extension of the interpretation of the scope of the internal market rules by EU institutions, most notably the European Court of Justice. The classic conflict in the area of internal market law is one of a Member States measure that restricts cross-border economic movement. In non-harmonised contexts this type of 'classical conflict' scenario is generally perceived as *vertical*. That is to say, the national measure will need to be justified within a higher order rule that simply has precedence on the basis of the supremacy of EU law. From the moment that the Court began to approach social

[27] Giubboni (n 21). See also further S Giubboni, *Diritti sociali e mercato. La dimensione sociale dell'integrazione europea* (Bologna, Il Mulino, 2003).

[28] R Dukes, *The Labour Constitution—The Enduring Idea of Labour Law* (Oxford, Oxford University Press, 2014).

[29] Costamagna, 'The Internal Market and the Welfare State' (n 26) at 386.

[30] S Liebfried and P Pierson, 'Semisovereign Welfare States: Social Policy in a Multitiered Europe' in S Liebfried and P Pierson (eds), *European Social Policy: Between Fragmentation and Integration* (Washington, Brooking Institution, 1995) 43–77.

[31] See further eg B Lange, F Haines and D Thomas (eds), *Regulatory Transformations: Rethinking Economy-Society Interactions* (Oxford, Hart Publishing, 2015). One of the soon to become dominant organisational rationales that developed in response to the 1970s crisis was that of new public management. This movement sought to replace the national welfare rationales inspired by public-spiritedness and collectivity with market-enabling rationales that installed managerial standards of efficiency. It was at the time part of a wider programme which seeming ambition was to expediently install economic efficiency and cost-benefit rationales as the main consideration for the development of socio-economic policy. This rationale has been adopted with some fervour by the European Commission as well.

structures within Member States as potential restrictions and *vertical* conflict constellations, the mediation of these conflicts started to raise fundamental questions with respect to the legitimacy of internal market law. The Court has started, at times, to reach deep into the fundamental structures of nationally embedded and differentiated social structures. This has been characterised as the steady 'infiltration'[32] of internal market rules towards the social spheres of Member States. An infiltration the Court started, albeit tentatively, in the 1990s,[33] at that time still employing a skilful self-restraint to assess the compatibility of previously isolated Member States social spheres with the functioning of a competitive internal market. It did so at first with respect to the potential application of competition law to health insurers that were operating in environments based on solidarity principles and reviewing compulsory membership rules with respect to pension schemes.[34] It is today, however, commonplace to see EU state aid rules applied with respect to the national compensation schemes for welfare services' providers.[35] Moreover, and paradigmatically, the European Court of Justice in the area of free movement law today simply considers that Member States' social law and policy may qualify as measures taken by a Member State which affect access to the market for companies from other Member States and have to be justified within a proportionality mould that often employs market-enabling rationales.

On this basis, the two once separated spheres have become connected in the case law of the Court and many consider that the connection has been made at the cost of the social.[36] This has become, again, particularly visible in the case law of the European Court of Justice. Methods of hierarchical balancing that are employed by the Court suggest national social law and policy can only exist insofar as it can be considered a reasonable correction to the functioning of the market.[37] Case law in recent years has interpreted minimum social rights as ceilings[38] and has given pre-emptive effects to partial-social-harmonisation directives within the internal market by forbidding more favourable national treatment for workers.[39]

[32] G Lyon-Caen, 'L'infiltration du droit du travail par le droit de la concurrence' (1992) *Droit ouvrier* 313–59.

[33] Augustin Menéndez traces this 'positive standard of constitutionality' back to *Cassis de Dijon*, Case C-120/78 *Rewe v Bundesmonopolverwaltung für Branntwein* [1979] ECR I 00649. Menéndez provides a compelling argument that this shift explains much of the abrasiveness of post 1970s CJEU case law and that from this moment internal market conflicts have become relevant, primarily, in policy substantive terms; A Menéndez, 'United they Diverge? From Conflicts to Constitutional Theory? Critical Remarks on Joerges' Theory of Conflicts of Law' RECON WP 2011/6 (Oslo, 2011) at 24.

[34] Case C-67/96 *Albany* [1999] ECR I-5751; Case C-160/91 *Poucet and Pistre* [1993] ECR I-637; Case C-218/00 *Cisal and INAIL* [2002] ECR I-691; Case C-264/01, C-306/01, C-354/01 and C-355/01 *AOK Bundesverband* [2004] ECR I-2493; and Case C-355/00 *Freskot* [2003] ECR I-5263.

[35] Case T-289/03 *BUPA* [2008] ECR II-00081.

[36] eg Davies, 'Democracy and Legitimacy in the Shadow of Purposive Competence' (n 15) 2–22.

[37] *cf* specifically L Niglia, 'Eclipse of the Constitution' (2016) 22 *European Law Journal* 132–56.

[38] Case C-341/05 *Laval* [2007] ERC I-11767; Case C-346/06 *Rüffert* [2008] ERC I-01989.

[39] Case C-426/11 *Alemo-Herron*, ECLI:EU:C:2013:521. See further C Kilpatrick, 'Laval's Regulatory Conundrum: Collective Standard-Setting and the Court's New Approach to Postal Workers' (2009) 34 *European Law Review* 844.

This whole development has put increasing relevance on the question that this section started out with and guides the substantive chapters of this book. How can the diversity of Member States' 'social systems' and the varying normative infrastructure of their economies be sustainably accommodated within the internal market?

II. THE ARGUMENT

At the heart of the paraphrased social critiques lies a fundamental tension and irreconcilability between market integration and 'social values'. Somehow, enabling the market and enforcing principles that would allow for its smooth functioning threaten the social fabric of the Member States. It is this fundamental tension between 'the market' and 'the social' that will be dissected and continuously investigated as it arises in the core areas of internal market law adjudication (free economic movement, competition and state aid). This book presents several case studies with respect to this oft-considered adversarial relationship and offers a rationalisation with respect to the means to mediate conflicts between these spheres. Instead of perceiving the market and the social as *necessarily* requiring one to trump the other in situations of conflict, or to perceive the social merely as *ancillary* to economic objectives (as is the case with regards to flexicurity and so forth), this book advances a more reconciliatory approach that conceives the market and the social as 'communicating vessels'.[40]

In this book I will come to a typology of the different types of reasoning adopted by the Court and the General Court in order to adjudicate so-called diagonal conflicts. That is to say, in the context of the argument presented in this book, cases that are right at the intersection between unity and diversity. In contrast to vertical conflicts, diagonal conflicts arise where the objectives that are pursued by Member States are restrictive of trade integration or competition but cannot be fully internalised within the functional rationales that underlie those of market integration. For example, a system of solidarity in the healthcare market of a Member State may fundamentally conflict with the objective of competition. The underlying normative rationales pursue potentially irreconcilable ends. In contrast to vertical conflicts that can be resolved by referring to the supremacy of EU law because they take place within the 'core nucleus' of internal market law, diagonal conflicts are reflective of conflicts which cannot, or should not, be so easily resolved, as they not only pit levels of government against each other—supranational versus national—but because the norms in conflict pursue radically different ends. As such, they cannot be easily reduced to one single balancing scale. Thus, diagonal conflicts represent the constitutionally most challenging type of conflict. How does the Court manage to reconcile (or not) the uniform application of internal market law with the socio-economic diversity of the Member States? Central to

[40] *cf* C Crouch, *Making Capitalism Fit for Society* (Cambridge-Malden MA, Polity Press, 2013) at 37.

this much-explored ambivalence of the integration project is the fact that these post-national interdependencies are at the same time the objective of market integration *and* the source of a plethora of conflict constellations. The argument that I will develop submits that the social purpose of internal market law is predicated on the ability to provide for a socially responsive legal infrastructure where conflicts of norms that result from the integration process can be resolved.

This may raise the immediate question of whether this seemingly modest aim should indeed be the primary social purpose of the internal market. Rather, should the internal market not aspire to such larger ideals as peace, well-being and prosperity for its peoples? And of course it should, but peace, well-being and prosperity in Europe depend on, and are intrinsically connected to, the issue of how conflicts between nation states are resolved and this is the quintessential social purpose of the internal market. The overriding normative perspective of this book therefore is that internal market law derives its legitimacy from its ability to provide a socially responsive platform for conflict resolution. The overarching concern is that the internal market, perceived as a project that promotes market integration amongst a diversity of social systems, will only endure with political support in the presence of a constructive interplay between market integration and social (non-market) objectives.

The scope of the argument is limited to the field of adjudication within the internal market. This requires some justification. At the outset it is important to consider why conflicts between supranational trade integration objectives and national social policy would need to be resolved at the supranational level to begin with. This is especially the case if one would favour the reconstruction of EU law from a federal constitutional perspective, which would arguably be more in line with some of the constituent features of the European Union.[41] From that perspective, it could be argued that the Court of Justice would simply have to refer a matter back to the national level as soon as a conflict between, for example, a free movement right and a socially relevant national measure is identified. A solid case can be made that this form of 'self-restraint' would be more in line with the fundamental idea behind the division of competences that is inherent to the whole idea of embedded liberalism and thus a more efficient means to ensure social legitimacy.[42] The book adopts a normative justification for the Court to adjudicate and resolve the many complex conflicts stemming from the dynamics of European integration on the basis of its capacity to perform a 'compensatory' function.[43] That is to say, the 'post-national' legitimacy of governance within

[41] *cf* Niglia, 'Eclipse of the Constitution' (n 37) at 139 and specifically fn 28. Also B Bercusson, 'The Trade Union Movement and the European Union: Judgment Day' (2007) 13 *European Law Journal* 279–308.

[42] J Mulder, 'Responsive Adjudication and the Social Legitimacy of Internal Market Law' (September 2016) *European Law Journal* 597–620.

[43] See C Joerges, 'Unity in Diversity as Europe's Vocation and Conflicts Law as Europe's Constitutional Form' in R Nickel and A Greppi (eds), *The Changing Role of Law in the Age of Supra- and Transnational Governance* (Baden-Baden, Nomos, 2014) 125.

constitutional states is flawed, insofar as it is unable to ensure that 'foreign' identities and 'foreign' interests are taken into account within national decision-making processes and the legitimacy of supranational institutions such as the Court can be derived from a compensatory function (ie its forcing national processes to take into account foreign interests and parties).

This idea is now most aptly described as the 'argument from containment' or the 'argument from transnational effects'.[44] The argument qualifies the process of integration as an exercise whereby traditional, outdated and unrepresentative manifestations of national forms of decision-making are progressively removed because they are hostile to transnational interests and inappropriate within an integrating European market. An integrating market to which the Member States have committed themselves in the Treaties. The point here is that internal market law is conceived as a tool that forces reconsideration and sometimes emancipation from outdated and unrepresentative institutional and procedural structures. For this purpose, the argument proposes that internal market provisions should be placed in 'dialogue' with restrictive regulatory contexts. Importantly, Member State contexts are not always worth defending, and the process of economic integration may foster emancipation by weakening traditionally entrenched forms of privilege. In this vein, the EU internal market is, or should be, a supple and constructive means towards a new transnational and more responsive democratic nation state, one that is sensitive towards the interests of entities that fall outside of its direct political reach and procedures.[45] In this respect, as an ideal type, the argument from transnational effects cannot justify dismissing the basic structure of competence allocation behind embedded liberalism. Instead, the version of the argument that I defend below recognises that the interdependencies between integrating national economies raise conflicts, which require coordination and resolution because of the overarching commitment of Member States to a process of internal market integration.

Within the perspective of the argument from transnational effects, the internal market is infused with a clear social purpose, namely as a platform for inter- and intra-societal dialogue. This is, however, a fundamentally underdeveloped part of the theory and an important part of the objectives of this book is to bring the preconceived social purpose to its full fruition. In this respect, it has been argued that Europe needs a better infrastructure and rationale to accommodate social conflicts and that the suppression of social conflict on the basis of a 'consensus culture' has hampered further integration. Moreover, the re-emergence of social conflict now poses fundamental 'challenges to the current institutional setting' which is in need of a new conceptual language for social conflicts within the internal market.[46]

[44] See also further A Somek, 'The Argument from Transnational Effects I: Representing Outsiders through Freedom of Movement' (2010) 16 *European Law Journal* 315–44. Also seminally in Maduro, *We the Court* (n 21).

[45] Somek, 'The Argument from Transnational Effects I' (n 44) at 320.

[46] Dani, 'Rehabilitating Social Conflicts in European Public Law' (n 15) at 621.

This book aims to develop a common language for internal market law on the basis of a dialogue of *mutual responsiveness.*

The social legitimacy issues across the free movement, competition and state aid rules that the case studies in the following chapters illustrate share some striking commonalities. Firstly, the means of valuation that are implicit within the adjudicative rationales applied by the European Court of Justice are similar even though they take place with regard to different techniques of adjudication (eg proportionality versus categorisation) or with regard to different legal categories (eg undertaking versus public authority). Similar lines of reasoning can be connected around a principle of substantive efficiency on the basis of evaluations that consider the least restrictive (free movement), most efficient (competition) or most profitable (state aid) course of action. The focus in this stage of the Court's reasoning is prescriptive with regard to the chosen course of action on the basis of substantive outcomes. The studies in the next chapters will find common problems in the manner in which evaluative standards based on substantive efficiency can value societal realities within a metric that risks doing violence to potentially genuine social objectives and pacts that are pursued at a Member State level. For example, the evaluative adjudicative method such as strict proportionality applied in free movement adjudication may seek the more efficient or less restrictive state measure and exclude a relevant and genuine political compromise. Efficiency-based exemption criteria in competition law value competition restrictive sustainability initiatives in terms of the willingness of consumers to pay for a price increase and may exclude the inherent value of a sustainable environment. The market-based evaluative standards in state aid law may nudge public bodies towards actions that are justified exclusively on the grounds of their commercial self-interest and crowd out potential alternative visions regarding the appropriate role of public authorities.

As such, problems of social legitimacy across the different fields of internal market law arise with respect to the unchecked application of the principle of substantive efficiency. I will argue that this is not in alignment with the current values and objectives structure of the EU that points towards the importance of institutionalising diversity. The unchecked and expedient use of the principle of substantive efficiency validates much of the social critiques that were introduced in the foregoing. However, is the picture indeed so straightforward? Has the Court lost its skilful self-restraint?

The analyses of case law amongst all internal market law fields in the next chapters will unveil a fragmented answer to this question. The Court has in different ways found means to value divergent social context by developing different rationales of valuation, going beyond a mere purposeful utilitarian standard. On the basis of applying margins of discretion, areas that are considered sensitive or important for Member States are, within all areas of the internal market, provided with a certain space where Member States can determine regulatory objectives and ways to get there without infringing the internal market rules. This is completed with standards of procedural good governance through which the

Court has progressively provided yardsticks that require integration-restrictive interests to be pursued on the basis of transparency, consistency and coherence. For example, regulatory choices for a monopoly system in the gambling market restricting the free movement of services and completely foreclosing access to the market, is allowed provided that the wider public law infrastructure is transparent and coherently tuned towards a high level of consumer protection. The focus of good governance is on procedure and the coherence of the broader regulatory context, rather than on the rationality, efficiency or profitability of the outcome. Private initiatives that restrict competition in the pursuit of a social objective is allowed, provided that the regulatory context sufficiently enables private actors and ensures affirmative political oversight. Selective advantages for undertakings that flow from a broader more general regulatory framework are allowed, provided that they are in accordance with the logic of a wider reference system, and, again, genuinely pursued by Member States. The studies in the next chapters reveal that the Court has constructed and applied, albeit incoherently, a mixture of three evaluative principles to adjudicate internal market conflicts: substantive efficiency, margins of appreciation and good governance standards. Therefore, although the chapters will highlight that there are differences and nuances in the way that social legitimacy issues and solutions arise within the different areas of the internal market, it will also be submitted that they can all be connected on the basis of an interplay of these three principles.

In reconstructing this case law I will submit that the key to social legitimacy lies in finding the balance between applying these principles; the substantive reach of the internal market and the 'switch' towards an evaluative framework that allows for a diversity (a margin of discretion), and plurality of legitimate *substantive* outcomes, provided that they are pursued in a transparent, coherent and systematic fashion. In effect this means that, to the extent that social diversity can be accommodated within the substantive scope of the market, the evaluative principle applied by the Court to assess restrictive national or local interests can be substantively oriented and require the more efficient or less restrictive measure. Where the interest pursued is legitimate and based on normative principles that fall outside of 'the scope of the market' the evaluative principle should, however, switch to a procedural assessment that is concerned with principles of good governance. The exercise of the Court to find this 'switch' between evaluative principles that are congruent with the underlying social context, without losing sight of internal market objectives, is coined as responsive adjudication and the studies in the following chapters have traced fragments of such responsiveness, albeit incoherently, in the case law of the Court in free movement, competition and state aid rules. Subsequently, the intention of this study is to consistently reconstruct the evaluative principles within the case law into a coherent model of social legitimacy.

In sum, this will allow the Court to implement an 'operational rationale' whenever it has to adjudicate a conflict between the objectives of market integration and restrictive domestic (social) interests. All the chapters demonstrate how the terms of substantive efficiency, margins of discretion and good governance can provide a common language within a dialogue of mutual responsiveness.

III. APPROACH

I approach internal market adjudication as a separate field of social ordering within the European Union. Court rulings determine how the relationship between the social and market sphere is to be governed and such rulings may enter in some degree into the future relationship between these two spheres in the internal market.[47] This provides a negative form for the qualification of the social sphere within the internal market. The following main research questions undergird and structure the book: (i) what are the adjudicative rationales that govern internal market conflicts between interests of a social nature and market integration objectives?; (ii) how can these adjudicative rationales be critiqued within a normative perspective of social legitimacy?; and (iii) if found lacking, what is a better alternative based on social legitimacy?[48]

The book will focus exclusively on the adjudicative rationales that have been developed to govern the interplay between the objectives of the internal market and restrictive social interests within the three pillars of internal market law: the book focuses on (economic) free movement, competition and state aid case law.[49] Occasional reference will of course be made to relevant policy and legislative contexts, which may already pre-determine and influence the extent to which adjudication can have an impact on Member States' social spheres.

The book constructs a normative framework around the idea of social legitimacy, which finds its origin in the 'embedded liberalism' compromise that stands at the basis of the legal infrastructure of the internal market. This infrastructure responded to a social urgency and common understanding that pressure of markets on societal structures should be kept in check by allowing domestic concerns to restrict free trade objectives if deemed necessary. The intellectual father of the idea that markets can harm social structures by rearranging them within a self-regulating, market-enabling rationale is Karl Polanyi and the first chapter develops a normative framework that is inspired by his ideas. As such, the normative argument that is developed is multidimensional as even though it contributes to an important and continuing constitutional narrative, it is nevertheless infused with ideas from another discipline. This is particularly aspired to with respect to

[47] L Fuller and K Winston, 'The Forms and Limits of Adjudication' (1978) 92 *Harvard Law Review* 353–409.

[48] This approach and these research questions can of course also be applied to an area of social ordering such as internal market legislation and some would argue that this is the field of internal market law that has a more profound impact on the 'social sphere' within Member States. Including the internal market legislation dimension would involve another kind of study, perhaps even a whole other PhD. Therefore, for the simple reasons of space and time I have chosen to focus on the adjudicative sphere.

[49] As such the citizenship case law of the ECJ is not discussed. Although this represents a line of case law where the Court has unmistakably formulated new principles with respect to the way the tension between unity and diversity with the internal market is approached that moves beyond market rights I consider it a line of case law that is largely autonomous and insulated from the other areas of free movement law where economic movement and market access provide the evaluative rationales of the Court.

the question of how the knowledge that economic action, is and always has been, deeply embedded in social relations should affect the interplay between supranational market integration and the remaining locality of the social within the legal framework of the internal market. Social legitimacy is developed as a requirement that connects the legitimacy of internal market law to the extent that it can respond and integrate social practices and values.

The approach of this book can be best understood as the construction and application of a normative legal argument. The concept of social legitimacy is constructed in the first chapter and is injected with the normative preconceptions about how the relationship between supranational law and 'embedded' social choices within the Member States should take place. As such, social diversity is valued over administrability or legal certainty and the explicit articulation of genuine normative conflicts is valued over an approach that suggests that 'everything can be reconciled' which is dishonest. We have to face the truth that there are genuine normative conflicts in the internal market and that choices have to be made. Although these are normative preconceptions, the book also argues that such conceptions are justified on the basis of the (evolution) of the legal infrastructure within the internal market, which points towards a higher valuation of institutionalising diversity as an autonomous EU value. Again, it has to be emphasised that this should be considered as one of the fundamental 'challenges to the current institutional setting', which is in need of a new conceptual language to accommodate social diversity within the internal market.[50]

Indeed, it is on the basis of this normative framework that the book approaches the areas of free movement, competition and state aid respectively. Each chapter follows the same structured argument and sets out: (i) where and how the normative concerns of social legitimacy arise; (ii) what the starting points are within existing adjudicative approaches for an alternative that is in accordance with social legitimacy; and (iii) what a coherent rationale on the basis of a dialogue of mutual responsiveness would look like. Each of the substantive chapters is characterised by a mixture of rigid black letter analysis of the case law and a discussion and reconstruction of that case law within the normative framework of social legitimacy. As such, the intention within each chapter is to combine theoretical reflections with a sound analysis of case law. The 'dialogue of mutual responsiveness' is based on the idea that internal market law is a means to start a conversation with Member States on the normative choices of restrictive laws and regulatory schemes. This dialogue requires on one side responsiveness within the application of internal market law to social context in Member States. Concomitantly, it also seeks to incite a clear understanding and articulation of restrictive objectives within the Member States. The normative concerns of social legitimacy and the potential of mutual responsiveness to address these normative claims are the central and connecting elements throughout the book. The substantive chapters

[50] Again Dani (n 15).

shall unveil that an overarching dialogue of mutual responsiveness is possible on the basis of a shared language of substantive efficiency, margins of discretion and good governance.

IV. OUTLOOK AND CONTRIBUTION

The contribution of the book to the literature can be discussed with respect to its separate parts and as a whole. Regarding its separate parts, Chapter 1 develops a normative outlook based on the work of Karl Polanyi and contributes to earlier debates, which have attempted to develop a 'Polanyian' approach to EU internal market integration.[51] I find in these contributions that the case law of the Court of Justice is too selectively analysed and commented on without a sufficient eye for detail. Often, these accounts seem to underestimate the quite subtle balancing work and adjudicative techniques offered by the Court of Justice, which provide for a more nuanced outlook. Furthermore, this debate is connected to a development of the constitutional narrative of the argument of transnational effects. Specifically, the chapter sets out the importance of the fundamental question that was posed by Alexander Somek with respect to the theory by asking: '*what might be done to prevent the argument from transnational effects from slipping into a free-wheeling rampage of economic due process*?'[52] One of the contributions of this book is to provide an answer to this question on the basis of mutual responsiveness. Moreover, the introduction of the normative framework based on social legitimacy introduces a novel method to critically assess case law along the lines of the interrelated terms of valuation, indeterminacy and incommensurability, as introduced above.

The chapters regarding the internal market all separately engage and contribute to specific and insulated debates on the basis of a novel reading and reconstruction of case law within a model of social legitimacy. Each of the chapters clarifies the

[51] A very early version of this chapter has partly been published in J Mulder, 'Re-embedding EU Governance Fields: A Research Agenda' in C Joerges and C Glinski (eds), *The European Crisis and the Transformation of Transnational Governance. Authoritarian Managerialism versus Democratic Governance* (Oxford, Hart Publishing, 2014), and further J Mulder, 'Finding the Public Interest and the Case of the Friesian Horse' 2013 ACLE Conference Paper http://acle.uva.nl/events/competition—regulation-meetings/conference-papers-9th-cr-meeting-2013.html.

[52] Somek (n 44) at 332. 'Economic due process' originates from the Unites States as the idea that substantive due process protects some rights from deprivation. In simple terms this means that government may not hamper the exercise of certain 'rights', even where due processes have been adopted. In the famous Supreme Court decision *Lochner v New York*, a New York State law that regulated the hours and working conditions of bakery employees was held to intrude too far into the 'fundamental right for an employee and an employer to freely contract'. This 'fundamental right' to contract freely could not be limited, even by fair legislative processes. And came to be known as having established 'economic' substantive due process. It was later overturned in the context of the aftermath of the Great Depression and the New Deal rationale which may have inspired the Supreme Court in its decision of *West Coast Hotel*, which overturned the *Lochner* jurisprudence. See further MJ Lindsay, 'In Search of Laissez-Faire Constitutionalism' (2010) 3 *Harvard Law Review* 55.

nature of the conflict *between* the 'market and the social', which manifests differently in each area of internal market law.

Specifically, Chapter 2 on free movement, contributes to the widely held debate on the legitimacy of the social impact and reach of free movement law by developing a prescriptive model of adjudication, allowing the Court to speak to a range of social interests and actors.[53] Claims to originality have to face the daunting amount of literature in this area of internal market law and certainly, many of the observations made with respect to free movement case law have been made before. The fact that an unqualified market access test is potentially problematic is obviously not new.[54] Similarly, the observation of the emergence of a procedural proportionality test in certain lines of case law and its potential importance for deciding salient issues within the internal market has been made before.[55] However, the novelty of the argument presented in this chapter lies in the reconstruction of 'ideal type' standards of adjudicative reasoning that the Court adopts in its proportionality analysis, combined with a wider contextualisation of these adjudicative means within a dialogue of mutual responsiveness. In particular, the adoption of the 'inherently irreconcilability test' as a means to adopt evaluative standards that are congruent with underlying social context is a novel view.

Chapter 3 on competition adds to the longstanding and ongoing debate regarding how, and to what extent, so-called non-competition or non-efficiency interests have a role to play within the legal framework of the competition rules and the literature on the wider constitutional *function* of EU competition law.[56] The chapter identifies a policy-induced trend in competition law, which requires social actors to implement a narrow efficiency-based framework in their behaviour within the market, especially when they pursue wider social objectives. This allows for a largely novel critique on the social impact of competition law, which should resonate within the adjudicative rationales of the courts.[57] The subsequent discussion of the case law provides for some novel understandings and a distinct

[53] A shortened version of the argument presented in this chapter has been published in Mulder, 'Responsive Adjudication and the Social Legitimacy of Internal Market Law' (n 42) 597–620.

[54] eg J Snell, 'The Notion of Market Access: A Concept or a Slogan?' (2010) 47(2) *Common Market Law Review* 437–72.

[55] eg D Damjanovic, 'The EU Market Rules as Social Market Rules: Why the EU Can Be a Social Market Economy' (2013) 50(6) *Common Market Law Review* 1685–717; F de Witte, 'Sex, Drugs & EU Law: The Recognition of Moral and Ethical Diversity in EU Law' (2013) 50(6) *Common Market Law Review* 1545–78; G Mathisen, 'Consistency and Coherence as Conditions for Justification of Member State Measures Restricting Free Movement' (2010) 47(4) *Common Market Law Review* 1021–48.

[56] This chapter has partly been published as a conference paper, Mulder, 'Finding the Public Interest and the Case of the Friesian Horse' (n 51) and 2 Dutch journal articles: J Mulder, 'Een duurzame maatschappij, wat mag dat kosten?' (2015) 1400 *NJB* 1912–20 and J Mulder, 'Op het snijvlak van onafhankelijkheid en openheid: wat is de rol van de ACM in een duurzamemaatschappij?' (2014) *SEW* 565–78.

[57] In close proximity to arguments presented first by H Schepel, 'Delegation of Regulatory Powers to Private Parties under EC Competition Law: towards a Procedural Public Interest Test' (2002) 39 *Common Market Law Review* 39 31–51. For a development of that view, see W Sauter and H Schepel, 'State and Market in European Union Law: the Public and Private Spheres of the Internal Market before the EU Courts' (Cambridge, Cambridge University Press, 2009) at 114.

reading of seemingly unconnected lines of case law that can be connected on the basis of the normative perspective of social legitimacy and the dialogue of mutual responsiveness. The chapter finds that the dichotomy between market and non-market, or economic and non-economic, is there to allow or even force a deliberative space for broader than monetary- or efficiency-based criteria.[58] Important considerations that range from sustainability, the integrity of certain professions or the ethical treatment of animals harbour important social values that do not necessarily speak in terms that can be captured in monetised terminology. However, when applied in a supple manner it can be applied to initiate a social dialogue on the validity and systemisation of regulatory choices within the Member States. Competition law should seek to incorporate the means by which to value different social contexts differently in accordance with the underlying normative commitments of those contexts. Such responsiveness ultimately depends on institutional design within Member States.

Chapter 4, the chapter on state aid, engages with the potential impact of the EU state aid rules on the pursuit of social objectives by Member States. It is fair to say that of all areas of internal market law, state aid rules are the least theorised. Nevertheless, in recent years some *important* contributions have been made to the discussion of the EU state aid rules concerning their wider function and constitutional status within the internal market,[59] in a field of internal market law that is otherwise primarily dominated by insulated and practitioner-led specialised debates. The salience of this chapter, in light of the existing contributions, is claimed to be particularly pertinent in two ways. Firstly, in the discussion of the structural social legitimacy concerns with regard to the potentially expedient nature of market based evaluations in state aid cases. Secondly, with the introduction of the idea of mutual responsiveness to state aid law. This allows a connection between state aid law and the wider debate on the social legitimacy of the internal market.

Chapter 5 concludes that as a whole the argument presented in this book aims to contribute to the debate and the legitimate role and social purpose of the internal market within the European Union. It should be noted that the literature that aims to contribute to this debate on the internal market tends, with notable exceptions,[60] to focus primarily, if not exclusively, on the impact of free movement

[58] Mulder, 'Finding the Public Interest and the Case of the Friesian Horse' (n 51). Ch 3 was previously published in part in this conference paper.

[59] F De Cecco, *State Aid and the European Economic Constitution* (Oxford, Hart Publishing, 2013) and JJP Lopez, *The Concept of State Aid under EU Law—From Internal Market to Competition and beyond* (Oxford, Oxford University Press, 2015). See also M Ross, 'State Aids: Maturing into a Constitutional Problem' (1995) *Yearbook of European Law* 79; M Ross, 'State Aid and National Courts: Definitions and Other Problems—a Case of Premature Emancipation?' (2000) 37 *Common Market Law Review* 401; M Ross, 'Decentralization, Effectiveness, and Modernization: Contradiction in Terms?' in A Biondi, P Eeckhout and J Flynn (eds), *The Law of State Aid in the European Union* (Oxford, Oxford University Press, 2004).

[60] eg J Baquero Cruz, *Between Competition and Free Movement: the Economic Constitutional Law of the European Community* (Oxford, Hart Publishing, 2002) 123.

case law. In addition, competition law and state aid are mostly *subject* to specialised debates related to the limited insulated approaches within those areas of law. The latter fact must be related to the ever-increasing specialisation within each area of internal market law, in particular the fact that competition and state aid rules are subject to a high degree of practitioner-led debates, whereas free movement tends to be a mostly academic affair. Free movement is therefore more often subject to wider academic reflections, whereas competition and state aid are more inwardly focused. Nevertheless, a critique on the legitimate 'social impact' of internal market law, and the potential structurally distortive effects of economic integration on the fundamental structures of domestic societies, has to take an overall approach. The benefit of such an overarching approach has been demonstrated. The book extrapolates and reconstructs interlinkages between the three fields of the internal market on the basis of a shared language that takes place in the context of a dialogue of mutual responsiveness, which allows the social purpose of the internal market to become a structural part of the European legal space.

1

Social Legitimacy, the Social Sphere and Embeddedness within the Internal Market

I. THE NORMATIVE FRAMEWORK OF SOCIAL LEGITIMACY

CONVENTIONALLY, THE LEGITIMACY of governance in the European Union can be traced back or related to three core concepts: 'input legitimacy, 'throughput legitimacy' and 'output legitimacy'.[1] The conventional meaning of these concepts is to see 'input' as the potential openness of the decision-making process for citizens, 'throughput' as the quality of the processes that subsequently process the input and 'output' as the quality of the result of the decision-making process. In addition to this set of normative concepts, the concept of social legitimacy is conventionally conceived to encompass an empirical notion that measures, with tools provided by social science, the societal attitudes and acceptance towards a political or legal regime.[2] The idea behind the concept is that lacking *empirically* measurable societal acceptance, a political regime will eventually disintegrate and a law will, generally, not be effective since it is too unconnected from prevailing social norms. I will not adopt this empirical outlook on social legitimacy. What is less discussed is that social legitimacy as a premise entails a normative expectation, specifically, in the context of supranational trading regimes. That is to say, if one accepts that these regimes depend on a level of social legitimacy to be sustained in the long run, one has to accept that such legitimacy depends on the structural institutional design and rationales that embed the normative orientations of societies within those regimes and vice versa.[3] This aspect of social legitimacy embodies a commitment that can be translated into an expectation regarding the responsiveness of transnational regimes to conflicts

[1] V Schmidt, 'Democracy and Legitimacy in the European Union Revisited: Input, Output and "Throughput"' (2013) 61 *Political Studies* 2–22; FW Scharpf, 'Legitimacy in the Multilevel European Polity' (2009) 1 *European Political Science Review* 173–204.

[2] eg JHH Weiler, 'In the Face of Crisis: Input Legitimacy, Output Legitimacy and the Political Messianism of European Integration' (2012) 34 *Journal of European Integration* 825–41.

[3] A Rawi and JG Ruggie, 'The Principles of Embedded Liberalism: Social Legitimacy and Global Capitalism' in D Moss and J Cisternino (eds), *New Perspectives on Regulation* (Cambridge, Cambridge University Press, 2009) 151–62.

between spheres that are embedded within the national social structures of states and the more remote supranational trade objectives. It is this normative commitment of social legitimacy that I develop.

I argue that social legitimacy has a distinct normative meaning and function within the multilevel context of the EU and specifically with regard to the areas of law that are concerned with establishing the internal market. To contextualise this specificity we have to take a step back and look at the institutional structures that were developed for international trade regimes in the post-1945 world economy, which have been described as embodying a particular *social bargain*.[4] This social bargain stands behind the normative grounding of social legitimacy. Policymakers were looking to reinvigorate the world economy on the basis of open markets but within an institutional context that would mitigate their recognised adverse social consequences.[5] It was a shared concern that the absence of such a compromise had led to the collapse of international cooperation in trade and macroeconomic policy during the 1920s and 1930s.[6] One of the proponents of this latter idea was Karl Polanyi. In his 1944 book, *The Great Transformation*, he introduced the idea of 'embedded' versus 'disembedded' socio-economic orders.[7] Polanyi's historical inquiry led him to conclude that economic orders tend to be characterised by the values of societies in which they are situated. However, the middle of the nineteenth century had seen the rise of the idea of economy separate from society in the form of a collection of self-regulating and autonomous markets, which required social relation to be transformed within its own logic:

> the control of the economic system by the market is of overwhelming consequence to the whole organization of society: it means no less than the running of society as an adjunct to the market. *Instead of economy being embedded in social relations, social relations are embedded in the economic system.*[8]

In this market-run dystopia, markets had to be shielded against political intervention so as not to disturb the allocative flow of supply and demand, which was best safeguarded by separating politics and the economy. Disembedding the economy

[4] JG Ruggie, 'International Regimes, Transactions and Change: Embedded Liberalism in the Postwar Economic Order, International Organization' (1982) 36 *International Regimes* 392:

> [To] say anything sensible about the content of international economic orders and about the regimes that serve them, it is necessary to look at how power and legitimate social purpose become fused to project political authority into the international system. Applied to the post-World War II context, this argument leads me to characterize the international economic order by the term 'embedded liberalism.

[5] ibid, at 388. Also R Nurkse, League of Nations Report: *International Currency Experience: Lessons of the Inter-War Period* (League of Nations, Economic, Financial and Transit Department, 1944).

[6] ibid, at 392; also S Marglin and J Schor, *The Golden Age of Capitalism: Reinterpreting the Postwar Experience* (Oxford, Oxford University Press, 1990).

[7] K Polanyi, *The Great Transformation: The Political and Economic Origins of our Time* (Boston, The Beacon Press, 1944, 2nd edn reprinted in 2001).

[8] ibid, at 57.

implied a process of commodifying the 'very substance' of society, which was determined through market exchange rather than through political deliberation.[9] There was, in other words, no social legitimacy in its empirical understanding. This turned out to be politically unsustainable and Polanyi considered it to be one of the important contributing factors for the rise of fascist-like movements which resolved the problem by taking over control of markets completely.

Against this background it seems that the post-1945 US and European policy-makers aligned with the basic insights articulated by Polanyi.[10] On the basis of John Maynard Keynes' ideas, rules were shaped on the basis of which the international economy was to be reconstructed. Similar to Polanyi's concerns, Keynes considered that the role of the international monetary order had put politically unsustainable pressures on societies to adjust policy and accommodate the needs of financial markets. A driving notion behind this was, indeed, the idea that markets, which are not considered legitimate within societies, are not sustainable. Therefore, it was considered a necessity to reconcile open and free markets with the prevailing values of the social-economic systems that they affected: a reconciliation of markets and politics. This has been famously coined by John G Ruggie, relying on insights from Polanyi, as the reconciliation on the basis of the compromise of 'embedded liberalism':

> Unlike the economic nationalism of the thirties, it would be multilateral in character; unlike the liberalism of the gold standard and free trade, its multilateralism would be predicated upon domestic interventionism.[11]

The idea behind this 'social bargain' was that through domestic interventionism the socially disruptive effects of markets would be mitigated *without*, however, eliminating the economic gains that could be derived from open and transnational markets. Therefore, this idea of social legitimacy implicitly requires trade regimes to be *responsive* to a variety of social contexts. In Europe this concretised in the development of the European welfare state models and the laws of the EU internal market share an explicit concern for embedding markets in social foundations of the Member States.[12] Despite the norm-based 'Hayekian' revolution in public policy of the 1970s and 1980s, the idea of a European welfare state remains alive today as well as the fact that the European Treaties still reflect to a large extent the institutional set-up and rules that are reflective of the original embedded

[9] G Dale, *Karl Polanyi: The Limits of the Market* (Cambridge, Cambridge Polity Press, 2010); F Block, 'Karl Polanyi and the Writing of The Great Transformation' (2003) 32 *Theory and Society: Renewal and Critique in Social Theory* 275–306.

[10] J Ruggie, 'Taking Embedded Liberalism Global: The Corporate Connection', Institute for International Law and Justice Working Paper 2003/2, New York University School of Law; and J Ruggie, 'Multilateralism: The Anatomy of an Institution' (1992) 46(3) *International Organization* 561–98.

[11] Ruggie, 'International Regimes, Transactions and Change' (n 4) at 393.

[12] ibid.

liberalism compromise.[13] The internal market laws determine that, although there is a commitment to intra-European free trade, Member States retain control over domestic public interests that are able to override trade interests. Moreover, the Court of Justice of the European Union (Court of Justice) has repeatedly called for a balancing of both the economic and social objectives of the Union. In addition, the EU has a limited competence to produce rules with a 'social' dimension.

Nevertheless, as was alluded to in the introduction, the EU finds itself in what can be described as a crisis of social legitimacy. Many factors contribute to this crisis, not least the fact that the EU-induced austerity programmes have enforced the view that the EU is one of the main, if not 'the' key, driver in the dismantling of social protection within the Member States and only pushes for a very limited understanding of the balance between social and market objectives. The 'social' is within the context of the internal market perceived as a 'restriction' of the economic objectives of the Union or as merely ancillary to them. This ambiguous relationship is reflected in a passage of the Court of Justice where it held in one of its most contentious decisions in recent history:[14]

> Since the Community has [...] not only an economic but also *a social purpose*, the rights under the provisions of the Treaty on the free movement of goods, persons, services and capital must be balanced against the objectives pursued by social policy [...].[15] (emphases added)

The statement of the Court of Justice is ambiguous because in this and other cases 'the balance' was found by subordinating the right to strike to market freedoms.[16] Many consider that the social purpose of the EU remains aloof and the commitment of Member States to ever further integration cannot be taken for granted any longer.[17] Diverging interests of an increasingly heterogeneous Union increase the importance of some clear notion, a sense of purpose, that can be attached and serve as a focal point for challenges that lie ahead.

As was discussed, the firm belief behind the studies in the next chapters of this book is that this purpose can be constructed around a rationale of social

[13] Confirmed by the historical reconstruction of Giubboni who coined this as a 'historical compromise': S Giubboni, *Social Rights and Market Freedoms in the European Constitution. A Labour Law Perspective* (Cambridge, Cambridge University Press, 2006) at 7; more recently, see R Dukes, *The Labour Constitution. The Enduring Idea of Labour Law* (Oxford, Oxford University Press, 2014) at 130 ff.

[14] Although not related to the Lisbon Treaty and stated in one of the most socially controversial cases of the Court.

[15] Case C-438/05 *International Transport Workers' Federation and Finnish Seamen's Union v Viking Line ABP and OÜ Viking Line Eesti* [2007] ECR p I-10779 at paras 78–79. This statement of the Court is similar to the one formulated in 1976 in the case of *Defrenne* where the Court held that 'the social objectives of the community, which is not merely an economic union, but is at the same time intended, by common action, to ensure social progress and seek the constant improvement of the living and working conditions of their peoples'; Case 43/75 *Defrenne* [1976] ECR 00455, para 10.

[16] Case C201/15 *AGET Iraklis*, ECLI:EU:C:2016:972.

[17] See for a similar outlook also the Editorial Comments of (2015) 52 *Common Market Law Review* 881–88.

responsiveness within the structure of EU law or 'European legal space'. This responsiveness can be derived from the original embedded liberalism compromise. In short, on this basis, the social purpose of the internal market is to provide for an infrastructure for the conflict of norms within the Union that arise through the interaction between principles of economic integration and social spheres within Member States.[18] This understanding of the internal market as a constructive platform for social conflict is in need of reinvigoration. Along these lines, Dani has, for example, argued that the effect of internal market law is rather one of 'marginalising social conflicts'—something that will become apparent in particular in the next chapter on free movement adjudication.[19] Similarly, Dani submits that a development of a language for social conflicts within internal market law will be a main factor contributing to its stability and legitimacy. Section III discusses that this conceived social purpose is implicit in the constitutional form that is advanced on the basis of the constitutional argument from transnational effects.

II. THE SOCIAL SPHERE WITHIN THE INTERNAL MARKET

At this point it should be admitted that I have already employed the concept of the social in various instances and it is important to specify my usage of this terminology. The social is a fuzzy concept and is often assigned different meanings depending on different contexts. The social as understood in this book is by its nature dynamic because it is always connected to particular spheres where, for example, the norms of a professional group provide meaning, value and understanding regarding a certain economic activity that are considered prescriptive.[20] Such social spheres are abundantly varying within the Member States and can be found in styles of governing such as redistributive governance as an expressive relationship of solidarity between citizens, or a choice for market-enabling regulation of industrial relations. Additionally, social spheres may exist as part of professions (associations of law, medicine or French waiters), business conduct or university politics. These different meanings and contexts of the social sphere can be understood and limited in operational terms as a sphere that determines the *underlying normative infrastructure of (a segment of) the economy*. Importantly, these normative underpinnings and the underlying rationales may, for example, determine the nature of a social sphere in terms of being embedded within a

[18] KH Ladeur, '"Conflicts Law as Europe's Constitutional Form" … and the Conflict of Social Norms as its Infrastructure' in C Joerges and C Glinski (eds), *European Crisis and the Transformation of Transnational Governance: Authoritarian Managerialism versus Democratic Governance* (Oxford, Hart Publishing, 2014) 380–400, at 383.

[19] M Dani, 'Rehabilitating Social Conflicts in European Public Law' (2012) 18 *European Law Journal* 621.

[20] See for a similar approach DJ Galligan, *Law in Modern Society* (Oxford, Oxford University Press, 2010).

market (commodity) or non-market logic. For example, labour market rules may sometimes fulfil a market-enabling function by reducing transaction costs and information asymmetries in wage setting, and, consequently, are not necessarily antithetic to market making.[21] However, this is not the rule; a major tension normally exists between the right to strike and market interests. Depending on the normative orientation of the social sphere that regulates this relationship, the very essence of the right to strike is to shield workers from the power that capital owners can exercise as holders of capital (and thus of economic freedoms). The underlying normative infrastructure of the social sphere of both types of labour market rules are fundamentally different. One may be qualified as being embedded within a commodity logic since the underlying rationale follows the allocative logic of the market whilst the other is entrenched in non-market rationales and involves a structure of negotiated deliberative coordination.[22]

Now when EU law strives to create an internal market it may want to change or modify the behaviour of a profession or style of government and, consequently, enter the 'social sphere' within a Member State and confront the embedded conventions and value systems and understandings. In some cases EU law will render the social sphere compatible, at times reinforcing the conventions and understandings, for example by holding that competition restrictive practices of law associations may be considered to be legitimate when the integrity of the legal profession is at stake.[23] In other cases the object of internal market law is to expressly change the conventions and understandings, for example by holding that the right to strike within a Member State is only allowed if it is exercised in a proportionate manner.[24] Between these two examples there exist of course different shades of compatibility and incompatibility, depending on the normative interpretation of the law.

There exists an analogy on this point with the debate on the interaction between social norms and the law, which is governed by roughly two ideas. One concerns the idea that 'custom' or norm-based rules lack the flexibility and rational control that is considered desirable for some higher order reason. Law then could become the means to reform such 'old-fashioned' social norms.[25] Some social norms may not be desirable from a particular higher *rational* perspective, and law can then improve the situation by regulating the concerned behaviour in congruence with the desired rationally and correcting undesirable phenomena, such as

[21] A Ebner, 'Transnational Markets and the Polanyi Problem' in C Joerges and J Falke (eds), *Globalisation and the Potential of Law in Transnational Markets* (Oxford, Hart Publishing, 2011) at 28.

[22] The understanding of the social in these terms is inspired by Polanyi and shall be further contextualised below.

[23] eg Case C-309/99 *Wouters and Others* [2002] ECR I-1577.

[24] eg Case C-438/05 *International Transport Workers' Federation and Finnish Seamen's Union v Viking Line ABP and OÜ Viking Line Eesti* [2007] ECR p I-10779.

[25] As can be derived from HLA Hart, *The Concept of Law* (Oxford, Clarendon Press, 1961). Also R Posner, 'Social Norms and the Law: An Economic Approach' (1997) 87 *The American Economic Review* 365–69.

protectionist state aid schemes.[26] This is reflected in the core nucleus of EU law where there are some interests (however social they may be) that are simply not part of the accepted EU internal market values scheme and will therefore always have to give way to the objectives of market integration and competition. These include tariff/custom duties, national discrimination, the discriminatory subsidisation of national champions and price cartels. It appears that these bans are, today, congruent with prevailing norms within Member States and EU law has been effective in implementing the idea that blatant protectionism amongst the Member States of the Union is disruptive. However, outside of the core nucleus of mutually shared values, the balance between market integration and social interests that are restrictive of free movement and competition interests becomes more complex and in need of a subtler rationale. This is the idea that legal and social norms do their job in the 'best' way when they are somehow aligned.[27]

Law and social norms should in a way complement each other. This position harbours more challenges, in finding the right interplay between social norms and enforcing a specific rationality through law. What underlies it is the idea that law should not be alien to society but instead that there should be some form a mutual communication between law and society.[28] If law is completely alien it will risks losing its legitimacy and become irrelevant. As such, the supranational EU law rules have to some extent to align with social contexts within Member States and built-in mechanisms of responsiveness in order to retain their legitimacy. Simply said, outside of the core nucleus the internal market allows for social diversity in and between the Member States. The argument presented in this book presents a rationalisation with respect to the interpretation of the legitimate reach of internal market law into the social spheres of the Member States.

There are various ways to look upon the way that internal market law conditions the emergence of Member States' social spheres within its legal framework. Within the multilevel context of the EU, the social sphere as understood here is influenced in at least two ways that are relevant to distinguish from each other for the purpose of social legitimacy. On one level the EU produces legislation that influences the social sphere. This can be said to be the 'positive' form of influence on the social sphere. On another level the social sphere is contingent on the fulfilment of requirements that flow from the internal market rules. This can be said to be the 'negative' form of influence on the social sphere.[29] Both forms are of

[26] eg R Posner, *Economic Analysis of Law* (Boston, Little Brown, 1972) argues in favour of the higher economic rationale.

[27] eg RD Cooter, 'Three Effects of Social Norms on Law: Expression, Deterrence, and Internalization' (2000) 79 *Oregon Law Review* 1–22; JR. Hay, A Shleifer, and RW Vishny, 'Toward a Theory of Legal Reform' (1996) 40 *European Economic Review* 559–67; JR Hay, and A Shleifer, 'Private Enforcement of Public Laws: A Theory of Legal Reform' (1998) 88 *American Economic Review* 398–403.

[28] eg D Acemogluy and MO Jackson, 'Social Norms and the Enforcement of Laws' NBER Working Paper No 20369 (August 2004).

[29] *cf* Scharpf's distinction of positive and negative integration 'Negative and Positive Integration in the Political Economy of European Welfare States' in G Marks, FW Scharpf, P Schmitter and W Streeck (eds), *Governance in the European Union* (London, Sage Publications, 1996) at 15.

importance and can be approached on the basis of questions related to their social legitimacy. However, both are also governed by different dynamics, institutional contexts and from the perspective of legitimacy, touch on separate potential issues. The positive influence on the social sphere can be more easily discussed in terms the potential openness of the decision-making process for citizens, the quality of the processes that subsequently process that input and the quality of the result of the decision-making process.[30] The positive form exists on the level of EU policy and within specific EU institutional and legal contexts. Its sources are found in the legal provisions that govern the competence of different institutions to enact legislation for the functioning of the internal market.[31] Regulations, Directives and non-legislative acts including new forms of governance fall under this heading of the positive social sphere.

The negative provides a conditional form for the social sphere that is deemed contingent on the fulfilment of specific EU internal market requirements. Here adjudication of the Court, in determining the conditions under which certain policy within Member States is restrictive, becomes a form of social ordering.[32] It determines how the relationship between the social and economic sphere is to be governed and the adjudicative determinations of the Court regarding this relationship will normally enter in some degree into the future relationship between these two spheres in the internal market. This negative form of influence on the social sphere is the main focus of this book. I will nevertheless briefly discuss the positive constitutive form, which I consider to be for a large degree a commodified version of an idealised EU social sphere.

A. The 'Positive' Social Sphere in the Internal Market

In 1957 the principle of equal pay for men and women was part of the Treaty of Rome. Although undeniably of social content, this did, however, not influence, concretely the social sphere within Member States, nor did the Social Charter of 1986, which was at that time, only declaratory.[33] The first, more concrete positive influence concerned the Social Protocol of the Maastricht Treaty, which added social provisions on workers' safety and health and introduced obligations for the Commission to consult management and labour when proposing legislation.[34]

[30] Schmidt, 'Democracy and Legitimacy in the European Union Revisited' (n 1) at 2.

[31] TFEU, Arts 114, 115 and 352.

[32] LL Fuller and KI Winston, 'The Forms and Limits of Adjudication' (1978) 92 *Harvard Law Review* 353.

[33] M Savevska, 'Polanyian Reading of the Socio-Economic Transformations of the European Union' (2014) 22 *Journal of Contemporary European Studies* 395–410.

[34] See further J Goetschy, 'Taking Stock of Social Europe: is there such a Thing as a Community Social Model?' in M Jespen and AS Pascual (eds), *Unwrapping the European Social Model* (Bristol, Policy Press, 2006) at 66.

It also established the Social Dialogue.[35] The so-called European Employment Strategy was introduced with the Amsterdam Treaty in 1997, which also established the Employment and Social Policy Titles.[36] The Treaty of Nice (2001) also established some joint rights for the Community to take action in tackling social exclusion.[37] More generally, one can see a trend from the 1990s onwards of an increase of 'minimal standards' introduced at the EU level.[38] Moreover and in particular, the environmental policy output over the years has been impressive,[39] with Directives on a variety of topics.[40] Importantly, the 'Lisbon Strategy' in 2000 introduced and set out the Open Method of Coordination (OMC) in social policy. Environmental policy was added to the OMC one year after. The OMC introduced 'close coordination' between the Member States in areas that fall outside the exclusive competence of the EU.[41] The OMC is also used for the implementation of the new 2020 Strategy, which 'consists of quantitative targets aimed at securing smart, sustainable and inclusive growth'.[42]

These examples of a positive, constitutive impact on the social sphere have to be contextualised within the specific function and context that they emerge on an EU level. Simply said, it is often social content that can be seen as something ancillary to wider economic objectives.[43] An example is the definition of social inclusion as an employment objective such as employability, empowerment and the enablement of the individual.[44] The Lisbon Agenda that was continued in the new Europe 2020 Agenda equates social cohesion (normally defined as the bond

[35] See further C De Gryse, 'Historical and Institutional Background to the Cross-industry Social Dialogue' in AD Dufresne and P Pochet (eds), *The European Sectoral Social Dialogue* (Brussels, PIE, 2006) at 31.

[36] J Goetschy, 'The Lisbon Strategy and Social Europe: Two Closely Linked Destinies' in MD Rodrigues (ed), *Europe, Globalization and the Lisbon Agenda* (Cheltenham, Edward Elgar, 2009) 74–90.

[37] P Watson, *EU Social and Employment Law* (Oxford, Oxford University Press, 2009).

[38] See further the extensive overview in Savevska, 'Polanyian Reading of the Socio-Economic Transformations of the European Union' (n 33): minimum rules concerning gender equality, part-time regulation, fixed-term work, parental leave, consultation of labour, work councils, health and safety at work and transfer of social benefits.

[39] See further J McCormick, *Environmental Policy in the European Union* (Basingstoke, Palgrave, 2001); S Oberthür and M Pallemaerts (eds), 'The New Climate Policies of the European Union : Internal Legislation and Climate Diplomacy' (Brussels, VUB Press, 2010).

[40] See also the European Commission, Climate Action policy brief accessible at https://ec.europa.eu/clima/policies/eccp_en and Oberthür and Pallemaerts, 'The New Climate Policies of the European Union (n 39)

[41] L Tholoniat, 'The Career of the Open Method of Coordination: Lessons from a "Soft" EU Instrument' (2010) 33 *West European Politics* 93–117; CF Sabel and J Zeitlin, *Experimentalist Governance in the European Union towards a New Architecture* (Oxford, Oxford University Press, 2010).

[42] European Commission, 'EUROPE 2020: A Strategy for Smart, Sustainable and Inclusive Growth' (COM(2010) Brussels, European Commission).

[43] See further also the brilliant analysis of A Somek, *Engineering Equality: An Essay on European Anti-Discrimination Law* (Oxford, Oxford University Press, 2011).

[44] eg B van Apeldoorn, 'The Contradictions of "Embedded Neoliberalism" and Europe's Multi-level Legitimacy Crisis: The European Project and its Limits' in B van Apeldoorn, J Drahokoupil and L Horn (eds), *Contradictions and Limits of Neoliberal European Governance: From Lisbon to Lisbon* (London, Palgrave Macmillan, 2008) 21–43.

that brings people together in a given society) with activation, lifelong learning and flexicurity. Social cohesion is therefore sought not through protecting labour from market forces but to include labour in the market as much as possible.[45] Discourses are created that equate social cohesion with people's potential to participate in the labour market. Importantly, the discourse that is established in the pursuit of social cohesion and inclusion does not consider that there may exist a tension between transforming the Union into 'the most competitive and dynamic knowledge-based economy' and the development of social cohesion and inclusion policy.[46] Social policy is supposed to assist people into becoming successful market participants.[47] In this way the social objective of inclusion is 'regulated' in order to channel this interest through an institutional mechanism that makes it controllable with the ultimate objective to allow sectors of an economy to perform better. As an example, environmental regulation in the EU is shaped in the form of tradable rights to pollute, subjected to self-regulating market mechanisms.

This trend at the EU level followed a wave of reforms during the 1980s in many OECD countries that were inspired by market informed measures, that led to liberalisation of labour markets, capital markets, deregulation of industry and the privatisation of state enterprises.[48] Importantly, during this time, many public sector departments were restructured and downsized through outsourcing and the instalment of so called 'new public management' tools.[49] This basically installed a new rationality with respect to public management, introducing a move towards entrepreneurial systems of public management that were largely market informed. Although, over the course of the 1990s this trend became less radical through counter-reforms, today, a lot of public policy is still informed by and measured in terms of success through a market-based metric.[50]

It may very well be argued that within the context of EU internal market legislation a social sphere is mostly engineered instrumentally for the purpose of, essentially, economic objectives.[51] This is policy that is created mainly with the purpose of making markets work better by channelling social concerns within a model that renders the social sphere more *manageable*.[52] Hence, this emanation of the social

[45] ibid.

[46] ibid.

[47] See on this also D Ashiagbor, 'Unravelling the Embedded Liberal Bargain: Labour and Social Welfare Law in the Context of EU Market Integration' (2013) 3 *European Law Journal* 303–24.

[48] See further eg F Toth, 'Healthcare Policies over the Last 20 Years: Reforms and Counter-Reforms' (2010) 95 *Health Policy* 82; T Judt, *Postwar: A History of Europe since 1945* (London, Penguin Group) Inc, 2006) at 556.

[49] JE Lane, *New Public Management* (Abingdon, Routledge, 2002) at 147.

[50] eg OECD, Public Administration after "New Public Management": Value for Money in Government, vol 1, (Paris, OECD Publishing, 2010).

[51] ibid.

[52] See more generally NS Rose, *Governing the Present: Administering Economic, Social and Personal Life* (Cambridge, Polity, 2008).

sphere is generally considered as reconcilable with the EU's economic objectives:[53] if the social is engineered to function as a measure of increased productivity it qualifies as a *beneficial constraint* on the market because it actually lets the market function better than it would function without the constraint.[54]

The legislative powers conferred on the Union to harmonise laws for the purpose and benefit of the functioning of the Internal Market have been largely employed to pursue the creation of what may be called a commodified social sphere. There may be a simple reason for this since the Union legislature can often only seek recourse to a harmonisation measure at the moment that there are differences between national rules 'which are such as to obstruct the fundamental freedoms and thus have a direct effect on the functioning of the internal market'.[55] As explained, this influence from the internal market rules on the social sphere will not be addressed in this book. Normative concerns over the functioning of this positive impact on the social sphere may exist on the basis of the fact that they are largely established on the basis of a covert technocratic process that depoliticises the formulation and pursuit of social objectives and disregards the normative infrastructure of the economies within the Member States. This leads to concerns about its democratic legitimacy and can be seen as an encroachment on the constitutional space for Member States to develop social policy. Although, this commodified social content can in many ways be critiqued as being unresponsive to the idea of social plurality and diversity, it falls outside of the scope of this book because, as was explained above, this type of positive influence on the social sphere is governed by its own specific dynamic and actors that can be considered separate from the contingent influence on the social sphere, which is primarily governed by an adjudicative context.

B. The Internal Market Rules as a Negative Contingent Form for the Social Sphere

The positive influence on the social sphere should be differentiated from the more covert and contingent emanation of Member State social spheres within

[53] See also C Kaupa 'Maybe not Activist Enough? On the Court's Alleged Neoliberal Bias in its Recent Labor Cases' in B de Witte, E Muir and M Dawson, *Judicial Activism at the European Court of Justice: Causes, Responses and Solutions* (Cheltenham, Edward Elgar Publishing, 2013) 56–75.

[54] On the concept of beneficial constraints, see originally W Streeck, 'Beneficial Constraints: On the Economic Limits of Rational Voluntarism' in J Rogers Hollingsworth and R Boyer (eds), *Contemporary Capitalism: The Embeddedness of Institutions* (Cambridge, Cambridge University Press, 1997) 197–218. Further discussion in T Dobbins, 'The Case for "Beneficial Constraints": Why Permissive Voluntarism Impedes Workplace Cooperation in Ireland' (2010) 35 *Economic and Industrial Democracy* 497; W Streeck, 'Educating Capitalists: A Rejoinder to Wright and Tsakalotos' (2010) 2 *Socio-Economic Review* 425; E Tsakalotos, 'Market Constraints, Economic Performance and Political Power: Modernizers versus Leftists' (2004) 2 *Socio-Economic Review* 415.

[55] See Case C-58/08 *Vodafone and Others* [2010] ECR I-4999, para 32.

EU internal market law. The latter refers to situations where the internal market rules are functioning in their evaluative role and govern Member State social rules and structures by virtue of the fact that these social contexts can be considered as restrictive of the free circulation of economic factors and, from that point onwards, can only be considered to be in accordance with EU internal market law if they can be considered as 'legitimate' and 'proportionate' or, in the case of the competition rules, if they fulfil a set of efficiency criteria. These rules can be said, from an EU perspective, to be constitutive of 'legitimate' social spheres. If the test is passed then the social policy, although restrictive of trade interests, can be considered to exist in accordance with EU internal market law. The importance of this conditioned emanation of the social sphere within the legal frameworks of the EU internal market should not be understated. The increase of the scope of application of the EU free movement rules has led to a situation where, theoretically, all social policy measures that are capable of restricting access to a market of an economic operator, that are restrictive of competition or provide a selective economic advantage, are captured and in that sense the EU legal frameworks can to a large extent be seen as a constitutive framework of social realities that originate from a Member State level, targeting a wide variety of Member States' political regulations as obstacles to European law and not only political regulations but also the actions of private bodies such as firms or trade unions.[56] Moreover, the decentralised enforcement of the EU competition rules, which require self-assessments from undertakings, have the potential to significantly influence the content of 'private sphere' rules that are constitutive of local social spheres within the Member States.

Some would however argue that any conditioning effects of EU internal market law on social spheres within Member States are minimal in view of the fact that Member States' political authority in the determination of their own 'social identity' has been significantly impeded by the 'globalization of economic processes'.[57] Due to a threat of exit, the disciplining forces of markets, supranational monetary policy and fiscal oversight Member States no longer have the power to implement whatever 'social identity' they may desire. In the words of Streeck, 'the markets have begun to dictate in unprecedented ways what presumably sovereign and democratic states may still do for their citizens and what they must refuse them'.[58] Regardless of the dispersive effects that the global markets dynamics, undeniably, bring on Member States' regulatory options, there is a bulk of literature based on varieties of capitalism insights, which has established that, despite such globalising

[56] Case C-438/05 *International Transport Workers' Federation and Finnish Seamen's Union v Viking Line ABP and OÜ Viking Line Eesti* [2007] ECR p I-10779. See on horizontal effect H Schepel, 'Constitutionalising the Market, Marketising the Constitution, and to Tell the Difference: On the Horizontal Application of the Free Movement Provisions in EU Law' (2012) 18 *European Law Journal* 177–200.

[57] A Glyn, *Capitalism Unleashed: Finance, Globalization and Welfare* (Oxford, Oxford University Press, 2007); see also F de Witte, *Justice in the EU: The Emergence of Transnational Solidarity* (Oxford, Oxford University Press, 2015) at 37.

[58] W Streeck, 'The Crises of Democratic Capitalism' (2011) 71 *New Left Review* 26.

effects, the informal rules or common knowledge that is acquired by actors on the basis of the history and culture of nations leads to a variety of capitalist organisation.[59]

C. The Value of Social Diversity

Based on this literature it is suggested that the development of a particular type of institution will develop complementary, cohesive, institutions in other spheres of its socio-economic constellation.[60] One can see, for example, in countries that have adopted stock market liberalisation a tendency to have less labour protection. The overall idea behind the varieties of capitalism school of though is that the operation of capitalist market economies is not uniform. On the basis of the question how 'firms resolve the coordination problems they face' in different countries, Hall and Soskice found a distinction between the (Anglo-Saxon) liberal market economies and the northern European coordinated market economies.[61] Those two types could be distinguished on how firms coordinate with each other and other actors, such as trade unions. In liberal market economies firms will primarily coordinate on the basis of market mechanisms. In coordinated market economies firms will rely more heavily on non-market forms of interaction in the coordination of their relationships with other actors. Therefore, firms of liberal market economies and coordinated market economies tend to respond differently to a similar economic shock and its institutions have been characterised as 'socialising agencies' that go through a continuous processes of adaptation.[62] Some normative implications can and have been drawn from this literature. Firstly, that a transformation of one variety into another is hard to achieve and, secondly, that the selective insertion of elements of one variety into the fabric of the other can have disintegrative effects.[63]

[59] Also FW Scharpf, 'After the Crash: A Perspective on Multilevel European Democracy' (2015) 21 *European Law Journal* 384–405.

[60] See eg D Rodrik, *The Globalization Paradox* (London/New York, WW Norton, 2011) at 74:

> The considerable manoeuvring room afforded by [...] trading rules allowed advanced nations to build customized versions of capitalism around distinct approaches to corporate governance, labor markets, tax regimes, business-government relations, and welfare state arrangements. What emerged in a phrase coined by the political scientists Peter Hall and David Soskice, were 'varieties of capitalism'. The United States, Britain, France, Germany, or Sweden were each market-based economies, but the institutions that underpinned their markets differed substantially and bore unmistakably national characteristics.

[61] PA Hall and DW Soskice, *Varieties of Capitalism: The Institutional Foundations of Comparative Advantage* (Oxford, Oxford University Press, 2001); also specifically PA Hall, 'Varieties of Capitalism and the Euro Crisis' (2014) 37 *West European Politics* 1223–43.

[62] Hall and Soskice, *Varieties of Capitalism* (n 61) at 5.

[63] See eg A Hassel, 'Adjustments in the Eurozone: Varieties of Capitalism and the Crisis in Southern Europe' LEQS Paper No 76/2014; A Hassel, 'The German Model in Transition' in B Unger (ed), *The German Model* (Düsseldorf, Hans-Böckler-Stiftung, 2015) 105–34.

This builds on the idea that the social diversity of preferences and orientations in the EU is the product of specific historical experiences, political contestation, societal learning and continuous political decision-making.[64] As such, despite globalising trends Member States vary deeply in terms of institutional preferences and structural policy differences, resulting in a lush plethora of social spheres.[65] In similar terms the economic historian Werner Abelshauser has underlined the resistance of the varieties of capitalism against economic integration and argued that this resistance is an asset. Social diversity is economically beneficial, rather than detrimental.[66]

D. Social Legitimacy through Responsiveness

As was discussed in the introduction, the central issue pursued from the perspective of social legitimacy is how to adjudicate the potential irreconcilability between objectives of the internal market regime and variegating social spheres within the Member States. Irreconcilability occurs when social spheres cannot be translated within the internal market grammar without doing violence to potentially genuine and worthwhile aspects of those spheres. Adjudication that is based on strict proportionality, efficiency or market criteria that evaluate social spheres on the basis of the more efficient, less restrictive of more profitable course of actions carry this risk. If it is accepted that social diversity is a value to which the EU internal market is committed, then these functionalist modes of reasoning are not appropriate means to adjudicate conflicts, as they are likely to pre-empt a careful articulation of the actual conflict constellation. If applied to diagonal conflicts, an adjudicative technique such as substantive proportionality may inhibit and simply ignore legitimate policy choices that flow from the underlying normative infrastructure of each national socio-economic structure. A case in point is *Libert*, decided in 2013. The Court of Justice was asked to rule on Belgian social housing norms which restricted access to housing to those with a 'sufficient connection' to the geographical area and required property developers to meet social housing obligations.[67] The objective of this piece of housing regulation was to ensure

[64] As submitted by C Joerges, 'Market Integration and Europeanisation of Private Law', Jean Monnet Project Conference Paper (2015), on file with author.

[65] These can eg be classified in benefit structures, methods of financing, service intensity, family policy, employment regulation, logic of governance and the regulation of industrial relations in A Hemerijck, 'The Self-Transformation of the European Social Model(s)' in G Esping Andersen (ed), *Why we Need a Welfare State* (Oxford, Oxford University Press, 2002) at 178. See also P Beramendi, 'Inequality and the Territorial Fragmentation of Solidarity' (2007) 4 *International Organization* 783–820.

[66] See W Abelshauser, 'Ricardo neu gedacht: Komparative institutionelle Vorteile von Wirtschaftskulturen' in W Abelshauser et al (eds), *Kulturen der Weltwirtschaft (Geschichte und Gesellschaft)* (Sonderheft, 2012) at 24; W Abelshauser, *Europa in Vielfalt einigen. Eine Denkschrift* (2014). On this topic, see also G Majone, 'The Deeper Euro-Crisis or: The Collapse of the EU Political Culture of Total Optimism' EUI Working Paper LAW 2015/10.

[67] Case C-197/11, *Libert* ECLI:EU:C:2013:288.

access to housing in certain areas to low-income or otherwise disadvantaged sections of the local population, a measure designed to combat the phenomenon of gentrification. However, the Court considered after listing the restrictions on movement of capital, services and establishment that there were other means of pursuing Flanders' socio-economic objectives, which were less restrictive of the access to the local market. The Court even provided the example of 'subsidies for purchase or other subsidy mechanisms specifically designed to assist less affluent persons'.[68] In doing so, the Court did not take into account potential political compromises or budgetary restrictions but assumed a regulatory context that was largely *managerial*.[69] Moreover, the issue of gentrification in light of its potential to undermine social cohesion and the correlation with the free movement of capital and services of real-estate developers was not considered by the Court. As such, this mode of reasoning may lead to the denial that the diversity of preferences and orientations of Member States is the product of specific historical experiences, political contestation, societal learning and continuous political decision-making. As we discussed, Member States vary deeply in terms of institutional preferences and substantive policy choices and the evaluative standard that is used by the Court of Justice in such cases should express and acknowledge those differences. Rather, the approach adopted by the Court in this case is reflective of a mode of reasoning that suggests that 'everything can be reconciled', which potentially excludes the expressive value of conflict constellations within the internal market.[70]

Transplanting supranational trade objectives into local social spheres may eventually be disintegrative. It will be continuously emphasised in the studies of the next chapters that the legitimacy of EU law in the internal market in adjudicative settings depends on the capability to express instances of such irreconcilability before adopting evaluative principles that are congruent to the conflict that is being adjudicated.

The book joins streams with forms of critique that aim to show that EU law is capable of distorting social relations since objectives of pure economic integration carry the inherent risk to disregard the fundamental structures of domestic societies.[71] However, it is one thing to simply call for a substantial transformation of the European integration project, arguing that its laws and adjudication should be sensitive to social interests and local contexts; it is quite another thing to conceive of a rationale that accomplishes this, without completely forgoing the objectives of integration, free trade and legal certainty.[72] My argument in this book is

[68] ibid, at para 56.

[69] Perhaps it was, but is more than likely that it was not. See eg S Reynolds, 'Housing Policy as a Restriction of Free Movement and MSs Discretion to Design Programmes of Social Protection: Libert' (2015) 52 *Common Market Law Review* 259–80.

[70] *cf* Dani, 'Rehabilitating Social Conflicts in European Public Law' (n 19).

[71] See eg A Menéndez, 'Which Citizenship? Whose Europe?—The Many Paradoxes of European Citizenship' (2014) 15 *German Law Journal* 907–33; G Davies, 'Internal Market Adjudication and the Quality of Life in Europe' (2014) EUI Working Paper 2014/07.

[72] L Azoulai, 'The Court of Justice and the Social Market Economy: The Emergence of an Ideal and the Conditions for Its Realization' (2008) 45 *Common Market Law Review* 1335; L Azoulai,

that it is in developing a 'rationale of mutual responsiveness' that the EU internal market finds a social purpose; *a reconciliation of local social spheres with and within supranational market objectives.* Clearly, such a rationale of responsiveness will look different within the different governance fora of the European Union. As was highlighted in the general introduction, this book is specifically concerned with the development of a rationale of responsiveness for adjudicative contexts. The aim of this book then is to provide for means to make social responsiveness part of that legal space, concretely, within the adjudicative model and rationales of the Court of Justice in the application of internal market law.

I will further unfold the normative grounding of this theory of social responsiveness on the basis of social theory insights based on the idea of embeddedness in the work of Karl Polanyi. Any attempt to reinvigorate a Polanyian critique or to connect it to a contemporary normative account has to overcome the obvious fact that Polanyi's main work was written in the early 1940s and that today the orthodox market liberalism and social naturalism that formed the object of his critical, historical, investigations is without any (serious) intellectual support. More particularly, why and how should legal scholars, interested in legal issues in the EU internal market, be interested in the historical analysis of Karl Polanyi, who was by training an economic anthropologist? The next section explores this question, specifically with respect to the social *problematique* as it was previously introduced and contextualised within the argument from transnational effects.

III. THE INSTRUCTIVE VALUE OF EMBEDDEDNESS

The answer is that, primarily, Polanyi's study brings to the concept of social legitimacy a normative commitment based on his historical analysis of the effects of a structural disregard of domestic social spheres in the organisation of state-market-society relationships. In this way, Polanyi can be read as providing a historical narrative that provides a normative commitment to the conceptualisation of social legitimacy and for the idea that responsiveness in the governance mechanisms of the internal market is crucial for the social acceptance and hence political sustainability of the internal market project.

Karl Polanyi provides an appealing perspective that has increasingly been used and heralded as a moral framework for arguments of contemporary market critics.[73] Before diving into the central concepts that are of value for a discussion

'The European Court of Justice and the Duty to Respect Sensitive National Interests' in de Witte, Muir and Dawson, *Judicial Activism at the European Court of Justice: Causes, Responses and Solutions* (n 53) 167.

[73] Christian Joerges was one of the first to give Polanyi a serious and multifaceted consideration in a (transnational) law context. See C Joerges and J Falke (eds), *Karl Polanyi: Globalisation and the Potential of Law in Transnational Markets* (Oxford- Portland OR, Hart Publishing, 2011). See also J Caporaso and A Tarrow, 'Polanyi in Brussels: Supranational Institutions and the Transnational Embedding of Markets' (2009) 63 *International Organization* 593–620; M Höpner and A Schäfer,

of the social legitimacy of European market integration, the following section is aimed at familiarising the reader with the narrative and conceptual apparatus that Polanyi introduced with his much acclaimed work *The Great Transformation: the Political and Economic Origins of our Time* (TGT).[74]

A. Notes on Polanyi

TGT was written in the early 1940s and first published in 1944. In it Polanyi provides a theory for the origin of the political turbulence and economic collapse of nineteenth-century civilisation. These events puzzled Polanyi. A long period in Europe of peace and prosperity was quite suddenly exchanged for huge economic, political and human turmoil. His instinctive vision on these events qualifies 'world war—Great Depression—world war' not as disconnected events but as symptoms of one deep societal problem.[75] Polanyi argues that the main cause for the disaster is the utopian endeavour of market liberalism to set up a self-regulating market system. His core argument is that market liberalism requires everything to be tradable, including important ecological and societal phenomena such as labour, land and money. To place these within the alienating mechanisms of a self-regulating market is the main, and at the same time self-destructive, flaw of market liberalism. The self-regulating market requires a separation of politics and the economy and this plants a seed for political and economic unsustainability. The commodity fiction of societal and ecological interests led to a degree of social dislocation that no society can sustain. Eventually, a counter-movement against liberalisation would seek to de-commodify the commodity fiction. This process undermines the efficiency of the market and thus provides a major cause for further economic crisis, thereby opening up the political stage to fascist-like movements.

He traces the root of the mechanisms of a self-regulating market to the English Industrial Revolution, when market idealism becomes an organising principle of the world economy.[76] Polanyi's analysis of this event, in short, is that altered cost structures of producers, affected by the availability of new technologies, started to dictate market expansion and managed to bring elite opinion behind the political economist's case for a free market regime. This new order was then actively made by state policy.[77] In this order, the concepts of individual profit, gain and accumulation *had to* become inherent to human fulfilment and the market mechanisms *must* be allowed to function without outside governmental interference in order

'Polanyi in Brussels? Embeddedness and the Three Dimensions of European Economic Integration' (MPIfG Discussion Paper, 2010).

[74] K Polanyi, *The Great Transformation: The Political and Economic Origins of our Time* (Boston, The Beacon Press, [1944] 2nd edn 2001).

[75] See also Dale, *Karl Polanyi* (n 9) at 2.

[76] Polanyi, *The Great Transformation: The Political and Economic Origins of our Time* (n 74) at 35.

[77] ibid, ch 3.

not to disrupt the expectations of buyers and sellers.[78] What the producer sells is generally harmless to society but what he buys is raw material and labour. In Polanyian terms, he buys nature and man.[79]

Polanyi argues that the extent to which markets have control over society concerns a clear choice of design and institutional infrastructure:[80]

> Instead of economy being embedded in social relations, social relations are embedded in the economic system. [...] For once the economic system is organized in separate institutions, based on specific motives and conferring a special status, society must be shaped in such a manner as to allow that system to function according to its own laws.

It is important to note however that Polanyi argues not against markets. He states explicitly 'no society can exist without a system of some kind which ensures order in the production and distribution of goods'.[81] He considers markets excellent means to divide scarce resources in society and acknowledges that its mechanisms provide revolutionary means to achieve an increase in material wealth, but, so Polanyi argues, markets should always be merely *a function* of the social order. The potential for this function disappears because of the inherent system of fictitious commodification that is part of this market ideology.

At this point of the argument Polanyi introduces a key thesis: the double-movement. The idea of the self-regulated market appears as a very strong force. There is, however, a big flaw: it is simply unsustainable. The spreading of market idealism is accompanied almost instantaneously with measures and policies designed to check the impact of the market on the fictitious commodities of labour, land and money.[82] Human beings will not accept that their livelihoods depend on the needs and changing tides of supply and demand. Polanyi submits that consequent counter-movements occur spontaneously and pragmatically across societies whenever human or natural resources disproportionally fall into the grip of self-regulatory models and are diminished to input commodities within a market mechanism. Spontaneous interventions from society in the form of legislation, administration and associative self-organisation will be initiated in order to regain control over these things that Polanyi considers as 'fictitious commodities'.[83]

Polanyi records a high degree of diversity on the issues on which counter-action spontaneously arises, the common denominator being that they all deal with the safeguarding of some public interest against dangers in the market method of dealing with them.[84] Contrary to the artificial construction of free markets,

[78] ibid, at 74.

[79] ibid, at 44: 'Machine production in a commercial society involves in effect no less a transformation than that of the natural and human substance of society into commodities'.

[80] ibid, at 60.

[81] ibid, at 74.

[82] ibid, at 79.

[83] ibid, at 136.

[84] ibid, at 152. Polanyi provides the following examples: analysts of food and drink to be paid out of local rates; the inspection of gas works; making it penal to employ boys under 12 not attending school

subsequent restrictions on the mechanisms of the market do raise spontaneously out of society:[85] 'Laissez-faire was planned; planning was not'. Polanyi substantiates his point by showing how similar developments occurred in different countries in Europe. Each of Victorian England, the Prussia of Bismarck, the France of the Third Republic and the empire of the Hapsburgs experienced a period of free trade and laissez-faire followed by a period of anti-liberal legislation with regard to a variety of issues such as public health, factory conditions, municipal trading, social insurance, public utilities, trade associations etc. Polanyi sets out a clarifying timeline by which these 'double-movements' occurred.[86] Polanyi considers this universal 'collectivist' yet fragmented reaction against the expansion of market economy as conclusive proof of 'the peril to society inherent in the utopian principle of a self-regulating market'.[87]

Polanyi argues that social change such as protectionist movements generally result from external changes to societal structure as a whole. Whenever a new societal structure comes into existence, this necessarily impacts the interests of those groups most affected by the change. This is demonstrated by the various similar but diverging reactions of groups of people in different countries that experienced intense periods of laissez-faire politics, which impacted their position in society and consequently triggered a protectionist reaction. According to Polanyi, this protective movement should not be qualified as class interest but as spontaneous social interests and action imperilled by market mechanisms.[88] This can produce situations of societal instability and collapse. This is what Polanyi considers as the problem of the separation of politics and economics in an age of democratisation. Democracy and capitalism become irreconcilable enemies and society 'is inevitably doomed to collapse, or to revolution'.[89]

The capture of political power by the working classes provided effective means for protective movements to disrupt economic self-regulation.[90] Eventually, Polanyi concludes that the tension between capitalism and democracy became a disintegrating force.[91] Consequently, economic adjustments became impossible. The division of economy from society and the absence of change at a socially acceptable tempo caused a 'disembedding'. Social strains in society 'would transcend the

and unable to read or write; enforced vaccinations; local boards authorised to fix rates of hire for means of conveyance; inspectors for the wholesomeness of food; laws preventing the deaths of children that were set to sweep too narrow spaces; a contagious disease act; a public libraries act; and more examples of varying kinds.

[85] ibid, at 147.

[86] ibid, at 153.

[87] The other is that Polanyi rejects the idea of exclusive economic interests as drivers for social change. He argues that social change is generally driven by questions of social recognition.

[88] This a point where Polanyi clearly distinguishes himself from the social theory of Marx.

[89] Polanyi (n 74) at 207.

[90] M Höpner and A Schäfer, 'Embeddedness and Regional Integration: Waiting for Polanyi in a Hayekian Setting' (2012) 66 *International Organization* 429.

[91] Polanyi (n 74) at 235–36.

economic zone and the balance would have to be restored by political means'.[92] This necessitated a reuniting of economics and politics in a progressive and effective form. Short of that, workers were bound to deploy their electoral power to protective ends and capitalists to use their wealth and influence to weaken political democracy.[93] This was, however, an irreconcilable conflict and the time was ripe for the 'fascist solution'.[94]

This is roughly the analysis of Polanyi as regards the origins of the collapse of nineteenth-century civilisation. In the last part of the book Polanyi turns his outlook shortly to the future. He expected that markets would not be self-regulating and that political choice would fix prices for land, labour and money.[95] Importantly, abandoning the gold standard would free governments from the chains of the international monetary system and facilitate international cooperation: 'economic collaboration of governments and the liberty to organize national life at will'.[96] As was discussed before, these insights foreshadowed the idea and institutional construction of embedded liberalism in Europe.[97]

B. The Enduring Relevance of Polanyi

It is not a surprise that there has been a revival of interest in Polanyi's work in recent years, across disciplines.[98] Part of this popularity can be explained on the basis of his 'cite-ability' and eerie relevance for current and pressing themes, reflected, for example, in a passage such as the following where Polanyi discusses how the stabilisation of currencies became the focal point of political thought in the 1920s:

> the repayments of foreign loans and the return to stable currencies were [time and again] recognized as the touchstone of rationality in politics; and no private suffering, no restriction of sovereignty, is deemed too great a sacrifice for the recovery of monetary integrity. The repayment of foreign loans and the return to stable currencies were recognized as

[92] ibid, at 235.
[93] ibid, at 244.
[94] ibid, at 244.
[95] ibid, at 250.
[96] ibid, at 254.
[97] See Ruggie (n 4).
[98] See for a recent explanation of this resurfacing F Block and M Somers, *The Power of Market Fundamentalism: Karl Polanyi's Critique* (Boston, Harvard University Press, 2014). Examples related to the field of law include: Special Issue: 'New Directions in Polanyian Scholarship' (2014) 43 *Economy and Society*; D Ashiagabor, P Kotiswaran, and A Perry-Kessaris (eds), Special Issue: Towards an Economic Sociology of Law (2013) 40 *Journal of Law and Society*. Also, G Krippner et al, 'Polanyi Symposium: a Conversation on Embeddedness' (2004) 2 *Socio-Economic Review* 109; J Mulder, 'Re-embedding EU Governance Fields: A Research Agenda' in C Joerges and C Glinski (eds), *The European Crisis and the Transformation of Transnational Governance. Authoritarian Managerialism versus Democratic Governance* (Oxford, Hart Publishing, 2014) at 181.

> the touchstone of rationality in politics; and no private suffering, no restriction of sovereignty, was deemed too great a sacrifice for the recovery of monetary integrity.[99]

Today's market critics understandably derive a direct and profound normative and historically validated commitment from the work of Polanyi in critiquing contemporary atomistic austerity politics.[100] Other than drawing on similarities such as these, commentators have also picked up on Polanyi's core concepts of the double-movement, fictitious commodification and embeddedness and started working with those concepts in terms of a Polanyian-inspired research agenda.[101] In particular, Polanyi's conceptual apparatus has been used to qualify the process of European integration in terms of a double-movement, where 'disembedding' marketisation efforts are counteracted by 'embedding' re-regulation. Moreover, the separation of the political from the economic sphere resounds strongly with the advance of technocratic forms of decision-making within the Union.[102] However, a strong critique on the work of Polanyi is that his central concepts lack theoretical specificity.[103] In TGT they are defined sufficiently widely that the willing reader can interpret them in a way that captures most if not all social processes that involve a form of resistance or result in social policy of some kind as a response to 'the market'.[104] On this basis one legal commentator from the left went as far as to say that 'we are all Polanyians now'.[105] In adopting an explicit Polanyian vocabulary one should therefore carefully consider how that usage can be authentically traced back to Polanyi and from which point the conceptual apparatus needs to be extended to a post-Polanyian understanding in order to sufficiently capture the actual processes that are being described in order not to render Polanyi's valuable historical insights meaningless.

[99] Polanyi (n 74) at 148.

[100] eg DM Woodruff, 'Governing by Panic: The Politics of the Eurozone Crisis' (LEQS Paper No 81/2014, 2014).

[101] eg M Saveska, 'Polanyian Reading of the Socio-Economic Transformations of the European Union' (2014) 22 *Journal of Contemporary European Studies* 395–410; P Copeland, 'International Political Economy and European Integration—Applying Karl Polanyi's The Great Transformation' (2009) 40 *IPEG Papers on Global Political Economy* 1–26; N Lindstrom, 'Service Liberalization in the Enlarged EU: A Race to the Bottom or the Emergence of Transnational Political Conflict?' (2010) 49 *Journal of Common Market Studies* 1307–27; Caporaso and Tarrow, 'Polanyi in Brussels' (n 73); Höpner and Schäfer, 'Embeddedness and Regional Integration' (n 90); Ashiagbor, 'Unravelling the Embedded Liberal Bargain' (n 47).

[102] See also Saveska, 'Polanyian Reading of the Socio-Economic Transformations of the European Union' (n 101).

[103] C Holmes, 'Problems and Opportunities in Polanyian Analysis Today' (2012) 41 *Economy and Society Economy* 468.

[104] eg R Munck, 'Globalization and Contestation: A Polanyian Problematic' (2006) 3 *Globalizations* 175–86.

[105] H Schepel, 'Rules of Recognition: A Constructivist Approach to Transnational Private Regulation' in PF Kjaer, P Jurčys and R Yatsunami (eds), *Regulatory Hybridization in the Transnational Sphere* (Leiden, Martinus Nijhoff Publishers, 2013) at 193. See also J Beckert, 'The Great Transformation of Embeddedness: Karl Polanyi and the New Economic Sociology' in C Hann and K Hart (eds), *Market and Society: The Great Transformation Today* (New York, Cambridge University Press, 2009) 38–55.

C. Embeddedness and the Double-movement

Although the term 'embeddedness' is only occasionally used in the work of Polanyi, his work is clear on the dangers and, in particular, the social instability that results from attempts to 'disembed' the market from its fundamental socio-political settings and supports and 'to treat it as if it has no dependence on a wider social context'.[106] Embeddedness has become a, if not the, core concept of 'the new economic sociology'. However, Polanyi himself makes no effort to clarify, conceptually, how embeddedness is to be made tangible.[107] It is unclear if embeddedness is concerned with, for example, 'political institutions, legal controls, state policy or social conditions'.[108] Unsurprisingly, therefore, there is debate with respect to the exact meaning of embeddedness in Polanyian terms and it has been roughly described in two ways. Political economist Fred Block argues that markets are, necessarily, always embedded and that there can be no such thing as a pure and disembedded market economy: 'Economic processes cannot but result from a mix of cultural, political and economic forces'.[109] Block submits that Polanyi was mainly concerned with identifying this 'always embedded economy'. The 'always embedded economy' thesis recognises that markets are always and necessarily somehow related to other social and cultural elements of societies and therefore never fully autonomous from the start. This interpretation of the concept mainly allows for descriptive research with respect to why economic infrastructures and institutions function and look the way that they do.[110]

Another, reading of Polanyi's concept of embeddedness acknowledges that Polanyi identified the need to position markets in an institutional order that is 'always embedded' but distinguishes this from what Polanyi considered to be the *actual process of (dis)embedding markets.*[111] It is this process that is interesting for the development of a normative perspective on governance in the EU internal market. One lesson that can be taken from Polanyi's historical analysis is the 'trend' by which communities respond to atomised and under-socialised attempts to organise state-market-society relations on the basis of the self-regulating market rationale. The societal fragmentation and response occurs when such processes of societal change do not allow for pre-existing societal structures and choices to be recognised within those governance mechanisms. Hence, successful and enduring governance schemes will take account of the communities they regulate.

[106] R Cotterrell, 'Rethinking "Embeddedness": Law, Economy, Community' (2013) 40 *Journal of Law and Society* 49–67, at 53. *cf* with Granovetter, who uses the concept of embeddedness in a similar way in his famous M Granovetter, 'Economic Action and Social Structure: the Problem of Embeddedness' (1985) 91 *American Journal of Sociology* 481–93.

[107] See Beckert, 'The Great Transformation of Embeddedness' (n 105) at 38–55.

[108] ibid.

[109] F Block, 'Karl Polanyi and the Writing of the Great Transformation' (2003) 32 *Theory and Society* 275.

[110] See Dale (n 9).

[111] See Ebner, 'Transnational Markets and the Polanyi Problem' (n 21) at 28.

This reading emphasises the importance of a micro-community-based analysis of the actual content and object of socio-economic governance mechanisms.

Within the legal framework of the internal market this provides input for an evaluative rationale that needs to respond to diversity in approaches towards local social spheres. This is a reading of embeddedness that recognises the diversity and plurality of the central facets of organisational principles that determine the normative infrastructure of an economy. For example, relations of community can be based:

> (i) on a convergence of the participants' projects (instrumental community) which may be economic in nature; or (ii) on shared customs, traditions, physical environment or linguistic or historical heritage (traditional community) or (iii) on shared fundamental convictions (community of belief or values), or (iv) on essentially emotional attractions or rejections, likes or dislikes, loves or hatreds towards others (affective community).[112]

The point here is the connection between embeddedness and context specificity in economic regulation. Some of these communal contexts lend themselves easily to economic regulation. The instrumental community fits within a form of regulation based on an evaluative principle of efficiency. Problems may arise, however, when such economic substantive efficiency-oriented governance mechanisms would be installed to regulate traditional communities, communities based on belief or values and so forth. To do so would be to disembed the social sphere within a regulatory framework that remains under-socialised. Regulation of the organisational principles that govern these social contexts would need to be responsive in order to be recognised and accepted within the social networks that they aim to regulate. In this specific sense, there are requirements of institutional design and rationality that can be read into the normative concerns that Polanyi's notion of embeddedness and processes of disembedding provides.

Polanyi's more general point with respect to his coining of the double-movement is that accepting dominating principles of gain and profit as the sole organising principles in society contributes to the rise of unstable societies. This instability arises through the domination of one organising principle over, and to the exclusion of other, socially 'embedded' organising principles. Again, the point of Polanyi with a time-less relevance is that the structural disregard of important elements of the social sphere will at some undefined point in time, trigger opposition and contestation within society. A counter-movement against the submersion within a dominant rationale will seek to protect that which is not recognised in the dominating principle. If such opposition and contestation is not adequately channelled, then society may begin to fracture, lose cohesion and can ultimately collapse. This is the oversimplified, basic point of Polanyi but it is easy to point towards general trends in society that would validate the intuitive

[112] See Cotterrell, 'Rethinking "Embeddedness"' (n 106) at 55.

appeal of his framework.[113] Therefore, the specific relevance of the Polanyian 'double-movement' for the principle of responsiveness in the EU internal market is (i) the importance of the identification and recognition of different organising principles in society, whose treatment are directly related to the political sustainability and diversity of the European internal market project; and (ii) the need to develop a reciprocal dynamic between these different organising principles for any politically sustainable project, which relates directly to the need of an adjudicative rationale for situations where such organising principles might clash.[114]

D. A Rationale of Responsiveness: Moving beyond Polanyi?

The relevance of Polanyi's work for responsiveness in the EU internal market towards social diversity is not based on his analysis of naturalistic orthodox market fundamentalism but based on a concern with more general applicability for the effects of EU internal market law on the social sphere within the Member States. The historical narrative of Polanyi shows recurring trends within societies that respond to under-socialised attempts to reframe market-state-society relationships. Polanyi therefore provides a historically grounded commitment to the idea of social legitimacy in terms of its normative claims on the social responsiveness of a supranational trade regime. This concerns the idea that strong organising principles that adopt a dominant and strict rationality carry the inherent risk of disregarding conflicting principles in society that do not fit within that rationale. Therefore, thinking in terms of embeddedness allows a conceptualisation of the meaning of the social and diversity as they emerge within legal frameworks that translate their social meaning for regulatory purposes. The assumption is that dominating principles will tease out conflict and contestation and if structurally ignored will also challenge the social and political sustainability of the whole project. Polanyi therefore provides an urgency to develop a legal rationale that does not suppress but allows a diversity of embedding organisational principles to exist and communicate constructively within overarching legislative frameworks.[115] In this context, social legitimacy would be forgone when EU internal market

[113] A case in point would be the latest Greek election that responded directly to such an under-socialised and atomised system of decision-making that has the potential to destabilise the entire Eurozone.

[114] There is an interesting analogy here with the issue of functional rationalities and the complexities this brings for international law, which might be further explored; see G Teubner and A Fischer-Lescano, 'Regime-collisions: The Vain Search for Legal Unity in the Fragmentation of Global Law' (2004) 25 *Michigan Journal of International Law* 999–1046; AL Paulus in response to that article, 'Commentary to Andreas Fischer-Lescano and Gunther Teubner: The Legitimacy of International Law and the Role of the State' (2003) 25 *Michigan Journal of International Law* 1047–58, and again, G Teubner and A Fischer-Lescano, 'Reply to Andreas L. Paulus Consensus as Fiction of Global Law' (2003) 25 *Michigan Journal of International Law* 1059. More recently, see G Teubner, *Transnational Economic Constitutionalism in the Varieties of Capitalism* (Ms, Frankfurt, 2015).

[115] As in E Sternberg, 'Justifying Public Intervention without Market Externalities: Karl Polanyi's Theory of Planning in Capitalism' (1993) 53 *Public Administration Review* 100–09.

governance would apply an atomised, under-socialised conception of rational Member State action and ignores embedding social fabric that seeks to structure economic activities within the direction and values of a community.

As was touched on before, an issue that is often overlooked in the debates of the EU 'social deficit' is that it is important to be clear about the meaning of the social and how it *specifically* conflicts with, purposefully oversimplified, the 'economic'. To be clear means to understand the type of conflicts that may arise between clashes of different normative orders and the consequent need to have adjudicative and governance rationales that are able to deal with these different types of conflicts. Thinking in terms of embeddedness is instructive in this regard because it clarifies the nature of the social sphere for regulatory purposes. That is to say, to see the social sphere in terms of communal networks that *may* be dominated by economic objectives but *may* also be constituted on the basis of other normative principles. Regulating them will have to take into account the mixes of different types of normative infrastructures of economies that they may exhibit and thereby the internal market can be positioned within such '*legitimate* social purposes'.[116] This exercise of clarification, in itself alone, would benefit the functioning of the EU legal system.[117] Thus, the absence or presence of true or false conflicts in norms has consequences with respect to the means through which such conflicts should be resolved.

The Polanyian insights based on the societal phenomenon of the double-movement provide for direction and a normative commitment to essentially 'manage' the double-movement. That is to say, to develop governance rationales that do not suppress but allow a diversity of embedding organisational principles to exist and to develop a reciprocal dynamic between these different organising principles for a politically sustainable project. Dominating principles will tease out conflict and contestation and one way to 'discover' the nature of the social as economic or non-economic is through a residual approach. To define it through a process of opposition that allows elemental social fabric to be distinguished from market objectives. Indeed, this approach accepts the primacy of the market but then creates a space for everything else to be identified as a residual, conflicting and *potentially* legitimate objective.[118]

On the basis of the foregoing, a rationale of responsiveness, instructed by embeddedness has a procedural dimension that allows an evaluation of the social sphere in its specific context. It has a substantive basis that recognises the limits of evaluative principles that are unable to sufficiently weigh the objectives at stake.

[116] Caporoso and Tarrow (n 73).

[117] WN Hohfeld, 'Some Fundamental Legal Conceptions as Applied in Judicial Reasoning' (1913) 23 *Yale Law Journal* 16.

[118] This is partly an operationalisation of the perspective that Colin Crouch develops around the idea of assertive social democracy that accepts the value and priority of markets in the economy, but is aware of their limitations and deficiencies as inappropriate in some areas of life; see C Crouch, *Making Capitalism Fit for Society* (Cambridge-Malden MA, Polity Press, 2013) at 37.

It may for example be the way that certain objectives are pursued, and not so much their outcomes, that makes them socially relevant. Some objectives share a social and political pact that *underlies* the objectives that are pursued.[119] The distinction of Polanyi between embedded and disembedded markets allows reconciliation in the sense that markets as such are not rejected, but only the 'dangerous, disembedded market'.[120] It is in this sense a reconciliatory rationale that Polanyi advanced. Nevertheless, this raises the question: is all disembedding *necessarily* harmful? Local values may be reflective of forms of discrimination and a communitarian bias may be used to legitimise practices that are perhaps focused on entrenching privilege and exclusion.

What processes of commodification attack is therefore not always worth defending and a process of marketisation may very well foster emancipation by weakening traditional entrenched forms of privilege.[121] It is clear that Polanyi never set out to provide an idealised account of traditional society or favour domination of any sort. One of the main reasons for Polanyi's thesis is to avoid the rise of an authoritarian, fascist alternative by re-positioning markets within communities on the basis of democratic means. Polanyi made clear that not all regimes of protection were morally equivalent or worthy of protection. The point is that this was never concretised by Polanyi as part of his critical theory. That is to say, there is no concept that allows the distinction between good embedded markets or bad embedded markets (endorsing eg slavery and racial discrimination).

It is, in fact, on this point that a Polanyian-inspired critique stands to gain significantly from the theoretical foundations of the argument from transnational effects, which brings the *mutual* into the dialogue of responsiveness. As was discussed above, the traditional internal market obligations for Member States can be perceived as not being able to pursue their interests or laws without restraint. Instead they are

> obliged to respect the European freedoms; they are not allowed to discriminate and can pursue only legitimate regulatory policies; they must, in relation to the objectives that they wish to pursue through regulation, harmonise with each other, and they must reform their national systems in the most community-friendly way possible.[122]

In other words, the value of internal market integration is exactly to constrain national self-expression, 'so as to mitigate what are regarded as its potential excesses: the exclusion of certain interests from the political process, and its

[119] See similarly, R Bellamy, 'The Liberty of the Moderns: Market Freedom and Democracy within the EU' (2012) 1 *Global Constitutionalism* 141–72, at 168.

[120] N Fraser, 'Can Society Be Commodities All the Way down? Post-Polanyian Reflections on Capitalist Crisis' (2014)4 3 *Economy and Society* 541.

[121] ibid.

[122] See C Joerges and F Rödl, 'Informal Politics, Formalised Law and the "Social Deficit" of European Integration: Reflections after the Judgments of the ECJ in Viking and Laval' (2009) 15 *European Law Journal* 1–19.

capacity for sovereign violence in limiting permissible behaviour'.[123] In this way, the thesis aims to move beyond the communitarian bias through an emphasis on the *mutuality* that responsiveness requires within internal market governance mechanisms.

E. Polanyi in Luxembourg?

Quite a number of Polanyian accounts have been given about the enactment of internal market legislation and, in particular most recently, the European response to the debt crisis.[124] Interesting as such accounts may be,[125] this section focuses on Polanyian accounts and critiques on the case law of the Court of Justice.

The first serious attempt to connect the work of Polanyi to the dynamics of the internal market and specifically the case law of the Court of Justice was undertaken by Caporoso and Tarrow in 2009.[126] Caporoso and Tarrow take a Polanyian-inspired outlook by arguing that the Court of Justice has in its labour law case law started to develop what they describe as the structure for a supranational embedded liberal compromise. In its case law the Court of Justice has created a new social dimension where it recognises workers are 'human beings, with families, local commitments, and rights'.[127] The authors distinguish different phases in the case law of the Court of Justice in the application of free movement law for workers. Starting from a perspective of market failure the Court of Justice's first concern was to remove obstacles to the free movement of labour.[128] In a second stage the authors argue that the Court developed a supranational embedded liberal compromise by recognising that workers were not just commodities and 'the social standing of workers and people in general was taken into account' for the determination of their 'rights' based on the free movement of workers provisions in the Treaty.[129] Therefore, the authors argue that social content has been infused into the application of the free movement rules. This they argue is evidence for the idea that the Court is inspired by Polanyi and pursues an ideal of the supranational embedded liberal compromise.

This attempt at a Polanyian reconstruction of a single line of cases of the Court is unconvincing and demonstrates a confused understanding of the meaning of embeddedness. That is in itself not surprising, since as was discussed above,

123 See F de Witte, 'Sex, Drugs & EU Law: The Recognition of Moral and Ethical Diversity in EU law' (2013) 50(6) *Common Market Law Review* 1551.

124 See Woodruff, 'Governing by Panic' (n 100).

125 See esp Saveska (n 101).

126 See Caporaso and Tarrow (n 73).

127 ibid, at 600.

128 See a similar account for the free movement of healthcare services by M Krajewski, 'Commodifying and Embedding Services of General Interest in Transnational Contexts: The Example of Healthcare Liberalisation in the EU and the WTO' in Joerges and Falke, *Karl Polanyi* (n 73).

129 Referring to the *Carpenter* Case C-60/00 [2002] ECR I-06279.

the concept is never concretely grounded in the work of Polanyi. However, it is quite certain that Polanyi would not approve of Caporoso and Tarrow's use of his ideas. Their understanding of the embeddedness concept as the infusion of social rights-based content within the supranational trade regime is closer to the interpretation that Granovetter has given to the embeddedness concept, which is according to Granovetter himself not inspired by Polanyi in any way.[130] Granovetter argued that the perception of economic action within neoclassical economic accounts separated economics from society and culture in a 'under-socialised account' and atomised human behaviour. In a similar way, he argued that sociologists employed an 'over-socialised' view of economic actors, refusing to see the ways that rational choice could influence the ways they acted in traditional, 'embedded' social roles:[131]

> Actors do not behave or decide as atoms outside a social context, nor do they adhere slavishly to a script written for them by the particular intersection of social categories that they happen to occupy. Their attempts at purposive action are instead embedded in concrete, ongoing systems of social relations.

It seems to be this understanding of embeddedness that underlies Caporoso and Tarrow's attempt to reconstruct the free movement of workers case law of the Court into a structure for a supranational embedded liberal compromise. That is to say a free trade regime that is, on a supranational level, infused with social content. Therefore, the trade regime is not overly commodified nor socialised. I partly agree with Scharpf who forcefully responded to this idea in his famous piece on the asymmetry of European integration.[132] He argued that it is true that, as Caporoso and Tarrow argue, the rights-based case law of the Court of Justice has evolved in a way that it is no longer primarily based on economic interests but also serves non-economic interests. This development is, he argues, in no way evidence for the 'social embeddedness' of the European economy.[133] Instead, the case law of the Court is primarily concerned with 'individual rights of exit from, and entry into, democratically shaped and collectively financed systems of national solidarity'.[134] In this way, the case law is more likely to undermine the reciprocity that is needed for rights and obligations to have a social foundation in the first place.[135]

Martin Höpner and Armin Schäfer joined and extended this critique by discussing lines of case law from the Court of Justice that demonstrate a tendency to

[130] See Granovetter, 'Economic Action and Social Structure' (n 106) 481–93; also Krippner et al, 'Polanyi Symposium' (n 98).

[131] Granovetter (n 106) at 487.

[132] See Scharpf, 'After the Crash' (n 59) at 211.

[133] ibid, at 226.

[134] As argued by A Somek, *Individualism: An Essay on the Authority of the European Union* (Oxford, Oxford University Press, 2008).

[135] As argued by A Menendez, 'European Citizenship after Martinez Sala and Baumbast: Has European Law Become More Human but Less Social?' RECON Online Working Paper 2009/05 (Oslo, University of Oslo, ARENA—Centre for European Studies, 2009).

undermine national social foundations within Member States.[136] They recognise and acknowledge that the Court of Justice has established some significant anti-discrimination jurisprudence with an effect within all Member States. However, they see this case law as reflecting 'social' content in the wider sense, but not as an element of a Polanyian-inspired agenda: 'it aims to create free access to the market, unhampered by discrimination, in other words: free but fair markets'.[137] Instead the picture they paint is very similar to that of Scharpf. The argument is that the direct effect of market freedoms[138] has provided market agents with individual rights, which they have enforced, making use of the supremacy of those laws,[139] mainly to undermine regulatory systems within Member States.[140]

> Armed with direct effect and supremacy, European competition law became a live weapon in the hands of supranational actors, because, from that point on, it could potentially be used to liberalize economic sectors for which it had initially not been made, namely third sector areas providing public goods and services, such as telecommunications, energy, and transportation.

Moreover, they argue, the replacement of the principle of non-discrimination[141] by the principle of non-restriction[142] in the case law of the Court has accelerated and enforced a dynamic that structurally allows supranational market actors to successfully question regulatory choices within Member States.[143] In the words of Scharpf:[144]

> the only thing that stands between the Scandinavian welfare state and the market is not a vote in the Council of Ministers or in the European Parliament, but merely the initiation of [...] legal action by potential private competitors before a national court that is then referred to the European Court of Justice for a preliminary hearing.

It is this constitutional set-up that stands at the basis of the integration through law movement.[145] Höpner and Schäfer provide ample examples to justify their claim. For example, the liberalisation of corporate law by overturning the 'company seat theory' or 'real seat doctrine' in the *Centros*, *Überseering* and *Inspire Art* judgments of the Court of Justice on the basis of the free movement of establishment provisions.[146] This has led to a transformation of German co-determination

[136] See Höpner and Schäfer (n 90).

[137] ibid, at 446.

[138] As established in Case 26/62 *N.V. Algemeine Transport- en Expeditie Onderneming van Gend & Loos v Netherlands Inland Revenue Administration* [1963] ECR 1.

[139] As established in Case 6/64 *Costa v ENEL* [1964] ECR 586.

[140] See Höpner and Schäfer above (n 90) at 441.

[141] As established in Case 8/74 *Procureur du Roi v Benoît and Gustave Dassonville* [1974] ECR 837.

[142] As established in Case 120/78 *Rewe-Zentral AG v Bundesmonopolverwaltung für Branntwein* [1979] ECR 650.

[143] See also JHH Weiler, 'The Transformation of Europe' (1991) 100 *Yale Law Journal* 2403.

[144] FW Scharpf, 'The European Social Model: Coping with the Challenges of Diversity' (2002) 40 *Journal of Common Market Studies* 657.

[145] See also JHH Weiler, 'Van Gend en Loos: The Individual as Subject and Object and the Dilemma of European Legitimacy' (2014) 12 *International Journal of Constitutional Law* 94–103.

[146] See Cases C-212/97 *Centros*; C-208/00 *Überseering*; C-167/01 *Inspire Art*.

rules, which are now easily avoided. Secondly, they refer to the *Laval* and *Viking* judgments, where the Court effectively decided to limited the host countries' room to manoeuvre in preventing races to the bottom in the field of labour standards (*Laval*) and created a horizontal effect by deciding that the European market freedoms not only oblige Member States, but also private bodies to refrain from actions that might restrict market freedoms (*Viking*).[147] Thirdly, they provide the argument that decisions such as *Cadbury Schweppes* and *Marks & Spencer* prohibit national efforts to tackle tax-avoidance practices.[148] On the basis of these examples they argue that 'rather than socially embedding the market, this line of ECJ case law undermines policies that aim at correcting market outcomes to achieve redistribution'.[149]

Scharpf and Höpner/Schäfer provide a compelling argument about the structural effects of these lines of cases from the Court of Justice. The Polanyian outlook they provide on this basis is grim:[150]

> The 'permissive consensus' of the past has given way to a 'constraining dissensus' and a widespread distrust of elite-driven integration. In particular, those who have been negatively affected by stronger competition and integrated markets have adopted more skeptical views of integration. ... When the countermovement—protection against market forces—is not forthcoming at the EU level and is losing ground domestically, losers grow Euro-skeptical, endorse nationalism, and sometimes support extreme right parties.

I agree with Scharpf and Höpner/Schäfer on the potential detrimental effects of the seemingly one-sided case law of the Court of Justice in terms of its social legitimacy. Their normative outlook is therefore shared in this book. This does, however, not apply to the assessment of the case law. Too often the case law of the Court of Justice is too selectively analysed and commented on without sufficient eye for detail. These accounts seem to understate the quite subtle balancing work and adjudicative techniques offered by the Court of Justice, which provide for a slightly more positive outlook.[151] The next chapters shall substantiate this statement further. This book aims to complement such normative outlooks with a more complete analysis of the case law of the Court of Justice, if only because this study will include the important areas of competition law and state aid, which often are not mentioned in critical accounts of the case law of the Court of Justice but constitute two of the fundamental pillars of the internal market.

147 Cases C-438/05 (*Viking*); C-341/05 (Laval); C-346/06 (*Rüffert*).

148 Cases C-196/04 (*Cadbury Schweppes*); C-446/03 (*Marks & Spencer*).

149 Höpner and Schäfer (n 90) at 445.

150 ibid, at 450.

151 See eg analyses of D Damjanovic, 'The EU Market Rules as Social Market Rules: Why the EU Can Be a Social Market Economy' (2013) 6 *Common Market Law Review* 1685–717 and also de Witte, *Justice in the EU* (n 57); Ashiagbor (n 47) at 317: 'What these cases reflect is the Court's attempt to grapple with an issue over which the political institutions are similarly engaged: how to promote market liberalization without undermining the social values that national governments are perhaps best placed to protect'.

In the following I will reflect on the notion of social legitimacy and responsiveness from the perspective of a wider EU constitutional debate, more specifically as being an integral part of the argument from transnational effects. I will argue that 'social responsiveness' can be seen as a compulsory and constitutional feature of the internal market project that is built on the premise of embedded liberalism. As such, the normative framework that is developed in this chapter is not only grounded in 'external' demands that point to the urgency of social responsiveness for a stable legal framework but can also be found within the internal, primary law, framework of EU law.

IV. TRANSNATIONAL EFFECTS AND THE LEGITIMACY OF THE SOCIAL DEFICIT

A. Joerges and Maduro

As conceived most clearly by Christian Joerges, it is important to note that a divide between Member State social policy and the supranational 'economic constitution' has always been intentional and very much a part of the constitutional model of the Union:[152]

> This was its constitutional-supranational raison d'être. Social policy was treated as a categorically distinct subject. It belonged to the domain of political legislation, and, as such, had to remain national. The social embeddedness of the market could, and, indeed, should, be accomplished by the Member States in various ways.[153]

The Union's economic objectives were therefore to be seen as transnational and apolitical whereas the social remained national and political. This dichotomy led Joerges to conceptualise the EU internal market in terms of 'deliberative supranationalism'.[154] The argument of deliberative supranationalism is, roughly, that the 'post-national' legitimacy of governance within constitutional states is flawed to the extent that it is unable to include 'foreign' identities and their interests within national decision-making processes. Therefore, the legitimacy of supranational institutions can be derived from this compensatory function:

> We must conceptualise supranational constitutionalism as an alternative to the model of the constitutional nation-state which respects that state's constitutional legitimacy, but, at the same time, clarifies and sanctions the commitments arising from its interdependence with equally democratically legitimised states and with the supranational prerogatives that an institutionalisation of this interdependence requires.[155]

[152] Ruggie (n 4) at 393.

[153] Joerges and Rödl, 'Informal Politics, Formalised Law and the "Social Deficit" of European Integration' (n 122).

[154] C Joerges and J Neyer, 'From Intergovernmental Bargaining to Deliberative Political Processes' (1997) 3 *European Law Journal* 273.

[155] C Joerges, '"Deliberative Political Processes" Revisited: What Have we Learnt About the Legitimacy of Supranational Decision-Making?' (2006) 44 *Journal of Common Market Studies* 779, at 790.

Joerges' argument developed in what is now mostly, and arguably more aptly, coined as the 'argument from containment' or the 'argument from transnational effects'[156] and instructs to qualify the process of integration as an exercise whereby traditional, outdated, unrepresentative manifestations of national defective forms of decision-making are removed on the basis of the idea that these are hostile towards transnational interests and inappropriate within an integrating EU market, at least the one to which Member States have committed themselves in the Treaties.[157] For example, in the case of *Corbeau* the Court reviewed the Belgian postal monopoly created by laws in the 1950s and 1970s.[158] Demand for the courier service offered by Corbeau did not exist to the same extent then and the monopoly was considered to exclusively serve a privileged and entrenched group of interests. However, in 1993 societal developments had outgrown the basis for the law at that time and needed to be reconsidered, modernised. Similarly, in the case of *Albany*, certain individuals were concerned that they would be forced to join compulsory industrial pension schemes, despite the fact that the free market offered better deals.[159]

The intrinsic dynamic that internal market law creates on this basis can be compared with the effects of technological innovation on regulated embedded market structures. For example, the dynamic that the Uber app brings to regulated taxi sectors within countries across the globe. Uber develops, markets and operates a mobile app, which allows consumers with smartphones to book a trip which is then automatically routed to 'Uber drivers' who use their own cars for the service. Bills are automatically paid online and Uber is considered in many countries as a major threat to the vested taxi industries who have found themselves suddenly confronted with an army of competitors, who, unlike in many regulated taxi industries, are not required to finance their licence with significant funds. In effect, Uber has challenged many regulatory regimes and the responses of these regimes has revealed to some extent their 'producerist' or 'consumerist' orientations. By 'producerist' I refer to an orientation of the state on the supply side of a market. Producers are accorded a central function in society that goes further than merely an economic function but is able to provide a certain social identity to people. The protection of guilds (lawyers, waiters in France, pharmacists), certain

[156] To be traced back to Joerges and Neyer, 'From Intergovernmental Bargaining to Deliberative Political Processes' (n 154) 273–99. Also C Joerges, 'European Law as Conflict of Laws' in Joerges and Neyer (eds), 'Deliberative Supranationalism Revisited' 20 EUI Working Paper (2006). Most recently, C Joerges, 'Unity in Diversity as Europe's Vocation and Conflicts Law as Europe's Constitutional Form' in R Nickel and A Greppi (eds.), *The Changing Role of Law in the Age of Supra- and Transnational Governance* (Baden-Baden, Nomos, 2014) 125–76. See also A Somek, 'The Argument from Transnational Effects I: Representing Outsiders through Freedom of Movement' (2010) 16 *European Law Journal* 320 and MP Maduro, *We the Court: the European Court of Justice and the European Economic Constitution* (Oxford, Hart Publishing, 1998), who then proceeded to popularise the argument.

[157] D Schiek, 'The EU's Socio-economic Model(s) and the Crisi(e)s—any Perspectives?' in D Schiek (ed), *The EU Economic and Social Model in the Global Crisis* (Farnham, Ashgate, 2013).

[158] Case C-320/91 *Corbeau* [1993] ECR I-2533.

[159] Case C-67/96 *Albany* [1999] ECR I-05751.

ways of making products (pasta, wine, *reinheitsgebot*) or even the size of stores and their opening times thereby fulfil a social function that resonates with a certain culture, history and identity.[160] Obviously such functions are subject to social change. A (economic) consumerist orientation is, by contrast, focused on rights and interests on the demand side of the market—in particular, primarily as an interest in competitive prices and choice. Europe is traditionally perceived as oriented more towards the supply side (in particular the Netherlands, Germany and France) whereas the US harbours the fundamental consumerist interest. Perceived in this way the 'Uber app', which has gained ground and regulatory recognition in the US, can be framed as an attack on European 'producerist' orientations.

The dynamic is comparable with situations where, eg, service providers from a 'consumerist'-oriented Member State are restricted in their trade due to a 'producerist' regulatory framework and the 'producerist'-oriented legal system is unable to provide good arguments for its existence. The regulatory framework is then liable to be qualified as a restriction of free movement that cannot be justified and it can be overridden on the basis of market access rights. Although this is of course a slightly different situation, the inherent regulatory dynamic that Uber brings to the countries where it is launched seems to be essentially the same. That is to say that the existing regulatory protections of the taxi industry are being critically assessed with respect to the function that they actually provide and the suitability of the regulatory framework and restrictions they bring on competition.[161]

Maduro popularised this dynamic impact of the argument of transnational effects with respect to the fundamental internal market freedoms and applied this idea to demonstrate, in a structural manner, why and how the argument from transnational effects can be read into the application of the internal market rules and require states to internalise choices that affect outsiders.[162] Maduro notes for example, with regard to free movement case law, that even where the Court has adopted a wide interpretation of the scope of free movement provisions, it has done so in the belief for a need to place constitutional limits on state interventions

[160] See eg J Whitman, 'Consumerism versus Producerism: A Study in Comparative Law' (2007) 117 *Yale Law Journal* 340.

[161] Unlike as is the case in Britain, in the Netherlands an argument can be advanced that the social function of taxis is negligible if not negative. In some places you have to be careful not to be bullied away by groups of taxi drivers if you question their practices, if not even getting beaten to death as happened in 2009 to someone in Amsterdam complaining about the fare. The taxi industry in Amsterdam has been dominated by one operator that has used its dominance to bully away any attempts to open the market or increase the quality of service. None of the regulatory changes in the framework have really worked out owing to, arguably, the dominant economic presence of the vested player. In this situation it therefore seems that the 'producerist' focus on the industry has been mainly to do with interest capture and attempts to remedy a bad situation. In such a situation of bad regulation it can be argued that the consumerist breakthrough strategy of allowing Uber to rationalise the industry is not such a bad idea. In this way a concentration of economic power and interest capture of a regulatory framework can be circumvented.

[162] M Maduro, 'Reforming the Market or the State? Article 30 and the European Constitution: Economic Freedom and Political Rights' (1997) 3 *European Law Journal* 55–82.

in the market, not for the purpose of the market but for considerations related to the accommodation of interests that are not part of national democratic governance structures.[163] In other words, the ambitions of the EU free movement rules are not 'market' oriented but aim to achieve integration amongst otherwise defunct national democracies. This is a view that Maduro later, quite literally, tried to consistently include in his personal construction of a European legal space in many of his AG opinions that cover a significant amount of seminal case law of the Court of Justice.[164] The larger point here is that internal market law potentially allows reconsideration and emancipation from outdated, unrepresentative forms of institutions and schemes. Modern perspectives on life (no 'job for life', mobility and flexibility) have influenced people's identity, 'depending on their geographical proximity, collective history and experiences, common values and ambitions'.[165]

Within this view the EU internal market is or should be a subtle and constructive means towards a new transnational *more responsive* democratic nation state, one that is sensitive towards the interests of entities that fall outside of its direct political reach and procedures. The traditional internal market obligations for Member States fit within this perspective: they cannot implement their interests or laws without restraint, but are

> obliged to respect the European freedoms; they are not allowed to discriminate and can pursue only legitimate regulatory policies; they must, in relation to the objectives that they wish to pursue through regulation, harmonise with each other, and they must reform their national systems in the most community-friendly way possible.[166]

In other words, the value of internal market integration is exactly to constrain national self-expression, 'so as to mitigate what are regarded as its potential excesses: the exclusion of certain interests from the political process, and its capacity for sovereign violence in limiting permissible behaviour'.[167] Hence, the argument from containment conceptualises the intentions of the EU internal market not necessarily as 'pro trade' but as a means to engage in a dialogue with Member States on how their national systems can and need to be adjusted in order to accommodate the out of nation state interests that are to be made part of national processes of governing or governance structures. As such, this view is informed by

[163] Maduro, *We the Court* (n 156) at 150.

[164] eg his AG Opinion in the *Cipolla* case C-94/04, para 56:

> Member States are required to take into account the effects that measures they adopt to regulate their national markets will have as regards the exercise by providers established in other Member States of their right to freedom to provide services. In that context, it is not only discrimination on grounds of nationality that is prohibited but also discrimination imposing, in respect of the exercise of a transnational activity, additional costs or hindering access to the national market for service providers established in other Member States.

[165] E Horváth, *Mandating Identity: Citizenship, Kinship Laws and Plural Nationality in the European Union* (Alphen aan den Rijn, Kluwer Law International, 2007) at 126.

[166] Joerges and Rödl (n 122) 1–19.

[167] de Witte, 'Sex, Drugs & EU Law (n 123).

the most obvious empirical facts that characterise the European Union today: the diversity of socio-economic constellations of the Member States and the increasing asymmetry of interests amongst Member States.[168] Such diversity results in a need for communication and internalisation of their extraterritorial effects.

B. Somek's Fundamental Challenge

In an ideal form the argument from transnational effects conceptualises a type of European law that responds to differences in the laws of the EU Member States by resorting to principles that should respect and accommodate diversity. That is why, in the context of the social deficit issue, which leads to diversity in the way that social objectives are pursued amongst all individual Member States, the argument from transnational effects posits a supranational legal structure that is compatible with the social deficit. Not only that, it also provides for a theory of legitimacy for the social deficit, or in other words, a theory for the *social legitimacy* of the European internal market project. This would imply that the rules and principles that are applied through the argument of transnational effects are *responsive* to social context in the sense that social objectives can be legitimately challenged on the basis of the absence of representation of potential transnational effects they may have. However, as argued by Somek, on this point the argument from transnational effects is often far from the actual reality of the EU internal market project:

> In fact, this is clearly revealed in how its focus on transnational effects is mediated by the equal distrust of national regimes burdening, in one way or another, international economic mobility. Anchoring the mitigation of transnational effects in the facilitation of market access modifies the focus of the argument. It is thereby made subservient to an altogether different aim, namely, economic due process.[169]

The identification of the potential out of state interest that finds insufficient access within another Member State is identified, solely, on the basis of market access. Somek's point here is that despite the clear merit in the legitimising idea of EU internal market law as removing traditional, outdated, unrepresentative manifestations of national defective forms of decision-making, the grammar and language of this debate may contain inherent limits. This has led him, in his seminal discussions on the wider importance of the argument of transnational effects for European integration to pose a fundamental question: 'what might be done to prevent the argument from transnational effects from slipping into a freewheeling rampage of economic due process?'[170]

[168] Beramendi (n 65) at 783.
[169] Somek, 'The Argument from Transnational Effects I '(n 156) at 320.
[170] ibid, at 332.

Despite some interesting and promising attempts, this question has never been addressed in a structural way, across all fundamental areas of the internal market. The risk of 'slipping into a freewheeling rampage of economic due process' manifests differently within each area of internal market law and the following chapters will dissect how this risk materialises specifically. The argument from transnational effects is therefore better perceived as providing a normative perspective that sets out how the EU internal market laws *should* be applied, in order to be socially legitimate. The argument harbours an unfulfilled implicit understanding of the social purpose of the internal market. Roughly, that social purpose is the respect and accommodation of social diversity amongst Member States, whilst promoting the objectives of the internal market by scrutinising the internalisation of the transnational effects of Member State social measures. However, and importantly, Somek has demonstrated that the argument from transnational effect is incomplete as it has not provided us with the actual principles nor with the conceptual apparatus that EU law might resort to in order to govern the social diversity of the internal market. There is therefore a need to move beyond the argument from transnational effects for it to have real normative value.

The argument presented in this book can be contextualised, partly, as furthering the argument from transnational effects through a perspective that goes beyond emphasising either (i) the importance for EU law to respect the structures that are expressive of Member State choices, which embed the pursuit or protection of certain interests within social spheres, or (ii) the requirements for Member States or private actors to open up these embedded social structures in order to develop towards a post-national constellation that remedies potential democratic deficits or outdated unrepresentative or discriminatory structures. What is required and pursued, instead, is a more holistic approach to the issue, recognising the interdependence of both central facets for the structure and development of the internal market in a mutually responsive manner.[171]

C. The Constitutional Obligation of Responsiveness

Indeed, in terms of primary law, the EU internal market has evolved to become, constitutionally, more tuned towards accommodating interests that are of a broader concern than merely the creation of an area in which the components of trade move freely between the Member States.[172] As such, the centrality of

[171] See for a related discussion Schiek, 'The EU's Socio-economic Model(s) and the Crisi(e)s' (n 157).

[172] See also the historical account of P Craig, *The Lisbon Treaty: Law, Politics, and Treaty Reform* (Oxford, Oxford University Press, 2013). Although, the Maastricht Treaty (1992) already included, in one way or another, a majority of the social objectives that are include in the Lisbon Treaty (2007), a difference is that in the Maastricht Treaty these objectives were to be achieved mainly through the creation of an area without internal frontiers and through the establishment of economic and monetary union. In other words: through the creation of an internal market. As such, achieving certain market

the integrating market as a focal point for EU policy objectives has transformed. Whereas the 'internal market' of the Lisbon Treaty requires the abolition of the same barriers to trade, it appears that the connection to broader social values has evolved. Accordingly, it has been argued that, after the entry into force of Lisbon, the new constitutional balance towards broader social objectives should resonate in the adjudicative techniques employed by the Court.[173] Although the main objective spelled out in the Lisbon Treaty remains the establishment of the internal market,[174] this is combined with, compared to previous Treaties, increased emphasis on *sustainable* development of a Europe based on *balanced* economic growth and price stability, policies based on *a spirit of solidarity*, a competitive *social* market economy aimed at full employment and *social* progress, the pursuit of *social* cohesion and a high level of protection and improvement of *the quality of the environment*.[175] Moreover, from the Treaty of Amsterdam the coherence of EU policies is considered more important through the creation of cross-sectional clauses.[176] The Lisbon Treaty includes a requirement of consistency among Union policies (Article 7 TFEU), a duty to eliminate inequalities and

objectives was understood to bring forth other (social) benefits also. The idea of market progress was that it necessarily included a social purpose, a fulfilment inherent to achieving market objectives.

[173] Case C-515/08 *Santos Palhota* [2010] ECR I-000. AG Cruz Villalón suggested in this case:

> As a result of the entry into force of the Treaty of Lisbon, when working conditions constitute an overriding reason relating to the public interest justifying a derogation from the freedom to provide services, they must no longer be interpreted strictly. In so far as the protection of workers is a matter which warrants protection under the Treaties themselves, it is not a simple derogation from a freedom, still less an unwritten exception inferred from case-law. To the extent that the new primary law framework provides for a mandatory high level of social protection, it authorises the Member States, for the purpose of safeguarding a certain level of social protection, to restrict a freedom, and to do so without European Union law's regarding it as something exceptional and, therefore, as warranting a strict interpretation.

[174] Art 3(2) TEU.

[175] Compared with the objectives in previous Treaties one could argue that an important addition concerns the aim to work for a 'highly competitive social market economy' especially when compared with the objective of the 'open market economy'. The term 'social market economy' upon inclusion in the Constitutional Treaty was meant to summarise the EU's commitment to 'greater coherence between economic and social policies' (Working Group XI on Social Europe—CONV 516/1/03/ REV 1). Paul Craig argues that the reference to social market economy is specified by the phrase 'highly competitive' and hence 'a signal of compromise in the corridors of power'. He also notes, however, that this does not undermine the significance of use of the term 'social market economy' (Craig, *The Lisbon Treaty* (n 172) at 25). In a similar vein, JC Piris, *The Lisbon Treaty: A Legal and Political Analysis* (Cambridge, Cambridge University Press, 2010), relates this idea of the social in the economy to the system that was developed in Germany in the post-war Federal Republic also described as ordoliberalism. It aims for a balance between the market and social policy and Piris submits that it is comparable to the 'European Social Model' in that it enables the free play of forces on the market with the state creating the framework for competition to work and combining that with a complete system of social protection.

[176] M Dawson and B de Witte, 'The EU Legal Framework of Social Inclusion and Social Protection: Between the Lisbon Strategy and the Lisbon Treaty' in B Cantillon et al (eds), *Social Inclusion and Social Protection in the EU: Interactions between Law and Policy* (Cambridge, Intersentia, 2012) at 41; M Ferrera, 'Modest Beginnings, Timid Progresses: What Next for Social Europe?' in Cantillon et al, *Social Inclusion and Social Protection in the EU: Interactions between Law and Policy* (ibid) 17–39.

promote equalities between men and women in all activities (Article 8 TFEU), a duty to take into account employment, social protection, education, health, combating discrimination in the definition and implementation of its policies (Articles 9 and 10 TFEU), integration of environmental protection requirements and consumer protection requirements in defining and implementing Union activities (Articles 11 and 12 TFEU). Article 3(3) TEU's embrace of the 'social market economy' and the binding effect that is attributed to the Charter of Fundamental Rights could also be employed to argue that the constitutional character of the internal market has been altered by the Lisbon Treaty.[177] Relevant in this respect is also that pre-Lisbon Article 3(l)(g) TEC provided that the activities of the EC shall include 'a system ensuring that competition in the internal market is not distorted'. The Lisbon Treaty removed the reference to undistorted competition from the Treaty and placed it instead in a Protocol attached to both the EU Treaty and the TFEU, which states that the internal market referred to in Article 2 EU 'includes a system ensuring that competition is not distorted'. A Protocol is legally binding. However, the argument can be made that obscuring the reference to undistorted competition could adjust the constitutional balance in favour of socially responsive adjudication and regulation at the expense of market competition, and that this should be taken into account in the interpretation and application of the internal market provisions.[178] How to achieve this leads to an open question that is explicitly raised and left open in many contributions that critically analyse the future of the EU internal market project.[179]

I submit that a new balance of values is to be achieved through responsiveness. The developments in primary law have led to ground to argue for a constitutional obligation for the evaluative and constitutive frameworks of the EU internal market to become specifically responsive to social diversity and plurality. This is apparent when these developments are contextualised within Articles 3 and 4(2) of the Treaty on the European Union. As discussed, Article 3 TEU sets out a dual commitment to both promote the objectives of the internal market *and* the objectives of sustainability, social inclusion/cohesion and a social market economy.

[177] See D Schiek, *Economic and Social Integration: the Challenge for EU Constitutional Law* (Cheltenham, Edward Elgar, 2012) at 102–06.

[178] eg ibid, at 185.

[179] T Hervey, 'If only it were so Simple: Public Health Services and EU Law' in M Cremona (ed), *Market Integration and Public Services in the European Union* (Oxford, Oxford University Press 2011) at 247. Hervey sees the insertion of social objectives within the primary law framework as a reason to (collectively) (re)determine a balance of values, such as between competition and solidarity:

> EU law is no more (if it ever has been) simply, or even essentially or fundamentally about markets, leaving 'the social' to the Member States and national law. The roles of EU internal market and competition law are no longer (if they ever were) simply a means to achieve movement between markets, opening markets, and preventing nationality-based discrimination. Rather, EU free movement and competition law should become (or have become) a locus within which we collectively determine the balance of values, between (economic) freedom and (social) security; between competition and solidarity.

The objectives of the internal market are supranational and require responsiveness from Member States, whilst objectives normally associated with sustainability, social inclusion/cohesion and a social market economy predominantly find their origin within Member State social spheres and are therefore by nature diverse. It is the latter that Article 4(2) TEU is then particularly concerned with, by carving out the general commitment of the Union to 'respect' national identities of Member States that are inherent in their national, regional and local, fundamental political and constitutional structures.[180] In the 2010 Monti Report, addressing 'tensions between market integration and social objectives', it was stated that:

> These are even more vividly exposed, now that the Lisbon Treaty has introduced, even formally, the objective of achieving a 'highly competitive social market economy'. If the market and the social components do not find an appropriate reconciliation, something has to give in. Following the crisis, with the declining appetite for the market and the increasing concern about inequalities, it is by no means clear that it would be the market, i.e. the single market, to prevail.[181]

A reconciliation between the market and the social can be found within the perspective of responsiveness. Responsiveness advances a holistic approach that conceives the market and the social, literally, as 'communicating vessels'. Hence, this 'dialogue of *mutual* responsiveness' is based on the idea that internal market law is a means to start a conversation with Member States on the normative choices of restrictive laws and regulatory schemes. Within the multilevel context of the EU and specifically a context within which there exists a constitutional obligation to respect diversity and a plurality of social objectives it is imperative for legal review to become responsive to context.

V. SOCIAL LEGITIMACY IN THE CONTEXT OF INTERNAL MARKET ADJUDICATION

A. (E)valuation and the Expressive Function of Internal Market Law as a Dialogue of Mutual Responsiveness

The foregoing sections have discussed social legitimacy in a rather broad sense, that is to say, without making the normative claims of social legitimacy specific to the context of adjudication. However, as was explained before, this book will specifically explore social legitimacy in the sphere of internal market adjudication

[180] eg LFM Besselink, 'National and Constitutional Identity before and after Lisbon' (2010) 6 *Utrecht Law Review* 36; T Konstadinides, 'Constitutional Identity as a Shield and as a Sword: The European Legal Order within the Framework of National Constitutional Settlement' (2011) 13 *Cambridge Yearbook of European Legal Studies* 195; A von Bogdandy and S Schill, 'Overcoming Absolute Primacy: Respect for National Identity under the Lisbon Treaty' (2011) 48 *Common Market Law Review* 1417–53.

[181] M Monti, 'A New Strategy for the Single Market: at the Service of Europe's Economy and Society (2010) 26 available at http://ec.europa.eu/internal_market/strategy/docs/monti_report_final_10_05_2010_en.pdf.

and not cover legislation and other forms of internal market governance.[182] This section discusses how the normative claims that were developed in the foregoing concretise in the adjudicative context. This will be explored specifically with respect to the areas of free movement, competition and state aid in the following chapters but the normative framework can be discussed here in slightly more abstract terms in order to set out the lens through which adjudication will be approached in the following chapters.

The normative claim of social legitimacy in the context of the multilevel governance context of the EU and the internal market is that a reconciliation of local domestic social values within supranational market objectives requires a form of explicit responsiveness to the social context that is being adjudicated. Moreover, it was highlighted with reference to the historical analysis of Polanyi that in the context of market integration there is a risk that dominating market-based rationales will ignore and crowd out alternative legitimate social purpose. In the context of adjudication these normative demands boil down to the issues of valuation in law and the related problems of indeterminacy and commensurability.[183]

For example, in its evaluation of a regulatory intervention that restricts the movement of economic actors, the Court of Justice may exclude valuable social practices that contribute to social cohesion and capital within Member States. An evaluative adjudicative method such a strict proportionality, applied in free movement adjudication, seeks the more efficient or less restrictive state measure; potentially excluding a relevant and genuine political compromise (further discussed in Chapter 2). The efficiency-based exemption criteria in competition law value competition restrictive sustainability initiatives in terms of the willingness of consumers to pay for a price increase; potentially excluding the inherent value of a sustainable environment (further discussed in Chapter 3). The market-based evaluative standards that state aid law introduces may nudge public bodies towards actions that are justified exclusively on the grounds of their commercial self-interest; crowding out potential alternative visions regarding the appropriate role of public authorities and the direction that policy objectives take (further discussed in Chapter 4). The point is that these evaluative standards that are adopted in adjudicative contexts may translate social realities within a metric that risks doing violence to potentially genuine and worthwhile aspects of those objectives. This is the type of commensurability issue that is central to the normative lens in the thesis; when the evaluative standard adopted by the courts results in a situation where objectives pursued by Member States cannot be aligned along the evaluative metric without doing violence to the potentially genuine and worthwhile aspects of those objectives.

The metric that is adopted in these examples points towards instances where the evaluative standard that is implicit in the adjudicative rationale applied by

[182] Although the following chapters will shortly touch on those dimensions where relevant.
[183] CR Sunstein, 'Incommensurability and Valuation in Law' (1994) 92 *Michigan Law Review* 779.

the court is reflective of a utilitarian consequentialist standard. An analogy can be drawn on this point with the argument of Majone who would argue that such market-enhancing rationalities are based on the idea that they improve overall welfare and hence 'do not need a strong normative foundation' since they rely on output legitimacy.[184] Instead rationales that would imply choices between social objectives 'can only be legitimated by majority decisions and by virtue of that fact place too heavy a burden on the fragile normative foundations of a transnational polity'.[185] Moreover, these utilitarian standards are a, on first sight, clear and clean way of approaching otherwise obscure and complex objectives that are not easily translated into targets and means of achieving them. Therefore, the legal framework may well be willing to protect a particular non-market issue but also want a mechanism that allows the application of a clear and transparent standard of assessment. Thus, the use of a market rationale in order to evaluate a conflict between market integration and a particular regulatory choice may also partly just be about simplifying the application of the rules, rather than a way of saying that non-market issues only count if they can be perceived in terms of the market.[186] For example, in state aid, there can be no room for the subtler elements of the relationship between the state and a debtor in judicial review. There are good reasons for a purely functional, consequentialist evaluation of this relationship since recognising or allowing trust and informal considerations to rule the relationship between the state and its debtors would simply be too amorphous for judicial review to pick up and raise problems for the transparent application of the state aid rules.[187] That is to say, trust and informality are just a step away from the granting of advantages for protectionist aims.

However, this argument does run into difficulty, as pointed out by Höpner and Schäfer, if it is clear that the valuation that is implicit in market-derived standards has a direct and potentially structural impact on a variety of social measures and identity within Member States.[188] As was discussed before, the adjudication of the Court becomes a form of social ordering in so far as it sets the conditions under which certain policy within Member States is restrictive.[189] It determines how the relationship between the social and economic sphere is to be governed and the adjudicative determinations of the Court regarding this relationship will normally enter in some degree into the future relationship between these two spheres

[184] G Majone, *Dilemmas of European Integration. The Ambiguities and Pitfalls of Integration by Stealth* (Oxford, Oxford University Press, 2005) at 191.

[185] ibid.

[186] This is, as such, comparable to the so-called type I or type II errors that recognise the inevitable trade-off involved in the design of any system that pursues justice. We may attempt to set our standards as high as we can, but somewhere a balance must be struck, lest the system will become unworkable by making it too difficult to eg pass sentence on the majority of wrongful offenders.

[187] eg G Davies, 'Democracy and Legitimacy in the Shadow of Purposive Competence' (2015) 21 *European Law Journal* 2.

[188] Höpner and Schäfer (n 90) at 445.

[189] See Fuller and Winston, 'The Forms and Limits of Adjudication' (n 32) at 353.

in the internal market. Therefore, those who favour legal approaches based on unitary kinds of valuation must realise that this approach is only a means of overcoming institutional challenges and does not reflect a complete understanding of the nuances of the problems involved.[190] A completely functional and undersocialised model of adjudication could threaten the social cohesions, solidarity or identity that a state pursues. As has been argued consistently: a liberal society such as the EU aspires to be contains a diversity of social spheres—eg families, markets, politics, religious organisations—and (should) make, space for different kinds of valuation.[191]

As was discussed above, the literature on varieties of capitalism provides a further normative underpinning for the argument in favour of social diversity amongst Member States in the Union. In short, that literature demonstrates that institutions are shaped not only by a legal system. The informal rules or common knowledge that is acquired by actors on the basis of the history and culture of nations leads to a variety of capitalist organisation.[192] The development of 'institutional complementarities', ie the development of complementary institutions amongst different spheres means that the insertion of elements of one variety into the fabric of the other can have disintegrative effects.[193] This builds on the idea that the diversity of preferences and orientations in the EU is the product of specific historical experiences, political contestation, societal learning and continuous political decision-making.[194] Hence, consequentialist evaluations that demand a 'one-size-fits-all philosophy' are 'normatively flawed because of its disregard of the normative infrastructure of the economy'.[195] In this way, the normative fabric of the economic orders within Member States can be seen as their 'social *acquis*', which should be recognised within EU law.[196]

The above is to some extent reflected in the earlier cited words of Court of Justice judge Koen Lenaerts, highlighting the openness of the Court of Justice to accommodate value diversity beyond the core nucleus of EU law.[197] However, the point where exactly that dividing line falls remains the subject of much controversy.[198] Clearly, a problem for adjudication and a commitment to social

[190] See Sunstein, 'Incommensurability and Valuation in Law' (n 183).

[191] On social differentiation and valuation in law, see also Sunstein (n 183) at 782.

[192] Hall and Soskice (n 61); Hall, 'Varieties of Capitalism and the Euro Crisis' (n 61) 1223–43.

[193] See Hassel, 'Adjustments in the Eurozone' (n 63).

[194] As submitted by Joerges, 'Market Integration and Europeanisation of Private Law' (n 64).

[195] ibid, at 6.

[196] As defended by Scharpf (n 59); M Höpner and A Schäfer, 'A New Phase of European Integration: Organized Capitalisms' (2010) 33 *West European Politics* 344–68; W Streeck, 'E Pluribus Unum? Varieties and Commonalities of Capitalism' (2010) Cologne: MPIfG Discussion Paper 10 /12.

[197] K Lenaerts, 'The Court's Outer and Inner Selves: Exploring the External and Internal Legitimacy of the European Court of Justice' in H Clemens et al (eds), *Judging Europe's Judges: The Legitimacy of the Case Law of the European Court of Justice* (Oxford, Hart Publishing, 2013) 13–60.

[198] S Weatherhill, 'The Court's Case Law on the Internal Market: "A Circumloquacious Statement of the Result, Rather than a Reason for Arriving at It"?' in Clemens et al (eds), *Judging Europe's Judges: The Legitimacy of the Case Law of the European Court of Justice* (n 197) at 104.

diversity within the multilayer governance context of the Union is that plurality may be bought at the price of allowing too much. Internal market adjudication therefore needs coherent approaches to avoid that social diversity turns into a *carte blanche* for communities who prefer their own values at the expense of other Member States.

However, if we indeed accept the argument that social diversity is a value that the EU internal market is committed to then market-derived utilitarian standards are not appropriate means to adjudicate conflicts in every situation, despite the highlighted value of administrability. It can be discussed whether the fact that many restrictive Member State regulations perish within the evaluative framework of the Court is because Member States themselves do not really understand the functions of their own laws, nor defend them well,[199] or whether the problem is in the way the Court has chosen to frame things, in consequentialist, purposive terms,[200] which simply fails to capture and weigh the true social significance of some restrictive rules. It is probably a bit of both and the next chapter will explore how the adjudicative rationales of the Court can be made consistently more responsive to accommodate Member State social diversity *and* promote the objectives of the internal market; an integrated market that is responsive to a Member State's plural set of social contexts. Concomitantly, this approach will provide an answer to Somek's fundamental question and add to the constitutional debate based on the argument of transnational effects.

Another point of importance is that utilitarian standards tend to obscure the commensurability issue by assuming that different values or objectives are commensurable and thereby fail to reveal what is at stake in many areas of internal market law. There is on this point an *expressive function of internal market law* that is potentially lost if utilitarian standards dominate the legal analysis. This is directly related to the previously submitted social purpose for EU internal market law. It was submitted that the social purpose is concretised in the respect and accommodation of social diversity amongst Member States, whilst promoting the objectives of the internal market by scrutinising the internalisation of the transnational effects of Member State social measures. The expressive function of internal market law is then to unveil normative conflicts in order to illuminate what is at stake in internal market conflicts.[201] Questioning and demanding articulation of restrictive regulatory choices within legal frameworks may be an excellent starting point for a dialogue that aims to increase the distinct articulation, and thereby assists in the identification, of embedding organisational principles on the Member State level. The 'dialogue of mutual responsiveness' is therefore based on the idea that internal market law is a means to start a conversation with Member States on the normative choices of restrictive laws and regulatory choices, which

[199] See Davies, 'Internal Market Adjudication and the Quality of Life in Europe' (n 71).

[200] ibid.

[201] On the expressive functions of law, see also Sunstein (n 183). Also on this Dani (n 19) at 621.

requires on one side a responsiveness within the application of internal market law and, on the other side, a clear understanding and articulation of restrictive objectives that are pursued on a Member State level.

How responsiveness can be integrated within the legal framework of the internal market and what the proxies and requirements are for the articulation of regulatory choice shall be explored in the next chapters. The balance that needs to be struck therefore is to establish, with sufficient subtlety for the values at stake, which evaluative rationality is most suitable for the situation that is to be adjudicated. An understanding of problems of incommensurability within internal market adjudication will make it easier to see what is at stake and guide a court in its choice for an evaluative rationale that is congruent with the social context that is being adjudicated. The existence of a genuine norm conflict can guide the Court in choosing an evaluative rationale and instruct about the appropriateness of adopting an evaluative framework based on strict proportionality versus procedural proportionality; or instruct a categorisation definition regarding the pursuit of sustainability in terms of a restriction on competition; or, similarly, if the granting of selective regulatory advantages should qualify as state aid.[202] Each of these choices has an effect on whether the evaluative framework of the Court is based on utilitarian standards that prescribe certain substantive outcomes or whether the evaluative rationale shifts to a more procedurally based test.[203] In other words, each has an effect on the extent that diversity is tolerated in the internal market. This shall become clear in the following chapters which will discuss these choices and their effects extensively and more explicitly on the basis of case law of the European courts.

Therefore, the proposed normative-prescriptive model of adjudication seeks to serve various purposes. Above all, it seeks responsiveness to social context in the adjudicative model of the Court. However, in that process, the expressive value of internal market law will become apparent since the substantive scope and reach of the internal market will be established; to what extent the internal market can substantively accommodate local social spheres, and when objectives become inherently irreconcilable with the objectives pursued on the basis of market integration. The basic point then is that adjudicative rationales should respond to such a finding of irreconcilability. The exercise of the Court to find this 'switch' between evaluative principles that are congruent with the underlying social context, without losing sight of internal market objectives, is coined as responsive adjudication and the studies in the following chapters will aim to trace fragments of such responsiveness in the case law of the Court. Subsequently the intention

[202] On balancing and categorisation as adjudicative techniques adopted by the Court of Justice, see E Cloots, *National Identity in EU Law* (Oxford, Oxford University Press, 2015).

[203] On the latter, see also H Schepel, *The Constitution of Private Governance: Product Standards in the Regulation of Integrating Markets* (Oxford, Hart Publishing, 2005); H Schepel, 'Delegation of Regulatory Powers to Private Parties under EC Competition Law: Towards a Procedural Public Interest Test' (2002) 39 *Common Market Law Review* 31.

of this study is to consistently reconstruct that case law into a coherent model of social legitimacy in which the valuation that is reflected on the basis of an adjudicative rationale of the ECJ interacts constructively and in congruence with the social context that is being adjudicated. This allows the Court of Justice to implement an 'operational rationale' whenever it has to adjudicate a conflict between the objectives of market integration and restrictive domestic (social) interests.

VI. OUTLOOK

This chapter developed a normative outlook that shall be unfolded further in the coming chapters of the book. Social legitimacy has been dissected as to its meaning and function in a multilevel context such as the EU. It can be concluded that social legitimacy, as a concept, has been introduced specifically to emphasise the reciprocal relationship between global market integration and the locality of the social. Tracing the concept back to Polanyi, the idea of social legitimacy becomes a necessity for a political sustainable project that seeks supranational market integration. The balance between the requirements from the EU internal market for Member States' regulatory choices, whilst at the same time respecting the 'fundamental structures' that exist in the Member States (Article 4(2) TEU), through a recognition of a diversity of regulatory options, is one of the structural challenges faced by the internal market project. What is targeted in this book are the potential underlying fixed value choices that are implicit in the different modes of EU adjudication and may pull towards the adoption of rationalities in the evaluation of Member State action that disregards the social diversity and value pluralism that is inherent in the EU polity. This would not be in alignment with the current values and objectives structure of the EU that points towards the importance of institutionalising diversity. The quest for a combination of both an economic and social purpose for the EU has been there for a long time. It is argued that the 'key' to understanding this dynamic lies in terms of a dialogue of mutual responsiveness and it has a constitutional basis. The constitutional evolution has led to an obligation to integrate a rationale of responsiveness towards social diversity within the EU internal market governance mechanisms.

In a nutshell, within this context, social legitimacy places specific requirements on the selection and application of adjudicative rationales, depending on whether the objects of governance originate from different or within the same normative order(s) and provides a conceptualisation of a structural alternative model of internal market adjudication to account for social interests within an integrating EU market. Social legitimacy can be derived from a rationale that manages to distinguish voices within Member States that are embedding a social fabric from the voices that are to be embedded within the EU internal market fabric. Social legitimacy is foregone when rationales apply an atomised, under-socialised conception of, for example, rational Member State action and discards complex social context that embeds economic activities.

Foremost, clarity in the framing of the economic and social purpose and potential incommensurable conflicts between these potentially conflicting aims is needed in order to instruct adjudication. The following chapters illustrate that it is specifically *the lack of this clarity* that may undermine the required social legitimacy for the EU. In this way social legitimacy can be connected to the constitutional theory of transnational effects, which, as argued, derives the legitimacy of the internal market project from its ability to govern social diversity in a responsive manner, requiring explicit responsiveness both from Member States in view of their commitments to the internal market *and* from the internal market in the sense that *it* needs to be positioned within Member States' differing sets of social contexts. Indeed, implementing the idea of mutual responsiveness favours a constitutional conception of the EU legal system that is living, dynamic and a recognition that the EU Constitution can and should grow and adapt to changing circumstances without losing its identity and retaining its social legitimacy.[204]

It has been argued that, based on the social purpose of the EU internal market as one of providing an infrastructure for constructive interplay of norm conflicts, the idea of mutual responsiveness is an idea that should stand central to questions as regards the balance between market integration and social objectives. From the perspective of the supranational trade regime it is therefore necessary to answer the question what market integration can legitimately prescribe to Member States in terms of substantive outcomes, eg the less restrictive or more efficient measure and where the limit to that normative prescriptive power should be set and in what way in order to allow for social diversity. Conversely, social interests that are restrictive of the supranational trade interests will have to incorporate a certain responsiveness to integration objectives. The next chapters are concerned with developing a model of social legitimacy for the Court to adjudicate such conflicts and to provide an 'operational rationale' under the heading of responsive adjudication.

The following chapters of this book will look at the main areas of law of the EU internal market: free movement, competition and state aid. Each of these chapters shall identify how the social sphere manifests itself in that area of law and to what extent the supranational rules are able to accommodate social diversity and to what extent they threaten it. Each chapter shall identify, with regard to the mentioned areas of law, deficiencies in the extent that the dialogue of mutual responsiveness takes place. Questioning and demanding articulation of restrictive regulatory choices within legal frameworks may be an excellent starting point for a dialogue that aims to increase the distinct articulation, and thereby assists in the identification, of embedding organisational principles on the Member State level. Each chapter shall also develop a rationale of mutual responsiveness for the area of law under investigation. Developing this rationale of responsiveness in internal

[204] See also M Dawson and F de Witte, 'Constitutional Balance in the EU after the Euro-crisis' (2012) 76(5) *Modern Law Review* 817–44.

market law will be of discursive, formative value for the EU project as a whole. In developing a rationale of responsiveness the substantive scope and reach of the internal market will be established. That is to say, to which point the internal market can accommodate social claims and from which point objectives become inherently irreconcilable. Therefore, the overarching idea is that the struggle between market integration and social locality should be cherished as a potential source of deliberative and formative potential for the expressive value of internal market law.[205]

[205] As argued also by Dani (n 19).

2

Social Legitimacy in EU Free Movement Law

I. INTRODUCTION

CHAPTER 1 HIGHLIGHTED that the main requirements for Member States that flow from EU free movement law are clear, such as the textbook examples of the prohibition of quotas, customs duties and protectionist schemes. At the same time a lot of contentious questions remain regarding the resolution of cases that are right on the intersection of unity of EU free movement law and social diversity of the Member States. A lot of these contentious issues originate from the significant expansion in scope of all the free movement provisions over the last two decades.[1] Although Member States have been allowed to increasingly add categories to what can be considered as legitimate overriding objectives to market access rights, the Court of Justice has concomitantly been increasingly strict in the application of its proportionality analysis.[2] Moreover, the increase in scope has led to an increase of controversial outcomes in the case law of the Court.[3] In particular, the balancing of Member States' trade restrictive social spheres and the requirements of market integration are increasingly contested.[4] There is no apparent operational principle utilised by the Court to balance these types of conflicts.[5]

It is on this point, specifically, that this chapter seeks to contribute. Specifically, by offering a perspective that goes beyond emphasising either (i) the importance for EU law to respect the structures that are expressive of Member State choices,

[1] See eg E Spaventa, 'From Gebhard to Carpenter: Towards a (non-) economic European Constitution' (2004) 41 *Common Market Law Review* 743–73 and F De Cecco, *State Aid and the European Economic Constitution* (Oxford, Hart Publishing, 2013) ch 2.

[2] Inter alia C Barnard, 'Derogations, Justifications, and the Four Freedoms: is State Interest Really Protected?' in C Barnard and O Odudu (eds), *The Outer Limits of European Union Law* (Oxford, Hart Publishing, 2009) at 273.

[3] eg N Nic Shuibhne and M Maci, 'Proving Public Interest: The Growing Impact of Evidence in Free Movement Case Law' (2013) 50(4) *Common Market Law Review* 965–1005.

[4] eg C Joerges and F Rödl, 'Informal Politics, Formalised Law and the "Social Deficit" of European Integration: Reflections after the Judgments of the ECJ in Viking and Laval' (2009) 15 *European Law Journal* 1–19.

[5] See L Azoulai, 'The Court of Justice and the Social Market Economy: The Emergence of an Ideal and the Conditions for its Realization' (2008) 45 *Common Market Law Review* 1335.

which embed the pursuit or protection of social objectives[6] or (ii) the requirements for Member States to open up embedded social structures in order to develop towards a post-national constellation that remedies potential democratic deficits.[7] What is required and pursued, instead, is a holistic approach to the issue, recognising the interdependence of both central facets for the structure and development of the internal market in a mutually responsive manner. It is in EU free movement law that this field of tension, between supranational market integration and local structures, reflective of social identity and diversity, comes to fore most clearly. As such, this chapter speaks to what can be considered a—if not the—central point of tension in EU free movement law adjudication.

However, in the field of free movement adjudication, the EU internal market project has been a, seemingly, one-sided affair, primarily concerned with the question how social structures within Member States are required to accommodate market access rights that flow from the free movement rules.[8] Exemplary of this relationship is the syntax of the Court in the area of free movement law that, on the basis of an unqualified market access test, captures most regulatory structures and social interests as potential restrictions, whilst requiring justifications of these structures and interests within a strict evaluative framework. As argued in the previous chapter, the normative claim of social legitimacy in the context of the multilevel framework of the EU internal market is that a reconciliation of local domestic social values within supranational market objectives requires explicit responsiveness to social context within the Member States. The normative claims of social legitimacy were partly constructed on the basis of the ideas of Karl Polanyi, whose historical analyses of transformations in state-market-society relationships provides the normative foundation for the idea that an overly functional and under-socialised model of adjudication could threaten the social cohesion, solidarity or identity that a state pursues. The liberal society that the EU purports to be contains by its nature a diversity of social spheres and should incorporate different kinds of valuation of those spheres.[9] This chapter explores

[6] Most clearly F Scharpf, 'Negative and Positive Integration in the Political Economy of European Welfare States' in G Marks, FW Scharpf, P Schmitter and W Streeck (eds), *Governance in the European Union* (London, Sage Publications, 1996) at 15; FW Scharpf, 'The Asymmetry of European Integration, or why the EU Cannot be a "Social Market Economy"' (2009) 8 *Socio-Economic Review* 211–50.

[7] Inter alia M Maduro, *We the Court: the European Court of Justice and the European Economic Constitution* (Oxford, Hart Publishing, 1998); overview of this narrative and fundamental critique in A Somek, 'The Argument from Transnational Effects I: Representing Outsiders through Freedom of Movement' (2010) 16 *European Law Journal* 315, referring to C Joerges and J Neyer, '"Deliberative Supranationalism" Revisited' (2006) 2006/20 EUI Working Paper Law 2 as the 'inventors' of this perspective on EU free movement law. See also C Joerges and J Ney, '"Deliberative Political Processes" Revisited: What Have we Learnt About the Legitimacy of Supranational Decision-Making?' (2006) 44 *Journal of Common Market Studies* 779.

[8] The scope of the chapter is limited to 'market origin rights' versus regulatory choices of Member States. That excludes individual-based rights such as citizenship and some free movement of persons and workers lines of case law from the scope of this chapter.

[9] Chapter I, section II.

the adjudicative model(s) of the Court of Justice in free movement cases from this normative perspective. The need to find evaluative principles that are congruent with the underlying social context, without losing sight of internal market objectives, is coined as responsive adjudication.

Section II looks at the existing adjudicative template that the Court adopts in free movement adjudication and discusses how the 'valuation' of free movement conflicts within that template may lead to issues of incommensurability and consequent problems with the normative claims purported by social legitimacy. Section III looks more specifically at the current adjudicative techniques developed by the Court to govern this field of EU law in terms of ideal type models. It will be demonstrated that the Court has created different standards of evaluation towards restrictive social context but that responsiveness is currently lacking, in any coherent form, in the adjudicative models developed by the Court. Section IV gathers these approaches and considers how they could be reconstructed into a model of adjudication that is more in tune with the normative claims of social legitimacy. It turns out that the essential features of the proposed alternative are visible in the case law of the Court but in order to adjudicate in a socially responsive manner the Court will have to fundamentally reconsider its model of adjudication. The chapter submits a rationale of responsiveness that recognises manifest collisions between the objectives of free movement law and social spheres within the Member States. The submitted model instructs the selection and application of adjudicative reasoning, depending on the absence or presence of a *true* conflict.[10] On this basis the case law of the Court can be rationalised, restructured and become responsive to Member State diversity. The normative rationale of responsiveness leads to a restructuring of the case law on the basis of the notion that the social legitimacy of EU free movement law depends on an adjudicative model that allows a diversity of embedded organisational principles to exist and constructively interact within the internal market. Section V concludes that the development of this adjudicative rationale has the potential to contribute significantly to the social purpose of the EU internal market project.

II. VALUATION, INDETERMINACY AND INCOMMENSURABILITY IN FREE MOVEMENT ADJUDICATION

A. Organisational Principles within EU Free Movement Law

The supranational market rationale that EU free movement rules promote is concerned with an area without internal frontiers, in which the free movement of goods, persons and capital is ensured in accordance with the provisions of the

[10] Normative principles are understood in this context as justification narratives that reflect any system of rules and shared expectations governing a particular social context. See further J Scott and G Marshall, *A Dictionary of Sociology* (Oxford, Oxford University Press, 2009).

Treaties (Article 26 TFEU). Free movement rights promise market access and set out to challenge obstacles to trade. However, the EU Treaties and the Court have always allowed national measures to take precedence over free movement when they serve important interests recognised by the Union, including national identity. In addition, the Court has developed a range of mandatory requirements (*Cassis de Dijon*)[11] as 'public interest requirements' or 'objective justifications'. Free movement law recognises explicitly that in the absence of EU harmonisation and in so far as there are no national measures producing a protectionist effect, Member States enjoy leeway in safeguarding social objectives, which are deemed fundamental to their identity.[12] Beyond the 'core nucleus of shared values', the Court 'welcomes value diversity'.[13] However, controversy accumulates around the question where exactly that dividing line falls.[14]

The social critiques that were discussed in the previous chapter mostly originate from this controversial case law in the area of EU free movement law. As was discussed, these critiques tend to identify a structural bias of the Court in favour of market access and deregulation. In most cases before the Court, it is said, where there is found a restriction on free movement pursuant to the pursuit of a regulatory objective the conflict is decided in favour of EU free movement. Such claims are substantiated on the basis of controversial free movement cases such as *Centros*, *Überseering* and *Inspire Art*[15] that are critiqued for allowing companies to circumvent national co-determination procedures in Germany by establishing themselves in the UK or the *Cadbury Schweppes* type cases[16] that would allow tax-avoidance practices by companies, and perhaps most prominently in the socially salient cases of *Laval*, *Viking*, *Ruffert*, *Luxemburg*, *Occupational pensions*, *Herron* and, most recently, *AGET Iraklis*,[17] which have resulted in a strong belief that fundamental social interests are structurally valued as being subordinate to rights to free movement.[18] I shall argue, however, that there is another reading of these cases available.

[11] Case 120/78 *Rewe-Zentral AG v Bundesmonopolverwaltung für Branntwein* [1979] ECR 649.

[12] H Clemens et al (eds), Judging Europe's Judges: The Legitimacy of the Case Law of the European Court of Justice (Oxford, Hart Publishing, 2013).

[13] K Lenaerts, 'The Court's Outer and Inner Selves: Exploring the External and Internal Legitimacy of the European Court of Justice' in Clemens et al, *Judging Europe's Judges* (n 12) 13–60.

[14] S Weatherhill, 'The Court's Case Law on the Internal Market: "A Circumloquacious Statement of the Result, Rather than a Reason for Arriving at It"?' in Clemens et al (n 12) at 104.

[15] Case C-212/97 *Centros Ltd v Erhvervs- og Selskabsstyrelsen* [1999] ECR I-01459; Case C-208/00 *Überseering BV v Nordic Construction Company Baumanagement GmbH* [2002] ECR I-09919; Case C-167/01 *Kamer van Koophandel en Fabrieken voor Amsterdam v Inspire Art Ltd* [2003] ECR I-10155.

[16] C-196/04 *Cadbury Schweppes* [2006] ECR I-07995.

[17] Case C-341/05 *Laval un Partneri* [2007] ECR I-11767; Case C-438/05 *Viking Line* [2007] ECR I-10779; Case C-346/06 *Rüffert* [2008] ECR I-01989; Case C-319/06 *Commission/Luxemburg* [2008] ECR I-04323; Case C-271/08 *Occupational pensions* [2010] ECR I-07091; Case C-426/11 *Herron* ECLI:EU:C:2013:521; Case C-201/15 *AGET Iraklis* ECLI:EU:C:2016:972.

[18] A selection: C Barnard, 'Viking and Laval: An Introduction' (2007–08) 10 *Cambridge Yearbook of European Legal Studies* 464; A Dashwood, 'Viking and Laval: Issues of Horizontal Direct Effect' (2007–08) 10 *Cambridge Yearbook of European Legal Studies* 525; A Davies, 'One Step Forward, Two

The most obvious valuation bias is found to exist in the legal fact that restrictions on free movement of economic actors are applied so as to include almost all regulatory rules within Member States with a cross-border interest, which then have to be justified and accompanied by an analysis of the appropriateness and proportionality of the measures and by specific evidence, substantiating the claims made.[19] The argument is made that, as a result of the trade bias, there exists a structural preference in favour of deregulation that is targeted against specific, or perhaps better described as claims to, social organisational forms at the Member State level, which challenge the legitimacy of the EU internal market project.[20]

Chapter 1 posited how the argument from transnational effects attempts to (re) contextualise this as a subtle and constructive means towards a new transnational democratic nation state, one that is particularly sensitive towards the interests of entities that fall outside of its direct political reach and procedures. Within this perspective, a wide interpretation of the scope of free movement provisions is adopted for the purpose of placing constitutional limits on state interventions in the market, not for the purpose of the market but for considerations related to the accommodation of interests that are not part of national democratic governance structures.[21] In other words, the ambitions of the EU free movement rules are then not 'market'-oriented but aim to achieve integration amongst otherwise defunct national democracies. However, Somek highlighted that the conceptual apparatus to achieve this integration is based on economic due process or efficiency considerations, with the effect that social objectives within Member States may be forced to fit within a model that disregards their constituent features.[22] Structuring the dialogue on the basis of the notion of market access results often in a test

Steps Back? Laval and Viking at the ECJ' (2008) 37 *Industrial Law Journal* 126; S Deakin, 'Regulatory Competition after Laval' (2007–08) 10 *Cambridge Yearbook of European Legal Studies* 581; C Kilpatrick, 'Laval's Regulatory Conundrum: Collective Standard-Setting and the Court's New Approach to Postal Workers' (2009) 34 *European Law Review* 844; C Joerges and F Rödl, 'Informal Politics, Formalised Law and the "Social Deficit" of European Integration: Reflections after the Judgments of the ECJ in Viking and Laval' (2009) 15 *European Law Journal* 2–22; J Malmberg and T Sigeman, 'Industrial Action and EU Economic Freedoms: The Autonomous Collective Bargaining Model Curtailed by the European Court of Justice' (2008) 45 *Common Market Law Review* 1115; T Novitz, 'A Human Rights Analysis of the Viking and Laval Judgments' (2007–08) 10 *Cambridge Yearbook of European Legal Studies* 541; S Sciarra, 'Viking and Laval: Collective Labour Rights and Market Freedoms in the Enlarged EU' (2007–08) 10 *Cambridge Yearbook of European Legal Studies* 563; P Syrpis and T Novitz, 'Economic and Social Rights in Conflict: Political and Judicial Approaches to their Reconciliation' (2008) 33 *European Law Review* 411.

[19] N Shuibhne and Maci, 'Proving Public Interest' (n 3).

[20] See Joerges and Rödl, 'Informal Politics, Formalised Law and the "Social Deficit" of European Integration' (n 18); S Buckel and L Oberndorfer, 'Die lange Inkubationszeit des Wettbewerbs der Rechtsordnungen—Eine Genealogie der Rechtsfälle Viking/Laval/Rüffert/Luxemburg aus der Perspektive einer materialistischen Europarechtstheorie' in AF Lescano, F Rödl and C Schmid (eds), *Europäische Gesellschaftsverfassung. Zur Konstitutionalisierung sozialer Demokratie in Europa* (Baden-Baden, Nomos, 2009); see also Somek, 'The Argument from Transnational Effects I' (n 7).

[21] See Maduro, *We the Court* (n 7).

[22] See Somek (n 7).

of 'economic due process'.[23] Indeed, the question emerges 'what might be done to prevent the argument from transnational effects from slipping into a freewheeling rampage of economic due process?'[24]

This concern is in essence related to the 'mode of reasoning' adopted by the Court of Justice in resolving the conflict constellations generated by the integration project, particularly with respect to diagonal conflicts. Diagonal conflicts were introduced before as the constitutionally most salient type of conflict constellation within internal market law. They arise with respect to conflicts between the right to economic movement and areas where Member States have retained their competences, such as with regard to the development and implementation of social policies and a simple reference to supremacy of EU law to resolve possible conflicts is not available. Although it can be and has been argued that such policies should remain 'protected' on the basis of the principle of enumerated competences, the Court of Justice has decided that such measures may still conflict—diagonally—with the economic freedoms of movement and require a justification. Indeed, such conflicts arise abundantly and potentially endlessly, after the economic freedoms of the internal market have been interpreted by the Court of Justice so as to provide for a 'positive standard of constitutionality' because virtually all the social policy objectives within Member States can be framed as restrictions that require justification.[25] It is indeed from this moment onwards that many conflicts have become salient in policy *substantive* terms.[26]

The balance that is arguably to be found in EU free movement adjudication is exactly the dividing line between those organisational principles within Member States that are *embedding* a social fabric from those that *are to be embedded* within the EU internal market fabric. The Polanyian rationale, as it was introduced in Chapter 1, does not exclude the efficiency and liberty rationales of the market as an overarching framework to determine this. Questioning and demanding articulation of restrictive regulatory choices within legal frameworks may be an excellent starting point for the dialogue of mutual responsiveness that aims to increase the distinct articulation and thereby assists in the identification of embedding organisational principles on the Member State level. There exists an expressive function for free movement law in this respect. However, the argument presented in this chapter posits that the absence of a clear rationale to find this dividing line is exactly what undermines social legitimacy of the EU internal market

[23] ibid, at 320.

[24] ibid, at 332.

[25] eg also N Shuibhne and Maci (n 3).

[26] Augustin Menéndez traces this 'positive standard of constitutionality' back to *Cassis de Dijon*, Case C-120/78 *Rewe v Bundesmonopolverwaltung für Branntwein* [1979] ECR I 00649. Menéndez provides a compelling argument that this shift explains much of the abrasiveness of post 1970s CJEU case law and that from this moment internal market conflicts have become relevant, primarily, in policy substantive terms; A Menéndez, 'United they Diverge? From Conflicts to Constitutional Theory? Critical Remarks on Joerges' Theory of Conflicts of Law' RECON WP 2011/6 (Oslo, 2011) at 24.

project because it fails to identify genuine norm conflicts in free movement cases. This point shall be further developed below.

The normative claim of social legitimacy, as it was developed in the previous chapter, in the context of the multilevel governance context of the EU and the internal market, is that a reconciliation of local domestic social values within supranational market objectives requires a form of explicit responsiveness to the social context that is being adjudicated. Member States need to accommodate out of state interests by committing themselves to the integrating supranational market whilst the internal market principles concomitantly need to accommodate Member State diversity. The latter means, rather subtly, that the evaluating models that the Court adopts should be responsive to Member State objectives that are legitimate but incompatible with the rationale of the normative principle that the internal market promotes in a specific case. This responsiveness is to be found in the selection of an evaluative framework to come to a resolution of a conflict and the explicit articulation of irreconcilable conflicts between Member States' social spheres and the organisational principle pursued within the EU free movement rules.

The remainder of this chapter engages with this and seeks to develop an adjudicative rationale that can be regarded as socially responsive. The next section first explores more closely the legal reasoning adopted by the Court of Justice to govern the concerned conflict constellations on the basis of an ideal types approach. Although there are cases where the Court of Justice has arguably lost sight of the need for 'self-restraint' and the rationales that are adopted could lead to an 'unhindered right to cross-border movement', it is interesting to highlight some of the structural adjudicative rationales, which do not necessarily all point in the same direction. It will be demonstrated that the case law of the Court does not follow any particular settled adjudicative rationale to determine the more contested requirements that free movement law purports.[27] Nor is there any ideological agenda or explicit bias at work. Before making sweeping statements about the effects of this case law or the agenda of the Court, it is important to look in some detail at the structural adjudicative techniques that the Court employs in EU free movement law to distil some continuing and current trends in the adjudicative techniques employed by the Court.

B. The Expedient 'Rights Inflation' Proportionality Model in EU Free Movement Adjudication

There is a certain inherent and continuing structure in the free movement case law of the Court that follows partly from the structure of the Treaty and partly

[27] eg the 'centralised', 'competitive' and 'decentralised' models of Maduro (n 7).

from precedent-based case law.[28] The adjudicative template of the Court of Justice consists of three separate steps: (i) is there a restriction on a free movement right?; (ii) is there a legitimate justification for the restriction?; (iii) can the restriction be considered proportionate with regard to its legitimate objectives? Importantly, as has been discussed, the starting point of the adjudicative model developed by the Court is to apply a broad and unqualified market access test for all free movement rights,[29] which imposes jurisdiction over most Member State regulatory choices that can be considered restrictive to economic activities, and subsequently, in a second stage, resolve conflicts in the course of a proportionality exercise.

Whilst originating from the area of goods, the *Dassonville* formula, 'all trading rules enacted by Member States which are capable of hindering, directly or indirectly, actually or potentially, intra-community trade'[30] applies to all other freedoms as well.[31] Despite being concerned with the free movement of goods, the *Keck* approach provided for regulatory rules to fall outside of the reach of the free movement rules, in case they qualified as 'certain' non-discriminatory 'selling arrangements' and did not *completely prevent* market access;[32] today all freedoms appear to be converging towards a rather unqualified market access test.[33]

Indeed, the establishment of a restriction appears to be an important step in the adjudication of conflicts within free movement law, because as said, most regulatory rules that are tested within the traditional syntax tend not to fulfil the proportionality criteria that come later. The move of the Court towards the adoption of a rather unqualified market access has been frequently critiqued[34] and the contributions seem to agree that the Court has now 'refined' its approach in *Keck* in

[28] As highlighted eg in L Azoulai, 'The Court of Justice and the Social Market Economy: The Emergence of an Ideal and the Conditions for its Realization' (2008) 45 *Common Market Law Review* 1335.

[29] See for a recent analysis I Lianos, 'In Memoriam Keck: The Reformation of the EU Law on the Free Movement of Goods' (2015) 2 *European Law Review* 225–48. More discussion on this adjudicative tool in G Davies, 'Understanding Market Access: Exploring the Economic Rationality of Different Conceptions of Free Movement Law' (2010) 11 *German Law Journal* 671–704; Spaventa, 'From Gebhard to Carpenter' (n 1); J Snell, 'The Notion of Market Access: A Concept or a Slogan?' (2010) 47 *Common Market Law Review* 437–72. Whilst originating from the area of free movement of goods, the *Dassonville* formula (Case ECLI:EU:C:1974:82 (*Dassonville*), para 5).

[30] Case 8/74 *Dassonville* [1974] ECR 00837, para 5.

[31] For services in Case C-76/90 *Säger v Dennemeyer* [1991] ECR I-04221; for workers in Case C-415/93 *Union royale belge des sociétés de football association and Others v Bosman and Others* [1995] ECR I-04921; for establishment in Case C-55/94 *Gebhard v Consiglio dell'Ordine degli Avvocati e Procuratori di Milano* [1995] I-04165; for capital in Case C-367/98 *Commission v Portugal* [2002] ECR I-04731.

[32] Joined Cases C-267/91 and C-268/91, *Keck and Mithouard* [1993] ECR I-06097.

[33] See amongst others Spaventa (n 1).

[34] eg C Barnard and S Deakin, 'Market Access and Regulatory Competition' in C Barnard and J Scott (eds), *The Law of the Single European Market, Unpacking the Premises* (Oxford, Hart Publishing, 2002); Spaventa (n 1) at 914; Davies, 'Understanding Market Access' (n 29) at 671; Snell 'The Notion of Market Access' (n 29) at 437; MS Jansson and H Kalimo, 'De Minimis Meets "Market Access": Transformations in the Substance—and the Syntax—of EU Free Movement Law?' (2014) 51 *Common Market Law Review* 523.

favour of a market access test, although it seems that the Court in free movement of goods cases still uses part of its *Keck* rationale.[35]

In the two cases that have served as the main signalling point for the shift of the Court towards this market access test, what seems to have been decisive is the question whether the measures in question touched directly on cross-border movement. In *Commission v Italy (trailers)*,[36] the Court decided that the prohibition of specific trailers constituted a restriction (although it could be justified by reasons of road safety). The Court stated that, in addition to the principles of non-discrimination and mutual recognition, Article 34 TFEU reflects the obligation to 'respect the principle of ensuring free access of union products to national markets'.[37] As a result of the Italian rules, which completely banned motorcycle trailers from the road, the consumer demand for such trailers did not exist in Italy and, consequently, their importation to the market was directly hindered. The same approach was adopted in the case of *Mickelsson*.[38] Here the Court stated that Swedish rules, regulating areas where jet skis could be used, left only marginal opportunities for their use. Consequently, the restrictions could have considerable influence on the behaviour of consumers and, consequently, these rules affected market access.[39]

As such, it can be argued that the Court does provide for some qualifications to market access.[40] Indeed, it can be argued that the Court, to some degree, has focused on *the directness* of market access hindrance, as confirmed, for example, also in the field of services and workers.[41] For example, in *Bosman* the Court considered that a football transfer fee system qualified as a restriction by making a reference to the *direct impact* of a player's access to the employment markets of other Member States.[42] In *Alpine Investments*, the Court of Justice evaluated the legality

[35] See Case C-108/09 *Ker Optika* [2010] ECR I-12213, referring to *Keck* in para 51:

> For that reason, the application to products from other Member States of national provisions restricting or prohibiting certain selling arrangements is such as to hinder directly or indirectly, actually or potentially, trade between Member States for the purposes of the case-law flowing from Dassonville, unless those provisions apply to all relevant traders operating within the national territory and affect in the same manner, in law and in fact, the selling of domestic products and of those from other Member States. *The application of such rules to the sale of products from another Member State meeting the requirements laid down by that State is by nature such as to prevent their access to the market or to impede such access more than it impedes the access of domestic products.* (emphasis added)

[36] Case C–110/05 *Commission v Italy (trailers)* [2009] ECR I–519.

[37] ibid, para 34.

[38] Case C-142/05 *Mickelsson* [2009] ECR I-04273.

[39] ibid, para 28.

[40] See Jansson and Kalimo, 'De Minimis Meets "Market Access": Transformations in the Substance—and the Syntax—of EU Free Movement Law?' (n 34) at 523.

[41] See Snell (n 29).

[42] Case C-415/93 *Bosman* [1995] ECR I-04921.

of a Dutch measure preventing financial service providers from cold calling potential clients.[43] The regulation was defended on the basis of its non-discriminatory nature and that it could consequently be qualified as a selling arrangement. The Court disagreed, describing the measure as *directly* affecting access to the market in services in the other Member States. AG Tizzano agreed with this approach in *Caixa Bank* where he argued that the freedom of establishment is violated only if a measure either discriminates or *directly affects* market access. Therefore, importantly, this reasoning would imply that it is insufficient if a measure's only effect is to reduce profit margins and the attractiveness of the pursuit of an activity.[44] That is because the latter could be seen to mean that the market access test provides for unlimited economic freedom. Similarly, AG Tesauro argued in the case of *Hünermund* that 'Article 34 does not provide for a general freedom to trade or the right to the unhindered pursuit of commercial activities, but is aimed at restrictions on imports'.[45] AG Maduro built on this by arguing in *Alfa Vita* that market access should be restricted in the sense that differences between regulatory regimes as such cannot lead to restrictions that trigger the free movement rules, unless they lead to cross-border situations being treated less favourably than the national situation.[46] However, recent case law demonstrates that when pressed, the notion is still likely to collapse into a wide economic freedom assertion, much like the original *Dassonville* formula.[47] A recent application in the case *DKV Belgium* explicitly illustrates the workings of the market access test in this respect.[48]

The case concerned a Belgian authorisation requirement for certain insurance premiums. According to Belgian law, insurers could only alter annually the premium on the basis of the consumer price index. If they would require higher premium increases, this could only be done after authorisation from the banking, finance and insurance commission. These rules were aimed at protecting consumers, particularly with a view to preventing them from being faced with sharp, unexpected increases in insurance premium rates.[49] DKV Belgium was denied an increase of its premium and challenged the system, alleging that it disproportionately infringed the free movement of services. Regarding the existence of a restriction the Court repeated the mantra that 'the term "restriction" within the meaning of Articles 49 TFEU and 56 TFEU covers all measures which prohibit, impede or render less attractive the freedom of establishment or the freedom to provide services'.[50]

43 Case C-384/93 *Alpine Investments* [1995] ECR I-01141.
44 AG Tizzano Opinion in Case C-442/02 *Caixa Bank* [2004] ECR I-08961.
45 AG Tesauro Opinion in Case C-292/92 (1993) ECR I-06787.
46 AG Maduro Opinion in Joined Cases C-158/04 and C-159/04 *Alfa Vita* [2006] ECR I-08135.
47 Case 8/74 *Dassonville* [1974] ECR 00837, para 5.
48 Case C-577/11 *DKV Belgium* [2013] ECLI:EU:C:2013:146.
49 ibid, para 9.
50 ibid, para 31.

However, the Court then considered that

> a measure applicable without distinction, such as the system of premium rate increases at issue in the main proceedings, may come within that concept, it should be borne in mind that rules of a Member State do not constitute a restriction within the meaning of the FEU Treaty solely by virtue of the fact that other Member States apply less strict, or more commercially favourable, rules to providers of similar services established in their territory …

The logical step would have been for the Court at this point to qualify the market access test such as some form of differentiated impact,[51] selectivity,[52] de minimis[53] or a perhaps even a return to a *Keck*-type rule.[54] Instead the Court simply considered that 'the concept of restriction covers measures taken by a Member State which, although applicable without distinction, affect access to the market for undertakings from other Member States and thereby hinder intra-Community trade'.[55]

The Court's current approach to market access seems to have been inspired mostly by the idea of AG Jacobs who argued in his Opinion in the case *Leclerc/Siplec*, that the central concern of the treaty provisions on free movement is 'to prevent unjustified obstacles to trade between Member States and if an obstacle to interstate trade exists, it cannot cease to exist simply because an identical obstacle affects domestic trade'.[56] AG Jacobs held that 'restrictions on trade should not be tested against local conditions, which happen to prevail in each Member State, but against the aim of access to the entire Community market'.[57] This idea seems to have been the decisive one for the Court, whose main consideration is worth citing in full:

> a system of premium rate increases such as that at issue in the main proceedings is liable to dissuade insurance undertakings having their head office in a Member State other than the one which introduced such a system from opening a branch in that Member State or to offer their products there as part of the free movement of services. Those undertakings will not only have to change their terms and rates to meet the requirements imposed by that system, they will also have to determine their premium positioning and, therefore, their commercial strategy when they first set their premiums, with the risk that future premium rate increases will be insufficient to cover the costs with which they will be faced. It follows that insurance undertakings entering the market of a Member State

[51] Snell (n 29) at 448 argues in favour of a differential impact test combined with market access.

[52] Davies (n 29) at 685 offers selectivity as an alternative.

[53] Jansson and Kalimo (n 34) at 523.

[54] P Oliver, 'Of Trailers and Jet Skis: Is the Case Law on Article 34 TFEU Hurtling in a New Direction?' (2011) 33 *Fordham International Law Journal* 1469; see also P Oliver, *Free Movement of Goods in the European Community: under Articles 28 to 30 of the EC Treaty* (London, Sweet & Maxwell, 2003) at 111. Also JJW Weiler, 'The Constitution of the Common Market Place: Text and Context in the Evolution of the Free Movement of Goods' in P Craig and G De Burca (eds), *The Evolution of EU Law* (Oxford, Oxford University Press, 1999) at 372.

[55] Case C-577/11 *DKV Belgium* [2013] ECLI:EU:C:2013:146, paras 32–33.

[56] AG Jacobs Opinion in Case C-412/93 *Leclerc-Siplec* [1995] ECR I-179.

[57] ibid, para 40.

> which has introduced a system of premium rate increases such as that at issue in the main proceedings are obliged, if they want to be able to access that market under conditions which comply with the legislation of that Member State, *to re-think their business policy and strategy* [...]. In those circumstances, a system of premium rate increases such as that at issue in the main proceedings must be held to constitute a restriction on the freedom of establishment and the freedom to provide services.[58] (emphasis added)

The Court demonstrates here what unqualified market access entails and it is contradictory to the idea that regulatory differences as such do not entail, automatically, restrictions on freedom of movement as meant in the Treaty.[59] Thus applied, any rule preventing profit-maximising behaviour that an undertaking wishes to engage in, is likely to reduce 'profitability', which the Court considers the benchmark of the market access test. The Court considers that the basic fact that an undertaking will have to determine a commercial strategy that is 'specific to a Member State' and takes account of the differing regulatory circumstances in that Member State is sufficient to constitute a restriction on the freedom of establishment and the freedom to provide services. It is, thereby, automatically unfavourable towards the out of state trader. Interpreted in this way, market access is an open concept that will encompass all rules, which have an effect on an economic operator's *business policy and strategy*, which are introduced as the substantial criteria of market access in this case.[60] According to the Court, the issue is not whether the product can access the market at all but whether the measure is such as to make the offering of services less attractive because it reduces the possibilities or because it increases costs. In other words, the economic operator not only has a right to access the market, 'it has a right to access as wide and cheap a market as possible'.[61] Somek's concerns would be validated on this basis since it would turn free movement law into an unrestricted economic due process test. This reading of market access has recently been confirmed by AG Bot:

> According to the formula now usually employed in the case-law, Article 34 TFEU reflects the obligation to comply with the principles of non-discrimination and of mutual recognition of products lawfully manufactured and marketed in other Member States, as well

[58] Case C-577/11 *DKV Belgium* [2013] ECLI:EU:C:2013:146, paras 34–35.

[59] To the same effect: Case C-543/08 *European Commission v Portuguese Republic* [2010] ECR I-11241.

[60] See also Spaventa (n 1) 914–32. See also Case C-518/06 [2009] *Commission v Italy* ECR I-03491, paras 68–70, concerning an infringement action against Italy, in respect of regulatory rules on motor insurance. Insurance companies in Italy were required to provide insurance to any potential customer, under terms and rates that the company had to publish in advance and there were limitations on the freedom of the companies to set their premiums. In the view of the Court this affected market access:

> inasmuch as it involves changes and costs on such a scale for those undertakings, the obligation to contract renders access to the Italian market less attractive and, if they obtain access to that market, reduces the ability of the undertaking concerned to compete effectively, from the outset against undertakings traditionally established in Italy.

[61] See Spaventa (n 1) at 924.

> as the principle of ensuring free access of EU products to national markets. I infer from that standard formula that a national measure may constitute an obstacle not only when, as a selling arrangement, it is discriminatory, in law or in fact, but also when, *irrespective of its nature, it impedes access to the market of the Member State concerned*. It follows that, where an obstacle to market access is found to exist, there is no need to undertake a comparative examination between the situation of the domestic products and that of the imported products in order to establish the existence of a difference in treatment between them.[62] (emphasis added)

This approach can of course be critiqued, and it has been by many commentators.[63] For example, Juka Snell notes that since the term 'market access' lacks a clear content: 'the court may use it freely either to approve or to condemn measures that it happens to like or dislike. Market access may simply provide a sophisticated sounding garb that conceals decisions based on intuition'.[64] From the perspective of responsiveness, the potential danger of this method of adjudication is that the instalment of expedient concepts will lead to the quick disapplication of conflicting social objectives.[65] As Catherine Barnard submits, 'the moment collective action is found to be a "restriction". … the "social" interests are on the back-foot, having to defend themselves from the economic'.[66] It follows from the market access test that the assessment of the proportionality of a restriction to a right of free movement is triggered almost instantly and without any form of qualification as soon as access to potentially 'embedded' spaces of economic activities is restricted.

It is important to emphasise that the framing of the conflict that is being adjudicated at the proportionality stage in EU free movement cases lacks the traditional conflict that is adjudicated by the proportionality principle through resolving 'embedded' prima facie rights. Instead, the conventional method applied in EU free movement law is reversed. Namely, to assess an embedded public policy concern, such as, for example, a fundamental right, under the proportionality assessment versus an external right of free movement. At this point the restriction is seen as an exception to the fundamental Treaty principles and must be construed narrowly and the Court has established that 'those grounds must … be interpreted strictly, so that their scope cannot be determined unilaterally by each Member

[62] Opinion AG Bot in Case C-333/14 *The Scotch Whisky Association and Others v The Lord Advocate* [2015], nyr, para 58.

[63] See n 29.

[64] Snell (n 29) at 448.

[65] See also JHH Weiler, 'Fundamental Rights and Fundamental Boundaries' in JHH Weiler, *The Constitution of Europe: 'Do the New Clothes Have an Emperor' and other Essays on European Integration* (Boston, Cambridge University Press, 1999) 102–29; also JH Weiler, 'The Constitution of the Common Market Place: Text and Context in the Evolution of the Free Movement of Goods' in P Craig and G De Burca (eds), *The Evolution of EU Law* (Oxford, Oxford University Press, 1999). See also B de Witte, 'Community Law and National Constitutional Values' (1991) 18 *Legal Issues of European Integration* 1–22, at 19.

[66] C Barnard, 'Social Dumping or Dumping Socialism' (2008) 67 *Current Law Journal* 262, at 264.

State without any control by the Community institutions'.[67] A case in point is the *Omega* case concerning a prohibition imposed by the Bonn police authority on a games parlour at which players with the help of laser guns simulated killing each other. One of the reasons that was given by the authority for imposing this measure was the protection of public policy, which was qualified by the Bundesverwaltungsgericht to be protecting human dignity, a fundamental constitutional principle spelt out in Article 1(1) of the German *Grundgesetz*. Acknowledging that human dignity represented a fundamental societal interest, the Court nevertheless decided that human dignity would have to be justified as a derogation from the fundamental principle on the freedom to provide services, and thus interpreted strictly. The Court did not spend a lot of thought on the fact that in terms of hierarchy of norms, the freedom to provide services was considered, necessarily, as the higher norm since the protection of human dignity was able to 'restrict' the free movement right in this case. Although the Court in its subsequent assessment of the proportionality of the measures considered that human dignity was allowed to trump the free movement right, through a light substantive proportionality analysis, there remains something quite unsatisfactory with the way that the Court adjudicates these types of conflicts. This also seemed to be a concern of AG Trstenjak who argued in *Commission v Germany (occupational pensions)* that:[68]

> Such an analytical approach suggests, in fact, the existence of a hierarchical relationship between fundamental freedoms and fundamental rights in which fundamental rights are subordinated to fundamental freedoms and, consequently, may restrict fundamental freedoms only with the assistance of a written or unwritten ground of justification.

However, as pointedly commented on by Spaventa, whether this approach of the Court is truly problematic all depends on how the internal market is conceptualised: 'The broadening of the scope of the Treaty could be seen as a contribution not so much to deregulation but rather to better regulation, through a process of continuous self-reflection and of continuous dialogue between regulators, traders and the Court'.[69] This view is reminiscent of the argument from transnational effects, the main rationale of which is the opening up of the discursive value of exactly this dialogue. A broadening of the market access test thereby leads to a broadening of the dialogue and furthers the interests of European unity from that perspective. As aptly pointed out by Nic Schuibhne, 'the justification framework has evolved over time to become the prime space within which public interest arguments are aired. It is where the multifaceted construction of the internal market … is explored and contested'.[70] Indeed, the Treaty-permitted grounds for

[67] See eg para 17 in Case C-54/99 *Eglise de schientologie* [2000] ECR I-01335; para 47 in case C-503/99 [2002] ECR I-044809; para 48 in Case C-483/99; and para 72 in Case C-463/00 [2003] ECR I-04581.

[68] Opinion AG Trstenjak in Case C-271/08 [2010] ECR I-07091, para 184.

[69] Spaventa (n 1) at 925.

[70] NN Shuibhne, *The Coherence of EU Free Movement Law* (Oxford, Oxford University Press, 2013) at 26.

derogation from free movement rights[71] have for a long time been extended with a very expansive approach in the case law, which allows the propagation of most policy arguments as 'imperative requirements' or 'overriding reason in the public interest'.[72] Member States are only barred from adopting 'economic' justifications so as to highlight that only public interest objectives can override free movement rights.[73] However, in practice the 'economic' justifications have been interpreted mostly as 'protectionist' aims, which are, prima facie, not accepted as an overriding reason in the public interest.[74] Thus, the simultaneous increase of the reach and the potential justifications with regard to the free movement provisions can indeed be perceived as a tool to impose a view of *good governance*.[75] It may be argued that in this way, and on the basis of an unqualified market access standard a constitutional settlement is advanced in which the validity of *all* democratically enacted Member State legislation and regulatory regimes that restrict a free movement right are contingent on judicial approval through a proportionality standard.

Crucial for the argument advanced here is that, absent *explicit responsiveness*, and in the presence of normative evaluative frameworks, this adjudicative model of the Court would render the negotiation, compromise and agreement involved in the adoption of legislation and regulatory regimes on a Member State level potentially irrelevant. The model may lack social legitimacy because it will, in effect, recognise rights that may not be part of the constitutional or legislative contexts on the Member State level and instead require a justification for the existence of those contexts. As argued before, there are legitimate obligations that can be imposed on Member States' constitutional, legislative and regulatory contexts, that derive from the commitment of being part of an integrating European market; however, Member State legislative context reflects the choice and commitments of a political community that are significant and these choices must receive the explicit consideration of the judiciary. The 'culture of justification' for restrictions of economic activity as clearly purported by the Court of Justice on the basis of an unqualified market access test is therefore only acceptable within

[71] 'Public morality, public policy or public security; the protection of health and life of humans, animals or plants; the protection of national treasures possessing artistic, historic or archaeological value; or the protection of industrial and commercial property' in Art 36 TFEU for quantitative restrictions on the free movement of goods. Public policy, public security or public health in Artis 45(3), 52 and 62 TFEU for free movement of workers, free establishment and free movement of services. For restrictions on free movement of capital, specific restrictions are set out in Art 65 TFEU.

[72] See J Scott, 'Mandatory or Imperative Requirements in the EU and the WTO' in C Barnard and J Scott, *The Law of the Single European Market: Unpacking the Premises* (Oxford, Hart Publishing, 2002) at 269.

[73] Case C-141/07 *Commission v Germany* [2008] ECR I-6935, para 60; Case C-444/05 *Stamatelaki* [2007] ECR I-03185.

[74] See AG Jääskinen in Joined Cases C-105/12 to C-107/12 *Essent* ECLI:EU:C:2013:677, who provides a compelling argument for interpreting the economic justification in this way in para 89 ff.

[75] Spaventa (n 1) at 925.

the confines of the embedding context of Member States that allow for economic activity to take place at all.[76]

Therefore, the unqualified market access test, as a means to structure free movement conflicts can only be socially legitimate if it is merely a prima facie way to structure the conflict at hand. In a next stage, responsiveness should become a core and explicit part of the proportionality analysis. By adopting a rationale of responsiveness, at a preliminary stage, it will be possible to streamline the choices of the Court for a particular model of evaluation and intensity of proportionality assessment in a way that guarantees the responsiveness of legal review. We shall now move on to look at proportionality analysis from this angle.

C. The Structure of Proportionality

The three stages of proportionality assessment are standardised and consist of an inquiry into (i) whether a measure was *suitable* to achieve the desired end (in the form of a rational connection between means and end); (ii) whether it was *necessary* to achieve the desired end (in the form of a test if there was a less restrictive measure available); and (iii) whether the measure imposed a burden on the individual that was excessive in relation to the objective sought to be achieved (proportionality *stricto sensu*). The third part of the test is often not applied by the Court and, as Paul Craig has noted, the Court will normally only consider the third part when an applicant explicitly addresses an argument concerning this stage of the inquiry.[77] Otherwise the Court tends to resolve the assessment on the basis of the first two stages of the proportionality assessment.

The function of proportionality in a democracy based on the rule of law, traditionally perceived, incorporates some important elements of responsiveness. Traditionally perceived the connection between proportionality and democracy is 'to secure government not only by the people through representation but to secure it in a way that a common good can be advanced in recognition of which

[76] See further, more broadly, D Dyzenhaus 'Proportionality and Deference in a Culture of Justification' in G Huscroft, BW Miller and G Webber (eds), *Proportionality and the Rule of Law: Rights, Justification, Reasoning* (Cambridge, Cambridge University Press, 2014) 234–58. In the famous words of R Cover, 'Foreword: *Nomos* and Narrative' (1983) 97 *Harvard Law Review* 4–68:

> no set of legal institutions or prescriptions exists apart from the narratives that locate it and give it meaning. For every constitution there is an epic, for each Decalogue a scripture. Once understood in the context of the narratives that give it meaning, law becomes not merely a system of rules to be observed, but a world in which we live. In this normative world, law and narrative are inseparably related. Every prescription is insistent in its demand to be located in discourse—to be supplied with history and destiny, beginning and end, explanation and purpose.

[77] P Craig and G de Burca, *EU Law Text, Cases and Materials* (Oxford, Oxford University Press, 2011) at 551.

everyone can, in principle, collaborate by obedience to a legitimate regime of law'.[78] For such a regime it is important to have the law function in a way that a legal subject's treatment by the law must be capable of a justification that explicitly articulates a conception of the 'public good' that is context specific, dynamic and therefore open to debate and criticism.[79] Implicit in this conception is that the burdens that flow from the law must be measured with respect to the advancement of that public interest and that the social legitimacy of a legal regime is, in part, obtained through a process of reasoned deliberation through which abstract principles of law become concrete and constitutive in the course of application to specific situations.[80] From this perspective, the idea of proportionality can be perceived as a technique that considers that the resolving of conflicts between rights and general public interest is best resolved by responsiveness to context, allowing reasonable solutions to be found that are sensitive to all the relevant contextual considerations.[81]

Importantly, on the basis of the previously discussed unqualified market access test, the adjudicative model of the Court resembles what can be termed as a 'rights inflation' proportionality model.[82] The rationale behind this model is that the existence of a hierarchical relationship between competing objectives is purely *functional* and that proportionality, applied in this way, indeed merely structures the conflict in a prima facie way so that legitimate rights and policies can actually be established. For example, in the extreme, proponents expounding a wide understanding of rights in proportionality analysis may include murder at a prima facie stage as a potential right or interest, but there is no doubt that there are reasons of sufficient weight in favour of a prohibition of that prima facie right, which are to be taken into account at the justification stage. In fact, it may be argued that proportionality is ideally suited to conduct such an inquiry as it is an approach that acknowledges, first, that there is a right to murder and subsequently, at the justification stage, deals with the permissible limitations of this right, addressing all morally relevant considerations in order to reach the right conclusion.[83] Similarly, free movement rights are placed as a prima facie right above public interest concerns such as human dignity, merely to then at the justification stage, deal with all the permissible limitations of the free movement right on the basis of human dignity, and at that stage address all the morally relevant considerations to come

[78] TRS Allan, 'Democracy, Legality, and Proportionality' in Huscroft, Miller and Webber (eds), *Proportionality and the Rule of Law: Rights, Justification, Reasoning* (n 76) 205–33, at 209.

[79] Further Dyzenhaus 'Proportionality and Deference in a Culture of Justification' (n 76) 234–58.

[80] Allan, 'Democracy, Legality, and Proportionality' (n 78).

[81] Further, ibid, at 211.

[82] As in K Moller 'Proportionality and Rights Inflation' in Huscroft, Miller and Webber (n 76) 155–72.

[83] As argued, eg, by Moller (n 82). See also M Kumm, 'The Idea of Socratic Contestation and the Right to Justification: The Point of Rights-based Proportionality Review' (2010) 4 *Law & Ethics of Human Rights* 157.

to a resolution of the conflict.[84] The prima facie structuring of EU free movement conflicts in this way is a crucial part of the adjudicative model of the Court, as indicated before, allowing it to engage with a range of regulatory contexts and, as explained before within the constitutional construct of the internal market, to initiate a dialogue with Member States that promotes internal market integration.

However, as was argued, to avoid problems of social legitimacy, the model depends crucially on responsiveness and can only be perceived as an adequate and acceptable technique if, eventually, conflicts between rights and general public interest are resolved on the basis of responsiveness to context, which incorporates a type of valuation that is able to respond to all the relevant contextual considerations. In the first place, the basic adjudicative free movement framework of the Court requires, from the perspective of social legitimacy, determinacy on the basis of an identification of normative conflicts between complete market access and restrictive social context. In so far as genuine normative conflicts are resolved within a metric that too easily presumes that conflicting objectives are commensurable within a single metric, social legitimacy issues will arise. To see to what extent this applies in free movement adjudication we need to explore, in more depth, the actual evaluative rationales that the Court incorporates in its proportionality assessment. I turn to this in the next section.

III. THE PROPORTIONALITY ANALYSIS OF THE COURT

Recently, increasing reference has been made to two 'separate' versions of proportionality analysis that are applied by the Court.[85] One version is considered to be more substantively oriented, and the other oriented more towards assessing the procedural context in which the measures were taken. It would appear that these are not so much separate tests but rather instances where the Court has either put more emphasis on whether a measure is *suitable* to achieve the desired end, or on the question as to whether a measure is *necessary* to achieve the desired end.[86]

[84] For a critique on this, see JHH Weiler and NJS Lockhart, '"Taking Rights Seriously" Seriously: The European Court of Justice and its Fundamental Rights Jurisprudence' (1995) 32 *Common Market Law Review* 593, who challenge the rights denigration argument as an 'unjustified leap from a lexical equivalence to normative equivalence'.

[85] D Damjanovic, 'The EU Market Rules as Social Market Rules: Why the EU Can Be a Social Market Economy (2013) 50 *Common Market Law Review* 1685–717; F de Witte, 'Sex, Drugs & EU Law: The Recognition of Moral and Ethical Diversity in EU Law' (2013) 50 *Common Market Law Review* 1545–78.

[86] See also G Mathisen, 'Consistency and Coherence as Conditions for Justification of Member State Measures Restricting Free Movement' (2010) 47 *Common Market Law Review* 1021–48. The 3 stages of proportionality assessment are standardised and consist of an inquiry into (i) whether a measure was suitable to achieve the desired end (in the form of a rational connection between means and end); (ii) whether it was necessary to achieve the desired end (in the form of a test if there was a less restrictive measure available); and (iii) whether the measure imposed a burden on the individual that was excessive in relation to the objective sought to be achieved (proportionality *stricto sensu*). The third part of the test is often not applied by the Court, as Paul Craig has noted; Craig and de Burca, *EU Law Text, Cases and Materials* (n 77) at 551.

The criterion that stands behind the decision of the Court to place emphasis on procedural context or substantive rationality is largely unclear and mostly arbitrarily applied without explicit consideration. Indeed, the Court will sometimes engage in a comparative review of solutions adopted in other Member States on the basis of the principle of mutual recognition.[87] Then again, it is also often considered that 'the fact that one Member State imposes less strict rules than another Member State does not mean that the latter's rules are disproportionate'.[88] At times, the Court protects a space for Member State difference by referring to 'the circumstances of law and of fact, which characterize the situation in the Member State concerned'[89] and defers the proportionality assessment completely to the national court.[90] However, when looking at these seemingly incoherent techniques of the Court to adjudicate free movement conflicts it is possible to distil three 'ideal type' models.

A. Substantive Efficiency Model

The first model can be labelled the *substantive efficiency model* and, as an ideal type, comes to the resolution of a conflict by way of questioning whether a measure is *necessary* to achieve the desired end. If there exists a less restrictive measure then the test is failed. This substantive oriented variant of the proportionality test is prescriptive of the *content* of national choices and the legality of a particular measure, which will depend on the absence of 'policy alternatives that are less restrictive of the rights of mobile actors. It allows such actors to demand that Member State policies are re-assessed in light of less restrictive choices made by other Member States'.[91] The most standardised version is the one where the Court stipulates that '[i]f a Member State has a choice between various measures to attain the same objective it should choose the means which least restricts [free movement]'.[92] In goods cases the Court has seen labelling as the least restrictive instrument in many instances. Exemplary here is the *Beer Purity* case where the Court decided that informing consumers through linking the name '*Bier*' only to products brewed with malted barley, hops, yeast and water could equally well be achieved 'by means which do not prevent the importation of products which have been lawfully manufactured and marketed in other Member States and, in particular, by the compulsory affixing of suitable labels giving the nature of the products sold'.[93]

[87] eg Case ECLI:EU:C:2010:44 (*Commission v France*) para 105.

[88] eg Case C-141/07 *Commission v Germany* [2008] ECR I-06935, para 51; Case C-36/02 *Omega Spielhallen- und Automatenaufstellungs-GmbH v Oberbürgermeisterin der Bundesstadt Bonn* [2004] ECR I-09609, para 108.

[89] Case C-434/04 *Ahokainen and Leppik* [2006[ECR I-09171, para 40.

[90] eg Case C-405/98 *Gourmet International Products* [2001] ECR I-01795, paras 21–22.

[91] See De Witte, 'Sex, Drugs & EU Law' (n 85) at 1568.

[92] Case 261/81 *Walter Rau* [1982] ECR 03961, para 12.

[93] Case C-178/84 *Commission v Germany* [1987] ECR 01227, para 36.

Whenever the Court applies this model of substantive efficiency, it pursues the idea that there is a single normative principle at work and that all the interests in the conflict are therefore necessarily compatible, by insisting that the diversity of options which have led to a restriction can be subject to one rational judgement according to their weight and rankings. By virtue of this description it is immediately clear that this is a mode of reasoning that is not suitably applied in the presence of a 'true' diagonal conflict constellation. That is to say, with respect to conflicts where the objectives that are pursued by Member States cannot be fully internalised with the functional mode of reasoning that underlies 'blanket' market integration.

This mode of reasoning is illustrated in a case concerning Austrian restrictions on road transport for environmental reasons, where the Court of Justice stated that:

> Without the need for the Court itself to give a ruling on the existence of alternative means, by rail or road, of transporting the goods covered by the contested regulation under economically acceptable conditions, or to determine whether other measures … could have been adopted in order to attain the objective of reducing emissions of pollutants in the zone concerned, it suffices to say in this respect that, before adopting a measure so radical as a total traffic ban on a section of motorway constituting a vital route of communication between certain Member States, the Austrian authorities were under a duty to examine carefully the possibility of using measures less restrictive of freedom of movement, and discount them only if their inadequacy, in relation to the objective pursued, was clearly established.[94]

The Court eventually held that:

> it has not been conclusively established in this case that the Austrian authorities … sufficiently studied the question whether the aim of reducing pollutant emissions could be achieved by other means less restrictive of the freedom of movement and whether there actually was a realistic alternative for the transportation of the affected goods by other means of transport or via other road routes.[95]

When the Court chooses to apply this substantive efficiency model it approaches the context that underlies a conflict on the basis of an idea of *managerialism*[96] and internalises the social considerations of Member States within a functional mode of reasoning. A regulatory context is assumed where a rational assessment of a problem involving the gathering and collating of information, listing options, calculating the costs of each option, evaluating consequences and choosing the best course of action is available. The main limitation of this form of reasoning in terms of its responsiveness is that, as an evaluative frame for Member State regulatory choices, the model is unable to take account of the potential systemic

[94] Case C-320/03 *Commission v Austria* [2005] ECR I-09871, para 87.

[95] ibid, para 89.

[96] A term coined in W Enteman, *Managerialism: The Emergence of a New Ideology* (Wisconsin, University of Wisconsin Press, 1993).

effects of certain policy choices in Member States. That is to say, many legislative, regulatory choices and governance schemes are the product of a compromise between different interests. Hence, such choices can often be criticised for being inefficient.[97] However, if these choices reflect essential points of compromise that, for example, secure the necessary political capital for a specific regulatory choice, then a blanket substantive review may forgo the underlying social context that is embedded within a particular regulatory scheme.[98]

This is not particular to the Court of Justice. In principle, all (administrative or constitutional) courts by their very nature face the challenge that rulings to annul laws or political decisions on the basis of the necessity stage of a proportionality test lack democratic legitimacy and that the discretion of democratically legitimised institutions should be to some extent reflected in the rulings. Therefore, in national contexts, courts tend to rely on the supremacy of another law to justify an intervention or refer a matter back to the legislature for repairs, instead of imposing their own solution. At least with respect to the diagonal conflict constellation (where a mere reliance on supremacy is not acceptable), these are solutions which are not easily available to the Court of Justice. That is why it often resorts to a resolution of a conflict constellation, *in abstracto*, and refers a case back to the national court together with guidelines that need to be taken into account by the national court.

The point of the ideal type description of this mode of reasoning is that if it is accepted that social diversity is a value to which the EU internal market is committed, then this utilitarian mode of reasoning, even when applied *in abstracto*, is not an appropriate means to adjudicate conflicts without a careful articulation of the actual conflict constellation. If applied to diagonal conflicts, it may inhibit and simply ignore legitimate policy choices that flow from the underlying normative infrastructure of the economy within a Member State. A case in point is the 2013 *Libert* case where the Court of Justice was asked to rule on social housing regulation in Belgium, which restricted access to housing in certain situations to those with a 'sufficient connection' to the geographical area and required land developers to meet social housing obligations.[99] The objective of the housing regulation was to ensure access to housing in certain areas for low-income or otherwise disadvantaged sections of the local population, a measure designed to combat the increasingly unstoppable phenomenon of gentrification.[100] However, the Court considered after listing the restrictions on movement of capital, services and establishment that there were other means of pursuing Flanders' socio-economic

[97] See eg G Monti, 'EU Competition Law from Rome to Lisbon' in C Heide-Jorgensen et al (eds), *Aims and Values in Competition Law* (Copenhagen, DJOF Publishing, 2013) 27–66, at 34.

[98] G Davies, 'Democracy and Legitimacy in the Shadow of Purposive Competence' (2015) 21 *European Law Journal* 2.

[99] Case C-197/11 *Libert* ECLI:EU:C:2013:288.

[100] ibid, para 23.

objectives, which were less restrictive of free movement and provided the example of offering 'subsidies for purchase or other subsidy mechanisms specifically designed to assist less affluent persons'.[101] In taking this position, the Court did not take into account potential political compromises or budgetary restrictions but assumed a regulatory context that was largely managerial.[102] Moreover, the issue of gentrification in light of its potential to undermine social cohesion and the correlation with the free movement of capital and services of real estate development was not touched upon.[103] As such, this mode of reasoning is at risk of denying that the diversity of preferences and orientations of Member States is the product of specific historical experiences, political contestation, societal learning and continuous political decision-making. Member States vary deeply in terms of institutional preferences and structural policy differences[104] and the evaluative standard that is used by the Court of Justice in such cases is not able to express and acknowledge those differences. Rather, it is reflective of a mode of reasoning that suggests that 'everything can be reconciled', which potentially excludes the expressive value of conflict constellations within the internal market.[105]

The use of this utilitarian standard tends to obscure the commensurability issue by assuming that different values or objectives are commensurable and thereby fails to reveal what is at stake in many areas of internal market law.[106] There is, in other words, an *expressive function of free movement law* that is potentially lost. By way of illustration reference can be made to the recent Scottish minimum alcohol pricing case.[107] The Scottish Parliament passed a law in order to reduce the consumption of alcohol, specifically to create disincentives for lower-income groups, which were considered to constitute a majority of 'hazardous drinkers'. The law prohibited the sale of alcohol at a price below a minimum price that was to be calculated on the basis of the content in alcohol. The law was challenged and it was argued, inter alia, that the minimum pricing restricted access to the Scottish alcohol market because it factored out the potentially lower cost structures and the

[101] ibid, para 56.

[102] Perhaps it was, but is more than likely that it was not. See S Reynolds, 'Housing Policy as a Restriction of Free Movement and MSs Discretion to Design Programmes of Social Protection: Libert' (2015) 52 *Common Market Law Review* 259–80.

[103] eg S Sassen, 'On Concentration and Centrality in the Global City' in P Knox, L Taylor and J Peter (eds), *World Cities in a World-System* (Cambridge, Cambridge University Press, 1995) 63–75.

[104] These can eg be classified in benefit structures, methods of financing, service intensity, family policy, employment regulation, logic of governance and the regulation of industrial relations. See further A Hemerijck, 'The Self-Transformation of the European Social Model(s)' in G Esping Andersen (ed), *Why we Need a Welfare State* (Oxford, Oxford University Press, 2002) 174–218, at 178. See also P Beramendi,' Inequality and the Territorial Fragmentation of Solidarity' (2007) 4 *International Organization* 783–820.

[105] *cf* M Dani, 'Rehabilitating Social Conflicts in European Public Law' (2012) 18 *European Law Journal* 621–43.

[106] Davies, 'Democracy and Legitimacy in the Shadow of Purposive Competence' (n 98) at 2.

[107] Opinion AG Bot in Case C-333/14 *The Scotch Whisky Association and Others v The Lord Advocate* [2015] ECLI:EU:C:2015:845.

comparative advantages that existed in other Member States. AG Bot considered that the proportionality assessment boiled down to the question whether taxation could not be used as a 'more effective and less trade restrictive measure'.[108] AG Bot considered that on the basis of the principle of 'free formation of prices' an objective such as 'increased taxation that is less restrictive of trade while enabling the objective pursued to be attained must be preferred to a measure fixing a minimum price, which gives rise to a greater obstacle'.[109] AG Bot was of the opinion that this alternative would present a better '*cost-benefit outcome*' than the setting of a minimum price. The consequentialist rationale that is implicit in the utilitarian standard adopted by the AG in this case juxtaposes a measure of minimum pricing with general taxation without considering to what extent the social context allows such a cost-benefit choice for the legislator. The Court followed this reasoning in its judgment as well. For the Scottish authorities, there was no apparent alternative available to seek a normative choice for the regulation of alcohol consumption, since general alcohol taxation is controlled by the UK government. Therefore, underlying the cost-benefit analysis is a fundamental question regarding the balance of constitutional taxation powers between the UK and Scotland and the question to what extent Scotland has the ability to define the normative infrastructure of its own economy. This dimension of the conflict is obscured by the consequentialist analysis, which reduces such social complexities to a question of thinking in terms of the 'less restrictive' measure. This is directly related to the previously submitted social purpose of EU internal market law. It was submitted that the social purpose is concretised in the respect and accommodation of social diversity amongst Member States, whilst promoting the objectives of the internal market by scrutinising the internalisation of the transnational effects of Member State social measures. The expressive function of internal market law is then to unveil normative conflicts such as these in order to illuminate what is at stake in internal market conflicts.[110]

However, in other cases the Court does find itself granting a definite margin of discretion. Contrast the above findings with the Court's analysis in the *Trailers* case on road safety measures, where less restrictive measures had been brought forward by AG Bot but the Court nevertheless granted a wide margin of discretion to the Member State because

> [i]n the field of road safety a Member State may determine the degree of protection which it wishes to apply in regard to such safety and the way in which that degree of protection is to be achieved. Since that degree of protection may vary from one Member State to the other, Member States must be allowed a *margin of appreciation*. [...] Member States cannot be denied the possibility of attaining an objective such as road safety by the

[108] ibid, para 146.

[109] ibid, para 148.

[110] On the expressive functions of law, see also C Sunstein, 'Incommensurability and Valuation in Law' (1994) 92 *Michigan Law Review* 779.

> introduction of general and simple rules which will be easily understood and applied by drivers and easily managed and supervised by the competent authorities.[111] (emphases added)

However, such simplicity was not valued to the same degree in, for example, the invalidation of the Swedish monopoly system for the import of alcohol by persons younger than 20 years of age, on the basis of suggestions made by the Commission for less restrictive measures:

> the age check could be carried out by way of a declaration in which the purchaser of the imported beverages certifies, on a form accompanying the goods when they are imported, that he is more than 20 years of age.[112]

As such, there is a degree of variety in the application of the substantive part of the proportionality assessment by the Court, which is not directly clarified or justified in the case law. A strict application of the substantive proportionality assessment invalidates the measure before the Court immediately as in the Beer purity measures in Germany, the environmental measures of Austria and the import monopoly on alcoholic beverages in Sweden. The deferential version of the substantive review test allows for more discretion for the Member States in the selection of protective measures such as in the *Trailers* case and often involves a referral back to the national court to make the final assessment. This referral will then often be provided with more or less guidance as to the way that this assessment should take place. Suffice to say for now that the extent and the degree to which the substantive proportionality test is applied by the Court is not obviously consistent and appears to depend to some degree on the 'sensitivity' of the measure that is under review.

B. The Margin of Discretion Model

The second rationale can be coined as the *margin of appreciation model* and has been heralded as being of the highest significance for EU internal market law.[113] The model is based on granting a margin of discretion to Member States as soon as the restriction at stake is to be considered 'sensitive' and is mostly applied in cases where fundamental rights or values are at stake at the Member State level.[114]

[111] Case C-110/05 *Commission v Italy (Trailers)* [2009] ECR I-519, paras 65–66.

[112] Case C-170/04 *Klas Rosengren and Others v Riksåklagaren* [2007] ECR I-04071, para 56.

[113] S Weatherhill, 'Viking and Laval: the EU Internal Market Perspective' in M Freedland and J Prassl (eds), *Viking, Laval and Beyond* (Oxford, Hart Publishing, 2014) at 32. Also JHH Weiler, 'Fundamental Rights and Fundamental Boundaries' in JHH Weiler, *The Constitution of Europe: 'Do the New Clothes have an Emperor' and other Essays on European Integration* (Cambridge, Cambridge University Press, 1999) 102–29, at 104.

[114] See N Nic Shuibhne, 'Margins of Appreciation: National Values, Fundamental Rights and EC Free Movement Law' (2009) 32 *European Law Review* 230–56.

The more sensitive the matters advanced in the context of justifications are, the more generous the scope for justification becomes, as do the breadth of the margin of appreciation enjoyed by the regulator.[115] The normative principle at work in this model is that free movement rules will scrutinise Member State restrictions on free movement rights, in so far as justifications are not sensitive and allow a '*definite margin of discretion*' to Member States in the pursuit of objectives, when the interest at stake is for some reason considered to be sensitive.[116] The obvious shortcoming of the model is that there is no rationale for *when* an interest is to be considered sensitive, other than the vague notion that the further removed from 'trade' the interest is, the more leeway is provided to Member States. However, the model points in a promising direction in terms of responsiveness to the social context of a conflict. That is to say that the normative principle of the internal market, narrowly perceived as purporting technocratic managerialism, is related to trade interests and that Member State objectives which clearly fall outside of this 'trade sphere' will not be reviewed within a model of substantive efficiency that looks for a less restrictive measure. However, is the internal market then to be considered as forwarding only the narrow aims of substantive efficiency? This would imply that any interest, which is considered sensitive falls outside of the reach of the internal market, regardless of its transnational effects and potential democratic deficiencies. Interpreted in this way, the two models combined would take the mutuality out of the responsiveness that is required for a model of embedded liberalism to succeed. The Court of Justice provides a first answer to this in *Schmidberger*. In *Schmidberger*, the Court acknowledged a *wide margin of discretion* to Austria to decide whether or not to ban a demonstration, which resulted in the closure of a major transit route and hence restricted the free movement of goods but then proceeded to investigate how it came to that decision, noting that:

> various administrative and supporting measures were taken by the competent authorities in order to limit as far as possible the disruption to road traffic. Thus, in particular, those authorities, including the police, the organisers of the demonstration and various motoring organisations cooperated in order to ensure that the demonstration passed off smoothly.[117]

The Court, after acknowledging a wide margin of discretion for Austria to determine the best course of action in this situation, proceeded to investigate whether Austria respected basic 'good governance principles' in the decision to allow the

[115] ibid.

[116] eg Case C-112/00 *Schmidberger* [2003] ECR I-5659 and Case C-36/02 *Omega Spielhallen- und Automatenaufstellungs-GmbH v Oberbürgermeisterin der Bundesstadt Bonn* [2004] ECR I-9609. See further generally J Morijn, 'Balancing Fundamental Rights and Common Market Freedoms in Union Law: Schmidberger and Omega in the Light of the European Constitution' (2006) 12 *European Law Journal* 15–40.

[117] Case C-112/00 *Schmidberger* [2003] ECR I-05659.

protests to take place.[118] As such, the Court granted a margin of discretion but introduced also another standard of evaluation, which can be seen as the third 'ideal type' model of the Court.

C. The Procedural Good Governance Model

The third 'ideal type' type model of the Court can be coined as the *good governance model*. This section shall discuss the emergence of this model and the requirements that flow from it. This concerns a line of case law that focuses nearly exclusively on the suitability of procedural context surrounding specific regulatory choices of Member States. Conventionally, suitability in the proportionality test looks at the existence of a 'rational connection' between the measure and its objective. In the case of *Hartlauer*[119] the Court formulated what can be coined as the 'external suitability' of a measure. Not only must there be a rational connection between the measure and the objective, such as for example in *Bosman*,[120] there must also be a rational connection between the measure and its broader regulatory context. In *Bosman*, the Court held that transfer fee rules were not an *adequate means* of maintaining financial and competitive balance in football leagues because they neither precluded the richest clubs from securing the services of the best players nor did they prevent the availability of financial resources from being a decisive factor in competitive sport. As such, there did not exist a sufficiently deducible *rational connection* between the means and the end. This form of application of the suitability test can be seen as the 'inherent suitability' of a measure. In other words, there should be an inherent rational connection between the measure and the concerned objective. Then, in *Hartlauer*, a measure that made the right to operate a certain category of dental clinics subject to a prior authorisation, while another category of dental clinics was not subject to any such requirement, was considered unsuitable. The Court could not identify any rational basis for the disparate treatment of the two classes of establishment and, accordingly, dismissed the justification plea that the legislation was justified on public health grounds.[121] In other words, the measure did not make any sense in the wider regulatory context in which it operated. This 'externally oriented' suitability test has been developed by the Court in detail in various strands of case law and has crystallised

[118] See similarly W Sauter and H Schepel, *State and Market in European Union Law: the Public and Private Spheres of the Internal Market before the EU Courts* (Boston, Cambridge University Press, 2009) at 99; also D Chalmers, G Davies and G Monti, *European Union Law; Cases and Materials* (Boston, Cambridge University Press, 2010) at 760.

[119] Case C-169/07 *Hartlauer* [2009] ECR I-01721.

[120] Case C-415/93 *Bosman* [1995] ECR I-04921.

[121] Case C-169/07 *Hartlauer* [2009] ECR I-01721, paras 55–63.

in various requirements that can be placed on how Member States design their regulatory frameworks in a wider sense.[122]

The Court provided somewhat of an underlying rationale for looking at procedural context instead of on the substantive measure itself in the *Schindler* case regarding a UK ban on large-scale lotteries:[123]

> Even if the morality of lotteries is at least questionable, it is not for the Court to substitute its assessment for that of the legislatures of the Member States where that activity is practices legally. [...], lotteries involve a *high risk of crime or fraud*, given the size of the amounts which can be staked and of the winnings which they can hold out to the players, particularly when they are operated on a large scale. [...] they are an *incitement to spend which may have damaging individual and social consequences*. A final ground which is not without relevance, although it cannot in itself be regarded as an objective justification, is that lotteries may make a *significant contribution to the financing of benevolent or public interest activities* such as social works, charitable works, sport or culture. Those particular factors justify national authorities having a *sufficient degree of latitude* to determine what is required to protect the players and [...] it is for them to assess not only whether it is necessary to restrict the activities of lotteries but also whether they should be prohibited, provided that those restrictions are not discriminatory.[124] (emphases added)

The Court explicitly considers in *Schindler* the high risk of crime or fraud, damaging individual and social consequences and the link to public interest activities as reasons not to substitute the assessment of the Court with that of the legislature. As a result, the Court, did not refer at all to the possible existence of equivalent substantive safeguards in the Member State where the service provider was established—safeguards which AG Gulmann thought were sufficient in this case.[125] On various other occasions, whilst reviewing regulatory contexts surrounding gambling, the Court has stated explicitly that a system of protection that is less restrictive compared to the one that is adopted by other Member States *cannot* affect the proportionality of the system of protection that was implemented.[126] Instead, it matters in these cases whether or not a Member State policy reflects a *genuine concern* to limit gambling opportunities. The criteria to assess this will differ according to *the system* for which a Member State opts and results in what the Court itself has coined a 'global assessment', in the *Läärä* case, where the Court held that a system of protection must be *assessed as a whole*.[127]

As explained, the criteria to assess this will respond to *the system* for which a Member State opts. As described before, it is standard case law that whether some

[122] See generally S Van den Bogaert and A Cuyvers, 'Money for Nothing: The Case Law of the EU Court of Justice on the Regulation of Gambling' (2011) 48 *Common Market Law Review* 1175; also J Mulder, 'A New Chapter in the European Court of Justice Gambling Saga: A Stacked Deck?' (2011) 38 *Legal Issues of Economic Integration* 243–62.

[123] Case C-275/92 *Schindler* ECR [1994] I-01039.

[124] ibid, paras 60–61.

[125] Opinion AG Gulmann in Case C-275/92 *Schindler* ECR [1994] I-01039.

[126] eg Case C-124/97 *Läärä* ECR [1999] I-6067.

[127] ibid, paras 35–36.

types of games of chance are subject to a public monopoly whilst others are subject to a system of licences issued to private operators is not *in itself* capable of affecting the suitability of a public monopoly for achieving the objective of preventing citizens from being incited to squander money on gambling and of combating addiction.[128] Member States are free to disregard other Member States' systems of protection when choosing *the level of* protection they want to ensure in their territories. The Court made this very explicit in *Stoss and others*:

> having regard to the discretion which Member States enjoy in determining the level of protection for consumers and public order which they intend to ensure in the gaming sector, *it is in particular not necessary*, with regard to the criterion of proportionality, *that a restrictive measure decreed by the authorities of one Member State should correspond to a view shared by all the Member States concerning the means of protecting the legitimate interest at issue.*[129] (emphases added)

Hence, a system of protection must solely be assessed by reference to the objectives pursued by the Member State and the level of protection the Member State concerned intends to provide. The Court has kept to this intention in all but two subsequent rulings concerning gambling holding that:[130]

> moral, religious or cultural factors, as well as the morally and financially harmful consequences for the individual and for society associated with betting and gaming, may serve to justify a margin of discretion for the national authorities, sufficient to enable them to determine, in accordance with *their own scale of values*, what is required in order to ensure consumer protection and the preservation of public order. (emphases added)

The Court considers that 'in the specific area of the organisation of games of chance'[131] national authorities enjoy a 'measure' of discretion to enable them to determine what is required in order to ensure consumer protection and the preservation of order in society and it is then for each Member State to assess whether, in the context of the legitimate aims which it pursues, it is necessary to prohibit betting and gaming wholly or in part or only to restrict them and, to that end, to lay down more or less strict supervisory rules. There is in these cases a role for mutual recognition only where a system under review concerns a 'hybrid' policy. For example, in the *Gambelli* case the Italian government pursued a policy based partly on exclusive—monopoly—licensing and partly on an expanding liberal licensing policy.[132] The Court takes the position that such 'hybrid' systems of protection can be tested on their necessity, taking into account principles of mutual recognition, if the supplier of the service is subject in his Member State of

[128] As in Case C-124/97 *Läärä* ECR [1999] I-6067.

[129] Joined Cases C-316/07, C-358/07 to C-360/07, C-409/07 and C-410/07, [2010] ECR I-08069 (*Stoss and Others*) para 80.

[130] ibid, para 76. See for the incoherency Case C-243/01 *Gambelli* [2003] ECR I-13031 and Case C-243/01 *Placania* [2007] ECR I-01891, where the Court did apply a light necessity test.

[131] Case C-390/12 *Pfleger* [2014] ECLI:EU:C:2014:281, para 45.

[132] ibid, para 73.

establishment to completely *comparable* regulations entailing controls and penalties. In contrast, policies that are based on a monopoly system can only be assessed on the basis of their own merits and potentially inconsistent policy objectives. This was explicitly confirmed by the CJEU in *Stoss and others*:

> where a public monopoly in the area of games of chance has been established in a Member State and it appears that that measure satisfies the various conditions permitting it to be justified having regard to the legitimate public interest objectives allowed by the case-law, any obligation to recognise authorisations issued to private operators established in other Member States is, ex hypothesis, to be excluded, simply by virtue of the existence of such a monopoly.[133]

It is certainly true that gambling in particular is subject to very different degrees of regulation between the Member States; a business practice classified as lawful in some Member States is liable to criminal prosecution and penalties as severe as imprisonment in others.[134] As a result, the Court has in these gambling cases mostly chosen to not apply the necessity test at all and instead focused on the procedural context of the measures, promoting a 'global assessment' of the circumstances in which legislation has been adopted and implemented. The idea of a global assessment originated in the *Läärä* case where the Court held that a system of protection must be *assessed as a whole*.[135] The Court considered that the mere fact that some games of chance were not prohibited is insufficient to show that the national legislation is not in reality intended to achieve the public interest objectives at which it is aimed. It was considered that a limited authorisation of such games on an exclusive basis has the advantage of confining the desire to gamble and the exploitation of gambling *within controlled channels*.[136] Since the objective of protecting consumers from gambling addiction is, in principle, difficult to reconcile with a policy of expanding games of chance characterised, inter alia, by the creation of new games and by the advertising of such games:

> such a policy cannot be regarded as being consistent unless the scale of unlawful activity is *significant* and the measures adopted are *aimed at channelling consumers' propensity to gamble into activities that are lawful*.[137] (emphases added)

This illustrates the 'global assessment' that the Court can make in these cases. In this type of assessment the Court will look at whether legislation actually pursues the objective of protecting gamblers or fighting crime and does so 'genuinely' and in a consistent and systematic manner. A global assessment involves a thorough evaluation of legislative context and intentions in order to reveal if the intentions of Member States are genuinely concerned with the objectives that are claimed to be pursued and the Court has on various occasions considered that Member State

[133] ibid, para 109.
[134] Case C-67/98 *Zenatti* [1999] ECR I-7289 para 36.
[135] Case C-124/97, *Läärä* ECR [1999] I-6067.
[136] ibid, para 37.
[137] ibid, para 30.

legislation lacked such genuine intentions through unveiling inconsistencies in the activities of the authorities concerned with the supervision:

> In so far as the authorities of a Member State incite and encourage consumers to participate in lotteries, games of chance and betting to the financial benefit of the public purse, the authorities of that State cannot invoke public order concerns relating to the need to reduce opportunities for betting in order to justify measures such as those at issue in the main proceedings.[138]

In relation to *monopoly systems* the Court in *Stoss and others* decided that:

> the establishment of a measure as restrictive *as a monopoly*, which can be justified only in order to ensure a particularly high level of consumer protection, must be *accompanied by a legislative framework suitable for ensuring that the holder of the said monopoly will in fact be able to pursue, in a consistent and* systematic *manner, the objective* thus determined by means of a supply that is *quantitatively measured and qualitatively planned* by reference to the said objective and subject to strict control by the public authorities.[139] (emphases added)

A choice for a monopoly-based policy has to be embedded in a general policy that is aimed at a high level of consumer protection. In addition, the choice for a monopolist is only genuine if the legislative framework that establishes a monopolist suitably (qualitatively) equips and limits the activities (quantitatively) of the monopolist in a way that genuinely reflects the chosen policy of a high level of consumer protection. This strand of case law of the Court makes clear that the fundamental choice for a system of protection affects the assessment of Member State policy along the consistency yardstick of the Court. As such, the Court has developed a number of concrete guiding principles that clearly illustrate when a Member State is genuine and when a Member State is hypocritical in its intentions to limit gambling opportunities. *Stoss and others* and *Carmen Media* best illustrate how far such an analysis can go. For example, advertising issued by the holder of a public monopoly has to remain *measured and strictly limited* to what is necessary in order to channel consumers towards authorised gaming networks. In *Stoss and others*, the Court limited the possibilities for advertisement, within a system of protection aimed at a high level of consumer protection, significantly:

> any advertising issued by the holder of a public monopoly remain *measured and strictly limited* to what is necessary in order thus to channel consumers towards authorised gaming networks. Such advertising *cannot*, however, in particular, aim to *encourage consumers'* natural propensity to gamble by stimulating their active participation in it, such as by *trivialising gambling* or giving it *a positive image* due to the fact that revenues derived from it are *used for activities in the public interest*, or by increasing the attractiveness of gambling by means of *enticing advertising messages depicting major winnings in glowing colours.*[140] (emphases added)

[138] Case C-243/01 *Gambelli* [2003] ECR I-13031, paras 67, 69.
[139] ibid, para 83.
[140] ibid, para 103.

The referring courts in *Stoss and others* and *Carmen Media* also noted, in relation to casino games and automated games, that the public authorities had been developing or tolerating policies of expanding supply despite the fact that the concerned forms of gambling (as follows from the judgment) presented a higher potential risk of addiction. Possibilities of casino games on the internet were tolerated and automated games could be exploited in a lot of establishments other than casinos, gaming arcades, restaurants and cafes.[141] These circumstances led the Court to conclude that the German courts:

> may legitimately be led to consider that the fact that, in relation to games of chance other than those covered by the public monopoly at issue in the main proceedings, the competent authorities thus conduct or tolerate policies aimed at encouraging participation in those other games rather than reducing opportunities for gambling and limiting activities in that area in a consistent and systematic manner, has the effect that the objective of preventing incitement to squander money on gambling and combating addiction to the latter, which was at the root of the establishment of the said monopoly, *can no longer be effectively pursued by means of the latter*, so that the latter can no longer be justified having regard to Articles 43 EC and 49 EC.[142] (emphases added)

Within this evaluative framework Member States are free to disregard other Member States' systems of protection when choosing *the level of* protection they want to ensure in their territories.[143] The Court considers in these cases that national authorities enjoy a 'measure' of discretion to enable them to determine what is required in order to ensure the level of protection they want and the means to pursue them. It will then, however, scrutinise the measures as to their genuine nature, systemacy and coherence in a global assessment of the regulatory context. The normative principle that is inherent in this model is that Member States enjoy the freedom, with respect to legitimate interests, to choose levels of protection as well as the substantive content of them as long as the measure fulfils a standard of good governance.

Another standard of good governance can be traced back to the 1980s.[144] The Court started formulating procedural guarantees, which had to be satisfied in relation to restrictive Member State measures. They related to judicial review and standards to be met by administrative procedures, which resulted in the granting or refusing an authorisation or a licence. For example, in the *Medien Vertriebs* case the Court considered that the procedure governing access 'must be one which is readily accessible, can be completed within a reasonable period, and, if it leads to

[141] Cases C-316/07, C-358/07 to C-360/07, C-409/07 and C-410/07 *Stoss and Others* [2010] ECR I-08069, paras 100 and 106 and Case C-46/08 *Carmen Media* [2010] ECR I-08149, paras 67 and 68.

[142] Joined Cases C-316/07, C-358/07 to C-360/07, C-409/07 and C-410/07 *Stoss and Others* [2010] ECR I-08069, para 106 and judgment of 8 September 2010 in Case C-46/08, *Carmen Media* [2010] ECR I-08149, para 68.

[143] ibid (*Stoss and Others*), para 80.

[144] See also S Prechal, 'Free Movement and Procedural Requirements: Proportionality Reconsidered' (2008) 3 *Legal Issues of Economic Integration* 201.

a refusal, the decision of refusal must be open to challenge before the courts'.[145] These types of requirements are reminiscent of a series of Court rulings that have established that, when awarding a services concession, a public authority is subject to EU Treaty principles of non-discrimination and equal treatment and that these principles imply an 'obligation of transparency'.[146] That obligation means that, before their award, services concessions must be subjected to a degree of advertising, which is sufficient to open them to competition. Small exceptions to these transparency requirements are allowed if:

> the Member State concerned decides to grant a licence to, or renew the licence of, a public operator whose management is *subject to direct State supervision* or a private operator whose activities are *subject to strict control by the public authorities*.[147] (emphases added)

Similar reasoning van be found in cases like *Radlberger v Land Baden-Wurttemberg* where legislation was held to run counter to the principle of proportionality on the grounds that traders were given insufficient time to adapt to it.[148] Similarly, the Court held in *Commission v Austria* (a case that preceded the other traffic ban of Austria on the Brenner pass discussed above) that:

> a transition period of only two months between the date on which the contested regulation was adopted and the date fixed by the Austrian authorities for implementation of the sectoral traffic ban was clearly insufficient reasonably to allow the operators concerned to adapt to the new circumstances.[149]

The same kind of requirement applies to administrative authorisation schemes, which must be based on 'objective, non-discriminatory criteria known in advance, in such a way as adequately to circumscribe the exercise of the national authorities' discretion'.[150] *Laval* can be seen as, partly, imposing a similar obligation on collective action that is restrictive towards foreign service providers and:

> cannot be justified in the light of the public interest [...], where the negotiations on pay, which that action seeks to require an undertaking established in another Member State to enter into, form part of a national context characterized by a lack of provisions, of any kind, which are *sufficiently precise and accessible* that they do not render it impossible or excessively difficult in practice for such an undertaking to determine the obligations with which it is required to comply as regards minimum pay.[151] (emphases added)

[145] Case C-244/06 *Medien Vertriebs* [2008] ECR I-00505, para 50.

[146] See eg Case C-324/98 *Telaustria and Telefonadress* [2000] ECR I-10745, paras 60–62; Case C-206/08 *Eurawasser* [2009] ECR I-0, para 44; and Case C-91/08 *Wall* [2010] ECR I-0, para 33.

[147] Case C-203/08 *Betfair* [2010] ECR I-04695, para 59.

[148] Case C-309/02 *Radlberger v Land Baden-Wurttemberg* [2004] ECR I-11763, similar reasoning with regard to the fulfilment of proportionality is applied in cases such as C-463/01 *Commission v Germany* [2004] ECR I-11705, paras 79–80.

[149] Case C-320/03 *Commission v Austria* [2005] ECR I-09871, para 90.

[150] eg Case C-367/12 *Sokoll-Seebacher* [2014] np, para 27; Case C-169/07 *Hartlauer* [2009] ECR I-1721 para 64.

[151] Case C-341/05 *Laval* [2007] ECR I-11767, para 110.

Another good example is *Commission v Spain* where the Court assessed regional measures in Catalonia that regulated the setting up of large retail establishments. Retail establishments of a certain size were subject to a system of prior authorisation.[152] Spain argued that the provisions related to town and country planning and environmental protection. By confining the location of large retail establishments to 'population centres', where the demand would be greatest, and by limiting the size of establishments in less populous areas, the legislation was seeking to avoid polluting car journeys, to counter urban decay, to preserve an environmentally integrated urban model, to avoid new road building and to ensure access by public transport. The Court first established that:

> taken as a whole, those specific restrictions laid down in the contested legislation significantly affect the possibility of opening large retail establishments on the territory of the Autonomous Community of Catalonia. In such circumstances, the reasons which may be invoked by a Member State in order to justify a derogation from the principle of freedom of establishment *must be accompanied by an analysis of the appropriateness and proportionality of the restrictive measure adopted by that Member State, and by precise evidence enabling its arguments to be substantiated.*[153] (emphases added)

The Court then considered that the introduction of preventative and therefore prior measures must be regarded as appropriate means of achieving the objective of environmental protection. A rational connection was established since the adoption of measures a posteriori, if the setting up of a retail establishment already built should prove to have a negative impact on environmental protection, would certainly be less effective and more costly as compared to a system of prior authorisation. However, then the Court investigated the procedural criteria and found that they required the application of ceilings as regards the market share and the impact on existing retail trade that the Retail Facilities Committee, which co-decided on the authorisation, was composed of potential competitors of the economic operator wishing to set up a new large establishment in Catalonia and that the only sectoral interest represented in that committee was that of the existing local trade and without representation of environmental or consumer interests.[154] As such, even though the substantive measures themselves were considered appropriate, the design of the authorisation procedure was considered misconstrued.

Floris de Witte has commented that the procedurally oriented version of proportionality, when correctly applied, could allow for the rationalisation of the implementation of national policy and argues that it is the ideal tool to be used by the Court to ensure the absence of discrimination and protectionism and to adjudicate conflicts between moral/ethical choices of Member States and the interests

[152] Case C-400/08 *Commission v Spain* [2011] ECR I-01915.
[153] ibid, paras 81–82.
[154] ibid, paras 109–11.

of free movement law.[155] One of the reasons being that the procedural proportionality test would respect the substance of national moral and ethical choices and instead focuses on 'teasing out discriminatory or protectionist biases' focusing on 'the normative coherence of national policies, the consistent application of sanctions, and legislative transparency'.[156]

The argument that is developed in this chapter is, on this point, largely in alignment with the conceptualisations of De Witte. It is, however, important to note that the orientation on procedure can have important and structural effects on the way that policy objectives come into existence on a Member State level. In the said gambling cases the Court, in addition to teasing out discriminatory or protectionist measures, also positively implements procedural due care obligations that are to be followed by the Member States. This goes further than teasing out discriminatory or protectionist measures. According to Barnard it is in fact a sign of the excessively rigorous scrutiny that the Court adopts in its evaluation of restrictive measures.[157] It is argued here that the procedural due care obligations, as well as the rationalisation and transparency requirements that the Court promotes are part of an emerging internal market principle of 'procedural good governance'.[158] Indeed, it is the way in which legislation is adopted or implemented that is becoming increasingly important in determining the compatibility of national rules with the Treaty. The rise of this interpretation of the principle of proportionality appears to reflect a shift towards a culture of justification, of the giving of reasons in due course within a framework that is transparent and calculable. However, it is correct that the 'global assessment' approach that the Court promotes in these cases allows for more social diversity in the internal market since it acknowledges that the normative infrastructure of gambling markets differs amongst Member States and shifts the analysis to procedural soundness and away from guiding the normative choices that a Member State makes.

It could very well be argued that the Court of Justice is ill placed to judge the transparency and coherence of national legal systems, which may be intricate, such as tax systems, and be evaluated erroneously based on a lack of insider knowledge of the policy measure that is under investigation. This would, however, be only really problematic if Member States themselves do not really understand the functions of their own laws because they will have the opportunity to illuminate all intricate connections of their restrictive laws within the procedure before or leading up to the Court of Justice. As to its more immediate shortcomings, the granting of a definite margin of discretion to the Member States appears loosely connected to the 'sensitivity' of the measure that is being evaluated. This has, however, not been connected to a coherent rationale that sets out *when* it is to be applied by the Court. It is unclear, for example, why the Court in the majority of gambling cases

155 de Witte (n 85) at 1551.
156 ibid, at 1573.
157 Barnard, 'Derogations, Justifications, and the Four Freedoms' (n 2) at 273.
158 Similarly, see Prechal 'Free Movement and Procedural Requirements' (n 144) 201.

has chosen not to apply a necessity test at all, whereas it does so in cases where regulatory differences between Member States exist, arguably to the same degree on the basis of, for example, cultural, historical and regulatory differences.[159]

D. Incoherence in the Application of the Different Rationales

Summarising the previous sections, the ideal type models developed by the Court are threefold: (i) the substantive efficiency model, which is concerned with the inherent rationality of a measure and its necessity that purports a normative principle of technocratic managerialism; (ii) the margin of appreciation model that balances conflicts through the allocation of a margin of discretion as soon as the interests at stake are to be considered removed from trade and valued as 'sensitive'; and (iii) the good governance model that looks at the measure in its procedural and governance context and advances principles of transparency, coherence and consistency. In the application of each of these 'ideal type' models, the Court seems to be without a clear rationale as to when a definite margin of discretion is explicitly granted to Member States, when interests are to be considered sensitive[160] and when a focus on procedural context is more appropriate than an evaluation of the necessity of the substantive measures themselves.[161]

For example, in *Medien Vertriebs* the Court decided with respect to the level of protection for which the German government opted in relation to minimum age requirements for watching Japanese Manga movies that were in free circulation in the UK that:

> it is not indispensable that restrictive measures laid down by the authorities of a Member State to protect the rights of the child, [...], correspond to a conception shared by all Member States as regards the level of protection and the detailed rules relating to it [...]. As that conception may vary from one Member State to another on the basis of, inter alia, moral or cultural views, Member States must be recognised as having a *definite margin of discretion.*[162] (emphases added)

However, the Court then moved on to evaluate the substantive scope of the prohibition, by establishing that the concerned measure did not preclude all forms of marketing of unchecked image storage media, considering that in the light of those factors, the protective rules did not go beyond what was necessary to attain the objective pursued. Its assessment was oriented on the substance of the

[159] *cf* eg with Case C-244/06 *Dynamic Medien* [2008] I-00505, concerning the level of protection for which the German government opted in relation to minimum age requirements for watching Japanese Manga movies that were in free circulation in the UK.

[160] *cf* also with Case C-137/09 [2010] *Josemans* ECR I-13019 eg where there was no explicit mention whatsoever of a margin of discretion despite similar intensity in differences in regulatory contexts between Member States as to the regulation of soft drugs.

[161] See on this also Damjanovic, 'The EU Market Rules as Social Market Rules' (n 85).

[162] C-244/06 *Medien Vertriebs* [2008] ECR I-00505, para 44.

measures. Equally, in *Omega* the Court considered that, despite, again the existence of a 'definite margin of discretion'[163] for Member States to define how economic activities should be exercised in a manner that respects human dignity, the justification for a derogation from the fundamental freedom to provide services must be interpreted strictly and considered justified 'only if they are necessary for the protection of the interests which they are intended to guarantee and only in so far as those objectives cannot be attained by less restrictive measures'.[164] The Court then considered very briefly that by prohibiting 'only the variant of the laser game the object of which is to fire on human targets' and thus 'play at killing' people, the contested order did not go beyond what was necessary in order to attain the objective pursued by the competent national authorities.[165]

As regards the suitability of the measure, the Court did not in these cases engage in any 'global assessment' of the regulatory context within which the measures were taken. I mention this merely to illustrate that the Court has not been willing or able to formulate an approach that can be considered coherent or consistent in cases where Member States are granted a definite margin of discretion in the formulation of their policy objectives.[166] In this respect Gareth Davies has submitted that

> The rules and principles stated by the Court are far better understood as embodying a series of compromises, perceptions of fact, and pragmatic approximations which aim to deal with the problems of evidence, workload, and legal clarity, rather than as an ongoing monologue about market philosophy. Looking in the case law for a coherent framework addressing these classical judicial concerns is … quite fruitful. Looking in the case law for clear or consistent guidance about the conceptual foundation of economic integration is, as internal market lawyers know, a hopeless cause.[167]

According to Davies the Court is unable or uninterested in defining a coherent approach in its case law.[168] However, the foregoing analysis has demonstrated that, if perceived as ideal types, there are certain clear trends in the rationales the Court adopts in adjudicating free movement conflicts, which allows the formulation of a normative critique that aims to reconstruct this case law into a more coherent and consistent model of adjudication. It will be argued that this can be achieved on the basis of a rationale of mutual responsiveness. The analysis will now start to move in that direction.

[163] Case C-36/02 *Omega* [2004] ECR I-9609, para 31.

[164] ibid, para 36.

[165] ibid, para 39.

[166] See Shuibhne, 'Margins of Appreciation' (n 114) at 31 ff for potential explanations for this incoherence.

[167] G Davies, 'The Court's Jurisprudence on Free Movement of Goods: Pragmatic Presumptions, not Philosophical Principles' (2012) 2 *European Journal of Consumer Law* 25, at 27.

[168] In contrast, see K Lenaerts, 'The Court's Outer and Inner Selves: Exploring the External and Internal Legitimacy of the European Court of Justice' in H Clemens et al (n 12) 13–60.

IV. A DIALOGUE OF MUTUAL RESPONSIVENESS

A. Between Managerialism, Margins of Discretion and Good Governance: A Responsive Model

This section argues that the mode of reasoning of the Court of Justice should be structured on the basis of the identification of the nature of a conflict as vertical or diagonal. As previously argued, the compromise of 'embedded liberalism', as conceived within the argument from transnational effects, depends on the constructive interplay between the objectives of transnational market integration with domestic social spheres. In its ideal form, a mode of reasoning based on the principle of embedded liberalism would therefore in a first stage adopt a narrow and functional rationale to tease out and understand the nature of regulatory choices that restrict free trade objectives and in a second stage adopt an evaluative rationale that is congruent with the context that gave rise to the restriction.

The identification of a conflict along the lines of this reasoning can be illustrated on the basis of the case *Commission v Germany (occupational pensions)*.[169] The Commission considered that Germany failed to respect the public procurement Directives. A collective agreement between an association of employers and a trade union reserved pension services to three specific groups of service providers and excluded a large number of insurance companies from the market, thus, the Commission argued, reducing competition and increasing the price for the service. The German authorities had argued that the procurement Directives could not apply because the collective agreement pursued social objectives and required reduced competition. The German system deprived employers from their authority to select providers by replacing it with 'a consensual solution arrived at by the social partners'. Therefore, the selection of the pension scheme providers was, in itself, and by virtue of the process, the relevant social concern. The Court did not accept this argument and demanded a revisit of the objective by looking specifically at the concrete objective that was sought within the German system of governance. For this purpose, the Court specifically assessed whether the social objective at stake could not be internalised within a tender procedure and found that:

> the pooling of risks, upon which any insurance activity is based, can be ensured by a body or undertaking that provides pensions which is selected following a call for tenders at European Union level. Nor is there anything in the public procurement directives to preclude a local authority employer from specifying, in the terms of the call for tenders,

[169] Case C-271/08 *Commission v Germany (Occupational pensions)* [2010] ECR I-07091. On the potential of this case, see also S Deakin, 'The Lisbon Treaty, the Viking and Laval Judgments, and the Financial Crisis: in Search of New Foundations for Europe's "Social Market Economy"' in N Bruun, K Lörcher and I Schömann (eds), *The Lisbon Treaty and Social Europe* (Oxford, Hart Publishing, 2012) 19–43. Also P Syrpis, 'Reconciling Economic Freedoms and Social Rights—The Potential of Commission v Germany (Case C-271/08, Judgment of 15 July 2010)' (2011) 40 *Industrial Law Journal* 222–29.

> the conditions to be complied with by tenderers in order to prevent, or place limits on, workers interested in salary conversion being selected on the basis of medical grounds.[170]

In other words, although it was argued that there was in this case a diagonal conflict between principles of solidarity and the internal market procurement rules, the Court found that there was *in concreto*, no such conflict—or rather that the conflict was vertical. That is to say, that the actual objective of the collective agreements could be internalised within the ambit of the procurement rules, without inhibiting the actual, specific, social policy objective. As such, the Court in this case set out the beginning of a 'compatibility rationale'.[171] Concomitantly, the Court demonstrated a means to qualify a vertical versus a diagonal conflict constellation. The vertical conflict constellation would be one where the rationales, as in this case between procurement and the concerned social objective, are reconcilable and therefore allow for a mode of reasoning that searches for the less restrictive measure. In contrast, the conflict constellation would be diagonal where the rationales aspire to different ends. In such a situation, the mode of reasoning would have to shift towards an assessment of the wider procedural context of the measures, provided of course that the ends pursue legitimate ends. As such, on the basis of this 'dialogue', objectives that cannot be internalised within the narrow aims of substantive efficiency are separated within a rationale of supranational market integration and to ensure that market integration objectives are pursued on the basis of procedural unity, transparency, consistency and coherence within those local structures. It is submitted that this approach would allow the Court to recognise legitimate normative principles on a Member State level that do not 'fit' within the utilitarian normative order of the free movement rules and accordingly guide the Court in its adoption of a suitable 'socially responsive' mode of reasoning. I shall expand on this by reframing three exemplary cases within the proposed rationale, with an emphasis on how this approach can improve the selection of an evaluative rationale that is responsive to social context.

B. *Volkswagen*: Valuing the '*Social acquis*' of a Member State within the Internal Market

Volkswagen is a paradigmatic case mainly because it showcases a free movement case where there is a conflict between a supranational rationale of free capital exchange with shareholder primacy and a local governance model, which is exemplary of the German social economic system of negotiated solutions and contrary

[170] ibid, para 58.

[171] See also the Opinion of AG Wahl delivered in Case C-113/13 *Azienda sanitaria* ECLI:EU:C:2014:2440.

to shareholder primacy.[172] The case demonstrates in principle how the adjudicative model of the Court is capable of valuing different normative orientations within economic systems of Member States.

Porsche had set out to take over Volkswagen but found its plans blocked by the control mechanisms that existed in the Volkswagen company, Volkswagenwerk, for the reason of safeguarding the interests of all affected stakeholders. Importantly, the Land of Lower Saxony had a blocking 20 per cent shareholder vote on the basis of the *Volkswagengesetz* (VW Law) that, inter alia, capped voting rights at 20 per cent for all shareholders. The VW Law has a complex and interesting history.[173] The law had been adopted in 1960 to put an end to the disputes between various groups of persons who had laid claim to private rights over the limited liability undertaking, which had basically become ownerless after the Second World War. The Commission brought proceedings against the VW Law for infringing the rules on the free movement of capital. The Court agreed with the Commission that the controlling rights in the VW Law derogated from general German company law and enabled the Land of Lower Saxony to exert considerable influence on Volkswagen, beyond that which it could exert under general company law. That considerable influence was liable to deter investors from other Member States.[174] Germany was unable to provide convincing arguments that demonstrated *in concreto* why the control mechanisms were necessary to protect the interests of workers and minority shareholders against the whims of a single shareholder, and how a company as big as VW could affect the general interest.[175]

After a similar prima facie structuring of the conflict, the preliminary step in the proposed responsive model of adjudication would inquire whether the social objectives at stake could be internalised within the substantive efficiency standards of free capital movement. Essentially, at the centre of the case stand two competing models of governance: shareholder primacy and free capital movement versus a model that negotiates stakeholder interests. The rationale of shareholder primacy and capital movement requires a governance model that puts shareholder interests as a first priority relative to other corporate stakeholders, including the power to intercede directly and frequently in corporate decision-making (one share, one vote). The stakeholder interest model cannot be accommodated within this rationale since it broadens the scale of interests that are relevant for the company and pulls the corporate decision-making process away from a model that can be validated purely on the basis of shareholder value towards a framework of non-market mechanisms of negotiated compromise. After the identification of

[172] See C Gerner-Beuerle, 'Shareholders between the Market and the State : The VW Law and Other Interventions in the Market Economy' (2012) 49(1) *Common Market Law Review* 97–144. Also J Snell, 'Varieties of Capitalism and the Limits of European Economic Integration' (2011) 13 *Cambridge Yearbook of European Legal Studies* 415–34; and F De Cecco, *State Aid and the European Economic Constitution* (Oxford, Hart Publishing, 2013) at 24 (chapter on the limits of constitutional adjudication).

[173] See the Opinion of AG Colomer in Case C-112/05 *Commission v Germany* [2007] ECR I-8995.

[174] Case C-112/05 *Commission v Germany* [2007] ECR I-8995, para 60.

[175] ibid, paras 72–82.

these competing principles and the identification of a diagonal conflict constellation,[176] the evaluative principle to be used in order to scrutinise the German governance model would be based on principles of good governance and not substantive efficiency. This would not necessarily lead to another outcome of the case but the object of the evaluation would be radically different. The scrutiny would concern the choice for the governance model; the coherence and transparency of the decision-making process; the availability of an appeal process and the broader coherence with the policy objectives of the German authorities. Moreover, the veto power of the Land would have to be specifically embedded within and limited to the protection of the general public interests at stake; the use of a veto would have to be articulated in a reasoned and open fashioned way as to what the justifications were; involve explicit consideration of alternatives; and all stakeholder interests would have to be considered. As such, the advantage of the responsive model is that it allows diverging governance models to exist in accordance with good governance principles, which explicitly allow for regulatory diversity, yet stimulate EU *procedural* unity in these matters which can be connected to market integration objectives (such as transparency, consistency and contemporaneousness).

C. *Omega*: The Importance of *Mutual* Responsiveness in the Pursuit of Legitimate Objectives

Another exemplary case to illustrate the responsiveness model is *Omega*.[177] The *Omega* case is often referred to as an example where the Court has been explicitly sensitive towards the specific Member State context since it restricted the market freedoms in favour of a fundamental right.[178] However, the proposed model would find the approach of the Court of Justice in *Omega* lacking from the perspective of *mutual* responsiveness. In *Omega*, the conflict at stake concerned the values of a local community that opposed the establishment of a British-based laserdome venue, where people would have fun shooting each other with laser guns. The police of the German Land North Rhine-Westphalia ordered a prohibition of these games as they constituted a danger to public order. It was considered that acts of simulated homicide and the trivialisation of violence were contrary to the fundamental values prevailing in public opinion. Omega argued instead that the order was contrary to EU law, in particular the free movement of services. The Court established first that

> the Community legal order undeniably strives to ensure respect for human dignity as a general principle of law. There can therefore be no doubt that the objective of protecting human dignity is compatible with Community law, it being immaterial in that respect

[176] And establishing that a governance model as pursued by the German authorities is a legitimate objective.

[177] Case C-36/02 *Omega* [2004] ECR I-9609.

[178] eg Weatherhill, 'Viking and Laval' (n 113).

that, in Germany, the principle of respect for human dignity has a particular status as an independent fundamental right.[179]

The Court considered that despite the existence of a 'definite margin of discretion' for Member States to define how economic activities should be exercised in a manner that respects human dignity, the justification for a derogation from the fundamental freedom to provide services, was to be interpreted strictly and could be considered justified, 'only in so far as those objectives cannot be attained by less restrictive measures'.[180] The Court then considered, albeit briefly, that by prohibiting 'only the variant of the laser game the object of which is to fire on human targets', the contested order did not go beyond what is necessary to attain the objective pursued by the national authorities.[181] As such, the Court applied a light *substantive* review of the restriction.

On the basis of the model of responsiveness as a first step, the Court would assess whether the economic activity that was sought in this case was inherently irreconcilable with the legitimate public interest concerning human dignity as expressed by the local authorities. The answer to this question would be 'yes', since the legitimate measure in question was supposed to be a reflection of local values, which opposed and specifically targeted the activity in question, and as such, was inherently irreconcilable with the principle of market access. The two objectives were, in that sense, incommensurable. Within the model proposed, that finding would then guide the Court in its choice for the subsequent evaluative principle. The incommensurability of the objective of market access with local values would guide the Court towards an application of good governance principles, which would assess the measure in its broader regulatory context. It would then be scrutinised whether the decree from a local police authority was sufficiently transparent, to determine whether the activity in question was genuinely contrary to fundamental values prevailing in public opinion, and whether it was a coherent policy response, or rather, an arbitrary process risking the complete exclusion of an assessment of transnational interests. Again, the advantage of this reasoning over the margin of appreciation model that the Court applied in this case is that local values are accommodated within a supranational market integration rationale, instead of a rationale that excludes such measures from the internal market dialogue completely.

D. *Viking*: Recognising the Substantive Limits of the Internal Market

The issues with *Viking* are well known and perhaps by now slightly over-explored.[182] The central question to address in *Viking* was balancing the right of trade unions

[179] Case C-36/02 *Omega* [2004] ECR I-9609, para 34.
[180] ibid, para 36.
[181] ibid, para 39.
[182] L Niglia has provided a new and quite innovative perspective highlighting the use of 'hierarchical balancing' by the Court; L Niglia, 'Eclipse of the Constitution' (2016) 22 *European Law Journal* 132–56. A selection from other discussions on *Viking* see above (n 18).

to initiate strikes with the right to reflag a ship for the purpose of acquiring lower wage employees. The judgment is slightly ambivalent because the Court emphasised, firstly, that the Union not only has an economic, but also a social purpose and that the rights under free movement must be balanced against the objectives pursued by social policy.[183] As such, this type of what has been termed as 'disclosed' balancing[184] would call for a rationale that reflects on the question to what extent objectives pursued by social policy can actually be internalised within a narrow and substantively orientated market efficiency rationale. Labour market rules do sometimes fulfil a market-enabling function by reducing transaction costs and information asymmetries in wage-setting, and, consequently, they do not necessarily originate from a principle that cannot be accommodated within a market enabling rationale.[185] Clearly, however, this does apply to a set of rules such as the right to strike that delegates components of wage-setting and features of industrial relations to an institutional domain that goes beyond a market-enabling rationale, since its objective is precisely to shield employee interests from market conditions.[186] The Court did not reflect on this balance in terms of substantive irreconcilability and considered that the strike had 'the effect of making less attractive, or even pointless, [...], Viking's exercise of its right to freedom of establishment',[187] thus necessitating an assessment whether no less restrictive measure was available. This framing of the conflict suggests the possibility of a *substantive reconciliation* of market access with the right to strike. The legal reasoning of the Court can in this sense be seen as indicative or symptomatic of the functional 'consensus rationale' which suggests that everything can be reconciled.[188] It is, however, impossible to conceptualise a situation where workers exercise a right to strike without disproportionately limiting the economic freedoms of a capital owner. Therefore, the Court has with its reasoning not acknowledged this important balance and did not recognise the impossibility of accommodating the social concerns within the rationale that it set out; it did not recognise a diagonal conflict. As such, the Court disregarded the social reality in which the conflict arose and undermined the social purpose of the right to strike within the specific regulatory context in Finland. Within the proposed model, the evaluative framework of the Court would, after concluding that the social interest at stake could not be accommodated within a rationale of the less restrictive measure, move towards the evaluative model of good governance. This would then involve an assessment of the concreteness of the employee interests at stake, the coherence and consistency

[183] Case C-438/05 *Viking Line* [2007] ECR I-10779, para 79.

[184] Niglia, 'Eclipse of the Constitution' (n 182).

[185] Further on this A Ebner, 'Transnational Law and the Polanyi Problem' in C Joerges and J Falke, *Globalisation and the Potential of Law in Transnational Markets* (Oxford, Hart Publishing, 2011) 19–41, at 28.

[186] ibid, at 28.

[187] Case C-438/05 *Viking Line* [2007] ECR I-10779, para 72.

[188] *cf* Dani, 'Rehabilitating Social Conflicts in European Public Law' (n 105) at 628.

of the protection of this interest within its regulatory context, and the transparency of the system itself.

Paradoxically, in part of its analysis the Court was concerned with a question of procedural good governance. In its referral, the Court indicated that the necessity of collective action was significantly hampered on the basis of the fact that the policy rules combating the use of flags was *misconstrued*. The *design* of the policy rules would, if triggered by one of its members, *always* lead to solidarity action against the owner of a vessel, irrespective of whether or not the flag owner's exercise of its right of freedom would actually be liable in a specific circumstance to have a harmful effect on the work or conditions of employment of its employees.[139] In other words, the design of the system of collective action was flawed, which consequently made the broader regulatory context inappropriate as a genuine means of worker protection. Therefore, the Court, in part of its assessment, applied a broader procedural review of the regulatory framework that led to the restriction. It is interesting in this respect to refer to a passage of the *Laval* judgment, which points in the same direction:

> collective action … cannot be justified in the light of the public interest objective […] where the negotiations on pay […] form part of a national context characterised by a lack of provisions […] which *are sufficiently precise and accessible* […] to determine the obligations with which it is required to comply.[190] (emphasis added)

These considerations of the Court of Justice seem to imply that the balance in these cases might have turned out differently *if* the wider regulatory context within which the collective action was exercised would have been 'more transparent', in line with what can be considered as good governance requirements. At this specific point, we can by analogy refer back to *Schmidberger*, where the Court allowed for a margin of discretion to Austria in order to decide whether or not to ban a demonstration and then proceeded to investigate how Austria came to that decision on the basis of a number of good governance requirements.

However, the Court of Justice in *Viking* approached the case on the basis of a flawed qualification of the conflict, which suggested that there was a possibility for *substantive* reconciliation by subordinating the right to strike to the objective of market access. On this basis it can be argued that the Court has 'restyled' EU law and introduced a form of hierarchical balancing, which no longer reflects the constitutive features and division of competences that are inherent to the embedded

[189] Case C-438/05 *Viking Line* [2007] ECR I-10779, para 89:

> [required to] initiate solidarity action against the beneficial owner of a vessel which is registered in a State other than that of which that owner is a national, irrespective of whether or not that owner's exercise of its right of freedom of establishment is liable to have a harmful effect on the work or conditions of employment of its employees.

[190] Case C-341/05 *Laval un Partneri* [2007] ECR I-11767, para 110.

liberalism compromise.[191] What I would argue instead is that a form of hierarchical ordering *can* be conjugated with the embedded liberalism compromise, provided that it only serves the purpose of framing a conflict in a prima facie manner, in order for legitimate rights and policies to be established and *optimised* in accordance with a principle of good governance.

It seems to me that this is also the rationale put forward by the Court in the important *AGET Iraklis* case.[192] AGET Iraklis wanted to reorganise its business and to shut down one of its three plants. It sought ministerial authorisation to carry out collective redundancies, as required by Greek law. Greek law provided that the Minister of Labour could refuse to authorise some or all of the projected redundancies on the basis of 'the conditions in the labour market'; 'the situation of the undertaking'; and 'the interests of the national economy'. With reference to the socio-economic crisis in Greece, the Minister of Labour refused to provide the requisite authorisation. In turn, AGET Iraklis argued that the national rule was inter alia not compatible with Articles 49 (freedom of establishment) and 63 (free movement of capital) of the TFEU. This case is interesting from many perspectives. The main point for the purpose of illustrating a rationale of mutual responsiveness is that the Court (grand chamber) held that when pursuing social policy Member States are justified in considering the existence of a mechanism that imposes a framework to ensure enhanced levels of protection of workers provided that criteria are formulated in concrete and precise terms:

> it is clear that, in the absence of details of the particular circumstances in which the power in question may be exercised, the employers concerned do not know in what specific objective circumstances that power may be applied, as the situations allowing its exercise are potentially numerous, undetermined and indeterminable and leave the authority concerned a broad discretion that is difficult to review. Such criteria which are not precise and are not therefore founded on objective, verifiable conditions go beyond what is necessary in order to attain the objectives stated and cannot therefore satisfy the requirements of the principle of proportionality.[193]

Although I have presented it in a simplified manner, the message of the Court appears clear. Member States have the option to introduce socio-economic governance mechanisms that ensure high levels of workers protection and significantly restrict the freedom of establishment provided that a standard of good governance is met.

V. CONCLUSION

Chapter 1 pointed out that it can be discussed whether the fact that many restrictive Member State regulations perish within the evaluative framework of the

[191] Niglia (n 182) at 154. *cf* also B Bercusson, 'The Trade Union Movement and the European Union: Judgment Day' (2007) 13 *European Law Journal* 279–308.

[192] Case C-201/15 *AGET Iraklis*, ECLI:EU:C:2016:972.

[193] ibid, para 100.

Court is because Member States themselves do not really understand the functions of their own laws, nor defend them well, or whether the problem concerns the way that the Court often chooses to frame things, in consequentialist, purposive terms,[194] which simply fails to capture and weigh the true social significance of some restrictive rules. The culture of justifications that the Court of Justice pursues in its proportionality model requires a clearer articulation of the requirements and the limits of market integration. Social legitimacy requires the Court to be consistently responsive to accommodate Member State diversity *and* promote the objectives of the internal market; an integrated market that is responsive to a Member State's differing sets of social contexts.

The balance between the requirements from the EU internal market for Member States regulatory choices, whilst at the same time respecting the 'fundamental structures' that exist in the Member States, through a recognition of a diversity of regulatory options, is one of the structural challenges faced by the internal market project.[195] The different ways in which the Court has balanced these conflicts in the area of free movement, by granting margins of discretion in some cases and not in others, and by focusing exclusively on procedural context in some cases and not in others, demonstrates how the Court is struggling and in need of an operational principle. This need is clearly related to the social legitimacy question that stands central in this book. Looking through the lens of social legitimacy at EU free movement adjudication tells a mixed story. On the one hand there is clearly a responsiveness, which shows a concern for diversity and respect for local social context. On the other hand, there are plenty of cases where the Court forgoes social context and pushes a normative perception of the way in which social objectives and market integration relate to each other. What is missing is a consistent use of the rationales by the Court that move between principles of managerialism and good governance. In the application of each of these 'ideal type' rationales, the Court seems to be without a clear rationale as to when a definite margin of discretion is explicitly granted to Member States, when interests are to be considered sensitive and when a focus on procedural context is more appropriate than an evaluation of the necessity of the substantive measures themselves. This incoherence threatens the application of mutual responsiveness and thereby social legitimacy. On the one hand a normative metric of evaluation may be adopted that is unresponsive to legitimate social context within a Member State. On the other margins of discretion may be granted to Member States whereas regulatory measures could potentially have been implemented in a more Union-friendly way.

The rationality of responsiveness in the adjudicative model of EU free movement law is to find the societal basis of a conflict through a discursive process that allows market rationality to question Member States' protective organisations but allows non-market rationales to exist and remain an embedding fabric on the

[194] ibid.

[195] See on this point also A Somek, 'The Social Question in a Transnational Context' LSE 'Europe in Question' Discussion Paper series, June 2011.

Member State level. The social purpose of the internal market is not to condition choices that require the market to trump the social or its opposite. The approach suggested in this chapter purports a more holistic idea that conceives the market and the social sphere as 'communicating vessels'. Market-derived evaluative standards serve as a tool to tease out discriminatory, disingenuous regulatory choices within Member States but allow for genuine social objectives to exist in accordance with good governance principles that focus on the quality and systemacy of a governance process instead of on the rationality and efficiency of its outcome. In this way there is neither a sacrifice of the market or a sacrifice of the social and, instead, both social diversity and market integration are accommodated within the internal market.

There are a few clear advantages in the proposed model of adjudication that adopts an *inherently irreconcilable* test as a means of a preliminary qualification of the nature of a conflict before the Court of Justice. First, by 'using' the market access restriction in this way the Court avoids subsequent narratives that assert that the Court is engaged in the pursuit of a neoliberal biased agenda. A finding of 'reconcilability' will guide the subsequent evaluation on the basis of an assessment of the less restrictive measure. A finding of 'irreconcilability' will guide the subsequent evaluation on the basis of an assessment of the wider coherence and consistency of the procedural context. Consequently, the requirements flowing from the integrating European market will be more explicitly articulated, leading to more unity in the interpretation of these requirements.[196] It should be noted that, as a result, a particular measure may be considered as illegal in one country, depending on whether it is embedded in principles of good governance but not in another. Consequently, each case will need to be decided individually, on its own merits. The clear normative preference here is therefore to further context sensitivity over legal certainty in EU adjudication.[197]

As such, the proposed normative-prescriptive model of adjudication seeks to serve various purposes. Most of all, it seeks responsiveness to social context in the adjudicative model of the Court. However, in that process it will also establish the substantive scope and reach of the internal market. That is to say, to which point the internal market can accommodate social claims and from which point objectives become inherently irreconcilable. Therefore, the struggle that the Court faces in determining this balance should be cherished as a potential source of deliberative and formative potential for both the EU internal market and the Member States. The process of determining whether objectives are inherently irreconcilable will necessarily lead to a clearer articulation of what is required from Member

[196] Instead of as was the case in the aftermath of the *Viking* case which led to various and widely differing national responses as highlighted in M Blauberger's analysis, 'With Luxembourg in Mind … the Remaking of Policies in the Face of ECJ Jurisprudence' (2012) 19 *Journal of European Public Policy* 109–26.

[197] For the reverse argument, see Snell (n 29) at 437.

States in the organisation of their regulatory concerns. That is to say, the model will result in the creation of a discursive field that allows for the articulation of Member State prerogatives and the requirements flowing from European integration. This more context-specific model of adjudication will, as an effect, also provide for a clearer instruction to Member States to follow specific good governance principles. It is a model that is sensitive to the problem of judicial review in order to take account of the potential systemic effects of certain policy choices and stimulates a clearer articulation of what is required from Member States in the organisation of their regulatory concerns. As such it will improve awareness, identity and, importantly, dialogue regarding EU relevant matters not just before the EU courts, but also within the political arenas of the Member States. Concomitantly, interests and values will be better articulated, voiced and eventually picked up by the Court.

3

Social Legitimacy in EU Competition Law

I. INTRODUCTION

IN THIS CHAPTER I will explore how a certain economic rationality is created, entrenched and mobilised through European competition law and policy. More particularly, I will explore a question regarding European competition law's role in the construction, maintenance and transformation of frameworks of knowledge in particular market contexts and reflect on this through the normative lens of social legitimacy.[1]

The particular market context of interest for this discussion concerns that of (quasi) self-regulation. Competitors meet and may be stimulated or required to self-regulate within state governance systems in order to set standards for the pursuit of—often deontological—objectives.[2] This may happen for technical standards, environmental objectives, labour conditions, minimum trade standards and so forth. Agreements that flow forth from the pursuit of such objectives may restrict competition, for example through output restrictions, pricing agreements and prohibitions on trading in products that have been produced beneath certain trade standards.[3] From a 'traditionalist'-based understanding of competition law such private regulatory contexts raise issues since they are likely to restrict the independent operation of the undertakings in the markets concerned.[4]

Where self-regulation leads to restrictions of competition there exist, roughly, two 'escapes' within the European competition rules. Firstly, on the supply side of the market where the self-regulation takes place. The supply side may be

[1] *cf* research agenda of A Lang, 'The Legal Construction of Economic Rationalities?' (2013) 40 *Journal of Law and Society* 155–71.

[2] See eg L *Ankersmit, Globalization and the Internal Market: Process-based Measures Within the EU Legal Order* (PhD thesis, Vrije Universiteit Amsterdam, 2015); also H Schepel, 'The Constitution of Private Governance: Product Standards in the Regulation of Integrating Markets' (Oxford, Hart Publishing, 2005).

[3] ibid.

[4] G Monti, *EC Competition Law* (Boston, Cambridge University Press, 2006) 20–52; R Nazzini, 'Article 81 EC between Time Present and Time Past—A Normative Critique of "Restriction of Competition" in EU Law' (2006) 43 *Common Market Law Review* 497–536; G Monti, 'Article 81 EC and Public Policy' (2002) 39 *Common Market Law Review* 1057–99.

organised in a manner such that the companies involved are sufficiently restricted in their ability to regulate in a self-serving manner. This may be because the public law framework installs sufficient oversight and thus channels the private decision-makers towards exclusively serving public interests or because the objectives pursued are legitimate and necessitate and justify some restrictions on competition.[5] In this case the restrictions on competition can be excepted from the scope of the cartel prohibition. Secondly, the demand side of the market may be sufficiently 'compensated' for the resultant restrictions of competition owing to an increase in consumer welfare. Certain minimum technical standards may restrict competition on those standards but lead to quality increases of products that consumers are willing to pay for and thus positively contribute to consumer surplus. In this case the restrictions on competition can be exempted from the cartel prohibition.

I will argue that the modernisation and economisation processes of European competition law have at their core a programme that seeks to entrench a rationality that is based on the demand side of markets, ie of a consumerist nature. This may clash with rationales that do not necessarily accord with existing socio-economic organisational principles within economic sectors that have historically been organised to serve *producerist* objectives or interests. By 'producerist' I refer broadly to an orientation of the state on the supply side of a market. Producers are accorded a central organising function in society that goes further than 'merely' an economic function but is enabling in providing a certain socio-economic identity. The protection of guilds (lawyers, waiters in France, pharmacists), certain ways of making products (pasta, wine, *reinheitsgebot*) or the size of stores and their opening times may fulfil a social function that resonates with a certain culture, history and identity. Although the Court of Justice has explicitly created avenues to accommodate such producerist interests within European competition law, there is a clear (economic) consumerist orientation within the modernisation and economisation processes that has shaped the European competition rules over the last decade or two. The consumerist turn in European competition law focuses solely on purposive rights and interests on the demand side of the market in particular, primarily as an interest in competitive prices and choice for consumers.

I discuss the potential clash of organisational logics by reviewing how the structure and application of EU competition law has been employed to tilt EU Member States governance systems from producerist towards consumerist socio-economic orientations. I shall do so on the basis of a critical reflection of attempts by the European Commission to 'liberate' the liberal professions and more recent examples in The Netherlands that demonstrate how EU competition law may install a logic of (economic) consumer welfare as a primary principle of social organisation whenever firms cooperate to achieve public interest objectives.

[5] Based on eg Case C-185/91 *Reiff Bundesanstalt für den Güterfernverkehr* [1993] ECR I-5801, para 22 and Case C-309/99 *Wouters* [2002] ECR I-1577.

I will reflect on these findings from the normative perspective of social legitimacy. The normative claims of social legitimacy that were developed and applied in the previous chapters can be pointedly summarised as follows. Taking as a point of departure the compromise of embedded liberalism, the argument has been submitted that the social purpose of the EU internal market is to provide an infrastructure for the conflict of norms within the Union that arise through the interaction between principles of economic integration and the pursuit of social interests on a Member State level. In turn, this conceptualisation has allowed for the development of a model of social legitimacy that provides normative instructions to the Court of Justice in order to adjudicate conflicts within the internal market infrastructure in tune with a variety of social contexts.

With regard to the application of the competition rules this concerns the extent to which the 'competition interest' that is advanced through the competition rules can be prescriptive with respect to the social interests that are worth pursuing, without inhibiting social diversity and accommodating the constructive interplay of norm conflicts within the Union at the same time. Until late in the 1990s the competition rules were not deeply embedded within the Member States. The Netherlands, for example, was considered as a 'cartel paradise' and there were cartels in all sectors and branches of the economy until the introduction of more stringent legislation in 1998, which only then could be considered to be in closer proximity to the objectives of the EU competition rules. Today the principle of competition has rapidly become one of the primary departure points of public policy and, as Whish and Bailey note

> competition laws will be found in all continents and in all types of economies—large, small, continental, island, advanced, developing, industrial, trading, agricultural, liberal and post-communist. Quite apart from its geographical growth, competition law is now applied to many economic activities that once were regarded as natural monopolies or the preserve of the state: telecommunications, energy, transport, broadcasting and postal services, to name a few obvious examples, have become the subject of competition law scrutiny.[6]

The competition rules require, in relative comparison to the EU free movement rules, a clear commitment from both Member States and private economic operators, and the effects of this normative order on social spheres, which are not blatantly contrary to competition objectives, soon becomes potentially problematic from a social legitimacy perspective. In comparison with EU free movement, the competition rules more directly value social relations in a particularly formative manner. As will be discussed further below, the competition rules, in particular Article 101 TFEU, place emphasis on the benefits that consumers accrue from the process of competition. Solely by virtue of this fact, social relations between producers, which collectively pursue interests on that level, are on the back foot. This amounts to a significant formative effect of the competition rules with

[6] R Whish and D Bailey, *Competition Law* (Oxford, Oxford University Press, 2012) at 1.

regard to social relations in countries that, traditionally, have a more 'producerist' orientation and involve the supply side of markets in the formation of socio-economic policy objectives.[7] Moreover, an important facet of the competition rules is the obligation for subjects of competition law (undertakings) to self-assess their competition law status on the basis of the numerous position and guidance papers that are issued by (national) competition authorities on the basis of, inter alia, the case law of the Court of Justice. In this way competition law becomes, covertly, formative of social spheres, particularly when guidance is issued on the way that companies should (jointly) pursue public goods such as sustainability. These formative effects will become clearer in the case studies that are discussed throughout the chapter.

The question I reflect on in this chapter is to what extent this impact on social spheres can be considered to be problematic from the perspective of social legitimacy. Should competition in all cases prevail? I will discuss that the Court is not necessarily always clear in its guidance. For example, it has branded Irish beef producers that collectively aim to reduce the overcapacity in their sector in order to create an economic climate in which their businesses will be able to survive as measures with the object of restricting competition, which exposes them to significant sanctions.[8] On the other hand, associations of lawyers that prohibit cooperation between accountants and lawyers and thereby restrict competition in order to protect the integrity of the profession are granted a certain leeway to do so.[9] On the basis of what principles does the Court of Justice decide to impose a normative view of competition on social spheres? A question that becomes particularly salient whenever such principles are embedded within a context that is expressive of a Member States' socio-economic identity. To what extent should and can such context be recognised and accommodated within the EU competition rules?

Adam Smith famously prophesised that

> people of the same trade seldom meet together, even for merriment and diversion, but the conversation ends in a conspiracy against the public, or in some contrivance to raise prices. It is impossible indeed to prevent such meetings, by any law, which either could be executed, or would be consistent with liberty and justice. But though the law cannot hinder people of the same trade from sometimes assembling together, it ought to do nothing to facilitate such assemblies; much less to render them necessary.[10]

[7] See J Whitman, 'Consumerism versus Producerism: A Study in Comparative Law' (2007) 117 *Yale Law Journal* 340.

[8] Case C209/07 *BIDS* [2008] ECR I-08637. The starting point for the fine is the percentage of a company's annual sales of the product concerned in the infringement (up to 30%). This is then multiplied by the number of years and months the infringement lasted. In cartel cases, the fine is increased by a one-time amount equivalent to 15–25% of the value of one year's sales as an additional deterrent. The maximum level of fine is capped at 10% of the overall annual turnover of a company.

[9] Case C-209/07 *Competition Authority v Beef Industry Development Society Ltd and Barry Brothers (Carrigmore) Meats Ltd* [2008] ECR I-8637, paras 34–36 and Case C-309/99 *Wouters* [2002] ECR I-1577.

[10] A Smith, *An Inquiry into the Nature and Causes of the Wealth of Nations* (London, George Routledge & Sons, 1776; reprint, 1893) at 137.

It is, however, a fact that undertakings do meet and sometimes are also necessitated by national governments to meet, particularly in economies with a producerist orientation, and set standards for the pursuit of public goods.[11] This happens for environmental reasons, labour conditions, minimum trade standards and so forth. Agreements that flow forth from the pursuit of such objectives may restrict competition, for example through output restrictions, pricing agreements and prohibitions to trade in products that have been produced beneath certain trade standards.[12] From a 'traditionalist'-based understanding of competition law such private-led initiatives may raise issues since they are likely to restrict the independent operation of the undertakings in the markets concerned.[13]

The diversity of objectives and the requirement for competition law to accommodate the pursuit of diverse social objectives by members of the same trade leads to specific challenges. The chapter finds that the application of the EU competition rules by the Court of Justice and, concomitantly, competition authorities is insufficiently developed to accommodate the pursuit of a diversity of social objectives.[14] Consequently, on the basis of the normative framework that was introduced in Chapter 1 they are liable to impede the social legitimacy of EU competition law. This chapter shall develop this finding on the basis of three case examples in the Netherlands, which demonstrate how competition-based rationalities carry the inherent risk to disregards relevant and legitimate social spheres within Member States.

As was discussed in Chapter 1, there exists an analogy on this point with regard to the formative relationship between law and social norms. Roughly two ideas dominate the debate on the interaction between social norms and the law. One concerns the idea that 'custom' or norm-based rules lack the flexibility and rational control that is considered desirable for some higher order reason—in this case competition. Law then could become the means to reform such 'old-fashioned' social norms. Some social norms may not be desirable from a particular rational perspective, and law can then improve the situation by regulating the concerned behaviour in congruence with the desired rationally and correcting undesirable phenomena, such as price agreements between competitors. As was discussed in Chapter 2, this is somehow reflected in the core nucleus of EU law where there are some interests (however social they may be) that are simply not part of the accepted EU internal market values scheme and will therefore always have to give way to the objectives of market integration and competition. Outside of the core nucleus of mutually shared values, the balance between market integration and

[11] See eg Ankersmit, *Globalization and the Internal Market*' (n 2); also H Schepel, 'The Constitution of Private Governance' (n 2).

[12] ibid.

[13] Monti, *EC Competition Law* (n 4) at 20–52; Nazzini, 'Article 81 EC between Time Present and Time Past' (n 4) 497–536; Monti, 'Article 81 EC and Public Policy' (n 4).

[14] This chapter necessarily extends these normative views on competition authorities in their capacity as 'quasi'-like adjudicators.

social interests that are restrictive of competition interests becomes more complex and in need of a subtler rationale. To refer back to the previous analogy, this is the idea that legal and social norms do their job in the 'best' way when they are somehow aligned. The idea here is that law and social norms should in a way complement each other. This position harbours more challenges, in finding the right interplay between social norms and enforcing a 'dynamic' and flexible rationality through law. What underlies it is the idea that law should not be alien to society but instead that there should be some form of mutual communication between law and society. This reflects the basic point of the normative claim of social legitimacy, which is to say that if law is completely alien it risks losing its legitimacy and become irrelevant. As such, the supranational EU law rules have to some extent to align with social contexts within Member States and built-in mechanisms of responsiveness in order to retain its legitimacy. Since the application of the EU competition rules is mostly decentralised and applied within Member State contexts and institutional structures, it would seem that responsiveness is more easily obtained. This chapter reflects on these questions in the area of the competition rules from the perspective of social legitimacy.

The outline of this chapter is as follows. In section II, I will discuss the related issues of valuation, indeterminacy and incommensurability in the application of the EU competition rules. This section starts with a discussion on how these issues speak to the existing literature in EU competition law that deals with the objectives of competition law and to what extent competition rules should or can incorporate 'non-competition' interests. Three case studies will be discussed in this section that problematise the application of EU competition law in view of the social legitimacy requirement. Section III gathers and discusses the case law where the Court has demonstrated responsiveness to social context. Section IV reconstructs this case law into a coherent model of social legitimacy and demonstrates how this approach will be able to accommodate social diversity within the Union on the basis of the highlighted case studies. Section V concludes.

II. VALUATION, INDETERMINACY AND INCOMMENSURABILITY IN EU COMPETITION LAW

A. Economisation and Modernisation of EU Competition Law

The EU competition rules set out a strong and seemingly clear normative framework.[15] Article 101(1) TFEU prohibits 'all agreements between undertakings,

[15] As discussed further below the objectives associated with EU competition law are nevertheless often considered as plural: economic efficiency, consumer welfare, 'fair' competition, market integration, innovation, economic freedom etc. To give an indication of the sheer volume of contributions to this topic over the years, just a selection: P Akman, 'Consumer Welfare and Article 102 EC: Practice and Rhetoric' (2009 31 *World Competition* 71–90; P Akman, 'Searching for the Long-Lost Soul of

decisions by associations of undertakings and concerted practices which may affect trade between Member States and which have as their object or effect the prevention, restriction or distortion of competition within the internal market'. As an exception to this rule, Article 101(3) TFEU provides that the prohibition contained in the first paragraph may be declared inapplicable in case of agreements which contribute to improving the production or distribution of goods or to promoting technical or economic progress, while allowing consumers a fair share of the resulting benefits, and which do not impose restrictions which are not indispensable to the attainment of these objectives and do not afford such undertakings the possibility of eliminating competition in respect of a substantial part of the products concerned.[16]

In the late 1990s, the European Commission initiated the so-called 'more economic approach' in European competition law.[17] This approach implies inter alia that only 'economic efficiencies' or 'pro-competitive effects' of restrictive agreements are accepted in order to fulfil the exemption criteria.[18] One of the important effects this has had on the legal assessment of restrictions on competition is that decisive value is attached to the objective qualification and concretisation in economic terms of claimed benefits that may be effectuated by restrictive agreements in order to qualify for an exemption.[19] On this basis, the exemption

Article 82 EC' (2009) 29 *Oxford Journal of Legal Studies* 267–303; O Andriychuk, 'Dialectical Antitrust: An Alternative Insight into the Methodology of the EC Competition Law Analysis in a Period of Economic Downturn' (2010) 31 *European Competition Law Review* 155–64; O Andriychuk, 'Rediscovering the Spirit of Competition: On the Normative Value of the Competitive Process' (2010) 6 *European Competition Journal* 575–610; E Buttigie, 'Competition Law: Safeguarding the Consumer Interest. A Comparative Analysis of US Antitrust Law and EC Competition Law' in J Drexl, W Kerber and R Podszun, (eds), *Competition Policy and the Economic Approach—Foundations and Limitations* (Cheltenham, Edward Elgar, 2010); I Lianos, 'Some Reflections on the Question of the Goals of EU Competition Law' (2013) CLES Working Paper Series 3/2013; Monti, 'Article 81 EC and Public Policy' (n 4); P Nihoul, '"Freedom of Choice": The Emergence of a Powerful Concept in European Competition Law' (2012) 3 *Concurrences* 55–70; L Lovdahl-Gormsen, 'The Conflict Between Economic Freedom and Consumer Welfare in the Modernization of Article 82 EC' (2007) 3 *European Competition Journal* 329–44; O Odudu, 'The Wider Concerns of Competition Law' (2010) 30 *Oxford Journal of Legal Studies* 599–613; C Townley, *Article 81 EC and Public Policy* (Oxford, Hart Publishing, 2009); B van Rompuy, *Economic Efficiency: The Sole Concern of Modern Antitrust Policy? Non-Efficiency Considerations under Article 101 TFEU* (Alphen aan den Rijn, Kluwer, 2012); D Zimmer (ed), *The Goals of Competition Law* (Cheltenham, Edward Elgar, 2012).

[16] Guidelines on the application of Article 81(3) of the Treaty [2004] OJ C101/ 97; Guidelines on the applicability of Article 101 of the Treaty on the Functioning of the European Union to horizontal co-operation agreements [2011] OJ C11/1.

[17] *cf* AC Witt, *The More Economic Approach to EU Antitrust Law* (Oxford, Hart Publishing, 2016).

[18] Guidelines on the application of Article 81(3) of the Treaty [2004] OJ C101/ 97; Guidelines on the applicability of Article 101 of the Treaty on the Functioning of the European Union to horizontal co-operation agreements [2011] OJ C11/1.

[19] Whish and Bailey, *Competition Law* (n 6); Commission Guidelines on the application of Article 81(3) of the Treaty [2004] OJ C101/97; Commission Guidelines on the applicability of Article 101 of the Treaty on the Functioning of the European Union to horizontal co-operation agreements [2011] OJ C11/1; L Kjølbye, 'The New Commission Guidelines on the Application of Article 81(3): an Economic Approach to Article 81' (2004) 25 *European Competition Law Review* 566–77.

criteria of Article 101(3) TFEU provide a common 'monetised' scale to evaluate restrictive objectives of competition. In principle, all competition restrictive interests shall have to be evaluated on the basis of Article 101(3) TFEU.

In addition and importantly, what is known as the 'modernisation' of EU competition law has involved a decentralisation of the application of the competition rules. This had two significant and immediate effects. Firstly, the European competition rules were to be applied and enforced by national competition authorities and the European Commission simultaneously. This raised the need for uniform application of the competition rules and a subsequent explosion of instruments and knowledge-sharing instruments (such as the creation of the European Competition Network) in order to ensure that Article 101 TFEU would be applied by national competition authorities in congruence with the uniform guidelines of the European Commission. Secondly, undertakings themselves were from now on to 'self-assess' their status under the competition rules, whereas formerly they were able to request official 'exemption decisions' from competition authorities. Again, to that end the European Commission issued a plethora of guidelines, block exemptions and other soft law instruments to provide firms, and in particular their lawyers, with the tools to conduct such self-assessments.

Two important aspects can be derived from the dual development of economisation and modernisation of EU competition law. Firstly, competition authorities within Europe pursue cases on the basis of the idea that where competing firms jointly pursue, for example, fair trade standards, they should only do so if they can demonstrate efficiencies and that consumers will directly benefit from potential restrictions on competition. Hence, their actions should be completely in accordance with an understanding of what matters and can be validated in terms of the market's willingness to pay for certain restrictions of competition. Secondly, in the process of self-assessments, informal opinions and individual guidance, competition authorities aim to internalise this economic, consumer-led market rationale all the way down into the minds and calculus of the undertakings themselves.

The entrenchment of this economic rationality may have formative effects considering the fact that the importance of private regulation on the supply side of markets is increasing and non-state actors determine a growing part of the conditions, rules and regulations that govern transnational trade.[20] In addition, increasingly so, private regulatory initiative pushed by NGOs and enhanced consumer awareness, incorporates a responsiveness with respect to the pursuit of public—global—policy challenges, such as the protection of the environment, animal welfare and human rights. Examples range from sustainability initiatives in the forestry sector to the setting of minimum standards for labour conditions in the clothing industry and physical integrity rights in the extractive industry.[21]

[20] F Cafaggi, 'Transnational Private Regulation. Regulating Private Regulators' in S Cassese (ed), *Research Handbook on Global Administrative Law* (Cheltenham, Edward Elgar, 2016).

[21] Respectively, the Forest Stewardship Council (FSC), the Bangladesh Accord, the Voluntary Principles on Security and Human Rights and the International Licensing Platform.

Such initiatives with wider welfare effects are costly and require investments that companies are often only willing to make if free-rider problems and first mover disadvantages are resolved.[22] However, within this economic rationale, a group of companies that collectively adopt 'social objectives', such as a minimum fair trade standard, shall have to demonstrate that these measures are eventually beneficial for consumer welfare.[23] A group of firms that collectively decide to not to buy from suppliers that violate human rights is allowed only if consumer welfare increases in a quantifiable manner.

Many economists will argue that this would be good law and posit that where public interests are at stake that society wants to protect: regulation is the answer. The state can legislate and, on that basis, take issues away from the market. However, regulation may not always be a realistic or feasible option. Moreover, governance structures may enable, stimulate or require the private sector explicitly to incorporate public interest objectives. Often, private regulation is a generic response from the private sector to a failure or unwillingness of the nation state and conventional international law-making to effectively address cross-border challenges.[24] It is clear that applied in this manner and context, the European competition rules have the potential to enforce and entrench a specific economic rationality. Below I will discuss how this potentially transforms organisational principles in specific market contexts.

B. Goals of Competition Law

Debates with respect to the goals of competition law are vast and wide and the intention of this section is not to provide a very nuanced overview of all strands and perspectives. For the purpose of this chapter the debates can instead be roughly split in two categories. One line of debate looks inward and asks what competition law, as an insulated autonomous field of law aims to achieve. Here different goals are conceived, such as consumer welfare; total welfare; the process

[22] The first mover disadvantage concerns a situation where just one company decides not to offer certain unsustainable (often cheaper) products and may consequently lose a critical amount of customers to its competitors which remain selling the cheaper product. Such 'coordination' problems can be resolved if companies pursue welfare initiatives collectively. The free-rider problem concerns a situation where a company invests in sustainability—such as, eg, by virtue of a marketing campaign intended to inform consumers of the importance of fair trade—that may consequently benefit competitors which do not make such investments but nevertheless do benefit from consumers that are more willing to purchase sustainable goods.

[23] The starting point for the fine is the percentage of a company's annual sales of the product concerned in the infringement (up to 30%). This is then multiplied by the number of years and months the infringement lasted. In cartel cases, the fine is increased by a one-time amount equivalent to 15–25% of the value of one year's sales as an additional deterrent. The maximum level of fine is capped at 10% of the overall annual turnover of a company.

[24] P Schleifer, 'Creating Legitimacy for Private Rules: Explaining the Choice of Legitimation Strategies in Transnational NON-State Governance' EUI Working Paper 2015 RSCAS 2015/62.

of competition; the protection of competitors; consumer protection; innovation; economic freedom and redistribution of power. Each of these goals is then in itself, again, subject to debate since some economists may, for example, view consumer welfare so as to encompass not just merely low prices but as the product of a well-functioning overall process of competition. The latter is in that case perceived as a necessary means to achieve total welfare, innovation and economic freedom. Regarding the idea of 'welfare', questions arise to what extent 'economic welfare' should be central and which rules are the best to advance welfare. Here there is debate on issues such as the extent that total welfare should be the objective or whether only consumer welfare should count.[25] Should issues of regional policy or unemployment be allowed to play a role and in what way?[26] The inward debate is largely undecided and in flux. Importantly, one can find emanations of different goals in different lines of case law and areas of competition law. For example, Article 101 TFEU can be said to be concerned mostly with consumer welfare since agreements that restrict competition can only be exempted on the basis of the criteria in Article 101(3) TFEU if there are tangible positive effects for consumers. Article 102 TFEU can be said to be mostly concerned with protecting the process of competition and, specifically, competitors since certain lines of case law restricts dominant undertakings in engaging in behaviour that may exclude smaller, less efficient competitors.

The second line of debate is more outwardly oriented and asks what the goals of competition law are in the wider context of the world and, in the EU, with respect to European integration, specifically, what the relationship is or can be between competition and the social objectives pursued in the Lisbon Treaty.[27] Is competition law a threat to these objectives, which should lead to the exclusion of competition law in certain areas of social life within the Member States?[28] Can competition law contribute as a means to the achievement of the wider objectives of market integration?[29] These questions speak to a line of literature within competition law that concerns the issue if, to what extent, and how so-called

[25] eg Bork approaches consumer welfare and total welfare as being the same thing and serving the same objectives: RH Bork, *The Antitrust Paradox: A Policy at War with itself* (New York, Basic Books, 1978). For a recent critique, see DA Crane, 'The Tempting of Antitrust: Robert Bork and the Goals of Antitrust Policy' (2014) 79 *Antitrust Law Journal* 835–53.

[26] Whish and Bailey (n 6) at 23.

[27] eg G Monti, 'EU Competition Law from Rome to Lisbon—Social Market Economy' in C Heide-Jorgensen, C Bergqvist, U Neergaard and ST Poulsen (eds), *Aims and Values in Competition Law* (Copenhagen, DJØF Publishing, 2013); N Dhondt, 'Integration of Environmental Protection into other EC Policies: Legal Theory and Practice' (Brussels, Europa Law Publishing, 2003); D Casey, 'Disintegration: Environmental Protection and Article 81 EC' (2009) 15 *European Law Journal* 362–81; H Vedder, *Competition Law and Environmental Protection in Europe: Towards Sustainability?* (Brussels, Europa Law Publishing, 2003).

[28] *cf* Case C-67/96 *Albany* [1999] ECR I-5751.

[29] See D Ehlermann 'The Contribution of EC Competition Policy to the Single Market' (1992) 29 *Common Market Law Review* 257; Cases C-403/08 and C-429/08 *Football Association Premier League Ltd v QC Leisure* [2011] ECR I-000 and Case C-439/09 *Pierre Fabre Dermo-Cosmétique SAS v Président de l'Autorité de la Concurrence* [2011] ECR I-000.

non-competition or non-efficiency interests have a role to play within the legal framework of the competition rules. It is on this point of the discussion that this chapter seeks to contribute. More specifically, the remainder of the chapter will be concerned with this question in the context of the application of Article 101 TFEU. Article 101 TFEU promotes the idea that the relationship between undertakings including the actions of associations of undertakings, such as, for example, guilds or sector-based organisations, should be governed on the basis of competition. Moreover, as was highlighted in the introduction, the modernisation process of the competition rules incorporated the obligation for subjects of competition law (undertakings) to self-assess their competition law status on the basis of the numerous position and guidance papers that are issued by (national) competition authorities.[30] As such, I consider the application of Article 101 TFEU as the most relevant part of competition law from the perspective of the potential effects on the social sphere and the social diversity amongst the Member States.[31]

C. Non-competition Interests within Competition Law Assessments

The discussion on the issue if, to what extent, and how so-called non-competition or non-efficiency interests have a role to play within the legal framework of the competition rules exists within a spectrum where different arguments move between one of two seemingly opposing positions. On one side of the spectrum stand those who argue that non-competition interests can only play a role within a competition law framework if those interests can be translated and measured in strictly economic terms and, as such, can only override a competition interest if they contribute to consumer welfare.[32] This line of argumentation perceives

[30] R Wesseling, *The Modernisation of EC Antitrust Law* (Oxford, Hart Publishing, 2000) at 20.

[31] That is not to say that Art 102 TFEU or mergers have no relevance for his issue. Big corporations such as Google have of course a huge social impact and perhaps sometimes will restrict competition for the self-proclaimed advancement of a public interest (*cf* Case T-30/89 *Hilti AG v Commission* [1991] ECR II-1439). The enormous Google project on the digitisation of books is a real-life example of this. Moreover, merger policy can be discussed from a perspective of social legitimacy. eg, are hospital mergers to be assessed only from a narrow perspective of efficiency benefits? Such questions are, however, excluded from the scope of this chapter, if only for reasons of space. It is, however, also not necessary to include these interesting examples, which will be reserved for later research projects, in this chapter for the more theoretical argument to stand on its own feet. That is the wider discussion of the role and function of competition in society and the chapter proceeds to make a normative claim about this on the basis of a discussion of Art 101 TFEU only (a normative claim that can also be transposed to other areas of competition law).

[32] eg G Amato, *Antitrust and the Bounds of Power* (Oxford, Hart Publishing, 1997) at 117; O Odudu, *The Boundaries of EC Competition Law: The Scope of Article 81* (Oxford, Oxford University Press, 2006) at 7; L Kjølbye, 'The New Commission Guidelines on the Application of Article 81(3): an Economic Approach to Article 81' (2004) 25 *European Competition Law Review* 566; P Lugard and L Hancher, 'Honey, I Shrunk the Article! A Critical Assessment of the Commission's Notice on Article 81(3) of the EC Treaty' (2004) 25 *European Competition Law Review* 410; AC Witt, 'Public Policy Goals under EU Competition Law: now is the Time to Set the House in Order' (2012) 8 *European Competition Journal* 443. For a comparable argument, see also K Mortelmans, 'Towards Convergence in the Application of the Rules on Free Movement and Competition?' (2001) 38 *Common Market Law Review* 613.

the function of competition law in narrow terms and as exclusively relevant for the advancement of consumer interests and efficiency. 'True' non-competition or non-efficiency interests will fall completely outside of the reach of the competition rules and have to be discussed and addressed within a political context. Roughly, the line of argumentation here is that the competition rules are insufficiently equipped to be applied to a broad range of societal issues and that the added value of competition law as an instrument for the promotion of consumer welfare will be inhibited and obscured if non-competition interests were to play a prominent role in the application of the competition rules. Importantly, this view is advanced by the European Commission, which also makes sure that national competition authorities will approach this issue in the same way. According to the Commission, the purpose of the exemption provision of Article 101(3) TFEU 'is to provide a legal framework for the economic assessment of restrictive practices and not to allow application of the competition rules to be set aside because of political considerations'.[33] As a result, public interest goals 'pursued by other Treaty provisions can be taken into account' but only in so far as they can be subsumed under the four conditions of Article 101(3) TFEU 'by using the economic methodology employed by it'.[34] The case studies that will be discussed later shall demonstrate how this narrow view is liable to exclude valuable social content from the framework of analysis.

This line of literature does not argue that other, wider, social interests do not matter. The argument is merely made that competition law exists as a separate field and competition authorities are specialised and independent authorities, above all, with the purpose of ensuring the competition rules and it is not the competition authority but another (specialised or politically legitimised) entity that would have to make the assessment if non-competition interests were to become crucial in a balancing process. If the interest at stake does not qualify as an efficiency concern, an alternative evaluative rationale should allow for the inclusion of a public interest decision by an actor with political legitimacy (for example within a deliberative governance model).[35] For example, in mergers raising certain public interest considerations in the UK, the Secretary of State for Department for Business, Energy and Industrial Strategy may intervene.[36] Such intervention enables the Secretary of State to assume responsibility for determining whether or not to refer a merger to the Competition and Markets Authority and to take

[33] Guidelines on the application of Article 81(3) of the Treaty [2004] OJ C101/ 97; Guidelines on the applicability of Article 101 of the Treaty on the Functioning of the European Union to horizontal co-operation agreements [2011] OJ C11/1.

[34] ibid, para 42.

[35] Anna Gerbrandy has made suggestions to include more public stakeholders *within* the competition law *procedure* (instead of the analysis) in order to increase the legitimacy of competition law decisions to take account of non-competition objectives in A Gerbrandy, 'Addressing the Legitimacy Problem for Competition Authorities Taking into Account Non-Economic Values: The Position of the Dutch Competition Authority' (2015) 40 *European Law Review* 770.

[36] Whish and Bailey (n 6) at 728.

the ultimate decision in respect of mergers when defined public interest considerations are potentially relevant. In these cases, there is no longer a competition assessment rationale at play but instead the assessment made is confined to the relevant public interest consideration within a political and democratically legitimated arena. Some consider this as a choice in terms of *jurisdictional conflicts* between policy areas that can be solved through a procedural test. For example, Lavrijssen qualifies non-competition interests as 'aimed at the promotion of horizontal and flanking policy interests and sector-specific public service interests, such as the quality of healthcare'.[37] Similarly, Monti has argued for the addition of an Article 101(4) TFEU enabling public policy considerations to be integrated, separately, in the competition law assessment.[38]

What could be considered an opposing view argues that non-competition interests do (have to) play a prominent role *within* the competition law framework and are also able to set aside competition objectives if certain conditions are fulfilled.[39] This line of argumentation is in favour of an approach whereby a quantifiable value is attributed to a non-competition interest. The latter would then involve a calculation of some sort to determine, within the exemption criteria, whether the balance should turn out in favour of the competition or non-competition interest.[40] This approach may use a plethora of economic methodologies to quantify and place a value on both the costs and benefits of restrictive agreements.[41] The approach that assigns a quantifiable value to a non-competition interest, which then allows a subsequent balancing within the exemption criteria, is perhaps most clearly developed by Townley, who proposes that all interests (being competition or non-competition) can be assigned a money value.[42] The difference between this position and the line of argumentation that was firstly introduced is that the quantification method would disagree with the idea that there are interests that are not quantifiable for the purpose of a competition analysis, whereas the former acknowledges that there are simply some non-efficiency interests that can override competition objectives on the basis of societal/political priorities but turns that into a political decision, which has to be legislated.

[37] S Lavrijssen, 'The Protection of Non-Competition Interests; What Role for Competition Authorities after Lisbon?' (2010) 5 *European Law Review* 635.

[38] See Monti, 'Article 81 EC and Public Policy' (n 4) at 1096.

[39] eg S Kingston, 'Integrating Environmental Protection and EU Competition Law: Why Competition Isn't Special' (2010) 6 *European Law Journal* 790; S Kingston, *Greening Competition Law and Policy* (Boston, Cambridge, 2012); Townley, *Article 81 EC and Public Policy* (n 15); Casey, 'Disintegration' (n 27) at 362; A Gerbrandy, 'Competition Law and Private-Sector Sustainability Initiatives' in ALB Colombi Ciacchi et al (eds), *Law & Governance—Beyond the Public-Private Divide?* (The Hague, Eleven International Publishing, 2013) at 81; Wesseling, *The Modernisation of EC Antitrust Law* (n 30) at 173; S van Hees, *A Sustainable Competition Policy for Europe. A Research on how the European Cartel Rules Can Make a Stronger Contribution to Europe's Sustainable Development Goals* (Utrecht, Utrecht University, 2013).

[40] Townley (n 15); Kingston, *Greening Competition Law and Policy* (n 39).

[41] The use of environmental and ecological economics is a prominent example of such an approach, which goes beyond the use of a narrow welfare analysis. See Kingston, *Greening Competition Law and Policy* (no. 39) 163–93.

[42] Townley (n 15).

In summary, the first approach as discussed above resolves the integration of non-competition objectives on the basis of a rationale of 'exclusion'. The approach is *static* and wider objectives are not integrated in the substance of the competition law assessment. Instead, a conflicting interest will trump Article 101 TFEU completely or vice versa. The second approach that was discussed aims to resolve a potential conflict with wider objectives *within* Article 101(3) TFEU and, as such, they become an inherent part of the competition law assessment by virtue of a quantification approach, which allows for a concretisation of the advancement in the production or distribution of goods or to promoting technical or economic progress and are necessary proportionate to the attainment of those objectives.[43]

Somewhere in between these two positions, leaning more towards the exclusion than the quantification reasoning lies another approach, which excludes restrictive agreements from the scope of Article 101(1) TFEU, if they can be considered necessary for the pursuit of a public interest goal, primarily based on the seminal cases of *Wouters* and *Albany*.[44] This approach leans more towards the first position because it is also based on a rationale of exclusion. It differs mostly from the quantification approach because consumers do not require a 'fair share' of the benefits of the agreement, and instead is based on a more proportionality type of reasoning instead of the cost-benefit analysis which is the basis of the quantification approach in Article 101(3) TFEU. As such it will be discussed further below that this approach is most closely related to the normative claim of social legitimacy, which requires adjudicative rationales to be context specific. However, there are some important shortcomings of this approach, which are not fully addressed in the case law or the literature. These can be addressed on the basis of the idea of mutual responsiveness as will be further discussed below. For now, the potential and shortcomings of this approach are parked. I will return to them in section III below.

D. The Problem of Indeterminacy and the Expressive Value of Competition Law

This debate and the positions that were introduced above are closely related to the problem of incommensurability and the expressive value of competition law. It was discussed in the foregoing that certain evaluative standards carry the risk of excluding or wrongly valuing social context. In free movement it was discussed that this risk materialises, for example, in the application of strict proportionality to a social context, which cannot be completely captured in terms of the less restrictive measure. The normative concern is that evaluative standards may

[43] See van Rompuy, *Economic Efficiency* (n 15) at 218.

[44] Cases C-309/99 *Wouters* [2002] ECR I-1577 and C-67/96 *Albany* [1999] ECR I-5751.

translate social realities within a metric that risks doing violence to potentially genuine and worthwhile aspects of those objectives. Moreover, an additional point of normative concern is that where an evaluative standard adopts a unitary metric, the balancing of competing values becomes simply a matter of calculation. This is not to say that the calculation will be a simple one, but to indicate that the nature of the problem is fundamentally transformed into one of quantification.[45] Thereby, in situations where there is a manifest irreconcilability between normative orders, quantification risks losing the expressive value that is inherent in a normative conflict and the consequent potential for social learning that arises from it. It forgoes the question when competition objectives and non-competition objectives are actually and genuinely irreconcilable. It is submitted that the answer to this question matters because it provides instruction as to how evaluative rationales should deal with the interaction between competition and non-competition concerns. It answers the question, in simple terms, whether a non-competition interest can be incorporated within Article 101(3) TFEU or not.

However, the framing of competition concerns on the one side and wider social objectives on the other is underdeveloped and basically fails to discuss what is at stake when potential genuine norm conflicts arise. It was discussed in Chapter 1 that social interests are often constructed and pursued as enabling market interests. That is to say that the social interest concerned is often (more or less covertly) voicing a market-related interest. Such 'economic' social interests can be achieved on the basis of a market-based model based on the allocative logic of supply and demand and also would, for example, not necessarily conflict with the efficiency-driven exemption criteria of Article 101(3) TFEU. In those situations, there is no genuine normative conflict between a competition and non-competition objective. For example, the *CECED* case is often discussed in terms of a demonstration of the incorporation of non-competition objectives within the competition law framework of Article 101(3) TFEU.[46] The *European Committee of Domestic Equipment Manufacturers* (*CECED*) case concerned the evaluation by the Commission of an agreement amongst European dishwasher manufacturers to stop producing or importing high electricity-consuming appliances.[47] Since this affected 63 per cent of all dishwashers manufactured in Europe and would involve a price increase of up to 14 per cent in order to improve the energy efficiency, it was considered as a restriction on competition.[48] However, the Commission considered that the restriction could be exempted on the basis of Article 101(3) TFEU partly because

[45] See on this also BG Scharffs, 'Adjudication and the Problems of Incommensurability' (2001) 42 *William & Mary Law Review* 1367.

[46] eg. AP Komninos, 'Non-competition Concerns: Resolution of Conflicts in the Integrated Article 81 EC' (2008) The University of Oxford Centre for Competition Law and Policy Working Paper (L) 08/05; Whish and Bailey (n 6) at 158.

[47] *CECED* (Case IV.F.1/36.718) Commission Decision 2000/475/EC [2000] OJ L187/47.

[48] ibid, para 34.

'the new electric water heaters and dishwashers will be more efficient and enable consumers to reduce their energy bills. Moreover, lower electricity consumption will indirectly help the Union achieve its environmental objectives'.[49]

The case is often discussed as an example of how Article 101(3) TFEU has been used to incorporate non-competition, non-efficiency or non-economic considerations.[50] However, looking at the interests that were pursued in this case it does not appear that it is appropriate to frame it in terms of a case where the competition law framework was stretched to accommodate non-competition interests. In fact, the main objective of the agreement in question was to pursue the efficiency of washing machines and nothing of those objectives was lost or translated within the exemption framework of Article 101(3) TFEU in a way that would disregard fundamental aspects of those objectives. Instead the Commission assessed, on the basis of the exemption framework, the extent to which such efficiencies would materialise and, subsequently, benefit consumers.

Hence, when one speaks about norm conflicts between economic and social policies, this is not necessarily a conflict of different normative orders but, rather, reflects a disagreement with respect to the best design of one largely economic issue.[51] Often, in the use of terminology such as the 'economic versus the social' or 'competition versus non-competition' there is *no conflict of irreconcilable* normative orders. Therefore, a better conceptual understanding of the non-competition interest may solve or render more understandable some of the *apparent* problems within competition and non-competition balancing by clarifying whether a *true conflict is actually present.* A disentanglement of this kind could show more clearly when there is no real conflict of norms but rather a disagreement *over the construction of one norm* or when there is actually a conflict of different normative orders and hence indicate the need to adopt an evaluative legal rationale that does justice to pluralistic normative order conflicts.

To different degrees then, against this background, both previously discussed positions on the integration of non-competition objectives within the competition law assessment harbour some problems that are related to the lack of a clear understanding on the potential for norm conflicts between competition and non-competition objectives. There exists some terminological debate on the market versus non-economic objectives debate and specifically with respect to the question of what concerns an economic activity and the legitimate reach of the EU competition law provisions,[52] or the way that EU competition law should deal

[49] Commission Press Release IP/01/1659, 26 November 2001. As such, the Commission recognised the environmental benefits of the agreement in a broad sense.

[50] eg Komninos, 'Non-competition Concerns' (n 46); and Whish and Bailey (n 6) at 158.

[51] See eg C Kaupa 'Maybe not Activist enough? On the Court's Alleged Neoliberal Bias in its Recent Labor Cases' in B Witte, E Muir and M Dawson (eds), *Judicial Activism at the European Court of Justice* (Cheltenham, Edward Elgar, 2013) 56–75.

[52] eg O Odudu, 'Interpreting Article 81(1): Object as Subjective Intention' (2001) 26 *European Law Review* 60–75; Odudu, 'The Wider Concerns of Competition Law' (n 15).

with public policy concerns that limit competition.[53] These narratives are largely unfulfilling because of the lack of any serious attempt to clarify the key terms that play the most important role in the evaluation of conflict situations as introduced above. The 'nature' of such conflicts, ie the question where competition starts and non-competition begins, is therefore, purely conceptually, relatively untouched.[54] However, the key academic contributions that aim to provide a better understanding of how non-economic interests can and should be dealt with in competition law lack this discussion as a starting point to frame the issue. Key contributions in this area for example interchangeably use the terms public or social interest as representing non-economic, non-market or non-competition interests.[55]

The point is that many proclaimed non-competition interests such as the environment, consumer protection, quality and fair trade are quickly qualified as non-competition or public interests but can, from the perspective of a competition perspective, be perfectly translated in terms of a competition rationale since they may be factors that allow for a certain singularity in the market. The setting of a collective standard by retail stores to buy exclusively fair trade products eliminates a competitive factor amongst those retailers. In this sense fair trade is something to compete with and it qualifies as a competition-relevant benchmark, which can be quantified in terms of efficiencies.[56] Therefore, when an environmental interest is pursued and competition is concomitantly restricted in the relevant market, it is not a given that this concerns a normative conflict between a competition and non-competition interest. The risk of such indeterminacy in the framing of competition *versus* non-competition interests is that a conflict of different norms is suggested, whilst in reality there is only one norm at play (false conflict). The first position introduced above, that advances a strict and static application of the competition rules, is problematic in this respect because it more or less assumes a distinction between competition and non-competition interests, and submits that questions of priority between the two require different fora. The second, quantification, position that was introduced is problematic because there exist social interests that may get lost when they are quantified too easily within an efficiency rationale. Moreover, by artificially replacing the conflict between normative spheres through a process of quantification, a potential platform for

[53] eg F Kieran, 'A Separation of Powers Approach to Non-efficiency Goals in EU Competition Law' (2013) 19 *European Public Law* 189; I Colomo, 'Market Failures, Transaction Costs and Article 101(1) TFEU Case Law' (2012) 37 *European Law Review* 541; Townley (n 15); Gerbrandy, 'Addressing the Legitimacy Problem for Competition Authorities Taking into Account Non-Economic Values' (n 35).

[54] But also see B de Witte, 'Non-market Values in Internal Market Legislation' in N Shuibhne (ed), *Regulating the Internal Market* (Cheltenham, Edward Elgar 2006) at 63, who uses non-market for interests that may have economic effects but whose driving power is not economic, and Kaupa, 'Maybe not Activist enough?' (n 51).

[55] See eg Townley (n 15), Odudu (n 15), Monti, 'Article 81 EC and Public Policy' (n 4) and T Prosser, *The Limits of Competition Law* (Oxford, Oxford University Press, 2005).

[56] eg T-34-92 *Fiatagri and New Holland Ford* [1994] ECR II-00905 and T-35-92 *John Deere* [1994] ECR II-00957, paras 52 and 81 (confirmed by the Court in C-7/95P [1998] ECR I-03111).

societal learning and discussion concerning the (manner of) pursuit (of) worthwhile societal interest is removed from the table too quickly and without sufficient deliberation. It is submitted that, it is exactly on the intersection between market and non-market or competition and non-competition that it becomes possible to discover which societal interests matter and *how* they matter specifically.[57]

Again, if sustainable environmental objectives are pursued by lowering the output of an industry then, seemingly, there is no manifest conflict between normative principles. That is to say, the restriction on competition that follows from a collective and coordinated lowering of output can be measured against the efficiency valuation that is set out by the competition law framework. An efficiency rationale could be used to evaluate whether the lowering of output can be justified in terms of the effects it has on competition, without, at first sight, doing harm to the wider environmental objectives underlying the lowering of output. Both the problem and the solution can be quantified. However, if the same objective is pursued on the basis of a society-wide compromise, without a clear rational basis, then an efficiency evaluation may not be the most appropriate framework to structure and decide on the conflicting societal objectives that are at stake. The first situation may be properly characterised as technocratic or managerial in nature and does not require a political instruction on the priority of objectives. This may be different in the second scenario. The problem is how to distinguish one social reality from the other. I will return to this problem further below.

The normative demands of social legitimacy therefore require a mechanism within the competition law assessment to single out the non-competition interest. It is submitted that the non-competition interest is concerned with objectives that fall outside of concerns that are related with the efficient functioning of markets—it is in this sense residual and defined through a process of opposition *within* the competition law analysis.[58] Indeed, this approach accepts the primacy of

[57] As discussed in ch 1, section V. *cf* also with the elegant suggestion of Hervey in M Cremona, *Market Integration and Public Services in the European Union* (Oxford, Oxford University Press, 2011) at 310:

> EU law is no more (if it ever has been) simply, or even essentially or fundamentally about markets, leaving 'the social' to the Member States and national law. The roles of EU internal market and competition law are no longer (if they ever were) simply a means to achieve movement between markets, opening markets, and preventing nationality-based discrimination. Rather, EU free movement and competition law should become (or have become) a locus within which we collectively determine the balance of values, between (economic) freedom and (social) security; between competition and solidarity.

[58] The primary purpose of an exercise that tries to clarify the non-economic objective is therefore to provide an operational conceptualisation that allows elemental social fabric to be distinguished from market objectives. See also H Putnam, 'Meaning and Reference' (1973) 70 *The Journal of Philosophy* 699:

> no operational definition does provide a necessary and sufficient condition for the application of any such word. We may give an 'operational definition' [...] but the intention is never 'to make the name synonymous with the description'. Rather 'we use the name rigidly' to refer to whatever things share the nature that things satisfying the description normally possess.

competition but creates a 'responsive' space for the non-competition interest to be identified as a residual and conflicting objective.[59] It opens up a dialogue concerning the regulatory choices of Member States. There is therefore an implicit understanding that non-competition interests are dynamic because the underlying fabric can develop and evolve. This is reflective of the idea that competition law does not exist in a vacuum but should be able to respond to the current values and aims of society and is as susceptible to change as political thinking and social objectives are generally. Because views and insights shift over a period of time, competition law is infused with the need to move and adapt towards developing notions of what is to be perceived as a non-competition interest.[60] For example, technological advances or new theoretical insights regarding theories of market failure and state failure can influence the idea of the non-economic.[61] The EU case in point here is *Corbeau* where the Court reviewed the Belgian postal monopoly created by laws in the 1950s and 1970s.[62] Demand for the courier service offered by Corbeau did not exist to the same extent then. In 1993, societal developments had outgrown the basis for the law at that time. Similarly, in *Albany*, certain individuals were concerned that they would be forced to join compulsory industrial pension schemes, despite the fact that the free market offered better deals.[63] The point here is that institutions and schemes introduced in the post-war period as a formulation of solidarity and common identity amongst workers are not necessarily viewed in the same light any more.

It follows from these considerations that the non-competition interest is far from a fixed idea that can be determined ex ante or on the basis of a form of dominance reasoning. That is to say a type of reasoning which says that as 'x is better than y in all respects', if conflicts arise in practice, x will always have priority over y. Instead, the non-competition interest is a dynamic and residual concept that forces an open and inclusive outlook within competition law assessments. Therefore, it is suggested that a conceptual clarification may prove beneficial for the qualification of a conflict as a true normative conflict or a false normative conflict.[64] Both require different responses, both from the judiciary and the competition authorities. This will be the central theme running through the case studies that will be discussed further below.

For example, one of the case studies will discuss the Dutch competition authorities' (ACM) approach to a sector-wide and supply-side coordinated decision to no

[59] This comes close to the perspective that Colin Crouch develops around the idea of 'assertive social democracy' that accepts the value and priority of markets in the economy, but is aware of their limitations and deficiencies as inappropriate in other areas of life; C Crouch, *Making Capitalism Fit for Society* (Cambridge-Malden MA, Polity Press, 2013) at 37.

[60] Whish and Bailey (n 6) at 21.

[61] P Behrens, 'Public Service and the Internal Market' in T Einhorn (ed), *Spontaneous Order, Organization and the Law. Roads to a European Civil Society* (The Hague, Asser Press, 2003) at 43.

[62] Case C-230/91 *Corbeau* [1993] ECR I—2534.

[63] Case C-67/96 *Albany* [1999] ECR I-5751.

[64] W Hohfeld, 'Some Fundamental Legal Conceptions as Applied in Judicial Reasoning' (1913) 23 *Yale Law Journal* 16–59.

longer sell chicken in the supermarkets that is produced under conditions that are considered unacceptable from an animal welfare perspective. The measure specifically targeted so-called 'plofkip', which is a name to describe chicken that is made to grow unusually fast so as to speed up meat production (broiler chicken). The ACM considered animal welfare as a competition interest that was to be quantified by consumers. Only if consumers would be willing to pay for the removal of broiler chicken, would the measures then be considered legitimate from a competition law perspective. As such, the pursuit of animal welfare was put in the hands of the consumer and conceptualised as a monetary consideration. This is problematic for several reasons. In view of what was discussed before, mostly because societal interests are placed in the hands of consumers without proper societal deliberation. Is it desirable to have consumers place a number on the welfare of chickens or the way environmental objectives are pursued?[65] Is consumer indifference in their purchasing decisions towards social and environmental attributes of the products concerned overriding? If we accept that effective competition constitutes an important public interest, but only one of the worthwhile interests in society, forming part of a range of other interests that are worth pursuing, we should ask the question if effective competition and 'broader' societal interests can be aligned harmoniously within an evaluative framework that requires the 'net efficiency result' to be positive.

This argument becomes more pressing if perceived in the context of European integration. As was argued in Chapter 1, European integration is committed to value diversity. A liberal society contains a diversity of social spheres and (should) make space for different kinds of valuation.[66] Therefore, a competition law framework that lacks the tools to deal with social differentiation may lack social legitimacy. The case studies will demonstrate that this boils down, mostly, to a question of institutional design. This social legitimacy problem is not recognised nor addressed within the discussed academic narratives on the integration of non-competition interests within EU competition law. Supporters of a strict application of competition law would argue that this is 'simply' a competition issue or not. The legislator can address and prioritise the issue of eg animal welfare on the basis of legislation. On that basis the issue of animal welfare is kept outside of the 'competition sphere' and will be addressed within a democratically legitimate framework. In other words, lacking a clear political instruction, animal welfare as

[65] M Sandel, *What Money Can't Buy* (New York, Farrar, Straus and Giroux 2012) at 202:

> People disagree about the meaning of books, bodies, and schools, and how they should be valued. In fact, we disagree about the norms appropriate to many of the domains that markets have invaded—family life, friendship, sex, procreation, health, education, nature, art, citizenship, sports and the way we contend with the prospect of death. But that's my point: once we see that markets and commerce change the character of the goods they touch, we have to ask where markets belong—and where they don't. And we can't answer this question without deliberating about the meaning and purpose of goods, and the values that should govern them.

[66] See Ch 1, section V.

a non-competition interest is not able to overrule competition interests. My objection to this approach is that the black-white approach that is reflected in it is too simple. As said, I think the competition platform is well suited as a starting point for societal dialogue and exactly because of the struggle that takes place between competition and non-competition interests, societal preferences are articulated more 'sharply' because one or the other needs to justify itself. This requires a clear articulation of the interests at stake.[67]

The quantification approach would argue in favour of a monetary value to be attached to the objective of animal welfare in order to allow for measurement and the ordering of objectives within the competition law framework. This approach carries, in a similar way, the risk of a removal of deliberation and conflict between different normative objectives by a direct translation of the objectives at stake within a language and grammar that may be unsuitable for the objectives at stake. The approach is more problematic because of the previously mentioned system of self-assessments that is part of all competition law regimes across Europe. On this basis economic operators are compelled to reason in the one-dimensional language that a monetarisation approach entails also in the pursuit of, for example, sustainability initiatives and animal welfare.

E. Competition Law as a Platform for Societal Dialogue

The alternative perspective that is proposed can be seen as a requirement in competition law to incorporate a close and context-specific assessment with respect to the potential normative plurality that is rooted within the different objectives that are pursued and are in potential conflict with competition interests. Importantly, the potential for competition law as a platform for societal development is under-recognised in both positions that were introduced above. To contextualise competition law from a perspective of societal learning is related to its constitutional meaning within internal market integration. As was submitted in Chapter 1, the social purpose of the internal market is to provide for an infrastructure for the conflict of norms within the Union that arise through the interaction between principles of economic integration and the pursuit of social interests on a Member State level.[68] In this respect, the competition rules are a tool for social dialogue

[67] For further reading on social theory insights on the value of social interest conflicts, see G Simmel, 'The Sociology of Conflict. I' (1904) 9 *American Journal of Sociology* 491; R Dahrendorf, *The Modern Social Conflict: An Essay on the Politics of Liberty* (London, Weidenfeld and Nicolson, 1988) at 25; L Coser, *The Functions of Social Conflict* (New York, The Free Press, 1956); AO Hirschmann, 'Social Conflicts as Pillars of Democratic Market Society' (1994) 22 *Political Theory* 206–09; A Somek, 'The Social Question in a Transnational Context', LSE Discussion Paper June 2011, at 27.

[68] See Ch 1, section III. See also KH Ladeur, '"Conflicts Law as Europe's Constitutional Form" … and the Conflict of Social Norms as Its Infrastructure' in C Joerges and C Glinski (eds), *European Crisis and the Transformation of Transnational Governance: Authoritarian Managerialism versus Democratic Governance* (Oxford, Hart Publishing, 2013) at 383.

because of the expressive value that is unlocked with the potential conflict between competition and non-competition interests. As said, within this dynamic, societal preferences are both tested and newly articulated.

From this perspective, the function and potential pitfalls of competition law within the Union has been helpfully described by former Commissioner Monti who explained the liberalisation policy of the Commission with respect to liberal professions:

> The present level of rules and regulation of liberal professions owe some debt to historical convention. How many are still needed in the modem world? Do they hinder or favour the development of the sector? Let me be provocative: Do they protect the consumers or the professionals? I propose to assess whether existing rules and regulations, which, remember, were devised and enacted in a very different economic context to that which exists today, continue to serve the legitimate purposes of the protection of the public interest. I would also like to assess whether they are the most efficient mechanisms available in the current market situation. It is clear that across the [European Union] there are different regulatory mixes. As the study shows, different regulatory choices produce different outcomes in the market and it is possible that some regulatory mixes have more beneficial market outcomes than others. *It should be difficult to argue against those that have the least distorting effect on the workings of the market, while delivering the same, or even higher, turnover.*[69] (emphases added)

On the one hand, in the first part of the speech, competition law is perceived as a tool for societal dialogue, testing old conventions and requiring renewed articulation of the pursuit of public interests. On the other hand, in the second part of the speech, there is the emergence of the idea that regulatory systems should be tested on the basis of their 'efficiency' merits: 'It should be difficult to argue against those that have the least distorting effect on the workings of the market, while delivering the same, or even higher, turnover'. This is the potential pitfall of the application of competition law. Efficiency-dominated thinking threatens the idea that a diversity of social spheres requires space for different kinds of valuation. Therefore, the challenge is to combine the function of competition law—properly conceived—within the Union, in terms of its potential to serve as a tool for societal dialogue, with the need to allow for social diversity. It is exactly on this point that the dialogue of mutual responsiveness that is developed in this chapter, at the intersection of competition and non-competition interests, will add to the ongoing debate.

F. Irreconcilable Conflicts within Competition Law

The three case studies that will be discussed in this section aim to further concretise the slightly abstract issues that were discussed before. The three case studies

[69] M Monti, Commissioner for Competition: European Commission, 'Competition in Professional Services: New Light and New Challenge's, for Bundesanwaltskammer Berlin (2003) available at http://europa.eu/rapid/press-release_SPEECH-03-149_en.htm.

originate from the Netherlands. As was briefly indicated before, competition law in the Netherlands was introduced relatively late, in 1998. The competition law that was then introduced is fully based and informed by the EU competition rules. Although originating within the Netherlands, the case studies allow generalisation with regard to the theoretical issue of combining competition and non-competition interests within competition law assessments as it was introduced in the previous section.

The cases illustrate concretely how specific approaches can inhibit the emanation of social objectives within competition rationales. The political and institutional context in the Netherlands provides good examples of how competition law frameworks may struggle to incorporate social differentiation. Historically, the Dutch system of social and economic policy-making has always been seen as heavily consensus based, coined as the 'polder model'.[70] Consensus has always been institutionalised in the Netherlands, which is reflected in a plurality of advisory and consultative bodies that exist at all levels of policy-making. The polder model is best characterised by the cooperation between employers' organisations, labour and the government. These talks are institutionalised within the Social Economic Council (SER). The SER is the central forum to discuss labour issues and, again, completely consensus based. It is acclaimed to have defused labour conflicts and avoided strikes.

Moreover, the consensus-based policy-making used to be reflected in so-called 'product boards' that would include all interested parties in a production chain within a public institutional framework and would be involved directly in the development of social and economic policy-making, relevant to the economic sector involved. As such, policy concerning livestock would involve the product board for livestock, meat and eggs as an intermediary between government and industry to ensure a smooth transition between politics and industry. Recently, as part of a government programme to reduce administrative control and tax cuts for industry, the product boards have been cancelled. However, consensus-based policy-making remains a central feature of Dutch politics, which is reflected in all of the case studies. The implication of this institutional background is that the Netherlands is characterised by a high degree of quasi-public-private governance settings. As will be demonstrated in the case studies, this leads to challenges for the application of competition law that are directly related to the issue of social differentiation and valuation in competition law. Therefore, although the Netherlands has a governance context that can be considered quite singular, the issues that will be discussed further below are relevant for the broader theme of the book since it is a concrete example of how the legal framework of the competition rules is able to integrate social context and provide for a constructive interplay of norms without harming social objectives that are worth pursuing.

[70] J Woldendorp, *The Polder Model: From Disease to Miracle? Dutch Neo-corporatism 1965–2000* (PhD thesis, Vrije Universiteit Amsterdam, 2005) 267–69. Also B Bouwens and J Dankers, 'Competition and Varieties of Coordination' in K Sluyterman (ed), *Varieties of Capitalism and Business History—The Dutch Case* (Abingdon, Routledge, 2015) at 103 ff.

This is the recurring theme in the case studies. The first case study is an example of the quasi-public-private context for policy-making based on the old product board institutional context and focuses on the judicial review of rules of a studbook. These rules were aimed at the health of the horses within the studbook but restricted stud-owners in the amount of offspring they could produce. A classic output restrictions case from the perspective of a competition rationale. The second and third case study concern government-induced but privately led sustainability initiatives that resulted in restrictions on competition. These two latter case studies are interesting because of the clear approach the ACM has taken in these cases towards the issue of integrating non-competition interests in the competition law framework, which is part of a broader programmatic objective of the ACM to instruct undertakings how to pursue sustainability initiatives.[71] In a nutshell, the position taken by the ACM, based on legislative instructions,[72] is that of a monetisation approach, quantifying all objectives in order to balance them with restrictions on competition, whilst taking the position that there should be a strict difference between legislation and the market. That is to say that if the legislator would want to prioritise certain objectives over competition, it can do this on the basis of legislation. In the absence of legislative prioritisation, everything falls in 'the market sphere' and needs to be quantifiable for the purpose of an efficiency analysis to determine the balance of objectives. The following subsections set out the case studies in more detail.

i. The Friesian Horse: The Legitimacy of Private-led Public Interest Objectives

The Friesian horse case demonstrates some of the difficulties that arise in the context of the pursuit of social objectives in a private context if the pursuit of those objectives is liable to restrict competition in the relevant market.

[71] These guidelines are all in Dutch: ACM Visiedocument Mededinging & Duurzaamheid, May 2014, www.acm.nl/nl/publicaties/publicatie/12930/Visie-mededinging-en-duurzaamheid. This policy and resulting cases from the ACM are part of an ongoing discussion in Dutch competition law literature: eg L Ankersmit, 'Het einde van de kiloknallers? De grenzen aan zelfregulering van duurzaam vlees onder het kartelverbod' (2011) *Actualiteiten Mededingingsrecht* 149–55; Gerbrandy (n 35); A Gerbrandy, 'Duurzaamheidsbelangen in het mededingingsrecht' (2013) 9 *Nederlands Tijdschrift voor Europees Recht* 326–33; H Pijnacker-Hordijk, 'Beoordeling van duurzaamheidsinitiatieven onder het mededingingsrecht' (2013) *Markt & Mededinging*; J Mulder, 'Op het snijvlak van onafhankelijkheid en openheid: wat is de rol van de ACM in een duurzamemaatschappij?' (2014) *SEW* 565–78; J Mulder, 'Een duurzame maatschappij, wat mag dat kosten?' (2015) 1400 *NJB* 1912–20.

[72] Besluit van de Minister van Economische Zaken van 6 mei 2014, nr. WJZ / 14052830, houdende beleidsregel inzake de toepassing door de Autoriteit Consument en Markt van art. 6 lid 3 Mededingingswet bij mededingingsbeperkende afspraken die zijn gemaakt ten behoeve van duurzaamheid. At the time of writing there was a public consultation pending with new legislative instructions for the competition law assessment of sustainability initiatives, accessible at www.internetconsultatie.nl/mededingingenduurzaamheid. These new legislative instructions were created in response to the cases, discussed further below, where the ACM rejected sustainability initiatives from companies and the academic response referred to in the previous footnote. Within the new instructions, inter alia, future assessments of the ACM are to take account of 'long-term interests', 'measures as a whole' and potential broad 'societal interests'. The methodology to calculate these benefits remains, however, largely quantitative and based on consumer behaviour and 'willingness to pay' assessments.

The Friesian is a horse breed originating in a province, Friesland, in the Netherlands. It is easily recognised by its black coat colour and long, thick mane and tail, its long silky hair on the lower legs, deliberately left untrimmed. The breed has faced extinction many times and is considered one of the oldest breeds ever to be recorded. The *Friesch Paarden-Stamboek* (Friesian Horse Studbook) is traced as far back as 1879. Cross-breeding is not allowed and only the offspring of approved stallions can be entered into the main studbook registry. Stallions must be approved for breeding in order for their offspring to be eligible for registration with the Friesian Horse Studbook (FPS). A stallion's breeding approval is always conditional. The FPS was, at the time that the concerned measures were reviewed, recognised as an 'official pedigree' by the previously highlighted product board for livestock, meat and eggs. Within this context FPS had to adhere to requirements that were set for 'official' pedigrees across the Netherlands and this included the organisation of a pedigree in a way that would ensure that the preservation of the breed would be guaranteed on the basis of concrete breeding improvement programmes, to be determined by the FPS.

Historically, the Friesian horse has issues with inbreeding because the population of the Friesian went through a few so-called 'bottle necks' where the impact of just a few male horses was very big in the growth of the population. The FPS therefore strictly regulated the number of inseminations that the approved studs were allowed and forbids them to go above 180 per year until the offspring has been approved by the FPS. Members that would go above the 180 per year were liable to be sanctioned. In 2006, two of the approved studs that were owned by the same party, were particularly popular and surpassed the offspring limitation by 156 inseminations. The owner objected to the sanctions that were imposed on him, arguing that the restrictive pedigree rules qualified as output restrictions. Output restriction are generally considered as so-called 'hardcore' competition law infringements that are unlikely to be justified on the basis of Article 101(3) TFEU (and its Dutch equivalent). The question put on the table of an appellate court in the Netherlands was whether the FPS had indeed unduly restricted competition of its members by setting limits to the output of approved studhorses on the basis of concerns related to the health of the animal.[73]

More specifically, the question before the court was whether the health of the Friesian horse could be qualified as a restriction of competition that had to fulfil the efficiency requirements of Article 101(3) TFEU. The appellate court focussed on the 'legitimacy' question and posited in that respect that the nature of the non-competition interest at stake in this case could not be considered as a 'weighty public interest' and therefore it could not 'justify' an infringement on the competition rules without fulfilling Article 101(3) TFEU. The pursuit of the health of the Friesian horse could not be considered as a sufficiently 'special' public interest to be excluded from the scope of the competition rules. Hence, it had to fulfil

[73] Appellate Court of Arnhem 10-03-2010, Case nr 200.002.794.

the exemption criteria of Article 101(3) TFEU. Therefore, implicitly the appellate court valued the restrictions as falling within the competition-dominated sphere, which therefore had to be exempted on the basis of the potential efficiencies, which they produced. On this point lies the judgment's interest, specifically with respect to the question of the valuation of the restrictions as insufficiently 'weighty'. Which interests do qualify as sufficiently weighty or worthy and how should they be pursued? Apparently, the quasi-public-private governance context did not provide the measures with sufficient public interest weight. The appellate court did not expand on its reasoning and this makes the judgment weak but the judgment's interest lies exactly in this weakness as it indicates the clarification that is needed on this point and raises the issue of how private parties can pursue objectives that restrict competition but, concomitantly, potentially qualify as a genuine social objective.[74] This issue is further explored below in the following two case examples and section IV returns to it specifically from the perspective of mutual responsiveness.

ii. The Energy Agreement for Sustainable Growth: The Societal Relevance of the Process or the Rationality of its Outcome?

Another interesting case revolves around the so-called Energy Agreement for Sustainable Growth (EASG). The EASG involved 40-something organisations in the definition of a more sustainable energy and climate policy for the Netherlands.[75] Central government organised so-called round-tables with a wide array of organisations. These included regional and local government, employers' associations and unions, nature conservation and environmental organisations, and civil society organisations and financial institutions.[76] Central government has framed these round-table negotiations and the current outcomes as 'agreements' with and amongst the private sector with respect to the pursuit and attainment of sustainability objectives. Obviously, where such agreements include private actors that also compete in the market, issues with competition law may arise. From a competition law perspective, a problematic part of the early parts of the agreement concerned the closing down of coal-fuelled power plants from the 1980s. The energy companies that took part in the negotiations decided to close down the plants as part

[74] See on this issue specifically inter alia H Schepel, 'Delegation for Regulatory Powers to Private Parties under EC Competition Law: Towards a Procedural Public Interest Test' (2002) 39 *Common Market Law Review* 31–51. Also Gerbrandy (n 35) at 83; J. Mulder, 'Finding the Public Interest and the Case of the Friesian Horse', 2013 ACLE Conference Paper http://acle.uva.nl/events/competition--regulation-meetings/conference-papers-9th-cr-meeting-2013.html.

[75] The plan can be found at www.ser.nl/nl/publicaties/overige/2010-2019/2013/energieakkoord-duurzame-groei.aspx. See for the preliminary competition law assessment by the Dutch competition authorities ACM: ACM, 'Notitie ACM over sluiting 5 kolencentrales in SER Energieakkoord' www.acm.nl/nl/publicaties/publicatie/12033/Notitie-ACM-over-sluiting-5-kolencentrales-in-SER-Energieakkoord/.

[76] Interestingly, consumer interests were not represented.

of an incentive path that would encourage the development of more sustainable energy sources in the long-run. The trade association of the Dutch energy industry, Energie Nederland (EN) asked for an analysis from the Dutch Competition Authority (ACM) on whether the planned agreement on closing down the coal power plants could be reconciled with Article 101 TFEU (and its equivalent in Article 6 of the Dutch Competition Act). Despite the fact that the agreement was part of the wider overarching objectives of accord, the ACM qualified it simply as an agreement between undertakings within the meaning of the competition rules. The assessment of the ACM concluded that, firstly, the closing down of the coal power plants constituted an output restriction that would be caught under Article 101(1) TFEU. By reducing production capacity, the undertakings involved would have less capacity to produce energy than they would have had without the agreement.[77] Secondly, it could not be exempted on the basis of the exemption criteria of Article 101(3) TFEU.[78] For the latter analysis it conducted an extensive cost-benefit analysis in accordance with the more economic approach as set out by the European Commission. The value of the agreement's benefits was determined on the basis of the costs of other (efficient) measures that, as a consequence, would not have to be taken (ie avoided costs). The ACM concluded that comparing the estimated price increase with the environmental benefits revealed that the agreement's expected drawbacks to consumers in terms of price for electricity would be substantially higher than the estimated value of the positive effects in terms of avoided costs. Consequently, the closing down of the coal-fuelled power plants was removed from the accord.

The case of the EASG demonstrates the challenges for competition law frameworks in the valuation of a social interest, which is not necessarily quantifiable and, mostly, unveils a lacking institutional framework for the pursuit of social objectives by private parties. The interest at stake in this case, which cannot be valued completely within the competition law framework, concerns the process that has led to a specific organisational structure and brought together various societal actors in a way that has made them somehow co-responsible for these objectives, thereby creating mutual obligations to ensure that they operate according to the social value attached to these objectives. As was discussed in Chapter 1, this is a social value that is easily ignored within consequentialist, utilitarian-driven standards that clearly prefer evidence-based technocratic outcomes to 'political jostling and compromise that may lack evidence of a clear rational basis'.[79]

[77] The production capacity that is to be closed under the agreement represents approximately 10% of total production capacity available in the Netherlands.

[78] (i) the agreement contributes to the improvement of the production or distribution of goods or to the promotion of technical or economic progress; (ii) the agreement allows consumers a fair share of the resulting benefit; (iii) no restrictions that are not indispensable are imposed on the undertaking involved; and (iv) competition is not eliminated in respect of a substantial part of the products or goods in question.

[79] Monti, 'Article 81 EC and Public Policy' (n 4).

The application of competition law in these types of cases raises the question of the position and role of competition in society. Is competition an instrument or an overarching goal? The fact that the closure of the coal plants was a seemingly inherent part of the achievement of broadly supported societal objectives regarding the environment played no part in the analysis of the ACM. This narrow framework of analysis, combined with the way the ACM got involved in the discussion regarding the EASG illustrates how a socially relevant issue can be disembedded from its societal function through the narrow lens of an efficiency-driven framework. From the perspective of social legitimacy and mutual responsiveness this case mostly demonstrates the institutional lacuna in the way that societal interests and competition objectives can be aligned with each other. Economic operators that are in competition lack a framework within which private initiatives with a social component can be pursued in a way that there is not an inherent tension of a potential infringement of the competition rules.[80] One could also think of some more contentious issues.

In 2001, different producers of milk in the Netherlands initiated a plan to raise the price of a litre of milk by 10 cents for a period of two months as a response to the outbreak of the foot-and-mouth disease, and the extra income would be reserved for the farmers to partly compensate their damages.[81] This is an interesting example of a private initiative with a potentially genuine societal, redistributive aim, which was cancelled owing to its anti-competitive effects. The problem here and also in the other cases discussed is the legitimacy of the pursuit of the social objective to the detriment of competition. At some point the pursuit of these objectives in a private context needs to be fed by some kind of public legitimacy. As AG Jacobs noted in the *Albany* case, echoing the words of Adam Smith (cited in the introduction to this chapter):

> The rationale underlying the competition rules' wide scope of applicability *ratione materiae* is simple. It can be presumed that private economic actors normally act in their own and not in the public interest when they conclude agreements between themselves. Thus, the consequences of their agreements are not necessarily in the public interest.[82]

The point is that there are societal contexts where a more dynamic model is called for, within which, on the basis of public-private deliberation, both societal goals and effective competition can be aligned and pursued on constructive terms. I mean dynamic in the sense that some of these societal objectives arise as a response to a certain social reality or in the context of a process that engages different societal actors. This chapter argues that a dynamic model can be distilled from existing case law of the Court of Justice if one takes the perspective of responsiveness.

[80] See also Gerbrandy (n 35).

[81] Case 2432—17 April 2001. The ACM has a collection of cases on this topic: www.acm.nl/nl/onderwerpen/concurrentie-en-marktwerking/duurzaamheid-en-mededinging/kennisbank-duurzaamheid.

[82] A-G Jacobs Opinion in Case C-67/96 *Albany* [1999] ECR I-5751, para 184.

In a more harmonious setting, the ACM analysis concerning EASG could have taken place within an institutional representative context that could interrelate with the representative public stakeholders that have been part of the process that has led to the Energy Agreement. Instead, the fact that the closing down of the coal plants was part of a wider agreement concerned with bringing together various societal actors with the intention of creating co-responsibility for the objective of a sustainable environment was ignored. The narrow framework of analysis that the ACM applies illustrates how the application of the competition law framework can disembed a social agreement from its societal function and reduce it to efficiency benefits; failing to recognise the importance of the societal discursive process as an overarching value in itself. Ideally, there would be an institutional framework that allows the competition interests and a societal discursive process to align towards a common shared interest. This relates back to the social purpose of the internal market that was highlighted in Chapter 1; the constructive interplay of different normative orders within the European Union. Such institutional EU law framework is lacking at the moment and it remains difficult for (associations of) undertakings to develop or be part of a discursive process that pursues social interests, in congruence with competition law. This last point is clearly present in the third case example below.

iii. The Chicken of Tomorrow: The Market Rules When the State Retracts?

In the beginning of 2013 the main branch organisation on foodstuffs in the Netherlands announced that 'another chicken' would be introduced into the Dutch supermarkets. Most of the organisations from the poultry sector, the chicken meat producing industry and supermarkets came together during a round-table meeting to discuss a more sustainable production of chicken meat ('the Chicken of Tomorrow'). The aim of these negotiations was to introduce a sector-wide sustainability impulse on the basis of the introduction of a minimum standard for animal welfare. Dutch livestock holders responded to the increased attention within Dutch society to animal welfare and the explicit request from the Dutch government to incorporate animal welfare objectives within the supply chain.[83]

The Dutch government had indicated that the policy in this area should be informed and guided on the basis of sector-wide initiatives.[84] A sector-wide statement of intent was signed that committed the livestock sector, the meat producing industry and retailers to move towards a status quo where only sustainable produced meat would be sold in 2020. The Chicken of Tomorrow initiative was

[83] The case has led to quite some debate in the Netherlands: Ankersmit, 'Het einde van de kiloknallers?' (n 71); J Mulder, 'Een duurzame maatschappij, wat mag dat kosten?' (n 71).

[84] Letter with the position of the Dutch government, 'Toekomst van de intensieve veehouderij' Official parliamentary documents: 28973 nr 134 accessible at https://zoek.officielebekendmakingen.nl/kst-28973-137.html.

introduced within this context.[85] Again, the ACM was invited to assess this cooperation from a competition law perspective. The assessment of the ACM concluded that the sustainability initiative qualified as a restriction of competition on the retail market for chicken meat because 'regularly' produced chicken meat would no longer be for sale in Dutch supermarkets.

The ACM concluded that the initiative limited choice for consumers and removed a competitive benchmark. The analysis of the ACM aimed to provide guidance to companies that would want to implement such sustainability initiatives in the future as part of their self-assessment. For this purpose, the ACM by way of 'guidance' conducted a 'willingness to pay' analysis.[86] It considered that the first condition of Article 101(3) TFEU, ie the contribution to the production or distribution of goods or to promoting technical or economic progress, would only be fulfilled if the measure would eventually lead to a higher consumer surplus, which was to be determined on the basis of the willingness of consumers to pay more for the 'added' animal welfare. Consumer panels were asked to choose between different types of chicken meat that differed with regard to the level of animal welfare that was taken into account in the production of the meat. The economic analysis of the ACM concluded that the willingness to pay for the Chicken of Tomorrow was not enough to justify the increase in the consumer price.[87] On balance, according to the study, there would be a negative effect on consumer surplus of 0.64 euro per kilogram of chicken breast.[88] Moreover, the ACM considered that it would be preferable if, instead of introducing a minimum standard, consumers would be better informed about animal welfare on the basis of labels. This could then also become part of a broader commercial strategy of a supermarket to attract consumers who value these sustainable products. According to the ACM it would therefore be more appropriate if sustainability initiatives were to focus on measures to improve animal welfare by educating consumers and stimulating consumer confidence in other types of production, as part of a competitive process.[89] The initiative was, subsequently, disbanded.

[85] ACM assessment of the sustainability agreements 'Chicken of Tomorrow' (ACM/DM/2014/206028), January 2015, p 2. The minimum standards that were part of the Chicken of Tomorrow initiative concerned agreements on the keeping of a slower-growing breed of chickens, more space for chickens on the basis of a reduction of the number of chickens in a set space, improved conditions within the stables, stricter controls on animal welfare standards, a more natural day-night rhythm, lowering of the use of antibiotics, the use of 100% sustainable soya food and a number of other environmental measures. The initiative met with a lot of criticism, which according to animal welfare organisations, would improve the conditions of chickens only marginally. Indeed, at first sight, the measures do look minimal and the improvements in chicken welfare would not be ground-breaking.

[86] M Mulder, S Zomer (ACM), T Benning and J Leenheer (CentERdata), 'Economic Assessment ACM, Effects of the Chicken of Tomorrow—Costs and Benefits for Consumers' (October 2014) (accessible at acm.nl).

[87] ibid, at 26.

[88] ibid,.

[89] ACM assessment of the sustainability agreements 'Chicken of Tomorrow' (ACM/DM/2014/206028), January 2015, p 7.

This analysis of the ACM is problematic when framed within the introduced perspective. This is strikingly illustrated on the basis of the example of a consumer who does not buy chicken. All possible considerations that consumers may have not to buy chicken are reduced in the analysis of the ACM to a lack of willingness to pay for sustainable produced chicken. Moreover, the emphasis put on the artificiality of the assessment of consumer behaviour and explicitly not 'the actual selection process in stores' undermines the credibility of the whole assessment. The narrow framework of assessments values a multiplicity of intentions and social interests in terms of a monetary interest. Moreover, the actual selection process of consumers in supermarkets should be central in an analysis that looks for the 'reality' of consumer interests. Importantly, because there has been research suggesting that it is unlikely for the average consumer to consistently and consciously consider animal welfare in the actual purchase decision.[90] Secondly, there may be no real choice for consumers for whom the more expensive free-range chicken is not affordable but who think that animal welfare is important. Hence, a minimum standard constitutes a different measure and a different social purpose than to unveil the exact 'willingness to pay' of a consumer. More importantly, the introduction of a minimum standard does not inhibit the use of labels and commercial strategies for supermarkets to attract consumers who value sustainable products. As an aside, the position of the ACM regarding 'the better way' to achieve sustainability in the production of chicken meat is highly questionable. The use of eco-labels is assigned a very questionable role in securing sustainability goals.[91] The crucial point is that the analysis of the ACM is, explicitly, published as guidance material for undertakings to pursue these objectives in their self-assessments. On this point there is therefore an explicit and inherently limited valuation with respect to what matters and how things matter in society on the basis of a narrow competition-based perspective.

Therefore, from a broader societal perspective several question marks can be placed on the approach to animal welfare that the ACM supports in its analysis. By pursuing animal welfare on the basis of consumer preference and to conceptualise it as a monetary consideration, a choice is made for a particular type of society. That is a society where the consumer or the market largely determines whether and how to achieve certain societal interests. To put social objectives in the hands of the consumer is, however, a profoundly political decision. Is it socially desirable to place a number on the welfare of a chicken or the way we interact with the environment? Perhaps, but the point is that (i) this is not necessarily the case; (ii) it is socially relevant to discuss it exactly at the point that market and non-market interests intersect; and (iii) the competition platform constitutes a suitable starting point for this dialogue even if only to switch to another platform where competition will be but one of the interests at stake. The ACM, however, would

[90] eg RE Horne 'Limits to Labels: The Role of Eco-labels in the Assessment of Product Sustainability and Routes to Sustainable Consumption' (2009) 33 *International Journal of Consumer Studies* 175–82.

[91] ibid, at 181.

point to the fact that this is simply either a competition problem or not. The government can decide on this issue and prioritise animal welfare through legislation should it so desire.[92] Thus the issue would be taken outside the sphere of competition and it would be solved within a democratically legitimate framework.[93]

Importantly, the position of the ACM, again, points towards the institutional lacuna that has been now repeatedly discussed in the context of the previous case studies. The outcome in the cases led to calls from civil society actors and the concerned economic sectors for a reconsideration of the constraints of competition law with respect to sustainability initiatives. It initiated a broader debate within the Netherlands regarding the right balance between EU competition law and sustainability. Importantly, the Dutch government considered the way the competition law framework was applied as an ongoing obstruction to its ambition to increasingly involve non-state actors in the formulation of socio-economic policy as part of the future-proofing of its legislative agenda. Subsequently, the Ministry of Economic Affairs was tasked with the challenge to resolve this tension.

G. The Consumerist Push from the Commission

This resulted in a legislative instruction document that set out some amended conditions for the ACM to take into account in its assessment. The main changes concerned, firstly, the fact that positive long-term effects of initiatives would have to be considered with respect to the agreement, in so far as it was part of a wider package of measures, *as a whole.* Secondly, the potential positive effects would not only have to take into account the long-term—future—users but also the positive effects for *society as a whole.* These two criteria can be seen as a direct response

[92] It is important to note that the Chicken of Tomorrow case is in flux. The case has led to a political debate on the reach of the competition rules and, in particular the interaction between competition and sustainability initiatives. Currently, the Dutch Ministry of Economic Affairs is in the process, in coordination with the European Commission, of drafting new legislative guidance on how sustainability initiatives and competition law should interact.

[93] As a side note it is important to note that this position may not be tenable in light of EU case law. Dutch competition law is not applied in a vacuum but is part of the EU legal order and the ACM applies the EU competition rules. One of the important objectives for which the TFEU creates a legal basis is to denounce outdated national practices and legislation. eg, in the case of *Consorzio Industrie Fiammiferi* a royal decree of 1923 in Belgium was set aside that protected match manufacturers in Italy from competition. The Court decided in that case that the national competition authority is required to set national legislation aside as soon as it is established that such legislation is in conflict with EU competition rules. In the European context, the competition rules thus also apply to national legislation and serve as a strong crowbar to force national governments to reconsider restrictive competition practices, also if it is of a legislative nature. Especially now that the ACM has established that this sustainability initiative is in conflict with (EU) competition law, a state measure that would incorporate these commitments should, in principle, be put aside by the ACM on the basis of the CIF judgment. Case C-198/01 *Consorzio Industrie Fiammiferi*, [2003] ERC I-08055.

to the two cases that were highlighted before, potentially leading to different outcomes of the ACM assessment.[94]

However, when the draft instruction was put up for a so-called internet consultation, where interested parties could provide comments on the draft proposal, the European Commission stepped in.[95] The Commission objected to the new criteria and considered them to be contrary to EU competition law. In its letter the Commission emphasised that it considered the assessments of the ACM with respect to the two cases to be fully in accordance with EU competition law. Firstly, the Commission considered that the requirement to take into account the agreement as a whole was potentially confusing. The Commission acknowledges that it may be necessary to assess an entire package of agreements but posits that this is already part of the third condition of Article 101(3), which deals with the indispensability of the restrictions. Where an agreement that restricts competition is necessary for the benefits accrued by other parts of a package of an agreement, it may already fulfil the 'indispensability' condition of Article 101(3). This of course assumes that those benefits have been monetised. More revealing is that with regard to the new instruction the Commission also considered that it is not possible to consider the potential positive effects for *society as a whole*. This would be contrary to the text of Article 101(3) TFEU which explicitly refers to the positive advantages for the 'users' of the products or services:

> If certain policy goals are considered valuable for society as a whole, while not by the consumers in the relevant market, *regulation* is the right tool to safeguard them and not competition law. In other words, competition law does not stand in the way of regulation to achieve these goals, but cannot substitute for the absence of such regulation. (emphasis added)

Therefore, the Commission urged the government not to install the legislative instruction. In other words, the Dutch government could not simply ask or agree with the private sector to pursue public interest objectives if this would negatively impact competition. On the basis of the Commission's robust response, the Minister decided to disband the proposal and return to the drawing board.[96]

[94] Arguably, if the EASG would have been considered as a whole and, consequently, if the closing down of the coal plants would not have been considered in isolation, the outcome of the assessment may have been different. Perhaps, the fact that the closing down of the coal plants was an inherent part of a wider agreement, concerned with bringing together various societal actors with the intention of creating co-responsibility for the objective of a sustainable environment, could then have influenced the assessment. Moreover, with respect to the Chicken of Tomorrow, the willingness to pay for an assessment conducted by the ACM would have to be considered insufficient since the potential positive benefits for society as a whole would also have to be considered.

[95] Commission letter, attachment to Government Letter of Ministry of Economic Affairs to Parliament, 23 June 2016 (Kamerstukken II 2015/16, 30196, 463).

[96] See the official governmental communication to Parliament from the Minister of Economic Affairs to Parliament: Kamerbrief Minister van Economische Zaken aan de Tweede Kamer inzake Mededinging en Duurzaamheid, 24 October 2016 (*Kamerstukken II 2016/17*, 30196, 480, pp 1–6). The proposal that has since then been developed and now exists as draft legislation creates an option for

The Commission's response indicated that competition restrictive interests would have to be more actively regulated in case they served wider societal objectives. The rationale that lies underneath this response is concerned with a question of accountability. The competition rules provide accountability by way of the market. Private measures that aspire the achievement of public interest are provided with legitimacy because they can be accounted for in terms of the market. That is to say, if the measures on balance manages to achieve an outcome that leads to an increase in consumer welfare then there is no need for the political sphere to get involved and provide legitimacy to the development of measures that aspire to serve a public interest. If there is no such accountability for measures that aspire to serve the public interest but, in the process, limit competition, then they require another source of legitimacy in the form of direct government regulation.

As such the Commission clearly prefers a traditional command-and-control 'state-centred' perspective with respect to state-market-society relationships. This position of the European Commission is, however, not fully in accordance with the case law of the European Court of Justice. The Court of Justice has created avenues in its case law that do allow for deontological—producerist—structures to be exempted from the scope of the competition rules.[97] I will now turn to this line of case law.

III. RESPONSIVENESS IN THE CASE LAW OF THE COURT

The normative concern that underlies the discussed case examples is that the valuation that is implicit in the evaluative standards that may be applied to social realities on the basis of EU competition law are based on a metric that risks doing violence to potentially genuine and worthwhile aspects of those objectives. Moreover, the unitary metric transforms the balancing of competing values into an issue of calculation and the nature of the problem is thereby transformed into one of quantification. Quantification risks losing the expressive value that is inherent in a normative conflict and the consequent potential for social learning that arises from it. The following sections group together lines of cases from the Court that demonstrate a certain responsiveness to potential normative conflicts between the valuation that is implicit in the competition rules and the social realities addressed by these rules. These approaches from the Court serve the purpose of building

a *declaration of general effect* with respect to private sustainability initiatives that meet certain criteria. Private initiatives that pursue sustainability objectives can, on this basis, be turned into legislation. The explanatory memorandum accompanying the draft law notes that the potential EU competition law obstacles can thus be circumvented and resolved. The underlying rationale of the new proposal is comparable with the Dutch system of collective labour negotiations that operate on the basis of a similar process of declarations of general effect. See further on this G Monti and J Mulder, 'Escaping the Clutches of EU Competition Law' (2017) 5 *European Law Review* 635.

[97] Case C-209/07 *Competition Authority v Beef Industry Development Society Ltd and Barry Brothers (Carrigmore) Meats Ltd* [2008] ECR I-8637, paras 34–36 and Case C-309/99 *Wouters* [2002] ECR I-1577.

blocks that can be reconstructed into a coherent model of adjudication from the perspective of social legitimacy and address the institutional lacuna that was identified in the case studies above. Approaching the case law of the Court of Justice from the perspective of responsiveness provides a novel view, in particular, on requirements of institutional design within the Member States that are required to pursue EU competition restrictive social interests. As will be discussed in the subsections below, the perspective of responsiveness brings together lines of case law that are not normally considered to be related but, as will be demonstrated, can be grouped together from the perspective of responsive adjudication.[98]

A. The *Albany* Building Block: Valuation of Different Social Spheres

Firstly, it is important to emphasise that the Court at various times and in various ways has shown clear responsiveness towards the incompatibility between the rationale behind the pursuit of interests of a social nature and the normative concerns of the competition law framework. The Court has, for example, ruled in several cases that agreements in the context of collective bargaining between workers and employers may be excluded from the scope of Article 101 TFEU.[99] The Court held in *Albany* that some restrictions on competition are inherent in the pursuit of collective agreements between organisations representing employers and workers. Specifically, agreements entered into within the framework of collective bargaining between employers and employees that are intended to improve employment and working conditions must, *by virtue of their nature and purpose*, be regarded as not falling within the scope of Article 101(1) TFEU.[100] In the cases of *Drijvende Blokken* and *Brentjes*, which the Court issued on the same day, the same reasoning was used with respect to a supplementary pension fund set up for employees in the transport and dock industry and the building sector.[101] The reasoning of the Court to allow a genuine societal process some leeway from the competition rules was implicitly confirmed in *Pavlov*. In *Pavlov*, the Court refused to apply the *Albany* reasoning to self-employed medical specialists because the agreement was not concluded in the context of collective bargaining between employers and employees and aimed at improving employment conditions of workers, but was aimed at working conditions amongst self-employed persons.[102] In other words, the nature of the negotiations was not one of social protection.

[98] The lines of cases have been discussed similarly in earlier publications: Mulder, 'Op het snijvlak van onafhankelijkheid en openheid' (n 71); Mulder, 'Een duurzame maatschappij, wat mag dat kosten?' (n 71); Mulder, 'Finding the Public interest and the Case of the Friesian Horse' (n 74).

[99] Case C-67/96 *Albany* [1999] ECR I-05751; Joined Cases C-115-117/97 *Brentjens* [1999] ECR I-6025; Case C-219/97 *Drijvende Blokken* [1999] ECR I-6121.

[100] Case C-67/96 *Albany* [1999] ECR I-05751, para 60.

[101] Joined Cases C-115-117/97 *Brentjens* [1999] ECR I-6025, para 57; Case C-219/97 *Drijvende Blokken* [1999] ECR I-6121, para 47.

[102] Joined Cases C-180/98 to C-184/98 *Pavlov and Others* [2000] ECR I-6451, para 67; also Case C-222/98 *van der Woude* [2000] ECR I-7111, para 22.

It is, therefore, the nature and purpose of an agreement that may warrant its exclusion from the scope of the competition rules, specifically, because of the impediment of the social objectives that are pursued with these agreements, should they be subject to the competition rules. It is clear that certain restrictions of competition are inherent in collective agreements between organisations, representing employers and workers. However, the Court considered that some of the social policy objectives pursued by such agreements would be undermined if management and labour were subject to the liability of infringing the competition rules when seeking to adopt measures to improve conditions of work and employment. The Court, implicitly, recognises a tension between, in terms of the debate above, the competition and non-competition interests at stake in this case. The social value of the process of negotiation between employers and employees overruled the application of the competition law framework.[103]

In its decision the Court referred to the Treaty that provided that the EU Commission is to promote close cooperation between Member States in the social field, particularly in matters relating to the right of association and collective bargaining between employers and workers. Even though the Court refers to the *social objectives*, what is essentially protected with this legal analysis is the process of negotiation between management and labour. In other words, it is mainly the process that makes the exclusion of the negotiations necessary. The organisational structure that brings together these societal actors makes them co-responsible for these objectives, thereby, creating mutual obligations and ensuring that they operate according to the social value attached to these objectives. As such, this allows for a certain responsiveness to the process within which social objectives are pursued to be recognised and valued in the application of the competition law framework.

The Court, in *Albany*, exempted collective agreements from the application of the competition rules by reference to the objectives and values that are mentioned in the Treaty and thereby created an alternative type of valuation of this societal process within the legal framework of the internal market. It is through an extension of this rationale that the pursuit of other social objectives than the improvement of conditions of work and employment that a rationale of social legitimacy based on the idea that different types of social spheres require different kinds of valuation. The rise of non-economic objectives was discussed in the Chapter 1. In the Lisbon Treaty there is more emphasis on *sustainable* development of a Europe based on *balanced* economic growth and price stability, policies based on

[103] See also A Sangiovanni, 'Solidarity in the European Union' (2013) 196 *Oxford Journal of Legal Studies* 1–29; P Craig, 'Competence and Member State Autonomy: Causality, Consequence and Legitimacy' in HW Micklitz and B de Witte (eds), *The European Court of Justice and the Autonomy of the Member States* (Oxford Legal Studies Research Paper No 57/2009); J Shaw, *Social Law and Policy in an Evolving European Union* (Oxford, Hart Publishing, 2000); G de Búrca, *EU Law and the Welfare State: in Search of Solidarity* (Oxford, Oxford University Press 2005); M Dougan and E Spaventa (eds), *Social Welfare and EU Law* (Oxford, Hart Publishing, 2005).

a spirit of solidarity, a competitive *social market* economy aimed at full employment and *social progress*, the pursuit of *social cohesion* and a high level of *protection and improvement of the quality of the environment* combined with requirements of consistency among Union policies and consequent duty to take into account the environment, consumer protection employment, social protection, education, health, combating discrimination in defining and implementing Union activities. The reasoning in *Albany* provides for an argument that the evolution in scope of non-market interests within the primary law framework is not without legal consequences and should make space for different kinds of valuation of different social spheres. However, to the puzzle of social legitimacy, *Albany* provides only a limited answer since the analysis regarding the exact *nature* and *purpose* of the agreement is largely absent from the Court's analysis, which merely mentions that the category of agreements, ie collective agreements resulting in social dialogue, and the purpose, ie the establishment of additional pension funding, does not '*by reason of its nature and purpose, fall within the scope of Article* [101 (1) TFEU]'.[104] The reasoning of the Court on this point is therefore circular and incomplete. That is to say that the Court did not provide a rationale for the alternative valuation to be implemented but rather assumed that the process of negotiation between capital and labour served a purpose that was inherently outside the reach of the competition rules. This assumption lacks reasoning so as to distinguish the competition from the non-competition interest. The next subsections explore whether these gaps in the legal analysis can be addressed by reflecting on other lines of case law of the Court where it has been responsive to social context in different parts of the legal analysis.

B. *Poucet and Pistre* Building Block: A Rationale for the Alternative Valuation of a Non-economic Social Sphere (Part One)

The Court incorporates responsiveness in its legal qualification of an entity as 'undertaking' for the purpose of the competition rules. The legal definition of an entity as undertaking within the competition rules depends on the *economic nature* of the activity concerned. It is therefore possible for an entity to be treated as an undertaking with respect to part of its activities and not for others.[105] For example, universities that are partly operating within a market environment (eg with competitive tailored business courses) and partly fulfilling public educational tasks are only subject to the competition rules in so far it concerns activities that are in potential competition with other educational service providers. The definition

[104] Case C-67/96 *Albany* [1999] ECR I-5751, paras 62–64.

[105] Case C-222/04 *Cassa di Risparmio di Firenze* [2006] ECR I-00289; Case C-118/85 *Commission v Italy* [1987] ECR 2619. *cf* also Cases C-205/03 *P Fenin* [2006] ECR I-06295 and T-155/04- *Selex* [2006] ECR II-04797 for a situation where different activities could not be analysed separately.

of an undertaking is functional to the application of the competition rules.[106] Therefore, what is to be considered as an economic or non-economic activity cannot be given a priori status and requires a case-by-case analysis. It is not the formal status of an entity (eg a public undertaking) or an entire sector (eg health-care), nor the way in which it is funded, which determines whether its activities are deemed to be subject to the competition rules (economic or non-economic); it is the *nature of the activity itself*.[107] For the purpose of this analysis the Court has considered 'the nature, the aim and the rules' applicable to a given activity.[108] Participation in a market has been considered as representing activities of an economic nature, 'any activity consisting in offering goods and services on a given market is an economic activity'.[109] Therefore, it is not the mere fact that the activity may, in theory, be carried on by private operators that is decisive, but the fact that the activity is carried out *under market conditions*. On this basis, tasks that are exclusively exercised in the public interest, such as the maintenance of air navigation safety[110] and the conservation of nature,[111] have been excluded since those activities, in the concerned cases, were to be considered as inherent to 'the essential functions of the State'.[112] Cases that involve the 'exercise of official authority' for the purpose of regulating the market (as opposed to participating in it) do not fall within the scope of competition law.[113] The essence of this reasoning originates from the judgment in *Höfner and Elser*.[114] The Court there considered that the activity was economic in nature, since 'employment procurement has not always been, and is not *necessarily*, carried out by public entities' (emphasis added). Similarly, in the case *Ambulanz Glöckner* the Court reasoned that health organisations providing services on the market for emergency and ambulance services were held to be undertakings, because 'such activities have not always been, and are not *necessarily*, carried on by such organisations or by public authorities' (emphasis added).[115] On this basis the Court assessed Italian customs agents to be undertakings because: 'they offer, for payment, services consisting in the carrying out of customs formalities, relating in particular to the importation, exportation and

[106] Case 118/85 *Commission v Italy* [1987] ECR 2599, para 7: 'the State may act either by exercising public powers or by carrying on economic activities of an industrial or commercial nature by offering goods and services on the market'.

[107] Case C-82/01 *Aéroports de Paris* [2002] ECR 2002 I-09297.

[108] Case C-118/85 *Commission v Italy* [1987] ECR 2599, para 7.

[109] Joined Cases C-180/98 to C-184/98 *Pavlov and Others* [2000] ECR I-6451, para 75; and Case C-475/99 *Ambulanz Glöckner* [2001] ECR I-08089, para 19. See also Case C-309/99 *Wouters and Others* [2002] ECR I-1577, para 47; and Case C-82/01 *P Aéroports de Paris v Commission* [2002] ECR I-9297, para 79.

[110] Case C-364/92 *SAT Fluggesellschaft ('Eurocontrol')* [1994] ECR I-43.

[111] Case C-343/95 *Diego Calì & Figli* [1997] ECR I-1547.

[112] ibid, para 22.

[113] Case T-313/02 *Meca-Medina and Majcen v Commission* [2004] ECR II-0000, para 41.

[114] Case C-41/90 *Höfner and Elser* [1991] ECR I-1979.

[115] See paras 67 and 27, respectively, of the Opinions of AG Jacobs in *Ambulanz Glöckner* [2001] ECR I-08089 and Joined Cases C-264/01, C-306/01, C-354/01 and C-355/01 *AOK-Bundesverband and Others* [2004] ECR I-2493.

transit of goods, as well as other complementary services such as services in monetary, commercial and fiscal areas'.[116] Hence, there was, owing to the infrastructure that governed these activities, no 'necessity' for the exclusion of the competition sphere.

This reasoning is essentially responsive to social context since it has to be determined *when* an activity is carried out under market conditions. This responsiveness is demonstrated mainly in cases that involved a conflict between competition and what has been coined as principles of solidarity. The Court has established in these cases that conduct, which is undertaken *with the objective of capitalisation* is incompatible with the functioning of a sector on *the basis of principles of solidarity*. The Court has never truly developed this principle of capitalisation but the implicit reasoning suggests some manifest irreconcilability between, for example, 'capitalisation' and 'solidarity'. In *Poucet and Pistre*, the question arose as to the compatibility of compulsory membership of a social security scheme with competition law. In this case the Court referred to the nature of the organisations concerned: 'the concept of undertaking within the meaning of Articles [101 and 102 TFEU] does not encompass organisations charged with the management of social security schemes of the kind referred to in the judgments of the national court'. The Court decided, 'those schemes pursue a social objective and embody the principle of solidarity'.[117] The manner in which the principle of solidarity is embodied should form the basis of the classification and the '*exclusively social*' function fulfilled by those organisations 'is based on the principle of national solidarity and is entirely non-profit-making'. The Court also noted that 'the benefits paid are statutory benefits bearing no relation to the amount of the contributions'.[118]

This line of case law that originated with *Poucet and Pistre* is interesting because it demonstrates a rationale for the valuation of a different social sphere. A social sphere that is inherently irreconcilable with the sphere of competition because of the underlying rationales. There is responsiveness from the EU competition law framework in the sense that local rationales such as solidarity are recognised as the driving rationales of a particular social context and allowed an autonomous existence within an alternative type of valuation. There is, however, *mutual* responsiveness because the pursuit of these objectives is made conditional on the presence of certain institutional requirements and safeguards. Therefore, the Member States need to respond to requirements that set out the institutional conditions within which these objectives can be pursued. For example, in *Cisal*, the Court had to determine whether the compulsory membership of a national insurance scheme was subject to the competition rules.[119] The Court held that the Italian national

[116] Case C-35/96 *Commission v Italy* [1998] ECR I-3851, para 37.

[117] Joined Cases C-159/91 and C-160/91 *Poucet and Pistre* [1993] ECR I-637.

[118] ibid.

[119] Case C-218/00 *Cisal* [2002] ECR I-691. In paras 38 to 40 of *Cisal*, it is stated that solidarity was evidenced by the fact that contributions were not systematically proportionate to the risk insured against, nor were the benefits paid strictly proportionate to the insured person's earnings.

institute for insurance against accidents at work (INAIL), operated in accordance with the principle of solidarity. Importantly, it was also subject to the control of the state, which set the level of contributions and determined that membership was to be compulsory. That INAIL indeed operated in accordance with the principle of solidarity was determined on the basis of an analysis of a number of elements: 'that the insurance scheme was financed by contributions the rate of which was not systematically proportionate to the risk insured; the amount of benefits paid was not necessarily proportionate to the insured person's' earnings'.[120] The Court therefore held that the INAIL did not carry on an economic activity, with the result that competition law did not apply. In the case of *FFSA and Others*, the question related to the monopoly of management of an old-age insurance scheme conferred on a mutual fund.[121] In this case the Court considered that the entities, which managed the retirement scheme qualified as undertakings. The determining factors in this case concerned 'the fact that membership of the retirement scheme was optional, that the scheme was managed in accordance with the principle of capitalisation and that benefits were calculated on the basis of contributions made'.[122] In the second relevant part of the *Albany* judgment, a Dutch sectoral pension fund was held to be an undertaking for the purposes of competition law on the basis of the same reasons. The Court concluded that an element of competition was introduced, which impacted the assessment and opened up the sector to the competition rules. That there were also circumstances present, such as the pursuit of a social objective or the fact that the fund was non-profit-making were '*not sufficient* to "deprive" the activity carried on of its economic nature'.[123] Similar reasoning is adopted in other cases of the Court.[124]

The *nature of the activity* has thus both a formal and substantive component in the case law of the Court. The formal conditions relate to the existence of a market, state prerogatives or obligations of solidarity.[125] Most importantly, the formal notion of the non-competition interest determines that some rules or regulations do not enter 'the sphere of economic activity' because the state defines the public interest criteria and the essential principles with which its rules must comply and retains the power to adopt decisions. In that situation rules adopted by private associations remain *within state primacy* and are not covered by the Treaty rules applicable to undertakings. Other Treaty articles could of course then be triggered (internal market rules or Article 106 TFEU).[126] In the solidarity cases the formal

[120] ibid, paras 38–42.
[121] Case T-106/95 *FFSA and Others* [1997] ECR II-00229.
[122] ibid, para 21.
[123] Case C-67/96 *Albany* [1999] ECR I-5751.
[124] Joined Cases C-180/98 to C-184/98 *Pavlov and Others* [2000] ECR I-6451, C-355/01 *AOK-Bundesverband and Others* [2004] ECR I-2493.
[125] Case C-222/04 *Cassa di Risparmio di Firenze* [2006] ECR I-00289.
[126] For a given service to qualify as an economic activity under the internal market rules (free movement of services and freedom of establishment), the essential characteristic of a service is that it must be provided for remuneration. The service does not, however, necessarily have to be paid by those

criteria relate to the institutional safeguards that are in place and implement and necessitate entities to follow principles of solidarity. In substantive terms, solidarity has been identified as operating on the basis of another normative order. In the words of AG Fennelly in *Sodemare:*

> the existence of systems of social provision established by Member States on the basis of the principle of solidarity does not constitute, as such, an economic activity, so that any inherently consequent restriction on the free movement of goods, services or persons does not attract the application of Treaty provisions. Social solidarity envisages the inherently uncommercial act of involuntary subsidization of one social group by another. Rules closely connected with financing such schemes are more likely to escape the reach of the Treaty provisions on establishment and services. Thus, pursuit of social objectives on the basis of solidarity may lead Member States to withdraw all or part of the operations of social security schemes from access by private economic operators.[127]

Hence, solidarity constitutes a normative order that cannot be subsumed under a market order that operates on the basis of a principle of capitalisation. That is to say that the Court identifies that sectors that operationalise under a principle of capitalisation or under a principle of solidarity are representative of different normative spheres and that the normative sphere that is applicable in a sector that is organised on the basis of a principle of solidarity cannot be captured in a legal framework that is based on a competition rationale. That is *not* to say that the social and competition spheres are always irreconcilable. The interplay of the two, potentially irreconcilable principles is pointedly indicated by the Court in *AOK Bundesverband*, where sickness funds operated on the basis of a solidarity system but the German legislator introduced elements of competition for the purpose of attracting members:

> the legislature introduced an element of competition with regard to contributions in order to encourage the sickness funds to operate in accordance with principles of sound management, that is to say in the most effective and least costly manner possible, in the interests of the proper functioning of the German social security system. Pursuit of that objective does not in any way change the nature of the sickness funds' activity.[128]

In this short passage the Court demonstrates the expressive value of the interplay of competition and non-competition interests, which requires a specific and concrete articulation of the limits of both solidarity and competition. The moment of societal learning is reached where the Court establishes the limits of both spheres

benefiting from it. The economic nature of a service does not depend on the legal status of the service provider (such as a non-profit making body) or on the nature of service, but rather on the way a given activity is actually provided, organised and financed. In practice, apart from activities in relation to the exercise of public authority, to which internal market rules do not apply, it follows that the vast majority of services can be considered as 'economic activities'. For Art 106 it all depends on a procedural review of the organisation of the public service concerned.

[127] Case C-70/95 *Sodemare and Others v Regione Lombardia* [1997] ECR I-03395, para 29.

[128] Joined Cases C-264/01, C-306/01, C-354/01 and C-355/01 *AOK Bundesverband* [2004] ECR I-02493, para 56.

in a concrete manner. Hence, in these cases the Court is willing and able to implement a different kind of valuation towards a social sphere that is governed by the principle of solidarity.

The 'solidarity cases' have given impetus to a line of literature that considers solidarity as an independent principle within EU competition law[129] and the principle has been conceived as a potential 'buttress' against internal market law and competition law specifically.[130] Solidarity is generally framed as a principle that necessarily opposes the objectives of competition law and as a signalling post for an area where Member States have retained full control over national policy orientation. The discussion of case law, however, indicates that Member States do have to take into account principles of good governance in the organisation of sectors that are based on the principle of solidarity. The Court has limited the solidarity 'buttress' to situations where the exercise of solidarity is under strict state supervision and takes place within a legislative framework where objectives are installed by the state.[131]

In other words, these sectors have to be consistently organised in accordance with the solidarity principle in order to merit an existence outside of the scope of the competition rules. Moreover, as the Court noted above in *AOK Bundesverband*, there is no inherent irreconcilability between competition and solidarity. Instead, the Court assesses, *in concreto*, whether solidarity and competition are reconcilable. As such, solidarity is not necessarily a completely separate or 'unique' area, which is singularly able to act as a buttress against the evils of the internal market. Potential irreconcilable normative conflicts between societal organisational principles are not limited to these two spheres and it is submitted that the rationale employed by the Court in solidarity cases can be extended beyond the potential irreconcilability of just solidarity and competition. From the perspective of social legitimacy the Court of Justice has, with the *Albany* and *Poucet Pistre* lines of case law, established a rationale for context specific valuations of different social spheres and set out the beginning of a more comprehensive approach that, in a dynamic and context-specific way, instructs the constructive interplay between competition and non-competition spheres.

Below I explore a potential further extension of this rationale on the basis of another line of cases.

[129] A Winterstein, 'Nailing the Jellyfish: Social Security and Competition Law' (1999) 20 *European Competition Law Review* 324; M Ross 'Article 16 EC and Services of General Economic Interest: from Derogation to Obligation' (2000) 25 *European Law Review* 22; E Szyszczak, 'Public Services in Competition Markets' (2001) 21 *Yearbook of European Law* 35, at 64; M Ross, 'Promoting Solidarity: From Public Services to a European Model of Competition?' (2007) 44 *Common Market Law Review* 1057; N Boeger, 'Solidarity and EC Competition Law' (2007) 32 *European Law Review* 319; E Szyszczak, *The Regulation of the State in Competitive Markets in the EU* (Oxford, Hart Publishing, 2007).

[130] TK Hervey, 'Social Solidarity: a Buttress against Internal Market Law' in J Shaw (ed), *Social Law and Policy in an Evolving European Union* (Oxford, Hart Publishing, 2000) 31–47.

[131] Case C-437/09 *AG2R Prevoyance*, para 46; also Case C-222/04 *Cassa di Risparmio di Firenze* [2006] ECR I-00289.

C. *Wouters*: A Rationale for the Alternative Valuation of a Non-economic Social Sphere (Part Two)

The cases discussed above take into account the nature of the activity on the basis of the question whether they take place in market or non-market conditions to determine whether or not specific entities operate as undertakings. The rationale set out by the Court in *Poucet an Pistre,* which disapplies the competition law framework in cases where a sector is organised on the basis of principles of solidarity, is extended in case law where there is a potential conflict between the competition rules and private-led initiatives in the development and pursuit of social interests. Here we enter a line of cases, which starts with the *Wouters* case.[132] The central question in *Wouters* is to what extent and under what circumstances (associations of) undertakings can *themselves* formulate objectives as a public interest that can be pursued to the detriment of effective competition. In *Wouters*, the Court qualified a decision of the Dutch Bar to prohibit multi-disciplinary partnerships between attorneys and accountants as not infringing Article 101(1) TFEU. The Bar was charged on the basis of Dutch law to adopt deontological rules that assured the correct exercise of the attorneys' profession. The Court first established that the regulatory powers that were provided to the Bar were not strictly supervised by the Dutch state and there was scope for the Bar to define public interest criteria and the way to pursue them.[133] Consequently, the Bar qualified as an association of undertakings. Therefore, even though the Bar functions as the regulatory body of a profession, whenever it adopts its regulations, the competition rules apply. However, the Court of Justice considered that not every restriction of competition that flows forth from this necessarily falls within the prohibition laid down in Article 101(1) TFEU. The *overall context* of the restriction matters:

> More particularly, account must be taken of its objectives, which are here connected with the need to make rules relating to organisation, qualifications, professional ethics, supervision and liability, in order to ensure that the ultimate consumers of legal services and the sound administration of justice are provided with the necessary guarantees in relation to integrity and experience (…). It has then to be considered whether the consequential effects restrictive of competition are inherent in the pursuit of those objectives.[134]

The reasoning adopted by the Court calls to mind the reasoning adopted by the Court in *Albany* where it considered that certain agreements *by virtue of their nature and purpose* should be regarded as not falling within the scope of Article 101(1) TFEU. However, where in the *Albany* context it was the societal

132 Case C-309/99 *Wouters and Others* [2002] ECR I-1577. Three key pieces on Wouters: J Vossestein, annotation in (2002) 39 *Common Market Law Review* 841–63, Monti, 'Article 81 EC and Public Policy' (n 4) 1057–99; I Wendt, *EU Competition Law and Liberal Professions: an Uneasy Relationship?* (Leiden, Brill Academic Publishers, 2012).

133 Case C-309/99 *Wouters and Others* [2002] ECR I-1577, para 68.

134 ibid, para 97.

process that mattered and influenced the nature and purpose of the agreement, in *Wouters* the reasoning of the Court is specifically related to the rationality of the objectives of an agreement. The Court did not consider possible efficiencies of the restrictive agreements. The decisive question was whether the prohibition was *necessary* for the proper practice of the legal profession. Whether or not Dutch attorneys could provide more efficient advice to companies if one entity could provide legal and accounting services at the same time was not at stake. Instead, the Court created a possibility to lift a restriction on competition from the strict application of the competition law framework to a domain beyond the efficiency logic of the exemption framework and, consequently, towards another type of valuation. The objective of integrity was considered to be a legitimate objective and all the consequent restrictions on competition were to be evaluated on the basis of another test. This alternative valuation took place on the basis of the question whether the restrictions of competition are inherent to the pursued objective and do not go further than necessary.[135] Although not explicitly stated, the inherent logic at work here appears to be fairly clear. The Court assumes that integrity of a profession is not an objective that can be translated within the efficiency targets of the exemption conditions of Article 101(3) TFEU and hence merits an existence outside of this framework. Therefore, it can be said that the Court was explicitly responsive to the non-competition context and the potential negative impact of changing that context to the benefit of efficiency considerations.[136] Thus, the Court created a rationale to incorporate responsiveness in the legal review of restrictions on competition on the basis of a context-specific assessment of the rationale behind competition restrictive measures; a rationale that goes beyond competition versus solidarity conflicts. As was discussed with regard to *Albany*, the Court in that case did not provide a rationale for how an alternative valuation of a social sphere that potentially falls outside of the reach of the competition sphere

[135] ibid, paras 98–106.

[136] See for another opinion Vossestein (n 133) at 859:

> On the other hand, in my view it may not be excluded that the Court had competitive considerations in mind. The Court refers in paragraph 97 to the need '*to ensure that the ultimate consumers of legal services* and the sound administration of justice are provided with the *necessary guarantees in relation to integrity and experience*'. The Court may be viewing the regulation, looked at in an overall context, as improving quality, enhancing consumer choice and thus pro-competitive.

Whish sees Wouters mainly as the application of the inherent restrictions case law in a regulatory context:

> This seems to be a different application of the concept of ancillarity from that in earlier case law: the *Wouters* case is concerned with what could be described as 'regulatory ancillarity', whereas earlier judgments were concerned with 'commercial ancillarity'; perhaps the use of these two terms would be useful in, first, demonstrating a continuity with the earlier case law, through the common use of the idea of ancillarity, while also capturing the difference between the two situations, by distinguishing commercial and regulatory cases.
>
> Whish and Bailey (n 6) at 132.

is to be implemented but rather assumed that the process of negotiation between capital and labour served a purpose that was inherently outside the reach of the competition rules. As said, this assumption lacks reasoning so as to distinguish the competition from the non-competition interest. Similarly, in *Wouters* there is to some extent an assumption from the Court that the integrity of the attorneys' profession is irreconcilable with the exemption criteria of Article 101(3) TFEU.

An opinion of AG Wahl in the case *FNV Arts v the Netherlands* illustrates, how these gaps can be potentially addressed.[137] In this case, the Dutch ACM protested against provisions in a collective agreement that set the minimum rates of musicians who were employed on the basis of self-employed contracts for an orchestra in the Netherlands (so-called 'employee replacements'). The ACM had taken the view in this case that such provisions in a collective agreement were problematic and prohibited on the basis of Article 101 TFEU because the self-employed musicians qualified as undertakings for the purposes of the competition rules. Since the self-employed compete on the basis of their fees, the collective agreement was to be considered as a restriction on competition. The collective labour organisation FNV argued against this reasoning and submitted that the collective agreement for the self-employed was a necessary measure against strategies of social dumping. Employers that employ the self-employed for lower wages install incentive mechanisms that will eventually damage the regularly employed because it will negatively impact their willingness to pay higher wages to the 'normal' employees. Moreover, the self-employed are not truly independent agents because they are treated on the same basis as the regular employees. Because they therefore qualify as falsely self-employed, the *Albany* exemption would apply and the rates that are set would not be subject to competition enforcement.

The assessment proposed by the AG to determine whether the collective agreement was subject to the competition rules is relevant for a further development of the *Wouters* and *Albany* frameworks in the context of the mutual responsiveness model. In *FNV Arts v the Netherlands*, the AG argues that for the assessment whether a socially legitimate aim is subject to competition enforcement, it is required to determine *in concreto* whether a *real* and *serious* danger of social dumping exists and, if so, whether the designed provisions are necessary to prevent that dumping from taking place.[138]

Therefore, on the basis of this context-specific approach the social goals should manifest themselves concretely and are to be provided with a genuine right to exist before the application of the competition framework can be excluded and, hence, an alternative valuation should take place. This context-specific *in concreto*

[137] Opinion AG Wahl in Case C-413/13 np (*FNV Kunsten v Netherlands*).

[138] Opinion AG Wahl in case C-413/13, *FNV Kunsten v Netherlands*, paras 88–95. The Court did not go into this specifically but, instead tuned the judgment towards the conditions of the assessment that would have to determine whether the musicians qualified as employees or undertakings and it referred the case back with guidance on this question (paras 38–42).

approach advocated by AG Wahl is reminiscent of the Court's reasoning in *AOK Bundesverband*, cited above, where the Court considered to what extent an introduction of competition to part of the activities of a sickness fund was capable of concretely affecting the nature of its activities. The Court established whether the application of competition principles threatened the nature of solidarity in that specific situation. Equally, the approach of the AG puts emphasis on the expressive value of the interplay of competition and non-competition interests, which requires a specific and concrete articulation of the limits of both competition and genuinely irreconcilable non-competition interests. Again, a moment of societal learning is reached where the Court establishes the limits of both spheres in a concrete manner.

This part of the (extended) *Wouters* framework is concerned with the substantive interplay between the principles of competition and potentially irreconcilable non-competition interests. However, the framework of analysis applied by the Court should also include a formal component that is concerned with the public law infrastructure within which non-competition interests are pursued. This formal component would have to be concerned with the question whether the (association of) undertaking(s) in question is sufficiently embedded in a public law framework to be considered *enabled* to define the public interest it pursues and in what way. This boils down to the question if the *legitimate* interest can be defined independently by a private professional association or whether it has to flow as a compulsory obligation from a public law framework?[139] We can refer back on this point to the words of AG Jacobs that were cited above:

> It can be presumed that private economic actors normally act in their own and not in the public interest when they conclude agreements between themselves. Thus, the consequences of their agreements are not necessarily in the public interest.[140]

Thus, the formal requirement is concerned with the embedding of private actions within a public law framework. Can all private parties just set aside the competition rules on the basis of self-defined actions in pursuit of a non-competition interest?[141] As was explained before with respect to the case study on the Energy agreement, at some point the pursuit of these objectives in a private context needs to be fed by some form of public legitimacy. The Court's approach to this issue in *Wouters* is confused. The Dutch Bar association was governed by public law, established by statute, in order to further a public interest. For that purpose, it was endowed with regulatory powers, which required it to guarantee, in the public interest, the integrity (in terms of independence and loyalty to the client) of the legal services of its members. However, the Court approached this aspect of the case mainly to determine whether this public law context was sufficient to

[139] Similarly Whish and Bailey (n 6) at 135.
[140] A-G Jacobs Opinion in Case C-67/96 *Albany* [1999] ECR I-5751.
[141] See also Gerbrandy (n 35) at 81–103.

exclude it from the scope of competition law, such as with regard to public interest tasks that are exclusively exercised in the public interest, such as the maintenance of air navigation safety[142] and the protection of the environment.[143] Next, in its analysis of the social context these regulatory powers played a role for the Court to establish the singular position of lawyers vis-à-vis accountants in the Netherlands, which required the former to act exclusively in the interest of their clients. It remained, however, rather unclear what the facets of a public law institutional framework would have to look like, to accommodate the pursuit of private initiatives that pursue a non-competitive interest.

This aspect has also not been clarified in later case law of the Court where the *Wouters* analysis was applied. The Court did extend the *Wouters* approach by holding that Article 101 is not applicable for restrictive practices that: ensure the proper practice of the pharmaceutical profession *(Ordre national des pharmaciens)*;[144] safeguard the integrity of sports (anti-doping rules in *Meca Medina*);[145] ensure the quality of accountancy services (restrictions on entry in the market for professional training in *OTOC*);[146] provide guarantees to consumers about the services they receive (price control by an association of geologists in *Consiglio nazionale dei geologi*) and road safety measures *(API)*.[147] However, it is not easy to generalise from these instances. The Court's general approach is simply to discuss whether there is a 'legitimate objective' being pursued,[148] but it gives little clue as to the benchmarks by which one judges *legitimacy*.

Nevertheless, the *Wouters* type of assessment by the Court adds another factor to the potential social legitimacy model of the Court. The *Albany* and *Poucet Pistre* lines of case law have established the requirement for context-specific valuations of different social spheres and set out the beginnings of a more comprehensive rationale to determine, in a dynamic and context-specific way, the constructive interplay between competition and non-competition spheres. *Wouters* can be seen as an extension of this idea, widening the scope of potential irreconcilable non-competition interests to be transposed to a type of valuation outside of the strict application of the exemption criteria of Article 101(3) TFEU. At this point it becomes necessary to look more specifically at the institutional frameworks that would be required to legitimately restrict competition. As said, *Wouters* leaves a gap on this point, leaving it rather unclear what the facets of a public law institutional framework would have to look like, to accommodate the pursuit of private initiatives that pursue a non-competitive interest.

142 Case C-364/92 *SAT Fluggesellschaft ('Eurocontrol')* [1994] ECR I-43.

143 Case C-343/95 *Diego Calì & Figli* [1997] ECR I-1547.

144 In Case T-90/11 *Ordre national des pharmaciens* (ONP) ECLI:EU:T:2014:1049, para 38.

145 In Case C-519/04 P *Meca Medina*,ECLI:EU:C:2006:492, para 45.

146 In Case C-1/12 *Ordem dos Técnicos Oficiais de Contas* ECLI:EU:C:2013:127, paras. 94–95.

147 In Case C-136/12 *Consiglio nazionale dei geologi* ECLI:EU:C:2013:489, para 54.

148 In Case *ONP* ECLI:EU:T:2014:1049 reference is made to 'reasons of general interest' (para 38) and Case C-184/13 *Anonima Petroli Italiana* ECLI:EU:C:2014:2147, para 48.

D. The Requirements of *Mutual* Responsiveness in *Arduino, Cipolla* and *Mauri*

The gap that the *Wouters* case law leaves can be better understood and partly addressed if a connection is made with yet another but strongly connected line of cases, where the Court has established under what circumstances a restrictive state measure violates EU competition law, according to the *effet utile* principle.[149] These concern, inter alia, a number of cases that originated from conflicts between the Italian regulatory schemes for attorneys and the internal market rules. As was quoted above in section II, an important policy objective of the Commission in the period 2000–05 was to test potentially out-dated regulatory schemes within Member States concerning liberal professions. In particular, the Commission had targeted the regulatory systems of the legal profession around Europe. The Commission concluded that some regulations were affected by the 'weight of tradition', 'fail to see how things can be done differently', and did not or no longer regulate in the public interest.[150] This liberalisation initiative was partly triggered by two cases. One of these cases was actually *Wouters*, which, as was discussed above, provided quite some deference to the Dutch Bar on the issue whether a restrictive rule was necessary and proportionate to pursue the public interests involved, stating that 'the Bar of the Netherlands is entitled to consider that the objectives pursued by the … Regulation cannot … be attained by less restrictive means'.[151] The Commission was concerned that this deference would further restrict market access and competition in the sphere of liberal professions.[152]

On the same day as the *Wouters* judgment, the Court of Justice also issued a judgment in the case of *Arduino*, which further antagonised the Commission and provided impetus for its liberalisation agenda. This judgment concerned Italian legislation on the fixing of lawyers' fees. The Court of Justice reviewed this legislation in light of Article 4(3) TEU in conjunction with Article 101 TFEU. Since Article 101 TFEU applies to the conduct of undertakings, the Court of Justice had only by way of exception held that national measures can also be covered by Article 101 TFEU in situations where Member States can be seen as not cooperating in good faith in the application of Union law. On this basis the Court of Justice has held that such 'faithful cooperation' is infringed where a Member State requires, favours or reinforces an anti-competitive agreement or abandons its own

[149] For an extensive and deep analysis of this line of case law, see Schepel, 'Delegation of Regulatory Powers to Private Parties under EC Competition Law' (n 74).

[150] Communication from the Commission: Professional Services-Scope for More Reform: Follow-Up to the Report on Competition in Professional Services, at 10, COM (2005) 405 final (5 September 2005), available at http://eur-lex.europa.eu/LexUriServ/LexUriServ.do?uri=COM:2005:0405:FIN:EN:PDF. See for an extensive overview LS Terry, 'The European Commission Project Regarding Competition in Professional Services' (2009) 29 *Northwestern Journal of International Law & Business* 1.

[151] Case C-309/99 *Wouters and Others* [2002] ECR I-1577, para 108.

[152] See Terry, 'The European Commission Project Regarding Competition in Professional Services' (n 151) at 26.

regulatory powers and delegates them to private operators, who then infringe the competition rules.[153] In *Arduino*, the Court held that although part of the lawyers tariff scheme was delegated to the Italian Bar association, the scheme, nevertheless, never lost its character of a state scheme since in the Italian Bar submitted only a draft tariff scale to the Minister for Justice, who had the power to have the draft amended or defer its application.[154] It is important to highlight that because of the fact that these cases involve national regulation or some form of governmental validation, there is a connection to free movement law. This dimension was not addressed in *Arduino* but came to fruition in the *Cipolla* case, partly as a result of the Commission's arguments that were presented in the case.[155] In this case, the Court considered with regard to the same Italian tariff scheme for attorneys, that the fixing of minimum tariffs deprived lawyers that were established in another Member State of the possibility of competing effectively with lawyers established inside Italy who would have better opportunities for winning clients than competing lawyers established abroad (who would arguably have higher costs accessing the Italian market). As a consequence, the freedom to provide services was restricted. The Court considered that the restriction could be justified, provided that

> there is a correlation between the level of fees and the quality of the services provided by lawyers and whether, in particular, the setting of such minimum fees constitutes an appropriate measure for attaining the objectives pursued, namely the protection of consumers and the proper administration of justice.[156]

The Court indicated that this correlation was not unlikely on the basis of the specificities of the Italian market and the more general asymmetry of information between 'client-consumers' and lawyers: 'Lawyers display a high level of technical knowledge which consumers may not have and the latter therefore find it difficult to judge the quality of the services provided to them'.[157] The Court referred the case back to the national court on the basis of these guidelines. It can be argued that with the *Cipolla* case the Commission achieved at least partly its objective of creating a legal framework that is able to test whether historical regulatory schemes are still genuinely concerned with the protection of public interests.

The applicability of the free movement rules in situation where both Article 101 TFEU and the free movement rules apply has some implications for the model of adjudication that is developed in this chapter, which will be touched upon in the next section. However, what matters for current purposes is that the Court in this line of cases determines, inter alia, what is required from a public law framework, which involves the private sphere in the development of policy measures, if

153 Case C-35/99 *Arduino* [2002] ECR I-01529.
154 ibid, para 41.
155 Case C-94/04 *Cipolla and Others* [2006] ECR I-11421.
156 ibid, para 66.
157 ibid, para 68.

it is to retain the character of a government measure.[158] Therefore, this case law provides guidelines for situations in which states instruct private parties to take certain measures but the measures, nevertheless, *retain* the character of a government scheme. In *Arduino*, the Court ruled that this is the case, for example, when members of a professional organisation can be regarded as experts that can be considered *independent* from the undertakings that are involved in policy-making and when they are legally required to take into account not the interests of the undertakings or their associations but, mainly, to take into account the 'public interest' and the interests of undertakings in other sectors or the interests of those who use the services in question.[159]

In *Reiff*, the 'official character' of legislation was retained because the public authorities had to 'ensure that the boards fix their tariffs by reference to considerations of the public interest'.[160] In the *Mauri* case, the Court held that the emanation of the state in such proceedings can take place in several ways but, in any case, at key moments, should be potentially decisive within a process that shapes the measures. [161] Certainly, as far as the measure will only be binding after the state has approved it, then the measure retains the character of a government measure, provided that such approval is not just a rubber stamping exercise but has actually involved substantive engagement with the formation of the measure.[162]

The rationale that lies underneath most of the cases discussed in this section now becomes more apparent. That rationale is concerned with a question of accountability as a source of legitimacy. The competition rules provide accountability by way of the market. Private measures that aspire to the achievement of public interest are provided with legitimacy because they can be accounted for in terms of the market. That is to say, if the measures, on balance, manage to achieve an outcome that leads to an increase in consumer welfare then there is no need for the political sphere to get involved and provide legitimacy to the development of measures that aspire to serve a public interest. If there is no such accountability for measures that aspire to serve the public interest but, in the process, limit another public interest, then they require another source of legitimacy.

The emphasis of the Court in the discussed lines of cases (*Albany, Poucet and Pistre and Wouters*), on some level, all share a concern for unveiling this additional source of legitimacy and it becomes most apparent in the *Arduino* and *Mauri* types of cases.[163] The willingness of the Court to be responsive to social

[158] See also Case C-185/91 *Reiff Bundesanstalt für den Güterfernverkehr* [1993] ECR I-5801; Case C-153/93 *Delta* [1994] ECR I-2517; Case C-140/94-C-142/94 *DIP e.a.* [1995] ECR I-3257; and Case C-35/96 *Commission/Italy* [1998] ECR I-3851.

[159] Case C-35/99 *Arduino* [2002] ECR I-01529, paras 36–38.

[160] Case C-185/91 *Reiff Bundesanstalt für den Güterfernverkehr* [1993] ECR I-5801, para 22.

[161] Case C-250/03 *Mauri* [2005] ECR I-01267.

[162] ibid, paras 33–36.

[163] See also Schepel (n 2) at 51:

> the Court has fashioned a public interest test that transforms Community competition law into a rudimentary set of procedural norms of good governance for private regulation. It is

context, which is substantively irreconcilable with the normative framework of the competition rules, is therefore conditional upon the presence of another source of legitimacy, which can be found in the design of the public law framework surrounding private initiatives that restrict competition. In *Wouters*, the concerned measures were not of a nature that they could be considered, de facto, as measures from the state. However, it mattered, from this perspective, that the public law framework enabled the Dutch Bar to develop rules that would guarantee the integrity of the profession because this provided a degree of public legitimacy to the restriction on competition.

We will return now to the case studies with the insights that the discussed case law has provided.

IV. A DIALOGUE OF MUTUAL RESPONSIVENESS

A model of social legitimacy based on the idea of mutual responsiveness can be constructed on the basis of the case law of the Court. In summary, the *Albany* and *Poucet Pistre* lines of case law have established the need for context-specific valuations of different social spheres and set out the beginnings of a more comprehensive rationale to determine, in a dynamic and context-specific way, the constructive interplay between competition and non-competition spheres. The *Wouters* case law can be seen as an extension of this idea, widening the scope of potentially irreconcilable non-competition interests to be transposed to a type of valuation outside of the strict application of the exemption criteria of Article 101(3) TFEU.[164] However, the *mutual* responsiveness that is required for wider social objectives to be taken into account in determining whether or not there is a restriction on competition requires a source of legitimacy within a public law framework that feeds privately developed social objectives. Reading the *Arduino* cases by analogy provides insight with regard to the question how such frameworks can be organised.

The principles resulting from this case law can be reconstructed for the purpose of establishing a framework of assessment for competition authorities and judicial review to be responsive to social context and, concomitantly by extension, as a guide for legislators to set out their public-private frameworks in a way that ensures the public legitimacy of private sphere initiatives that aspire to achieve public interests but limit competition. As such and perceived as a whole, this framework is clearly reflective of a dialogue of mutual responsiveness.

a set of norms that recognises that the legitimacy of economic self-regulation depends on procedures that ensure the meaningful participation of all concerned parties rather than on hierarchical structures of formal political accountability. In that sense, the 'delegation' test contributes to the constitutionalization of private governance.

[164] The advocated approach therefore conceives the *Wouters*-type approach or the application of the Art 101(3) TFEU exemption criteria as mutually exclusive.

Firstly, the Court has demonstrated an explicit responsiveness towards the potential irreconcilability between objectives and rationales in competition law and social objectives that have been set up in pursuance of a broader public interest. In the submitted model this concretises in the form of a prior analysis of the 'market situation' regarding the nature of the activities, to determine whether the underlying normative framework of the restrictive activity in question is compatible with the underlying normative framework of the competition rules or not. In this way, a prior, *in concreto,* analysis of the market situation will take into account the nature of the activities and their authenticity with the intention to unveil whether the aspired aims are genuine and inherent to the pursuit of a public interest that is irreconcilable with the aims of the competition law framework. This context-specific *in concreto* approach puts emphasis on the expressive value of the interplay of competition and non-competition interests, which requires a specific and concrete articulation of the limits of both competition and genuinely irreconcilable non-competition interests. The moment of societal learning is reached where the limits of both spheres are established in a concrete manner. This does not exclude the competition interest from the process because the test involves an assessment 'whether the consequential effects restrictive of competition are inherent in the pursuit of those objectives'. In this way competition law can be applied as a tool for societal dialogue, testing old conventions and requiring the renewed articulation of the pursuit of public interests. On the other hand, it avoids the valuation of regulatory systems merely on the basis of their 'efficiency' merits and fulfils the normative promise of social legitimacy, which requires that a diversity of social spheres be subject to different means of valuation.

This is the first step in the submitted framework of assessment. In case there is genuine irreconcilability then the second step concerns an evaluation of the design of the public-private framework of deliberation. The design of the public-private framework would need to ensure that the aspired goals are, at important points, fed with public legitimacy and provided with affirmative political oversight. This part of the analysis would therefore unveil if the measures that aspire to serve the public, although inherently irreconcilable with the legitimacy of the exemption framework of the competition rules, are sufficiently provided with a source of legitimacy. On the basis of this second step, it would have to be determined to what extent the public-private partnership actually leads to the pursuit of a *legitimate* interest. Moreover, as was discussed with respect to *Arduino* there exists on this point a dimension that connects the pursuit of social objective within a public-private framework of governance to the scope of the free movement rules. The free movement rules play an additional part in the assessment of the potential restrictions that such frameworks establish in terms of market access. If there exists a market access restriction, an additional test will determine the potential justification of the regulatory framework from the perspective of the free movement rules. Pursuant to the model that was developed in Chapter 2, this assessment would then evaluate the restriction on the basis of questions relating to its coherence, transparency and systemacy in its wider regulatory context.[165]

Therefore, the second step in the submitted model emphasises the *mutual* responsiveness that is inherent in the dynamics of the internal market. Social diversity can be guaranteed within the Union, provided that Member States fulfil a standard of good governance in the organisation of their regulatory affairs. Hence, this approach fits the terms of the social purpose of the internal market that was developed Chapter 1. The social purpose of the internal market is not to condition choices that necessarily require the market to trump the social sphere or necessarily its opposite, to allow the social to always trump the market. The approach suggested in this chapter advances a more holistic approach that conceives the market and the social sphere as 'communicating vessels'. Competition-derived evaluative standards serve as a tool to tease out discriminatory, disingenuous regulatory choices within Member States but allow for genuine social objectives to exist in accordance with good governance principles that focus on the quality and systemacy of a governance process, instead of on the rationality and efficiency of its outcome. In this way there is neither a sacrifice of the market or a sacrifice of the social and, instead, both social diversity and competition can be accommodated within the internal market.

I will now briefly turn to the case studies to explore how this perspective copes with the highlighted issues in those cases.

A. A Return to the Case Studies on the Basis of Mutual Responsiveness

i. *The Friesian Horse*

We remember that the Friesian horse case concerned the question whether the pedigree could determine rules that would limit the commercial freedom of its members but was aimed at ensuring the health of the Friesian horse. Returning to this case with the perspective of mutual responsiveness leads to the following findings. As regards the normative interests at stake we would have to establish concretely that the nature of the measures was genuine and inherent to the pursuit of an interest that is irreconcilable with the aims of the competition law framework. This is not necessarily as straightforward as it may seem since the health of the Friesian horse could in this case plausibly be conceived as a 'quality' concern and addressed as such within the exemption framework of Article 101(3) TFEU, much like the environmental objectives within the *CECED* case, without damaging the objectives that are actually at stake. The proposed model would not object against that. It would have to be established, concretely, if there is anything in the pursuit of the health of the Friesian horse that would be damaged if tested within the exemption criteria. However, it may simply be the case that the required

[165] See II, section III.C.

data for the fulfilment of the Article 101(3) TFEU criteria is not available and that the exemption criteria cannot be fulfilled for, mainly, that reason. This is an issue that concerns a wider discussed problem of incorporating long-term, uncertain benefits of restrictive agreements within the efficiency-based rationale of Article 101(3) TFEU. As was touched upon before, in the application of Article 101(3) TFEU, competition authorities, such as the ACM, tend to attach decisive value to the objective qualification and concretisation in economic terms of claimed benefits that may be effectuated by restrictive agreements in order to qualify for an exemption.[166] However, in situations where the main focus is not the immediate but rather the long-term prevention of concerns that cannot be completely quantified, such as presumably in case of the studbook, would that be sufficient for the disapplication of the protective rules? Or is the absence of data in itself sufficient reason to move the evaluation to the alternative framework of analysis that was constructed above on the basis of concerns based on social legitimacy? The developed normative framework provides answers to these questions.[167]

First, the alternative valuation based on substantive irreconcilability and good governance requires that the valuation, which is inherent in the exemption criteria of Article 101(3) TFEU will damage or disregard essential features of the pursued objectives. If so there is an argument for the exclusion of Article 101(3) TFEU and to evaluate the restrictive non-competitive objective to establish whether the consequential effects, restrictive of competition, were inherent and the objectives sufficiently embedded within an overarching public law or regulatory framework. However, as said, it is unclear if the non-competition interest in this case is concerned with objectives that fall outside of concerns that are related with the efficient functioning of the studbook. Within the submitted model, this would be different if the rules of the studbook were reflective of choices related to concerns that could be traced back to a normative commitment and choice to the embedding of a market within a high standard of animal welfare in the Netherlands.

The studbook was, at the time of the measures, recognised as an official pedigree by the previously discussed product organisation for livestock, meat and eggs, which was a public-private entity, legally responsible for industrywide interests,

[166] S Kingston, Integrating Environmental Protection and EU Competition Law: Why Competition Isn't Special (2010) 16(6) *European Law Journal* 780–805.

[167] For an alternative idea, see Anna Gerbrandy who has submitted to include more public stakeholders *within* the competition law *procedure* (instead of the legal assessment) in order to increase the legitimacy of competition law decisions to take account of non-competition objectives. eg, an appealing version is that of a combination between a public stakeholder panel that is representative of various societal objectives combined with a form of political control that decides on the public interest that should take precedence; see Gerbrandy (n 35) at 770. The approach that is advanced here, instead, argues that competition and wider societal rationales should engage with each other within an institutional framework that is not instructed by an overarching competition law framework, which *includes* the non-market objectives within its institutional form, but instead initiates a broader societal dialogue which allows for an identification of normative conflicts and the disapplication of the competition law framework when appropriate.

including animal welfare. Within this context the FPS had to adhere to requirements that were set for 'official' pedigrees across the Netherlands and this included the organisation of a pedigree in a way that would ensure that the preservation of the breed would be guaranteed on the basis of concrete breeding improvement programmes. Moreover, the measures of inbreeding control that were pursued in the studbook were explicitly recognised by the Food and Agriculture Organisation (FAO) of the United Nations as essential for the health and survival of a race.

The public law framework therefore did to some extent embed the choices of the studbook within a wider, arguably social sphere, for the protection and preservation of the breed, which would qualify it as a non-competition objective. The analysis would in that situation still consider whether all restrictive effects on competition were inherent. It would therefore have to be established to what extent the preventive measures were indeed based on concrete evidence that there did exist a plausible threat to the health of the Friesian horse. However, the evaluation would not require the immediate objective qualification and concretisation in economic terms of the claimed benefits because the identification of the need to install protective rules would be connected and inherent to the normative societal, non-competitive, commitment to long-term animal welfare. However, the design of the public-private framework would then need to ensure that these aspired goals are, at important points, provided with affirmative forms of political oversight. This part of the analysis would therefore unveil if the measures that aspire to serve a public interest were indeed sufficiently and genuinely provided with a source of legitimacy.[168]

ii. Mutual Responsiveness in the Energy Agreement for Sustainable Growth

As described, the Energy agreement involved more than 40 organisations in the definition of an energy and climate policy and took place within a public law framework that was set up for the purpose of negotiations between various public stakeholders.[169] The interest-wide agreement was intended to offer long-term sustainable prospects and create trust and involvement on the part of individuals, businesses and civil society organisations.

The interest at stake in this case, which cannot be quantified within the competition law framework, concerns the process that has led to a specific organisational structure and brought together various societal actors in a way that would make

[168] As discussed before, the appellate court in Arnhem decided regarding the question of legitimacy that, unlike the situation in *Wouters*, this public framework context did not qualify the measure as 'special and weighty public interests'. Consequently, the pursuit of the health of the Friesian horse could not be considered a 'legitimate' purpose and should therefore be assessed on the basis of the exemption criteria of Art 101(3) TFEU. In terms of an accountability perspective, it was decided that this was to be provided by the market.

[169] The public stakeholders included central, regional and local government, employers' associations and unions, nature conservation and environmental organisations, other civil society organisations and financial institutions.

them co-responsible for these objectives on the basis of mutual obligations tuned towards a shared social value. By insisting on quantification, a narrow framework could disembed such an agreement from its societal function and reduce it to efficiency benefits; failing to recognise the importance of the discursive process as an overarching societal value in itself. Instead, mutual responsiveness would conceive the competition interest and the societal discursive in a way that they would align towards a common, shared interest.

A good argument can be made that the closing down of the coal plants was inherent for the existence of the agreement as a whole that in itself, as a process, reflected an *Albany*-type context and served a purpose that was broader and irreconcilable with the efficiency criteria of Article 101(3) TFEU. The inherent restriction test would then still provide this assessment with the means to assess concretely whether the societal narrative at stake was authentic and not used to disguise protective or merely anti-competitive measures.

Again, as regards the second requirement in the submitted model, it would have to be assessed if the public-private context within which the measures where shaped ensured the public legitimacy of the measures in question. The design of this framework would have to involve state involvement in the substantive formation of the objectives and a confirmation that the interests pursued were in accordance with the public aims and policy of the state, even though they were established in a dynamic public-private context. In this way competition law becomes very much a tool for societal dialogue, testing societal dialogue and requiring the concrete articulation of the pursuit of public interests. However, it avoids the valuation of socially relevant agreement merely on the basis of its 'efficiency' merits and fulfils the normative promise of social legitimacy, which requires that a diversity of social spheres be subject to different means of valuation.

iii. Mutual Responsiveness in the Chicken of Tomorrow Case

In the context of the Chicken of Tomorrow case, the *in concreto* assessment would determine if and how the 'embedding' of the economic activity on the basis of a minimum standard for the production of chicken meat would address an authentic societal interest that is irreconcilable with the exemption criteria of Article 101(3) TFEU. Again, similar to the Friesian horse, the case would have to be made that the introduction of a minimum standard was an expression of a normative commitment concerning the embedding of economic activity in this sector, which in a sense precedes the market. The exemption criteria, instead, strictly applied would lead the market decide. That is to say, to pursue animal welfare on the basis of consumer preference and to conceptualise it as a monetary consideration. This is a profoundly political decision. However, in the absence of an institutional framework that provides public legitimacy to the minimum standards of poultry trade, the sector cannot legitimately be left to decide on such matters. Hence, sustainability initiatives such as these are likely to suffer on the basis of a deferential government. The Dutch government had indicated that the policy in this area should be informed and guided on the basis of sector-wide and sector-based initiatives on the processing of livestock but this is clearly insufficient from the perspective of mutual responsiveness, which requires an active and aware government that institutionalises, to some extent, the pursuit of sustainability initiatives within the framework of good governance that the competition rules advance. Hence, with regard to the second limb of mutual responsiveness we would have to conclude that, despite the existence of a clear public-private deliberative framework, it was not transparent to what extent and on which points state involvement was present. Implicitly, it definitely was since the Dutch government had expressed its disappointment about the position of the ACM and also confirmed at that point that the policy was very much in line with the Dutch policy objectives. However, as was discussed above, in terms of accountability the public-private framework failed to provide sufficient clarity as to the public legitimacy of the interests that were pursued.

V. CONCLUSION

Mutual responsiveness in the context of EU competition law means accepting the primacy of a market-based rationale to initiate a dialogue with regard to the regulatory choices of Member States, whilst explicitly allowing space for the development of non-competition-based residual and conflicting objectives.

There are two main implication of this debate for the operation of competition law in the presence of non-competition-based public objectives. First, that the conventional framing of the conceptual dichotomy between the market on the one side and residual non-economic aspects of the social on the other is underdeveloped and fails to capture what is at stake when these spheres meet. Secondly, that clarity in the framing of competition and non-competition conflicts is needed to instruct balancing exercises in adjudication and tells something about how competition authorities should deal with (non-economic) social interest objectives in their decision-making process and, importantly, the institutional requirements for Member States to allow undertakings to pursue social objectives that are restrictive of competition in accordance with the EU competition law framework.

The dichotomy between market and non-market or economic and non-economic is there to allow or even force a deliberative space for broader than monetary or efficiency-based considerations of what matters in social relations. Sustainability, the integrity of a profession or the way animals are treated harbour important social values that do not necessarily speak market talk. However, such market talk is provided with a source of legitimacy within the EU competition rules and can be applied to initiate a social dialogue on the validity and systemacy of regulatory choices within the Member States. Competition law should then, however, incorporate means to value different social contexts differently, and in congruence with the underlying normative commitments of those contexts. Such responsiveness depends on institutional design.

The language of sustainability, animal welfare and professional standards, where voiced by private operators, needs a governance structure of legitimacy if they restrict the competition rules. The case law of the Court of Justice demonstrates a definite responsiveness to broader social values and has recognised it specifically with regard to collective negotiations, solidarity and, to a lesser extent, other types of non-competition interests that are pursued within quasi-public law frameworks by private entities with their own interests. The gap that the latter case law leaves is mostly concerned with the alternative source of legitimacy that is required from the perspective of mutual responsiveness. It was found in *Wouters* but in a way that would not allow any generalisations as regards its broader implications. By connecting the *Arduino*, *Cipolla* and *Mauri* types of reasoning to *Wouters*, a more general rationale of mutual responsiveness emerged. A responsiveness that allows on the one hand a finding of inherent irreconcilability between the normative order of the competition rules and the values with a broader social aim *but* which requires a source of legitimacy for the pursuit of those aims. It is only if both are present that the requirements, which EU competition law advances, can be met. As such, there is here a clear connection to the argument from transnational effects that installs requirements of good governance on the way that Member States pursue aims that have effects of a cross-border nature. In the area of competition law this translates into a double-sided requirement. If such measures can be accounted for on the basis of the efficiency criteria of the competition rules then the market provides legitimacy to cross-border effects. Alternatively, there should be another source of legitimacy that pursues genuine and authentic legitimate concerns within a transparent public law framework.

The case studies have demonstrated that there is a need for Member States to actively structure public-private frameworks where private initiatives are crucial in the development of social goals that restrict competition. Although the examples of the Energy agreement and the Chicken of Tomorrow cases demonstrate a clear involvement of the government, it was arguably not specific enough to infuse these initiatives with the public legitimacy that they require. Eventually, the identification of non-competition spaces could be structured as entrance points for forms of explicit democratic deliberation. In this way diversity can be cherished outside of efficiency logic and in accordance with the fundamental aims of the EU. Simply put, competition and public interest conflicts fall either within the scope of a competition rule, after which the method to resolve a conflict should be based on a weighing of efficiency merits, or outside the scope of the competition rule and the outcome should be based on a procedural review of the quality of the process that restricts competition. Competition authorities have in this latter stage a complementary and not an overarching role to play. They should be included in the societal narrative as the stakeholder of the public interest of competition and fulfil that role through providing a voice for competition that stands next to the other represented voices of public interest but not as an overarching and normative conditioner of these processes within society.

4

Social Legitimacy in EU State Aid Law

I. INTRODUCTION

WE ARRIVE IN the field of state aid after having developed and applied a normative framework based on social legitimacy. Internal market adjudication in the areas of free movement and competition law has been critically assessed and reconstructed in accordance with the perspective of social legitimacy. So far, the intention has been to unveil the potential normative concerns in these areas and to point towards ways to deal with them. It is submitted that this exercise has allowed for the development of a model of social legitimacy that enables the Court to adjudicate internal market conflicts in tune with a variety of social interests and actors. The idea of a dialogue based on mutual responsiveness was introduced to accommodate the normative claims of social legitimacy (and complete the argument from transnational effects). Mutual responsiveness means, simply, that, on the one hand the supranational market integration rationales have to incorporate responsiveness to Member State context and diversity and, conversely, that the pursuit of social interests on a Member State level have to be in some way responsive to the objectives of market integration within the institutional structures that pursue these social interests. The internal market rules are, from this perspective, to be conceptualised as the starting point of a dialogue, based on the shared values of market integration.

The previous chapters introduced how market access and competition can be used as tools for such a dialogue provided that these rules incorporate responsiveness towards social context, which may be restrictive of market integration objectives but reflective of important and legitimate societal fabric. If this responsiveness is absent, social legitimacy is at risk. This chapter explores these issues in the area of EU state aid law. Over recent years some important contributions have been made to the discussion of the EU state aid rules concerning their wider function and constitutional status within the internal market,[1] in a field of

[1] F De Cecco, *State Aid and the European Economic Constitution* (Oxford, Hart Publishing, 2013) and JJP Lopez, *The Concept of State Aid under EU Law—From Internal Market to Competition and beyond* (Oxford, Oxford University Press, 2015). See also M Ross, 'State Aids: Maturing into a Constitutional Problem' (1995) *Yearbook of European Law* 79; M Ross, 'State Aid and National Courts: Definitions and Other Problems—a Case of Premature Emancipation?' (2000) 37 *Common Market Law Review* 401; M Ross, 'Decentralization, Effectiveness, and Modernization: Contradiction in Terms?' (2004) in A Biondi, P Eeckhout and J Flynn (eds), *The Law of State Aid in the European Union* (Oxford, Oxford University Press, 2004).

internal market law that is otherwise primarily dominated by insulated and practitioner-led, specialised, debates.[2] The issue of the potential impact of the EU state aid rules on the pursuit of social objectives by Member States has also featured amongst these contributions.[3] As such, some of the approaches and adjudicative techniques of the Court and the General Court (GC) that will be discussed in this chapter have been touched on before. The salience of this chapter is twofold. Firstly, in the discussion of the structural social legitimacy concerns with regard to the potentially expedient nature of market-based evaluations in state aid cases. With 'expedient use' I mean, rather idiosyncratically, the quick adoption of market-based techniques when these may not be justified in light of the social context that is involved. Secondly, with the introduction of the idea of mutual responsiveness to state aid law. This allows a connection between state aid law and the wider debate on the social legitimacy of the internal market. By adopting the perspective of mutual responsiveness in reconstructing some lines of case law from the Court, it will become clear that regulatory space of Member States can certainly deviate and be excluded from the normative state aid objective of undistorted competition but needs to be infused with a variety of good governance requirements (in so far as selective advantages are granted to undertakings as part of broader social regulatory objectives).

The chapter develops further as follows. First, a description of the objectives of EU state aid law and an identification of the areas of potential normative concern from the perspective of social legitimacy (section II). Second, I will explore the case law of the Court and GC to trace fragments of mutual responsiveness in its case law (section III). Third, these fragments will be reconstructed into a coherent model of adjudication based on a dialogue of mutual responsiveness (section IV). Section V concludes.

II. VALUATION, INDETERMINACY AND INCOMMENSURABILITY IN STATE AID LAW

In this section I will discuss the state aid rules as a whole, describe important developments in the policy-making efforts of the European Commission and then

[2] Mostly with respect to tax issues: eg C. Quigley, 'General Taxation and State Aid' in A. Biondi, P. Eeckhout and J. Flynn (eds), *The Law of State Aid in the European Union* (Oxford, Oxford University Press, 2004) at 207; K Bacon, 'Differential Taxes, State Aids and the Lunn Poly Case' (1999) 7 *European Competition Law Review* 384; P Nicolaides, 'Fiscal State Aid in the EU: the Limits of Tax Autonomy' (2004) 27 *World Competition* 319. Also with respect to 'economic' issues: eg P. Crocioni, 'Can State Aid Policy Become more Economic-Friendly?' (2006) 29 *World Competition* 89; D Neven and V Verouden, 'Towards a more Refined Economic Approach in State Aid Control' in W Mederer, N Pesaresi and M van Hoof (eds), *EU Competition Law* (Deventer, Claeys & Casteels, 2008) at 99.

[3] See esp A Biondi and L Rubini, 'Aims, Effects and Justifications: EC State Aid Law and Its Impact on National Social Policies' in M Dougan and E Spaventa (eds), *Social Welfare and EU Law* (Hart Publishing, 2005) 79.

move to the area within state aid law that is most relevant from the perspective of social legitimacy.

In state aid law, similar to free movement and competition, the potential conflict between the objectives of market integration and Member State social spheres is reflected in the primary Treaty rules. EU state aid law is contained in Articles 107 to 109 TFEU. Article 107(1) TFEU is based on the assumption that selective economic advantages granted to undertakings by the state should be deemed 'incompatible with the common market'. However, under Articles 107(2) and (3) TFEU, potential socio-economic objectives of the measure may be considered with the result that an otherwise incompatible aid becomes compatible with the common market. Article 107(1) provides that:

> [s]ave as otherwise provided in the Treaties, any aid granted by a Member State or through State resources in any form whatsoever which distorts or threatens to distort competition by favouring certain undertakings or the production of certain goods shall, in so far as it affects trade between Member States, be incompatible with the internal market.

Preventing 'competition distortions' is the touchstone of the prohibition contained in Article 107(1) and it has five constituent elements: (i) there must be an intervention by the state or through state resources; (ii) this intervention must create an advantage for undertakings within the meaning of competition rules of the Treaty; (iii) the advantage must be granted to certain undertakings or to the production of certain goods selectively; (iv) the intervention must be likely to distort or to threaten to distort competition; (v) the intervention must be likely to affect trade between the Member States. If a measure cumulatively fulfils these criteria, it triggers a notification duty and a standstill obligation. Article 107(2) goes on to list categories of aid, which are compatible with the common market, and in Article 107(3) those categories of aid that may be considered by the Commission to be compatible. Examples of the former are aids with a social character granted directly to consumers (not undertakings) and aid to make good any damage caused by natural disasters or 'exceptional occurrences'; examples of the latter are aid to promote the economic development of areas where the standard of living is abnormally low or to 'remedy a serious disturbance in the economy of a Member State'. Hence, measures which are found to qualify as state aid within the meaning of Article 107(1) TFEU are subject to EU state aid *control* and that means that they are in principle prohibited. The Commission is then empowered to 'declare' them compatible under Article 107(3) TFEU, when it is deemed to be in the common interest. The general principle behind the Commission's compatibility assessment is to balance the positive impact of the aid measure (pursuing an objective of common interest) against its potential negative effects (the distortion of competition). For this assessment the Commission largely defers to pre-determined criteria or proxies. The conventional method taken in the block exemption regulations and in most enforcement guidelines is to predefine a set of objectives (eg aid for environmental projects) and the eligible costs (the costs of an environmental project) on the basis of which undertakings can then receive the state aid.

The central normative assumption behind the state aid rules is that the role of the state in the market should not lead to competition distortions between undertakings. As such it is reflective of a joint commitment of the Member States to ensure competitive markets. Traditionally the main concern of EU state aid law was to address specifically protectionist aims of Member States that were intent on financing sectors of the national economy or boosting national champions.[4] Still today, state aid is often applied to uncover protectionist aims of Member States. Thus, recently, the Commission decided that Luxembourg and the Netherlands had on the basis of a web of complex tax laws granted selective tax advantages to Fiat and Starbucks, respectively. DG Competition Commissioner Margrethe Vestager stated:

> Tax rulings that artificially reduce a company's tax burden are not in line with EU state aid rules. They are illegal. I hope that, with today's decisions, this message will be heard by Member State governments and companies alike.

Although these goals of state aid law are still part of the day-to-day state aid regime, the regime has significantly evolved, normatively, towards an area of law that is also concerned with ensuring that interactions between the state or emanations of the state and the market are efficient and take place with the least of costs to the Union.[5] This is quite a normative shift, which, as will be discussed further below, has taken place largely on the basis of a normative reading of existing legal categories within state aid law, on the basis of market-derived standards. The implementation of this idea has been achieved primarily on the basis of efforts from the European Commission,[6] which has been able to almost entirely proceduralise this area of internal market law.

A. The Proceduralisation of the State Aid Rules

Article 108 TFEU, crucially, provides for the supervision of state aid by the Commission, and imposes the duty on Member States to notify the Commission in advance of any plans to grant or to alter aid. The Commission has issued an extensive collection of guidance papers, forms for notifications and reporting, block exemption regulations, temporary rules, horizontal rules and sector-specific rules that Member States can rely on in their design of aid schemes or ad hoc individual aid actions.[7] These legislative documents all serve the purpose of minimising

[4] Lopez, *The Concept of State Aid under EU Law* (n 1) at 45; and further C Quigley, *European State Aid Law and Policy* (Oxford, Hart Publishing, 2015) at 270.

[5] The recent published monograph of Lopez (n 1) describes the evolution of the concept of state aid, from p 12.

[6] ibid.

[7] Including rules on procedure; forms for notifications and reporting; block exemption regulations; temporary rules in response to the crisis; horizontal rules; sector-specific rules; specific aid instruments; on the transparency of public undertakings; on Services of General Economic Interest (SGEI);

conflict and streamlining, in procedural terms, the allocation of governmental aid mechanisms.

In this respect it is important to note that over the past decade the state aid regime has been subject to what the Commission calls 'simplification and streamlining', first, under the Commission's 2005 State Aid Action Plan.[8] Second, and more importantly, the State Aid Modernisation (SAM) initiative, carried out by the Commission since May 2012. This has brought forward major changes with structural effects for the application of EU state aid law.[9] As a whole, the SAM initiative is targeted at 'enhancing the effectiveness of aid in supporting growth, in view of the Europe 2020 strategy's objectives'. For this purpose, the Commission is implementing a priority-based policy where enforcement of state aid is limited to cases with 'the biggest impact on the internal market'.[10] A big part of the SAM project involves a decentralisation of the state aid rules, which in some ways resembles the modernisation package that the Commission implemented with regard to the EU competition rules.[11] The SAM package focuses on 'common principles'. Aid measures should satisfy a certain number of criteria in order to be considered compatible with the Treaty. They need to contribute to a 'well-defined objective of common interest' and must be necessary and appropriate. Moreover, the beneficiary will need to undertake a project or activity, which he would not have done without the aid (the incentive effect) and the amount of aid has to be proportionate. Lastly, aid should avoid undue negative effects on competition and trade.[12] Key to the modernisation package is that the new state aid architecture

on rules applicable to state aid in the transport sector; on rules applicable to state aid in coal sector. See http://ec.europa.eu/competition/state_aid/legislation/legislation.html for an overview.

[8] Notable measures have included the General Block Exemption Regulation of 2008. Commission Regulation (EU) No 651/2014 of 17 June 2014 declaring certain categories of aid compatible with the internal market in application of Articles 107 and 108 of the Treaty.

[9] http://ec.europa.eu/competition/state_aid/modernisation/index_en.html.

[10] Communication from the Commission to the European Parliament, the Council, the European economic and social Committee and the Committee of the regions—EU State aid modernisation (SAM) (COM/2012/0209 final).

[11] See also X Boutin and R Peduzzi, 'Searching for "Good Aid": The Role of Evaluation' (2015) 14 *European State Aid Law Quarterly* 250–59.

[12] These principles have been implemented in all the main horizontal guidelines and frameworks: see Guidelines on regional State aid for 2014–2020 (OJ C 209 of 23.7.2013, p 1); Guidelines on State aid to promote risk finance investments (OJ C 19, 22.1.2014, p 4); Framework for State aid for research and development and innovation (OJ C 198, 27.6.2014, p 1); Guidelines on State aid for environmental protection and energy 2014–2020 (OJ C 200, 28.6.2014, p 1); draft Guidelines on State aid for rescuing and restructuring non-financial undertakings in difficulty (OJ C 249, 31.07.2014, p 1); and a new Communication—Criteria for the analysis of the compatibility with the internal market of State aid to promote the execution of important projects of common European interest (OJ C 88 of 20.6.2014, p 4). In addition, some important guidelines concerning specific sectors have been adopted in the context of modernisation and in line with the same common principles: EU Guidelines for the application of State aid rules in relation to the rapid deployment of broadband networks (OJ C 25 of 26.1.2013, p 1); Communication from the Commission on State aid for films and other audiovisual works (C 332, 15.11.2013, p 1); Guidelines on State aid to airports and airlines (OJ C 99, 4.4.2014, p 3); EU Guidelines for State aid in the agriculture and forestry sector and in rural areas 2014 to 2020 (OJ C 204, 1.7.2014, p 1).

requires, from the Member States, a higher level of transparency and, in some cases, a periodic evaluation. A central element of the modernisation package is the new General Block Exemption Regulation (GBER), which has been extended horizontally by adding several new categories of aid exempted from prior notification and vertically, with higher notification thresholds and numerous simplifications in the applicable conditions.[13] Estimates of the Commission claim that about three-quarters of state aid measures and some two-thirds of aid amounts can be exempted under the new GBER and up to 90 per cent, if Member States fully use the possibilities offered by the Regulation and design their aid schemes accordingly.[14] The Commission envisages a stronger role for Member States in correctly applying state aid rules and self-assessing their state aid measures. For this purpose, the Commission has introduced a simplification for Member States regarding the ex ante assessment of aid compatibility with some new or reinforced ex post safeguard mechanisms. These safeguards include monitoring (a periodic review of legality of a sample of state aid measures implemented by Member States), transparency (Member States will have to put in place national or regional public websites listing all the beneficiaries of individual aid) and, crucially, evaluation (an assessment of whether the aid actually achieved what it was meant to achieve and a verification of the balance between the aid's public objective and its impact on competition and trade between Member States).[15]

The set-up of the state aid regime and the consequent highly policy-driven nature of it has made it difficult to point out genuine normative conflicts between legitimate policy choices of Member States and the objectives that are pursued in the state aid framework. In this sense a lot of the potential conflicts that are of concern from the perspective of state aid have been 'negotiated' and Member States have agreed to follow certain procedures on when they grant state aid in specific sectors.[16] Clearly, protectionist aims of Member States conflict in normative terms with those of the state aid regime but such aims are, a priori, excluded as legitimate. Moving beyond such prima facie protectionist aims of Member States, it is difficult to identify genuine (*and* legitimate) normative conflicts *within* the EU state aid regime. This can, in part, be attributed to the Commission's effort to implement an expansive idea about the aims and objectives that can be addressed with state aid and combined with its proceduralisation efforts it has been able to largely streamline the way Member States finance public service missions and develop aid schemes. As said, a lot of the potential conflicts have therefore been

[13] Commission Regulation (EU) No 651/2014 of 17 June 2014 declaring certain categories of aid compatible with the internal market in application of Articles 107 and 108 of the Treaty Text with EEA relevance.

[14] Boutin and Peduzzi, 'Searching for "Good Aid"' (n 11).

[15] Commission Regulation (EU) No 651/2014 of 17 June 2014 declaring certain categories of aid compatible with the internal market in application of Articles 107 and 108 of the Treaty Text with EEA relevance.

[16] See V Verouden, 'EU State Aid Control: The Quest for Effectiveness' (2015) 14(4) *European State Aid Law Quarterly* 459–64.

resolved on the basis of the procedures that set out how Member States have to proceed if they want to provide state aid for certain social objectives. Moreover, the Commission has adopted a wide definition of (social) market failure around which to structure its policy. Simply said, the Commission's policy is essentially concerned with a normative procedural assessment of the optimum allocation of state resources, whilst allowing a broad range of policy goals, provided they serve a common/community interest. In the process the Commission perceives market failure to be very wide in scope, as a situation where the market does not achieve social welfare optimal outcomes. The approach in today's competition economics theory and the policy of the European Commission[17] is, for example, to *include* redistributive equity concerns within the market efficiency rationale of market failures. The idea behind it is that if market failure can be defined as a situation where the market does not achieve welfare optimal outcomes, it could perfectly encompass equity (redistributive) concerns. Consequently, social concerns are then internalised within the concept of a market failure. This is basically also reflected in the previously mentioned 'incentive effect' test, which is to say that the aid must be provided as an incentive to further develop activities or projects that serve a common interest and in which the beneficiary would not engage without the aid.

A narrower understanding of market failure would be concerned with fixing information asymmetries (so that consumers and producers take decisions taking into account all information), externalities (so that prices reflects all costs, including costs to third parties) and market power (so that firms cannot profitably charge prices in excess of marginal costs). However, the concept of a market failure as applied by the Commission is expanded to include situations where the market does not achieve *social welfare optimal outcomes* that can be defined along the lines of the common interests for the Union. As was identified in the first chapters, these common interests have evolved significantly and since Lisbon include a vast range of social objectives. However, the point in the first chapter was also that, in so far as these objectives were pursued on a EU level, in particular by the European Commission, they could best be perceived as 'commoditised' versions of the social. This emanation of the social, on the EU level, has a very specific meaning and context. Simply said, and as was argued in Chapter 1,[18] it is an understanding of the social that is often ancillary to or supportive of economic objectives.[19] It can be argued that this conception of the social has come to fruition within the area of the state aid rules. The modernisation package of the Commission is ultimately

[17] Restricting state aid to market failure situations is one of the main aims introduced by the 2005 State Aid Action Plan.

[18] See ch 1, section III.B.

[19] See further eg A Somek, *Engineering Equality: An Essay on European Anti-Discrimination Law* (Oxford/ New York, Oxford University Press, 2011) and M Saveska, 'Polanyian Reading of the Socio-Economic Transformations of the European Union' (2014) 22(4) *Journal of Contemporary European Studies* 395.

targeted to embed an idea of what constitutes 'good' aid, ie compatible aid.[20] The package will, according to the Commission, 'help designing *smarter* schemes with a better incentive effect and less competition distortions. Seen more broadly, it should be considered as part of a general move towards sound evidence-based policy making'.[21] In this context the Commission speaks about 'evaluation communities', which 'have a genuine interest in improving the effectiveness and efficiency of spending measures'.[22]

It is likely that the efforts of the Commission to nudge Member States towards the implementation of 'evaluation communities' that structure and implement a very specific idea of governance has systemic effects. That is to say that there are likely to be policies or objectives that are not developed because Member States are already thinking only in terms of the smart regulation rationale of the Commission.[23] In this way genuine norm conflicts are neutralised or depoliticised in the early stages of policy formulation by the Commission in a slightly covert way and it would require a challenging empirical research effort to quantify the actual effects of the Commission's state aid policy in terms of the limits it imposes on social diversity within the Union. As such, in purely conceptual terms, the wide approach to market failure leads to a partial politicisation of the economic concept and a depoliticisation of the social objectives involved.

This process in the state aid rules closely resembles the 'modernisation' and decentralisation efforts in competition law. As was argued in the previous chapter, the development and 'modernisation' of the EU competition rules went through two important developments that influence the ability of EU competition law to accommodate regulatory diversity. The previous chapter painted the following picture: a retracting state that increasingly defers socio-economic policy-making to undertakings; a European Commission that pushes for a one-dimensional idea of what matters in terms of socio-economic policy—at least whenever it infringes the competition rules—and undertakings that feel increasingly compelled to structure their potentially green and social objectives in accordance with what is efficient and for the sole benefit of a consumer.

The process and policy initiatives of the Commission in state aid policy are largely the same. Consequently, one would indeed expect to see less conflict as the social becomes part of a technocratic process of resolving market failures. This is confirmed with even a cursory glance at the overviews of EU state aid cases that lists the decisions of the Commission by type of decision from 2000 to 2013. Over 90 per cent of the Commissions' decisions approve notified aid measures.[24]

[20] See Boutin and Peduzzi (n 11).

[21] ibid.

[22] European Commission, Issues Paper 12/04/2013, 'Evaluation in the field of state aid', http://ec.europa.eu/competition/state_aid/modernisation/evaluation_issues_paper_en.pdf.

[23] See the better regulation initiative of the European Commission http://ec.europa.eu/smart-regulation/index_en.htm.

[24] http://ec.europa.eu/competition/state_aid/scoreboard/.

This excludes the aid schemes that are, additionally, exempted under the block exemption regulations. I think it is likely that the proceduralisation of a lot of state aid decision contributes to the fact that it is rare to see a negative decision from the Commission. It is therefore understandable why the Commission feels confident that the idea of evaluative communities on a Member State level, ie outsourcing state aid control, is now worth pursuing in full.

Within this context, normative claims over the functioning of the state aid regime as a covert technocratic process that depoliticises the formulation and pursuit of social objectives can be formulated on the basis of concerns about its democratic legitimacy and as an encroachment on the constitutional space for Member States to develop aid schemes.[25] It matters whether policy objectives developed by Member States are to be defined within the technocratic domain of the proceduralised world of the state aid rules or whether they are allowed to take shape within 'normal politics' and the democratic arenas of the Member States. Arguably, the political *process* of the pursuit of some regulatory objectives is what matters most. This is reminiscent of the normative concerns that were developed in the first chapter: some non-economic objectives tend to share or require a social and political pact that underlies the objectives that are pursued. As such, even if, theoretically speaking, a market or technocratic approach towards regulating access to public infrastructure would accommodate the functional features of an objective, there may be something lost in the process of pursuing the objective as part of a genuine political or regulatory process.[26]

The central issue pursued here is the potential incommensurability between the evaluative standards applied on the basis of the state aid regime with social objectives that are formulated on a Member State level. More specifically, incommensurability as discussed in Chapter 1 occurs in the application of state aid law when objectives pursued by Member States cannot be aligned along the metric that is pursued within those rules without doing violence to the potentially genuine and worthwhile aspects of those objectives. It was discussed that the social purpose of EU law in the internal market as applied by the Court is to express instances of such irreconcilability before adopting evaluative principles that are congruent to the conflict that is being adjudicated. Social legitimacy, in turn, depends on the extent that the Court is able to accommodate and identify genuine social objectives within its evaluative rationales. Hence, the moment of defining what can be defined as a state aid counts. It is at this juncture, where a decision is made whether a policy or regulatory framework can be developed *outside* of the state aid rationale or within the standards and justifications that are already prescribed in

[25] This is one of the main starting points of the study of De Cecco, *State Aid and the European Economic Constitution* (n 1). See also M Bovens, 'New Forms of Accountability and EU-Governance' (2007) 5 *Comparative European Politics* 104–20.

[26] See similarly R Bellamy, 'The Liberty of the Moderns: Market Freedom and Democracy within the EU' (2012) 1 *Global Constitutionalism* 141–72, at 168.

state aid *control*—that genuine norm conflicts come to the front and need to be adjudicated by the Court.[27]

B. Modes of Valuation in State Aid: Market versus Regulation

In a case that may have very well inspired the *Dassonville* formula, 13 years later, the Court determined already in 1961 that

> the concept of aid is … wider than that of a subsidy because it embraces not only positive benefits, such as subsidies themselves, but also interventions which, in various forms, mitigate the charges which are normally included in the budget of an undertaking and which, without, therefore, being subsidies in the strict meaning of the word, are similar in character and have the same effect.[28]

As will be further discussed below, the Court has since then consistently held that 'aid' is to be defined in relation to its effects, thus allowing the Court and the Commission to subject many forms of governmental 'interventions' to the Treaty provisions.[29] The wording of the Court is indeed similar to the *Dassonville* formulation, which subjects measures '*with equivalent effect*' to quantitative restrictions to the scope of the free movement rules.[30] The scope of the state aid rules is therefore wide, potentially covering all sorts of governmental interventions that lead to selective advantages for undertakings, and as will be argued further below, requires responsiveness to avoid problems of social legitimacy. It will be demonstrated that also in terms of responsiveness the Court has shown some overlap with the free movement rules in the development of evaluative principles to determine whether there is state aid or not. As will be discussed further below, different evaluative standards have been acknowledged by the Court for the purpose of evaluating governmental interventions of different kinds.

For example, as will be discussed further below, the Court has established that the application of a market-based evaluation of a governmental intervention should be preceded by an assessment of the 'nature of the measure'. In principle, only if the state is acting to participate on the market—eg as a shareholder—should market-based standards be used to evaluate whether any advantages have been granted. If, instead, the state is acting as a regulator, the 'market rationality' principle is replaced with evaluative standards based on questions whether regulation benefits a specific (group of) undertaking(s) or whether a measure involves a

[27] Similarly, De Cecco (n 1) at 1–3.

[28] Case 30/59 *Steenkolenmijnen v High Authority* [1961] ECR 1, 19.

[29] Such as direct subsidies, loans, guarantees, exemption from the ordinary rules concerning taxes and social contributions, under-price sales, capital injections, provision of market research and advertising activities or logistical and commercial assistance, payment of outstanding wages or redundancy costs, or exemption from the normal application of insolvency rules.

[30] As argued by Biondi and Rubini, 'Aims, Effects and Justifications' (n 3) at 89.

state resource. Social legitimacy then depends on whether the evaluative standard is congruent with the underlying social context. It shall be discussed below that the Court and the GC sometimes struggle in finding a coherent rationale for this distinction and that, as a result, market-based evaluations may become dominant and applied to social contexts that are unsuitable to be approached on that basis.[31] It was mentioned before that, for the definition of state aid, five constituent elements need to be fulfilled. The adjudicative technique of the Court in the definition of state aid is based on a rationale of categorisation. With this I mean that the Court has to establish if a certain context qualifies as a state resource; a selective advantage; a distortion of trade; an impact on trade between Member States. Such processes of categorisation harbour rationales that may result in qualifying a social reality in terms for which it is manifestly unsuited. Importantly, in order to determine what is the most efficient relationship between state and market, the state aid rules have to correctly distinguish the state from its role as a public authority and regulator from the state as a market participant.

For example, genuinely regulatory objectives concerning the regulation of public infrastructure may be qualified as forgoing state resources on the basis of a market-based valuation of the social context involved. It is on this point that market efficiency standards may be imposed as a yardstick of valuation for social contexts that do not fit (completely) within those evaluative standards.[32] From the perspective of social legitimacy the problematic areas of state aid law therefore concern those areas where genuine and legitimate policy choices are plainly rejected or simply not recognised within the evaluative rationales. That is to say, tensions between normative choices of Member States towards the functioning of their economy and the restrictions imposed by the state aid regime on political mechanisms such as subsidies and other forms of regulatory intervention to implement political choices. Such errors of wrong valuation may occur because in some crucial parts of its analysis the Court uses market-derived standards. These will be further discussed below.

C. The Expedient Nature of Market-derived Standards within State Aid Law

One of the most important and contentious criteria to establish state aid is the 'advantage' given to one or more undertakings. In simple terms, advantage means a benefit that could not have been obtained 'under normal market conditions; or in the absence of the intervention by the aid granting authority'.[33] As a consequence

[31] See also De Cecco (n 1) at 88.

[32] Interestingly, in the area of state aid law, the market standards are occasionally also 'used' by Member States to justify behaviour with seemingly protectionist aims; Case C-124/10 P *European Commission v Électricité de France* (EDF), nyp. Something I will return to further below.

[33] eg Case C-357/14 P *Electrabel and Dunamenti Erőmű v Commission*, nyp, para 144.

such advantages 'lighten the burdens normally assumed in an undertaking's budget'.[34] As was briefly discussed before, on the basis of the *Steenkolenmijn* judgment, the concept of advantage can be understood to be very wide and encompasses grants, subsidies, loans or guarantees by the state,[35] anything owed to the state (which the state would fail to collect),[36] anything the state gives up without objective reason,[37] services it purchases at excessively high prices[38] or any other types of advantages flowing from governance frameworks (provided they provide a selective benefit).[39]

To assess when the actions of a public authority qualify as conferring an advantage, the Court has, at the instigation of the Commission, accepted to adopt a test that is described as the market economy operator principle (MEOP—encompassing both the market economy investor and creditor principles).[40] On the basis of this principle the decision of a public authority to grant a subsidy, loan or guarantee, to forgo anything or purchase services is compared with the decision that a private market-operator would make under similar circumstances. According to some recent readings of the case law, the Court introduced the MEOP in order for it to become the main guiding principle upon which to assess whether an advantage has been granted.[41] This is contrary to subsequent case law where the Court has clearly stated the application of the principle should be preceded by an assessment of the 'nature of the measure'.[42] If, instead, the state is acting as a regulator, the 'market rationality' principle would have to be replaced with evaluative standards based on questions as to whether regulation benefits a specific (group of) undertaking(s) or whether a measure involves a state resource.[43] However, it shall be discussed below that the Court and the GC sometimes struggle in finding a coherent rationale for this distinction and that, as a result, market-based evaluations may become dominant and applied to social contexts that are unsuitable to be approached on that basis

[34] eg Case 173/73 *Italy v Commission* [1974] ECR 709, para 26; Case C-387/92 *Banco Exterior de España* [1994] ECR I-877, paras 12 and 13; and Case C-280/00 *Altmark Trans and Regierungspräsidium Magdeburg* [2003] ECR I-0000, para 84.

[35] eg Case C-559/12 *France v Commission (La Poste)* [2014] nyp and Case C275/10 *Residex Capital IV* [2011] ECR I-13043, para 39.

[36] eg Case C-271/13 P *Rousse Industry v Commission* [2015] nyp.

[37] eg Case C-279/08 P *Commission v Netherlands* [2011] ECR I-07671; Case C-39/14 *BVVG Bodenverwertungs- und -verwaltungs GmbH [BVVG] v Landkreis Jerichower Land* [2015] nyp; Case C-214/12 P *Land Burgenland v Commission* [2013] np.

[38] eg Case T-98/00 *Linde v Commission* [2002] ECR II-03961.

[39] eg Case C-518/13 *Eventech* [2015] nyp; Case C-357/14 P *Electrabel and Dunamenti Erőmű v Commission* [2015] nyp.

[40] First in Case C-234/84 *Kingdom of Belgium v Commission of the European Communities (Meura)* [1986] ECR 02263. See Lopez (n 4) at 75.

[41] eg Lopez (n 4) at 101.

[42] In Case C-124/10 *P European Commission v EDF and others* [2012] ECR nyp.

[43] As argued by De Cecco (n 1).

Fransesco de Cecco describes that the market operator principle pursues, in effect, substantive equality.[44] That is to say, to achieve a situation in which undertakings, regardless of their relationship with the state compete on an equal footing. In this sense, an important objective of state aid law is to neutralise the effects of state intervention by 'subjecting it to scrutiny based on market drawn criteria'.[45] As such, one of the main objectives of the MEOP is to bring transparency and clarity into the Member States' activity on the market. It is clear that this is, more generally, one of the main objectives of the state aid rules, which was clearly established by the Court in *Altmark* where it held that in order for compensation for public service obligations not to constitute state aid, 'the recipient undertaking must have public service obligations to discharge and these must be clearly defined'.[46] Moreover, 'the parameters on the basis of which the compensation is calculated must be established in advance in an objective and transparent manner'.[47] It can be said that in *Altmark*, the Court sought to eliminate any possibility of manipulation of state resources to the benefit of selective undertakings.[48]

Crucially, in this respect, the Court has rejected the idea that certain aims of fiscal or social policies would fall outside of the ambit of Article 107 TFEU. The Court has always insisted that the question of aid does not distinguish between the measures of state intervention concerned by reference to their causes or aims but defines them in relation to their effects.[49] It is therefore not possible for a Member State to only invoke the legitimacy of the aim pursued in order to avoid the application of the state aid regime.[50] Instead, by requiring that market 'rationality' is to inform the decision of public authorities, MEOP indeed turns market standards into regulatory standards, whose scope, depth and intensity can be illustrated by way of discussing some recent case law. Hence, the following discussion of some recent approaches of the Court of Justice and the General Court will serve as a problematisation of the application of the MEOP from the perspective of the social legitimacy of the EU state aid regime. The MEOP can become expedient and pervasive at the moment that there is not a clear rationale to separate the role of the state in its actions that pursue regulatory interests from the role of the state in

[44] ibid.

[45] ibid, at 74.

[46] Case C-280/00 *Altmark Trans and Regierungspräsidium Magdeburg* [2003] ECR I-0000, para 89.

[47] ibid, para 90.

[48] Opinion of AG Mazak in Case C124/10 P *European Commission v Électricité de France (EDF) and Others*, para 95.

[49] eg Case C39/14 *BVVG* [2015] nyp; Case C-417/10 *3M Italia* [2012] nyp, para 36; Case C-487/06 P *British Aggregates v Commission* [2008] ECR I-10515, paras 84 and 85; Case C-6/93 *Belgium v Commission* [1996] ECR I723, para 79; Case C-241/94 *France v Commission* [1996] ECR I-04551, para 20; Case C-75/97 *Belgium v Commission* [1999] ECR I-03671, para 25; and Case C409/00 *Spain v Commission* [2003] ECR I-01487, para 46.

[50] Case C-487/06 P *British Aggregates v Commission* [2008] ECR I-10515, para 84, Case C241/94 *France v Commission* [1996] ECR I-4551, para 21; Case C342/96 *Spain v Commission* [1999] ECR I-2459, para 23; and Case C75/97 *Belgium v Commission* ECR I-03671, para 25.

its actions that pursue participation in the market. The following sections set out how and why this might be problematic.

D. The Potential Expedient Scope of the Market Economy Operator Principle (Part One): The Absence of Rationale for Genuine Regulation versus the Clear Rationale of a Private Investor/Creditor

As was briefly touched on above, the Court has established that the MEOP should be applied after an assessment of the 'nature' of an aid giving measure. Arguably, in clear regulatory contexts concerning the exercise of public authority, it would not be applied. That this can be a topic of discussion is illustrated in, for example, the case of *The Netherlands and ING v the Commission*, which concerned a measure by virtue of which a Dutch bank was granted favourable conditions for the repayment of state aid that it had received in the wake of the financial crisis.[51] It was favourable because the rate of remuneration was lower than what had been originally agreed between the Dutch government and ING. The argument was made that this could not be considered state aid because a private investor would never find itself in the same situation as the Dutch government in relation to ING. The GC rejected this argument. Instead the GC decided that a hypothetical private investor could very well agree to accept repayment on different terms than initially agreed, for example, 'if it could benefit from avoiding the risk of holding shares whose future value was unknown'. The Commission failed to assess such potential benefits. The Court agreed with this and held that

> an economic advantage must, even where it has been granted through fiscal means, be assessed in the light of the private investor test if, on conclusion of an overall assessment, it appears that, notwithstanding the fact that the means used were instruments of State power, the Member State concerned has conferred that advantage in its capacity as shareholder of the undertaking belonging to it … It follows that the applicability of the private investor test to a public intervention depends, not on the way in which the advantage was conferred, but on the *classification of the intervention as a decision adopted by a shareholder of the undertaking* in question.[52] (emphases added)

The Court went on to observe that any holder of securities, in whatever amount and of whatever nature, may wish or agree to renegotiate the conditions of their redemption

> What is decisive … is whether the amendment to the repayment terms of the capital injection has satisfied an economic rationality test, so that a private investor might also be in a position to accept such an amendment, in particular by increasing the prospects of obtaining the repayment of that injection.[53]

[51] Case C-224/12 P *Commission v The Netherlands* [2014] nyp.
[52] ibid, paras 30–31.
[53] ibid, para 36.

In view of what was discussed before, the Court raises here, implicitly, the question of the rationale of a public authority versus the rationale of a private investor. In the absence of a rationale that can bring such measures within a general regulatory framework, the authority in effect concedes that it grants state aid unless it can claim that it acts as a private investor and positively provide evidence to establish that its transactions with undertakings can generate a return that would be acceptable in market terms. I will discuss in section III to what extent the reasoning of the Court harbours a potential for responsiveness to social context. What matters here is that the potential scope of the MEOP is, as interpreted by the Court, wide, especially if one takes into account how regulatory intervention takes place in post-Thatcher Europe.[54] Essentially those processes have obscured the difference between market and non-market approaches in regulatory intervention.

As was discussed in Chapter 1, processes of privatisation and liberalisation have spread over Europe and led to new forms of regulatory intervention and the gradual process by which the role of the state as a direct provider of public services disappeared has led to the creation of 'new regulatory tools' that are aimed at safeguarding the public interest on the basis of terms set by new public management reforms.[55] Outside of general schemes, state support to undertakings charged with public service obligations, providing services of general economic interest, as regulators or as a shareholder in undertakings with public responsibilities is among those new regulatory tools. The goals of the new public management wave have been to 'improve the effectiveness and efficiency of the public sector; to enhance the responsiveness of public agencies to their clients and customers; to reduce public expenditure; and to improve managerial accountability'.[56] This was undertaken by 'doing away with hierarchy, monolithic systems, politically neutral administrative bodies, standardized personnel system and standardized regulation of citizens and companies for the benefit of a market-like, deregulated system of pseudo-corporate, autonomous service providers and enthusiastic public managers'.[57] Therefore, one of the key features of these reforms has been to not make any distinctions between the public and the private sector when it comes to how the public sector is managed; separating commercial activity from non-commercial activity and emphasising financial reporting and accountability.[58]

[54] See also B Lange, F Haines, and D Thomas (eds), *Regulatory Transformations: Rethinking Economy-Society Interactions* (Oxford, Hart Publishing, 2015).

[55] See further E Szyszczak, *The Regulation of the State in Competitive Markets in the EU* (Oxford, Hart Publishing, 2007) 3–4; S Picciotto, 'Liberalization and Democratization: The Forum and the Hearth in the Era of Cosmopolitan Post-Industrial Capitalism' (2000) 63(4) *Law and Contemporary Problems* 157–78.

[56] T Christensen and P Laegreid (eds), *The Ashgate Research Companion to New Public Management* (Farnham, Ashgate, 2011) at 1.

[57] T Beck Jorgensen and L Bogh Andersen, 'An Aftermath of NPM: Regained Relevance of Public Values and Public Service Motivation' in Christensen and Laegreid (eds), *The Ashgate Research Companion to New Public Management* (n 56) at 335.

[58] Z Hoque and J Moll, 'Public Sector Reform: Implications for Accounting, Accountability and Performance of State-Owned Entities—An Australian Perspective' (2001) 14 *International Journal of*

Moreover, on the basis of the state aid rules the relationship between the state and the provider of public services in many of these regulatory bonds has to be based on the behavioural standard of the prudent investor in every action that brings forth an advantage or, alternatively, to notify the state aid. This has led to a new reality for authorities pursuing regulatory intervention in the market.[59] Although the Court recognises explicitly that the private investor principle has to be excluded in the event that the state acts as a public authority, since such situations can never compare to those of a private investor in a market economy, the new regulatory tools and implementation of principles of new public management make it increasingly obscure to understand what public authority actually entails outside of the traditional functions that have always been strongly associated with state authority (police, public health, public security).[60]

Take *Ryanair v Commission*, which concerned the setting of airport charges by regulation of the Walloon Region. The GC held that the setting of airport charges was closely connected with the use and operation of Charleroi airport, which was an economic activity and that it was necessary to differentiate between that specific economic activity and activities that fell strictly under public authority powers.[61] The GC held that the regulatory powers of the Walloon Region to fix airport charges did not mean that its regulatory decision to lower those charges would not fall in the sphere of the private investor principle, 'since such a scheme could have been put in place by a private operator'.[62] Just to have the regulatory power is therefore not enough to exclude the validity of the MEOP as a evaluative principle unless the activities in question can somehow be connected 'by their nature, their aim and the rules to which they are subject, are connected with the exercise of powers … which are typically those of a public authority'.[63]

These examples point out that in view of the development in public management it is likely that the MEOP is of increasing importance in regulatory contexts. However, the reasoning based on the connection to the 'traditional' exercise of public power is outdated and, as will be discussed further below, should be exchanged for a more dynamic approach, one that is responsive to potential genuine regulatory intentions of Member States.

Public Sector Management 305. See also P Dibben and P Higgins, 'New Public Management: Marketization, Managerialism and Consumerism' in P Dibben, G Wood and I Roper (eds), *Contesting Public Sector Reforms* (London, Palgrave Macmillan, 2004); W Dunn and D Miller, 'A Critique of New Public Management and the Neo-Weberian State Advancing a Critical theory of Administrative Reform' (2007) 7 *Public Organization Review* 345–58.

[59] Also E Szyszczak, 'Public Services in Competition Markets' (2001) 21 *Yearbook of European Law* 35, at 64.

[60] Such as eg in Case C-364/92 *SAT Fluggesellschaft* [1994] ECR I-00043. See also L Hancher, 'Towards a New Definition of a State Aid under European Law—Is there a New Concept of State Aid Emerging' (2003) *European State Aid Law Quarterly* 365–73, at 366–68.

[61] Case T-196/04 *Ryanair v Commission* [2008] ECR II-03643.

[62] ibid, para 101.

[63] Case C-364/92 *SAT Fluggesellschaft* [1994] ECR I-00043, para 30.

E. The Scope of the Market Economy Operator Principle (Part Two): Control over Economic Assets or Public Infrastructure

Moreover, and increasingly challenging, where the state acing as a regulator *creates or has control over an asset*, it may be necessary to determine whether that asset has an economic value and whether that value may constitute a transfer of state resources.[64] This was at stake in *Bouygues Sa v Commission*, where the GC held that the exercise of state functions does not preclude the taking into account of economic facts in connection with the management of a scarce public resource such as radio frequencies constituting the public airwaves, to which a right of access or a right of usage *may* be granted.[65] Again, the argument that the assets in question had no equivalent in the hands of private managers was not sufficient for excluding them as a state resource. Some economic value could be assigned to it and it therefore was an asset, which the state should approach on the basis of prudent market operator principles, if it would want to avoid the applicability of a state aid notification obligation.[66] A similar rationale applied with regard to the Netherlands which allowed the transfer by undertakings of trading emission allowances, free of charge.[67] The GC held that 'those assets are put at the disposal of the undertakings concerned free of charge, whereas they could have been sold or put up for auction; The Kingdom of the Netherlands has thus forgone State resources'.[68] On appeal, this was confirmed by the grand chamber of the Court of Justice, which added that

> the tradability of the NOx emission allowances depends above all on the fact that the State, first, authorises the sale of those allowances and, second, allows those undertakings which have emitted a surplus of NOx to acquire from other undertakings the missing emission allowances, thereby agreeing to the creation of a market for those allowances ... by making those allowances tradable the Kingdom of the Netherlands confers on them a market value.[69]

An analogy can be drawn on this point with the distinction between economic and non-economic activities and the application of the competition rules in Article 101 TFEU. As was discussed in Chapter 3, the Court has consistently held that any

[64] Also A Biondi, 'Some Reflections on the Notion of "State Resources" in European Community State Aid Law' (2007) 30 *Fordham International Law Journal* 1426.

[65] Case C-431/07 *P Bouygues and Bouygues Télécom v Commission* [2009] ECR I-02665.

[66] Although the Court decided in para 110 that

> the amount payable as a fee can constitute State aid only if, all other things being equal, there is a difference between the price paid by each of the operators concerned, it being recalled that, according to the Court of Justice, it is the time when each of the operators concerned entered the market that must be taken into account [...]. On the other hand, if the national authorities decide as a general principle that licences will be awarded free of charge, or awarded by means of public auctions or awarded at a standard price, there is no aid element, provided these terms are applied to all the operators concerned without distinction.

[67] Case T-233/04 *Netherlands v Commission* [2008] ECR II-00591.

[68] ibid, para 70.

[69] Case C-279/08P *Commission v Netherlands* [2011] ECR I-07671, paras 88 and 107.

activity consisting in offering goods and services on a market is an economic activity.[70] However, the question whether a market exists for certain services may depend on the institutional means through which those services are organised in the Member State concerned.[71] Similar as with the competition rules, the state aid rules only apply where an activity is provided 'in a market environment'. Therefore, the economic nature of certain services may differ between the Member States since this remains subject to political choices or Member State-specific economic developments, which may also change over time. At the same time, however, simply the decision of an authority not to allow third parties to provide a certain service (such as with in-house services) does not rule out the existence of an economic activity. In spite of such *market closure*, an economic activity can exist, simply, 'where other operators would be willing and able to provide the service in the market concerned'.[72] This rationale is potentially expedient in the sense that the potentiality of private operators providing the service in question can be increasingly wide, especially in a context of increasing liberalisation and privatisation. Similarly, the reasoning of the Court in the *Dutch NoX* case and other cases is potentially expedient since, if read in a certain way, there is, with regard to public infrastructure, always the potential of a resource and the actions of states may therefore quickly be qualified as forgoing that state resource.

F. The Potential Crowding out Effects of the Market Operator Principle

After having established that the MEOP harbours a risk of being adopted too easily and without sufficient context-sensitivity, we can say something about the potential effects of applying that principle to social contexts, which may pursue objectives that are potentially damaged or ignored within the evaluative standard of the market economy rationale. By way of introduction, the case of *Rousse Industry* provides some insights into what MEOP actually entails. Rousse is a Bulgarian manufacturing company specialising in metal constructions. It received state aid that the Commission found to be incompatible with the internal market in the form of loans it could not repay to the Bulgarian state.[73] The GC stated that a 'prudent and diligent private creditor', which is faced with a situation where a debtor's financial situation is worsening and is not making payments on its loan, would make a choice between launching proceedings against the debtor or reaching an amicable arrangement if that would recover more or at least part of the debt.[74] The Court

[70] Case 118/85 *Commission v Italy* [1987] ECR 2599, para 7; Case C-35/96 *Commission v Italy* [1998] ECR I-3851, para 36; Joined Cases C-180/98 to C-184/98 *Pavlov and Others* [2000] ECR I-06451, para 75.

[71] Joined Cases C-159/91 and C-160/91 *Poucet and Pistre* [1993] ECR I-637.

[72] See also the Opinion of AG Geelhoed in Case C-295/05 *Asociación Nacional de Empresas Forestales (Asemfo) v Transformación Agraria SA (Tragsa) and Administración del Estado* [2007] ECR I-2999, paras 110–16.

[73] Case C-271/13 P *Rousse Industry v Commission* [2014] ECR nyp.

[74] Case T-489/11 *Rousse Industry v Commission* [2013] ECR np.

agreed that the Bulgarian authorities had not acted as a private creditor because they limited themselves exclusively to the amicable route. Only 'reminders' for the payment were sent. There was, however, no specific evidence that Rousse Industry would eventually return to a viable status.[75] At this point the Bulgarian authorities would have to provide evidence of the profitability of the scenario it was following at that time. The Court decided that a public authority, which is owed money must exhaust all the options available to recover the loan and if necessary force the debtor into liquidation 'whenever a forced sale of assets would result in a higher yield in terms of recovered money'.[76]

In terms of behavioural standards, the prudent private investor represents a fundamental benchmark and has been defined as an 'an investor who wishes to maximise his profits but without running excessive risks' as well as being 'guided by prospects of profitability'. In a similar tone, AG Jacobs underlined in *Spain v Commission* that state aid is granted whenever a Member State makes available to an undertaking funds which in the normal course of events would not be provided by a private investor applying ordinary commercial criteria and 'disregarding considerations of a social, political or philanthropic nature'.[77] In cases where a company in financial distress proposes its creditors to rearrange its debt, each creditor acting as a private investor is expected to 'make a decision having regard to the amount offered to it under the proposed agreement, on the one hand, and the amount it expects to be able to recover following possible liquidation of the firm, on the other'.[78] Therefore, in the absence of *specific and credible evidence of return to profitability*, it is unrealistic to imagine that a private creditor placed in a similar situation could be persuaded that chances of successful recovery are maximised with deferring repayment. The burden of proof supporting that the Member State authorities in fact acted in accordance with the private creditor test lies with the Member State.[79]

Therefore, relationships based on 'trust' or 'informal relations' are not recognised within the world of the prudent private investor, unless they can be specifically quantified in terms of profitability. A private investor should be motivated solely by the possibility of making profits or return on investment and ignore all other policy objectives of a public nature at that stage.[80] Should any social ambitions be present then the Member State is to notify this as a state aid to the Commission, where these ambitions shall be reviewed. Simply said, the hypothetical private investor may not wilfully forgo any obvious opportunity for profit.[81]

[75] ibid, paras 60–61.

[76] ibid, para 65.

[77] AG Jacobs in Joined Cases C–278/92, C–279/92 and C–280/92 *Spain v Commission* [1994] ECR I–4103, para 28.

[78] Case T-152/99, *Hamsa v Commission* [2002] ECR II-3049, para 166.

[79] Case T-318/00 *Freistaat Thüringen v Commission* [2005] ECR II-4179, para 180.

[80] Case C-278/92 *Spain v Commission* [1994] ECR I-4103; Case T-358/94 *Air France v Commission* [1996] ECR II-02109.

[81] Case T-228/99 *WestLB v Commission* [2003] ECR II-435.

He may be guided by the same objective as a group of companies that tolerate short-term losses by one of the subsidiaries in order to achieve long-term profits for the group as a whole, possibly because this protects the image of the group.[82] However, when a public authority invests at the same time similar amounts on equal terms with a private investor, there is the presumption that the authority is acting rationally to earn a reasonable return on its investment. This is the case even when the firm in which the authority invests has suffered losses. In this eventuality the public authority and the private co-investor should be investing on the basis of a plan that can turn the firm around and return it to long-term profitability.[83]

Since the test of the private investor is a comparison of the behaviour of a public authority and a hypothetical investor, the corroborative evidence that is accepted by the Commission consists of analyses, reports or declarations from independent banks, venture capital companies, consultants or other economic experts.[84] It should be noted that the private investor concept as applied in state aid law is narrower than the likely actual behaviour of real investors. We know, for example, that market participants often act on far more than mere efficiency considerations. Often, as eg Macaulay has demonstrated, the non-contractual relations and factors influence business relationships to a great extent, regardless of the formal contracts and relationships that are in place.[85] To what extent the market operator principle therefore actually reflects behavioural market rationality is questionable. This adds to the argument that the MEOP should not be applied carelessly but should be preceded by an analysis of the societal context to which it is being applied.

Moreover, there is no room for the subtler elements of the relationship between the state and undertakings that receive advantages in judicial review and the application of the state aid rules. There are of course good reasons for a purely functional evaluation of such relationships since recognising or allowing trust and informal considerations to rule the relationship between the state and its debtors would simply be too amorphous for judicial review and raise problems for the application of the state aid rules.[86] That is to say, trust and informality are just a step away from the granting of advantages for protectionist aims. On the other hand, a completely functional and under-socialised model of adjudication could threaten the social cohesions, solidarity or identity that a state perhaps pursues and applies in social situations. Hence, there is a potential loss to be considered

[82] eg Case C-303/88 *Italian Republic v Commission* [1991] ECR I-01433. A private investor who already owns shares in a company may tolerate short-term losses and behave differently than a new investor in order to protect his existing investment or in order to avoid paying any extra costs or incurring penalties from liquidating his shareholding; Case C-42/93 *Spain v Commission* [1994] ECR I-4175, paras 13 and 14; Case C-323/00 P *DSG Dradenauer Stahlgesellschaft v Commission* [2002] ECR I-03919, para 42.

[83] ibid.

[84] Case T-228/99 *WestLB v Commission* [2003] ECR II-00435.

[85] S Macaulay, 'Non-Contractual Relations in Business: A Preliminary Study' (1963) 28 *American Sociological Review* 55.

[86] G Davies, 'Democracy and Legitimacy in the Shadow of Purposive Competence' (2015) 21 *European Law Journal* 2.

there. It is generally understood that a social fabric where economic actors are repeatedly in contact with each other allows for the development and dissemination of trust to develop.[87] This form of *embeddedness*, highlighted in Chapter 1, concerns the role of concrete personal relations based on reciprocity in generating trust and discouraging opportunistic behaviour. It has been shown that the quality and intensity of social relations may facilitate the strengthening of trust and discourage opportunistic behaviour.[88] This responds to the functional idea that society can be identified on the basis of its individual interests and merely seeing those individuals as freely contracting economic and social agents. A simple convergence of individual interests creates bonds that are too weak and superficial to give stability to social relations.[89]

The social relationships that the state can maintain on the basis of the MEOP are, however, individualistic, mechanistic and based, exclusively, on self-interest. The concept harbours a reductionist view of the variety of organisational principles that may govern certain social contexts.[90] Social legitimacy is concerned with the social value that can be lost in the perception of state market relationships within purely functional terms. However, it must also be clearly recognised that this is to some and perhaps a large extent a necessity since judicial or administrative review cannot be expected to integrate all social subtleties of these relationships. The tools available to adjudicate in state aid matters may simply lack sufficient refinement to take account fully of diverse kinds of valuation.[91] It may follow that state aid in some cases ought to operate on the reductionist and functional assumptions of the prudent investor when it approaches certain contexts. Section IV shall further explore the possibilities and limits in this regard.

This discussion of the case law in the previous sections was not to suggest that the setting of airport charges, granting of radio licences to operate or regulating the tradability of emission allowances is, necessarily, a typical public authority activity that should be allowed to exist outside of the scope of application of the MEOP but merely to point to the potentially expansive scope of the private investor rationale, which when combined with the idea that the state is under an obligation to actively pursue profit where it has control over an asset, becomes profoundly pervasive *in some regulatory contexts*. Mainly within many new

[87] M Granovetter, 'Economic Action and Social Structure: The Problem of Embeddedness' (1985) 91 *American Journal of Sociology* 481.

[88] M Tulio, F Zanin and CP Migueles, 'Trust as an Element of Informal Coordination and its Relationship with Organizational Performance' (2013) 14 *EconomiA* 77.

[89] See also E Durkheim, *The Division of Labor in Society* (New York, Free Press of Glencoe, 1964) at 152: 'for where interest alone reigns, as nothing arises to check the egoism confronting one other, each self finds itself in relation to the other on a war footing'.

[90] It is in this sense a rationale very close to Adam Smith's dictum: 'It is not from the benevolence of the butcher, the brewer, or the baker, that we expect our dinner, but from their regard to their own interest. We address ourselves, not to their humanity but to their self-love, and never talk to them of our own necessities but of their advantages'; A Smith, *The Wealth of Nations* (ed RH Campbell and AS Skinner, *The Glasgow Edition of the Works and Correspondence of Adam Smith*, 1976), vol 2b, at 26.

[91] See more generally on this point CR Sunstein, 'Incommensurability and Valuation in Law' (1994) 92 *Michigan Law Review* 779.

regulatory and governance contexts, it becomes increasingly difficult to envisage an alternative rationale besides that of the prudent private market operator. As was discussed in this section, there is not a lot of margin of appreciation for the wider societal context once within the MEOP. One such alternative would, for example, be 'public-spiritedness,' based on the desire to provide certain goods communally as part of the state.[92] This is, obviously, an amorphous, fragile, difficult to quantify, form of social value. However, once organised on the basis of individualistic market incentives, it might be difficult to maintain such organisational forms.[93]

Therefore, if the limits between the market and legitimate regulation are not coherently drawn there is a risk of genuine norm conflict failure, which is to say that the market economy operator principle could be applied to govern or foreclose legitimate aims of a regulatory nature that are insufficiently captured or addressed in terms of a market economy operator test. This has some foreshadowing effects. For example, AG Wahl, in the *Eventech* case (to be discussed further below in section III), pointed to the danger, that if the state aid rules were to be interpreted as generally requiring Member States to charge for access to public infrastructure or state-controlled resources, this might deter states from creating or opening up areas to which there has previously been no, or only limited access.[94] Equally, it might deter undertakings from participating in that process since paying for the use of public infrastructure might deter requesting access, which might result in access being given only to the economically most resourceful, and possibly defeating the legitimate purposes of a certain redistributive policy objective.[95] In this way there is a clear risk that the rationale associated with the market operator principle crowds out other potentially legitimate objectives that are simply not considered relevant.

G. The Conditional Pursuit of Services of General Interest on the Basis of Adversarial Relationships

Similar concerns can be voiced with respect to the efficiency rationale that governs the financing of services of general economic interest (SGEI). The Treaties, secondary legislation and the institutions attribute to the SGEI a central role in promoting social and territorial cohesion and as being part of the shared values of the Union. The Court of Justice approach to the idea of SGEIs is that they 'exhibit special characteristics as compared with those of other economic activities'.[96] Member States have a wide margin of discretion in defining a given service as

[92] N Boeger, 'Solidarity and EC Competition Law' (2007) 32 *European Law Review* 319–40.

[93] ibid.

[94] AG Opinion Wahl in Case C-518/13 *Eventech* [2014] nyp, paras 30–33.

[95] ibid, para 30.

[96] Cases C-179/90 *Merci convenzionali porto di Genova* [1991] ECR I-5889, para 27; Case C-242/95 *GT-Link A/S* [1997] ECR I-4449, para 53; and Case C-266/96 *Corsica Ferries France SA* [1998] ECR I-3949, para 45.

an SGEI. The Commission's competence in this respect is therefore traditionally limited to checking whether the Member State has made *a manifest error* when defining the service as an SGEI and to assessing any state aid involved in the compensation. On what basis the Commission can question Member State's definition of an SGEI has not yet been tested before the Court of Justice.[97] The Commission is of the opinion, and indicates as such in its Communication on the topic, that it is in any case 'not appropriate' 'to attach specific public service obligations to an activity which is already provided or can be provided satisfactorily and under conditions, as defined by the State, by undertakings operating under normal market conditions'.[98] Again, as for the question of whether a service can be provided by the market, the Commission acknowledges that it is 'limited to checking whether the Member State has made a manifest error'. As such, with regard to the definition of SGEI, there is a similar dynamic, or operational rationale in place as has been identified in the previous chapters on competition and free movement. Meaning that there is a soft market primacy approach as towards state involvement in the market through the setting of policy objectives, which should first consider whether the objectives in question are pursued by the market and subsequently whether regulatory action should be pursued for the instances where the market does not achieve social welfare optimal outcomes. Regulatory action that deviates from this principle then has to fulfil procedural safeguards, for which the well-known *Altmark* case provides the central framework.[99]

The facts behind *Altmark* are widely known. In 1990, Altmark Trans (Altmark) obtained licences and subsidies for passenger transport by bus in the Landkreis (district) of Stendal. A competitor complained that Altmark Trans would not be economically viable but for the subsidies. The handling court in Germany had concerns about the compatibility of the subsidies and accordingly referred the issue to the Court of Justice. The Court then used this case to set out the conditions under which the financing of public services would be immune from a state aid challenge. It formulated four conditions for state aid to be excluded.[100]

[97] The issue has been before the GC recently in Case T-309/12 *Zweckverband Tierkörperbeseitigung v Commission* nyp and will be further discussed in section IV.

[98] In the 2011 SGEI Communication the Commission considers it would not be appropriate to attach specific public service obligations to activities provided by undertakings operating under normal market conditions; *cf* Communication on the application of the European Union State aid rules to compensation granted for the provision of services of general economic interest, OJ 2012 C 8/4, para 48. See T Müller, 'Efficiency Control in State Aid and the Power of Member States to Define SGEIs' (2009) 1 *European State Aid Law Quarterly* 8.

[99] Case C-280/00 *Altmark Trans GmbH and Regierungspräsidium Magdeburg v Nahverkehrsgesellschaft Altmark GmbH* [2003] ECR I-7747.

[100] Paras 89–93:

> the recipient undertaking must have public service obligations and the obligations must be clearly defined; the parameters for calculating the compensation must be objective, transparent and established in advance; the compensation cannot exceed what is necessary to cover all or part of the costs incurred in the discharge of the public service obligations, taking into account the relevant receipts and a reasonable profit; where the undertaking which is to discharge public service obligations is not chosen pursuant to a public procurement

The idea behind *Altmark* and the way that it has been mostly interpreted afterwards is that Member States retain their autonomy in designating certain activities as SGEIs, but are significantly constrained in the way that they structure them. Therefore, the assumption is that 'it is possible to question the efficiency of SGEI providers without questioning SGEIs'.[101] It has been argued that *Altmark* follows the *Glöckner* case law of the Court by holding that SGEIs should be delivered efficiently.[102] The reasoning in this case was that a limitation of the competition law framework would not be accepted if it could be shown that the undertakings charged with the delivery of public service mission were in practice unable to satisfy the existing demand in relation to those services. The emphasis that the Court put in *Altmark* on the condition that SGEIs will have to be delivered 'at the least cost to the Community' and the role of efficiency in the selection of the SGEI provider is reminiscent of this rationale.[103]

It has been argued that the use of public procurement would threaten to 'undermine some of the central values associated with the provision of public services, notably trust and the use of co-operative rather than conflictual, or adversary, relations'.[104] These concerns are related to the way that Member States are now obliged to structure the provision of SGEIs and the concern would be that the possibilities for Member States within the given scheme are inherently limited to the detriment of genuine and legitimate policy structures. Moreover, the efficiency requirement for when an undertaking is not chosen pursuant to a public procurement procedure can be considered as strict and its evidentiary burden is usually not met, therefore conditioning Member States to use public procurement procedures. As said, the key characteristic of public procurement procedures is that they are based on adversarial relationships, which create a principal and agent relationship based on a competition for capital.[105] That is to say, the parties to the contract are balancing between self-interest and their obligations under the contract. Moreover, where the contractor unbundles services into separate contracts and subcontracts, the same adversarial relations are recreated, compounding the self-interests involved and limiting opportunities for collaboration and trust to develop.[106] Again, the policy framework of the Commission in this

procedure which would allow for the selection of the tenderer capable of providing those services at the least cost to the community, the level of compensation needed must be determined on the basis of an analysis of the costs of a typical well-run company.

[101] See De Cecco (n 1) at 159.

[102] Case C-475/99 *Ambulanz Glöckner* [2001] ECR I-08089.

[103] See De Cecco (n 1) at 165.

[104] T Prosser, 'Competition Law and Public Services: From Single Market to Citizenship Rights' (2005) *European Public Law* 543, at 562.

[105] M Regan, 'Public Infrastructure Procurement: A Comparative Analysis of Adversarial and Non-adversarial Contracting Arrangements' (2012) *Public Infrastructure Bulletin* 3–4; J Boston, 'Basic NPM Ideas and their Development' in Christensen and Laegreid (n 56); D Osborne and T Gaebler, 'Reinventing Government: how the Entrepreneurial Spirit is Transforming the Public Sector' (New York, Addison Wesley Publishing Company, 1992).

[106] ibid.

area is both impressive and pervasive.[107] The Commission has taken the conditions that were set out by the Court literally and has tried to use that framework to push Member States in the structuring and financing of public missions.[108] However, there are only very few Commission decisions, in which contracts have been established without the use of a public procurement procedure, in which the Commission came to the conclusion that the *Altmark* test was satisfied and it is obvious that the Commission conditions Member States to the use of the procurement procedure in the structuring of their SGEIs.[109] The concerns in this area of the state aid regime are therefore similar to the concerns that were voiced with regard to the expedient nature of market-based evaluative principles for the actions of Member States. That is to say, the state aid regime may implement a reductionist view of the variety of organisational principles that may govern certain social contexts. Social legitimacy is concerned with the social value that can be lost in the perception of state market relationships within purely functional terms. The next section shall explore to what extent the European courts have incorporated mechanisms of responsiveness in its case law.

III. RESPONSIVENESS IN THE CASE LAW OF THE COURT

A. Introduction

The first chapter developed the idea that the social purpose of the multilateral EU internal market is to develop institutional rationales with sufficient sophistication to allow for communal diversity *and* promote the objectives of market integration. It is clear that the scope for communal diversity/social context, within the terms of most of the market-derived standards as were discussed in the previous sections are limited. The valuation of societal context is mostly functional and the scope for unprofitable courses of action seems limited. The point here, from the view of the normative expectations that were developed in Chapter 1, is the recognition of embedded social context within overarching governance rationales.

[107] JL Buendía Sierra, P Rivas and J Manuel, 'The Almunia Package: State Aid and Services of General Economic Interest' in E Szyszcak and JW van de Gronden (eds), *Financing Services of General Economic Interest* (The Hague, TMC Asser Press, 2013) at 125; TM Rusche, 'The Almunia Package' in Szyszcak and van de Gronden (eds), *Financing Services of General Economic Interest* (ibid) at 108.

[108] M Klasse, 'The Impact of Altmark: The European Commission Case Law Responses' in Szyszcak and Van de Gronden (eds), *Financing Services of General Economic Interest* (n 107) at 35.

[109] Notable exceptions include Commission, 16 December 2003, State aid N 475/2003 Security of Supply Ireland (CADA); Commission, 16 November 2004, State aid N 381/2004 Broadband Infrastructure Project Pyrénées-Atlantiques; Commission, 3 May 2005, State aid N 382/2004 Broadband infrastructure project Limousin (Dorsal); Commission, 30 September 2009, State aid N 331/2008 Broadband Hauts de Seine; Commission, 24 May 2007 Energy supply Slovenia OJ 2007 L 219/9; Commission, 15 September 2009, State aid N 206/2009 Financing of the public transport services in district of Anhalt-Bitterfeld; Commission, 15 September 2009, State aid N 207/2009, Financing of the transport services in district of Wittenberg.

Some communal contexts lend themselves easily to economic regulation. The 'instrumental community' context fits within a form of regulation based on an evaluative principle of efficiency. Problems may arise, however, when such economic substantive efficiency-oriented governance mechanisms would be installed to regulate social context based on trust, informal values, public-spiritedness and so forth. The balance from the perspective of state aid is therefore a difficult one since trust and informal relations are, perceived from a state aid perspective, important factors contributing to in-transparency and constitutive to relationships, which are likely to end up in granting covert advantages to some undertakings and not to others.[110] The rigidity of the prudent private investor standard *leaving aside all social, regional-policy and sectoral considerations*[111] is, at least partly, based on this idea of the need for administrability and transparency in state aid matters. On the other hand, there is an inherent reductionist view of the legitimate relationship between the state and the market at play. One that in its valuation of state action may exclude valuable social practices that in all likelihood contribute to social cohesion and capital within Member States. This is a potential effect of turning the market into *the* platform for accountability in state aid matters.[112] The market-based regulatory standards that state aid law introduces may condition public bodies towards actions that are justified exclusively on the grounds of their commercial self-interest and thereby crowd out potential alternative visions towards the appropriate role of public authorities and the direction that policy objectives take.

Consequently, it is likely that the state aid rules may further condition Member States towards the installation of a spectrum of a cost-benefit analysis, which may soon become the primary frame of reference for public authorities. Therefore, as was noted in the previous section, if the limits between the market and legitimate regulation are not coherently drawn there is a risk of genuine norm conflict failure, which is to say that the market economy operator principle is applied to govern or foreclose legitimate aims of a regulatory nature that are insufficiently captured or addressed in terms of that test. Moreover, there are clear instances where the EU state aid rules, as they are interpreted by the Commission, the GC and the Court neutralise potentially salient issues within a technocratic syntax that largely proceduralises the way Member State structure regulatory interventions in the market. There is a risk that thereby state aid rules systematically devalue or exclude possible alternative routes, which forgo the development of social capital on a Member State level.[113]

[110] This concern is reflected in the case law of the Court that identifies policy discretion for Member States in granting advantages or derogations from general applicable legislation as evidence for selectivity in cases: Case C-241/94 *France v Commission* [1996] I-04551, paras 23 and 24; Case C-200/97 *Ecotrade* [1998] ECR I-07907, para 40; Case C-295/97 *Piaggio* [1999] ECR I-03735, para 39; Case C-256/97 *DM Transport* [1999] I-03913, para 27; and Case C-6/12 *P*, np, para 27.

[111] Case C-234/84 *Belgium v Commission (Meura)* [1986] ECR 2263, para 14 (emphasis added).

[112] See on this also De Cecco (n 1) at 76.

[113] Similar concerns voiced by M Dani, 'Rehabilitating Social Conflicts in European Public Law' (2012) 18(5) *European Law Journal* 621.

The previous section has identified instances where the state aid rules impose norms on Member States which may exclude relevant social context from the state aid evaluation and force Member States to behave according to narrow market-derived criteria that are one-dimensional and under-socialised. This section discusses the state aid case law of the Court with a view to tracing instances where it has shown an explicit responsiveness to such context and allowing for the potential of social norm diversity. The next section IV shall reconstruct that case law into a coherent model of social legitimacy that allows the Court to implement an 'operational rationale' whenever it has to adjudicate a conflict between the objectives of state aid and restrictive domestic (social) interests that is in accordance with the dialogue of mutual responsiveness.

B. Mutual Responsiveness: Between Regulation and the Market

It was highlighted before that the Court has been quite explicit about the need to juxtapose cases involving Member States acting in their role as public regulators and cases where they act as market participants. Arguably, when the state acts as a regulator its actions cannot be held accountable on the basis of the behavioural standards as derived from the MEOP. For example, the Court held in *Spain v Commission* that 'a distinction must be drawn between the obligations which the State must assume as owner of the share capital of a company and its obligations as a public authority'.[114] In *Altmark*, AG Léger noted that the Court applies the MEOP only in situations where the intervention of the state is of an economic nature. Where 'the conduct of the State is capable of being adopted, *at least in principle*, by a private operator acting with a view to profit', it should apply.[115]

In these situations the conduct of the state should be evaluated on the basis of market-derived standards for the reason that a private operator that is operating on the basis of self-interest profit motives may have made similar decisions. However, the principle would not apply where the activity concerned falls within the exercise of *public powers* of the state, such as 'tax policy or social policy'.[116] Similarly in *Westdeutsche Landesbank Girozentrale and Land Nordrhein-Westfalen v Commission*, the GC noted that

> as regards the Land's argument based on increased tax revenue, the Court observes that the Land's position as a public body and its position as the owner of a business must not be confused. The line of argument based on an increase in tax revenue would be *wholly irrelevant* for a private investor.[117] (emphases added)

[114] Joined Cases C-278/92 to C-280/92 *Spain v Commission* [1994] ECR I-4103, par 22. See also Joined Cases T-129/95, T-2/96 and T-97/96 *Neue Maxhütte Stahlwerke and Lech-Stahlwerke v Commission* [1999] ECR II-17, para 119.

[115] Opinion of AG Leger in Case C–280/00 *Altmark Trans and Regierungspräsidium Magdeburg* [2003] ECR I-7747.

[116] Case T-228/99 *DEP—Westdeutsche Landesbank Girozentrale v Commission* [2003] ECR II-00435.

[117] Case T-196/04 *Ryanair v Commission* [2008] ECR II-03643.

In the previously discussed *Ryanair* case the GC annulled a Commission decision concerning aid granted by the Walloon regional government to Ryanair on the basis of an error of law resulting from the Commission's misinterpretation of the scope of the market operator principle, which consisted in holding that the setting of landing charges was not congruent to that principle. The GC focused on the question whether or not the activity consisted in offering goods and services on a given market. The GC reasoned in line with the previously discussed case law that if the state acted as a private investor, the market operator principle should apply. The GC sanctioned the Commission for not clearly distinguishing between the state acting as a 'public authority and the activities of a market participant'.[118] In a similar vein the GC annulled a Commission decision that had found that certain measures implemented by France in favour of the state-owned energy company EDF amounted to state aid.[119] At the time, EDF was a public undertaking, wholly owned by the French state. In 1997, within the framework of the opening up of the internal market for electricity the French state amended its legislation. As part of this process, EDF's balance sheets were 'restructured' so as to increase its capital. After the restructuring operation the Commission adopted a decision finding that by virtue of this restructuring the French state had in effect waived a tax claim. The GC annulled the decision, holding that the Commission was not entitled, only because the measure taken was fiscal in nature, to refuse to examine whether the French state had acted as a 'private investor in a market economy'.[120] In its reasoning, the GC maintained the distinction that it had traced in previous cases, between economic activities and activities connected with the exercise of public power. However, it added, the distinction could not be traced on the basis of just the legal form used by the state but should instead be based on the *nature, aim and the rules* to which the states activities were subject, and, crucially, of the *objectives* that they pursued.[121] The GC again underlined the need to determine whether the state pursued an 'economic objective' which might also be pursued by a private investor, in order to establish whether or not the MEOP would be applicable:

> the measure must be examined not solely according to its form, but on the basis of its nature, its object and its objectives, which presupposes that all aspects of it are examined and *that its context is taken into consideration.*[122] (emphases added)

The GC noted that, as the law in question sought to restructure EDF's accounts and to increase its capital, it did not have a fiscal nature, but was an accounting measure with fiscal consequences. In light of these considerations, the GC concluded that the measure at issue could not be regarded as the exercise of public

[118] ibid.

[119] Case T-156/04 *EDF v Commission* [2009] ECR II-04503; Case C-124/10 P *European Commission v Électricité de France (EDF)*, nyr.

[120] Case T-156/04 *EDF v Commission* [2009] ECR II-04503, para 233.

[121] ibid, para 234.

[122] ibid, para 236.

powers, but had to be examined through the lens of the private investor test. However, this formal approach was in turn rejected by the Court. The Court held, instead, that, in a situation where a Member State is both a fiscal creditor of a public undertaking and its only shareholder:

> The roles of the State as shareholder of an undertaking, on the one hand, and of the State acting as a public authority, on the other, *must be distinguished*. Consequently, for the private investor test to be applicable, it must be in its capacity as shareholder and not in its capacity as public authority, that the Member State concerned confers an economic advantage on an undertaking belonging to it.[123] (emphases added)

In other words, the Court insists on an assessment that is dynamic and specifically concerned with the context in question. The Court specified that, if a Member State relies on the applicability of the private investor test, it must establish, unequivocally and on the basis of objective and verifiable evidence, that the measure implemented falls to be ascribed to the state acting as shareholder.[124] The Commission argued that when the state imposes *taxes* in the exercise of its public authority it cannot be claimed that it does this in its capacity as a private investor and the same would apply to its corollary—the waiving of tax debts. This was also the argument of AG Mazak in this case:

> Consequently, fiscal activities of the State—the imposition, collection, refund or remitting of taxes—are undoubtedly undertaken in the exercise of its public authority and cannot *by definition* be undertaken as a private investor. (emphases added)[125]

However, the Court decided that if the Member State concerned produces such evidence, it is for the Commission to carry out *a global assessment*, taking into account all evidence enabling it to determine whether the Member State took the measure in question in its capacity as shareholder or as a public authority.[126] It is interesting that the Court mentions this global assessment. The Court also referred to this type of assessment in the context of free movement cases,

[123] Case C-124/10 *P European Commission v Électricité de France (EDF)*, nyr, paras 80–81.

[124] ibid, para 82. EDF had an interest that the MEOP would be applied because it considered that the French state had good economic arguments for the forgoing of a tax claim it had against EDF and that a shareholder would have done the same thing in a similar situation. It therefore argued that the fact that the instrument used by the state (the waiving of a tax claim) is inaccessible to the private investor cannot mean that the MEOP must be rejected because it was still, in theory, possible to imagine a situation where a private operator would have the possibility to forgo a tax claim, whilst being a shareholder. In that situation it would then be possible to determine how a private operator would act. Indeed, perhaps if acting in its own self-interest only, it could be argued that the French state would then forgo that claim since it would be of a direct benefit to the shareholder of EDF. In other words, EDF reasoned that instruments, which in themselves are not available to private investors, can still be compared to the behavioural principles of private operators. This case shows that the MEOP can in some instances be manipulated by Member States to escape from the application of the state aid rules for disingenuous reasons.

[125] Opinion of AG Mazak in Case C-124/10 P *European Commission v Électricité de France* (EDF), nyp, para 79.

[126] Case C-124/10 P *European Commission v Électricité de France (EDF)*, nyr, para 86.

where it established whether or not the pursuit of a regulatory objective was genuine, systematic and coherent with the overall regulatory context.[127]

Accordingly, the Court agreed with the GC in holding that the objective pursued by the French state could be taken into account for the purposes of determining whether the state had acted in its capacity as shareholder. It is important to note that the Court did not provide an explicit answer to the question whether in this specific case the Commission was wrong to decide that the actions of the French State could not be qualified as the prudent behaviour of a private shareholder. The Court only established the principle that the decision to apply or not to apply the MEOP should be subject to a preceding assessment that establishes whether the context and objectives of the measure in question *were specific to those of a shareholder or public authority*.

However, the Court did not provide guidance with regard to the question how to decide between the domains of the market and the regulator. The rationale that is confirmed by the Court indicates that economic activities that are inherent for the pursuit of 'public authority' objectives are not captured within the state aid rules. However, as said, this is a quite formalistic and limited approach towards the role of the state. The state is either exercising its 'public authority' or it is engaged in market activities. The Court of Justice has been hesitant to further the scope of this reasoning towards a more dynamic approach. In fact, the reasoning on distinguishing the roles of the state as shareholder of an undertaking and as a public authority has never been subjected to an explicit rationale. The highlighted case-by-case approach of the GC and the Court has identified activities that can be associated with the exercise of public authority such as issues of tax or social policy. At the same time, in the absence of an explicit rationale to distinguish the market from the non-market, the MEOP becomes potentially expedient, as was discussed in section II.

C. The Individual Aid Measure in its Wider Context

Although there is, clearly, a call for responsiveness in the case law discussed above, the fact that the actual test is often concerned with a single carved out activity makes it slightly problematic since the individual aid conferring action may very well *on its own accord* be perceived as market specific. For example, in *Chronopost I*, it concerned the transfer of a client base; *in P&O European Ferries*, the *sale* of ferry tickets; in *Bundesverband deutscher Banken v Commission*, the making available of assets; and, in Ryanair, the *fixing of airport charges*.[128] Perceived as

[127] See ch 2, section III.C.

[128] Joined Cases C-83/01P C-93/01P and C-94/01P *Chronopost and Others v Ufex and Others* [2003] I-04777; C-442/03 P *P&O European Ferries (Vizcaya) v Commission* [2006] ECR I-04845; T-163/05 *DEP—Bundesverband deutscher Banken v Commission* [2010] ECR II-00387; Case T-196/04 *Ryanair v Commission* [2008] ECR II-03643.

single activities these are all clearly economic, market-specific actions. In particular, the GC made it clear in *Ryanair* that the airport charges were to be qualified as 'fees' and not as 'taxes'.[129] It is questionable whether this carving out is the right approach since the dissociation of a single activity from a perhaps broader socially relevant context may be unjustified and forgo the true purpose of a single measure. The Court acknowledged this, for example, in *FENIN*, a competition law case concerning Articles 102 and 106 TFEU, where it confirmed that state bodies running publicly financed hospitals in Spain did not act as undertakings at the specific moment they contracted with the commercial sector to buy medical equipment for use in the hospitals under their management. The GC held that the purchases in question could not be considered separately from the equipment's subsequent use in their hospitals:

> the nature of the purchasing activity must therefore be determined according to whether or not the subsequent use of the purchased goods amounts to an economic activity.[130]

The Court concurred with the CFI and concluded that that there was

> no need to *dissociate* the activity of purchasing goods from the subsequent use to which they are put in order to determine the nature of that purchasing activity.[131]

This line of reasoning has been used by analogy in a specific state aid context. In the *Leipzig Halle* case the Court rejected the appeals brought by Mitteldeutsch and Flughafen Leipzig-Halle seeking the partial annulment of the GC's judgment concerning the financing of airport infrastructure.[132] Leipzig had managed to broker a deal with DHL, which would transfer its main hub from Brussels to Leipzig in exchange for the exclusive use of a newly build runway. Moreover, the airport promised to complete the runway, ensure 24/7 operations of the hub and provide sufficient capacity to ensure DHL's operation for an undisclosed period of time. In addition, the airport had an obligation to compensate DHL for resulting losses and damages resulting from the move. After the start of operations this liability would become unlimited.

The court procedure focused on the financing of the expansion of the airport infrastructure that was necessary to accommodate DHL. The Court considered whether the construction of the airport infrastructure should be qualified as an economic activity within the meaning of Article 107(1) TFEU. The appellants argued that the construction or extension of airport infrastructure should not have been considered as an economic activity in and of itself and its financing by means of public funds could not constitute state aid. The construction of such infrastructure would have to be placed within a broader political context

[129] Case T-196/04 *Ryanair v Commission* [2008] ECR II-03643.

[130] Case T-319/99 *Fenin v Commission* [2003] ECR II-00357.

[131] Case C-205/03 *P FENIN v Commission* [2006] ECR I-06295.

[132] Case C-288/11 *P Mitteldeutsche Flughafen and Flughafen Leipzig-Halle v Commission* [2012] nyr; Case T-443/08 *Freistaat Sachsen and Others v Commission* [2011] II-01311.

of transport, economic and regional policy. Moreover, a private investor would never engage in the activity because there is no possibility of profitability (airport charges require authorisation from the airport authority and private investors have no influence over their amount and they bear no relationship to investment costs). The Court, however, agreed with the Commission and the GC

> there is no cause to *dissociate* the activity of building or enlarging infrastructure, in the event, the southern runway from the subsequent use.[133] (emphases added)

The logical effect of this case is, *a contrario*, that infrastructure that *is* separable from the subsequent operation would according to the Court not fall within the scope of state aid rules. Moreover, infrastructure, which is inseparable and which subsequently is not used commercially would be exempt as state aid since it would be subsumed under the non-commercial nature of the main activities.[134] However, demonstrating the poverty of a rationale for what distinguishes economic from non-economic spheres, the Court in this regard, quite statically and formalistically, went back to pointing to the exercise of 'state authority' as the main non-commercial sphere and referred to security and police functions, fire protection measures and public security measures, operating security measures, the German meteorological service and the air traffic control service.[135] Although the Court demonstrates in its case law that context is important and also requires distinctions between acts from state authorities made in the capacity as a market participant and as a public authority it has not developed a principle whereby to distinguish one from the other. The Court refers to the MEOP as a flexible concept that can be adopted as a fluid mentality within contexts where states have exclusive regulatory power but, conversely, state authority is not accompanied by the Court with any distinguishing criteria, based on for example motivations based on non-profit or 'public-spiritedness'. Instead, here the Court refers back to the traditionally perceived minimal state functions such as those that are mentioned above. However, one can further enrich this rationale by linking it to a line of cases, which I submit can be coined as the Court's good governance model in state aid.

D. The Connection to the Wider Regulatory Context: A Good Governance Model

As was discussed before, the judgments of the Court have shown some overlap with the free movement rules in the development of evaluative principles to determine whether there is state aid or not. In its essence, the MEOP can be compared

[133] T-443/08 *Freistaat Sachsen and Others v Commission* [2011] II-01311, para 95.

[134] Inter alia T Wilson, 'Infrastructure Financing and State Aid Post Leipzig-Halle' (2004) 1 *European State Aid Law Quarterly* 24–27. For an application of the *Leipzig-Halle* principles in the case of sport infrastructure, see R Craven, 'State Aid and Sports Stadiums: EU Sports Policy or Deference to Professional Football' (2014) 9 *European Competition Law Review* 453–60.

[135] T-443/08 *Freistaat Sachsen and Others v Commission* [2011] II-01311, para 42.

with the substantive efficiency model of the Court in free movement cases. The Court has also developed valuations based on a margin of discretion, with respect to the chosen policy objectives of a Member State, provided that the regulatory context follows requirements of good governance. As was highlighted before, in principle, if the state is acting as a 'legislator', the 'market rationality' principle is not followed but instead the Court adopts an evaluative standard that is based on an assessment whether regulation benefits a specific (group of) undertaking(s) or whether a measure involves a state resource. For example, the Court reasoned in the case *Sloman Neptun* that a partial non-application of German employment legislation to foreign crews of vessels flying the German flag did not constitute a grant of aid to the ship owners since

> the system at issue does not seek, through its object and general structure, to create an advantage which would constitute an additional burden for the State or the above-mentioned bodies, but only to alter in favour of shipping undertakings the framework within which contractual relations are formed between those undertakings and their employees.[136]

Similarly, in the case *Kirshammer-Hack*, the Court concluded that the exclusion of small businesses from a legal regime requiring payment of compensation in the event of unfair dismissals did not amount to the grant of an aid to the businesses concerned, reasoning that it

> does not entail any direct or indirect transfer of State resources to those businesses but derives solely from the legislature's intention to provide a specific legislative framework for working relationships between employers and employees and to avoid imposing on those businesses financial constraints which might hinder their development.[137]

Regardless of the merits of these cases,[138] these evaluations allow for normative choices of Member States with regard to their economy to exist outside of the technocratic evaluation of the state aid rules and be developed on the basis of internal political choices that embed economic activities. This reasoning is part of a line of state aid cases where the Court has considered selective advantages as *inherent features of general regulatory schemes*. This reasoning was present, for example, in the *PreussenElektra* case.[139] In short, the Court decided in that judgment that Member States may, without it constituting state aid, require private electricity suppliers to purchase electricity from renewable energy sources at minimum prices that are higher than the real economic value and, subsequently, 'allocate the financial burden arising from that obligation amongst electricity

[136] Joined Cases C–72/91 and C–73/91 *Sloman Neptun* [1993] ECR I–887 para 21.

[137] Case C–189/91 *Petra Kirsammer Hack* [1993] ECR I–6185, para 17.

[138] Arguably in *Sloman Neptun* the Court overlooked the fact that Germany had made these changes in order to improve the competitiveness of its shipping industry. Such aims should fall within the state aid regime.

[139] Case C-379/98 *PreussenElektra* [2001] ECR I-02099.

supply undertakings and upstream private electricity network operators'.[140] The Court considered, in that judgment,

> that even if the financial burden arising from the obligation to purchase at minimum prices was likely to have negative repercussions on the economic results of the undertakings subject to that obligation and entail a diminution in tax receipts for the state, *that consequence was an inherent feature of such a legislative provision* (emphases added).[141]

This rationale of the Court can be interpreted as providing an area, which is reserved for the Member States, *in their legislative roles*, where they are not automatically subject to the behavioural standards of a prudent investor nor do they fall within the scope of the technocratic apolitical realm of state aid *control*.

The objection against applying such a rationale for state aid, in a context where a social objective, such as environmental protection, is pursued would be that this entails taking into account *the aims and objectives* of the policy of a Member State and as such inhibits the effects-based approach of the state aid rules.[142] Indeed, as was discussed briefly before, consistent case law of the Court has clarified that aid is to be defined in relation to its effects.[143] In theory this implies that the case law of the Court could never be truly responsive to regulatory intent. As such there are cases such as the *Maribel bis/ter* case, for instance, where the Court found that the increased reduction in social contributions for manual workers in certain industrial sectors, which were allegedly most affected by redundancies and restructuring, did constitute state aid.[144] The arguments of the Belgian government, which maintained that the scheme was a general measure reflecting a choice of economic policy consisting in the decision to promote the creation of jobs in industrial sectors because they employ mostly manual workers who earn low wages owing to their minimal qualifications, was rejected:

> The social character of such State measures is not sufficient to exclude them outright from classification as aid for the purposes of Article [107] of the Treaty ... Article [107] (1) of the Treaty does not distinguish between measures of State intervention by reference to their causes or their aims but defines them in relation to their effects.[145]

[140] ibid, para 59.
[141] ibid, para 62.
[142] As argued by eg Biondi and Rubini (n 3) at 89.
[143] See the following cases: Case C–387/92 *Banco Exterior de España* [1994] ECR I–877, para 13; Case C–241/94 *France v Commission (Kimberly Clark)* [1996] ECR I–4551, para 34; Case C–256/97 *DMT* [1999] ECR I–3913, para 19; Case C–251/97 *France v Commission* [1999] ECR I–6639, para 35; Case 56/93 *Belgium v Commission (Gasunie)* [1996] ECR I–723, para 79; Case C–75/97 *Belgium v Commission (Maribel bis/ter)* [1999] ECR I–3671, para 25; Case C–480/98 *Spain v Commission (Magefesa)* [2000] ECR I–8717, para 16; Case T–46/97 *SIC v Commission* [2000] ECR II–2125, para 83; Case C–5/01 *Belgium v Commission (Cockerill)* [2002] ECR I–11991, para 45; Case C–409/00 *Spain v Commission* [2003] ECR I–1487, para 46; Case T–109/01 *Fleuren Compost v Commission* (Judgment of 14 January 2004), para 54; Case 342/96 *Spain v Commission* [1999] ECR I–2459, para 23.
[144] Case C–75/97 *Belgium v Commission (Maribel bis/ter)* [1999] ECR I–3671.
[145] ibid, para 25.

It is settled case law that a measure, which has the effect of conferring a selective advantage on an undertaking or a sector, is not relieved of its quality as an aid *merely* because it was adopted for social purposes. This reasoning stands in a slight contrast to the other approach, which allows selective outcomes provided that it is an inherent part of a more general and legitimate aim. However, the cases can be reconciled if viewed from a perspective of governance. For example, in the *Maribel bis/ter* case the increased reductions in the social contributions could not be justified in terms of the logic of the Belgian general system of social protection, and its underlying objectives of employment policy, but had rather the 'sole direct effect of according an economic advantage to the recipient undertakings alone, relieving them from part of the social costs which they would normally have to bear'.[146] Therefore, the Court looked at the objectives of the Belgium scheme but concluded that the measure in question was *not coherent* since it derogated from the general system of social protection. If a differential impact can be connected inherently and genuinely to the nature or general scheme of a reference system, a measure can be excluded as state aid. Within this rule of reason type approach, some consideration of the objectives is necessary since only by doing so is it possible to decide *whether it is in line with the logic of the system.*

Well known is the approach of the Court in the *Aria-Wien Pipeline* case. Here, the Court further developed this idea of responsiveness towards the general logic of regulatory schemes. At stake in this case was a law in Austria that granted a rebate on energy taxes to undertakings that were primarily active in the manufacturing of goods rather than in the provision of services. The Austrian government had argued that the energy tax and the rebate was not adopted as an isolated measure but was inherent to the overall 'package of measures intended to consolidate the budget. That package, composed of general socially balanced measures affecting all socio-professional groups, [and therefore] should be considered as a whole'.[147] The Court was willing to entertain this argument

> the only question to be determined is whether, under a particular statutory scheme, a State measure is such as to favour 'certain undertakings or the production of certain goods' within the meaning of Article [107](1) of the Treaty in comparison with other undertakings which are in a legal and factual situation that is *comparable in the light of the objective* pursued by the measure in question.[148] (emphasis added)

However, the energy tax rebate for goods could not be justified on the basis of the nature or general scheme of the taxation system established under the legislative package of which the Austrian authorities considered it an integral part. It could not be established that such undertakings were more energy-intensive than those active in the provision of services, nor that the environmental objectives underlying the measure under review justified any differential treatment of

[146] ibid.
[147] Case C-143/99 *Aria-Wien Pipeline* [2001] ECR I-8365, para 43.
[148] ibid, para 41.

undertakings producing goods.[149] Moreover, the statement of reasons, which led to the enactment of the national legislation referred to the circumstance that the advantageous terms granted to undertakings manufacturing goods were intended 'to preserve the competitiveness of the manufacturing sector'. Therefore, the genuine intentions of the Austrian authorities to act in pursuit of environmental objectives were undermined.[150]

The Court did, however, confirm that objectives play a potentially crucial role and demonstrated responsiveness to potentially legitimate objectives pursued on a Member State level in its adjudicative reasoning. The gist of the evaluative test it applied is that the contested measures can be excluded as state aid, provided that they are pursued coherently and systematically and in alignment with regard to the general measures that are under review. The specific measures have to conform to the internal logic of the general system of which it forms part. That means that a difference in tax rates would have to be justified in the light of the environmental purpose of the legislative package in question. As such, the fundamental criterion for establishing the selective character of a measure lies in the nature of a derogation from the system in which it is set and a measure constitutes a derogation where it does not apply to all the undertakings which, *in view of the nature and the scheme of the system*, are capable of benefiting from it.

On the basis of this reasoning, selectivity is determined through an 'objective-based analysis' of a regulatory context that needs to fulfil some requirements of good governance. That is to say, it needs to be internally and externally coherent and genuine. Meaning that the objective of a measure is essential to understanding the relevant system, or so-called reference framework, on which the answer to the selectivity question is to be based. However, the Court has established that also the reference framework itself has to be set up in such a way that it genuinely and systematically pursues legitimate objectives. This was at stake in the *British Aggregates* case.[151]

In *British Aggregates*, the United Kingdom had imposed a levy on so-called 'virgin aggregates' extracted from nature, the so-called Aggregates Levy (AGL), whereas recycled aggregates were exempted from this. The AGL had sustainable intentions. The UK claimed that its background was concerned with the reduction and rationalisation of the extraction of minerals commonly used as aggregates. The tax exemption was meant to incentivise their replacement with recycled products or exempted virgin materials. The Commission held that the exemption of certain minerals did not constitute state aid, since the scope of the levy was justified *by the logic and nature of the tax*, ie the reference system. British Aggregates, an association of small independent quarrying companies in the United

[149] See also A Bartosch, 'Is there a Need for a Rule of Reason in European State Aid Law? Or how to Arrive at a Coherent Concept of Material Selectivity' (2010) 47 *Common Market Law Review* 729–52.

[150] Case C-143/99 *Aria-Wien Pipeline* [2001] ECR I-8365, para 54.

[151] Case C-487/06 P *British Aggregates v Commission* [2008] ECR I-10515.

Kingdom that could not benefit from the exemption, brought an action seeking the annulment of the Commission decision. The GC roughly agreed with the reasoning of the Commission and added:

> An environmental levy is an autonomous fiscal measure which is characterised by its environmental objective and its specific tax base. It seeks to tax certain goods or services so that the environmental costs may be included in their price and/or so that recycled products are rendered more competitive and producers and consumers are oriented towards activities which better respect the environment. It is open to the Member States, which, in the current state of Community law, retain, in the absence of coordination in that field, their powers in relation to environmental policy, to introduce sectoral environmental levies in order to attain certain environmental objectives. In particular, the Member States are free, in balancing the various interests involved, to set their priorities as regards the protection of the environment and, as a result, to determine which goods or services they decide to subject to an environmental levy.[152]

The GC found that, in the absence of Community measures for harmonisation, the decision to introduce an environmental levy such as the AGL falls 'within the power of the Member States to set their priorities in the environmental fields' (based on Article 11 TFEU). The crucial point in this analysis was that the GC considered the AGL to constitute its own reference system. It was on this point that the Court, on appeal, disagreed and, in effect, determined that the selectivity analysis also involves an assessment as to *how* the Member State has drawn up the scope of a reference system.[153] The Court found that the fact that the levy did not apply to all similar activities which have a comparable impact on the environment meant that the activities which are not subject to the levy necessarily benefited from a selective advantage.[154] As a whole it made the scope of the regulatory measures inconsistent with the broader environmental objectives of the measure. This inconsistency was further established on the basis of the fact that the scope of the measures appeared, as in *Austria Wien*, to have been established on the basis of a desire to maintain the international competitiveness of certain sectors.[155] Therefore, the Court did not reject the proposition of the GC that Member States are free to draw the scope of their fiscal measures in accordance with environmental objectives but it established that such regulatory measures would have to be consistent with the objectives that they pursue.[156] The objectives of environmental protection could not be reconciled with the effects of the regulatory measures that excluded or included aggregates that were not considered on the basis of their environmental effects.

[152] Case T-210/02 *RENV-DEP—British Aggregates v Commission* [2006] ECR II-02789, para 114.

[153] Also De Cecco (n 1) at 103.

[154] Case T-210/02 *British Aggregates v Commission* [2006] ECR II-2789 and Case T-233/04 *Netherlands v Commission* [2008] ECR II-591; Case C-487/06 P *British Aggregates v Commission* [2008] ECR I-10505, para 186.

[155] Case C-487/06 P *British Aggregates v Commission* [2008] ECR I-10515, para 88.

[156] Also De Cecco (n 1) at 89.

These inconsistencies in the logic and nature of the tax system strengthened the idea that the AGL in fact reflected a desire to exclude some sectors from the levy in order to protect their competitiveness. The faith of the AGL was then basically sealed on the basis of a UK regulatory impact assessment on the taxation of aggregates which stated that 'some of the [exempted] materials form significant constituents of products that are traded internationally, whose [United Kingdom] producers would be put at a competitive disadvantage against importers and in export markets'.[157]

Therefore, the Court appeared to set out some principles of good governance in its assessment of the reference system to the effect that Member States are required to minutely and transparently pursue objectives and they have to analyse those objectives according to their effects. The discussion of this case law illustrates that if a policy measure is consistent with, for example, general environmental objectives, based on a global approach that considers the regulatory system as a whole and scrutinises the treatment of comparable situations on the basis of the guiding principles that the regulatory systems itself sets out, the generality of the system is ensured and will fall outside of the realm of the state aid rules.[158] It requires, however, the fulfilment of good governance principles in the exercise of those roles and a minute understanding from the Member States of their own regulatory systems as a whole.

The question then becomes which objectives the Member States can attach to their reference frameworks. Clearly, they must be contemporaneous and cannot be added with the benefit of hindsight. As such the Court held that

> a distinction must be made between, on the one hand, the objectives attributed to a particular tax regime, which are extrinsic to it, and, on the other hand, the mechanisms inherent in the tax system itself, which are necessary for the achievement of such objectives.[159]

Although the Court has consistently adjudicated on the basis of an effects-based approach, it has also provided for a consideration of objectives, already at the stage of defining a measure as state aid. Some impermissible goals can of course be derived from the primary objectives of the state aid regime, such as considerations related to improving the competitiveness of certain undertakings, industries, sectors or regions. These are from the very outset impermissible and will have to be notified and justified within one of the existing state aid programmes. In addition, objectives that are harmonised in a state aid context, and hence for which specific state aid programmes have been developed, should be part of the notification process as well.

[157] Case T-210/02 *British Aggregates v Commission* [2006] ECR II-2789 and Case T-233/04 *Netherlands v Commission* [2008] ECR II-591; Case C-487/06 P *British Aggregates v Commission* [2008] ECR I-10505, para 186.

[158] See also B Kurcz and D Vallindas, 'Can General Measures be … Selective? Some Thoughts on the Interpretation of a State Aid Definition' (2008) 45 *Common Market Law Review* 159–82.

[159] Case C-487/06 P *British Aggregates v Commission*, [2008] ECR I-10505, para 43.

Taking all of this into account, there is a structural area carved out for the Member States, in their legislative or regulatory roles, where there is responsiveness towards objectives pursued by Member States. In this way the 'call' for responsiveness of the Court with respect to the decision to apply or not to apply the MEOP can be subjected to a more dynamic rationale that evaluates a measure within its wider regulatory context and excludes it from the state aid rules if it forms a coherent and consistent part of a general and legitimate regulatory framework. Although it is not explicitly stated by the Court all the examples discussed in this section, where the Court has considered a measure to be an inherent part of a more general legislative framework, regarded instances where the Member State concerned, in one way or another, aimed to 'carr[y] out its task towards its population in the social, cultural and educational areas'.[160] It is for such measures and context that there exists a genuine irreconcilability between subjecting such legislation to a technocratic rationale of state aid control or allowing it to take shape as part of domestic political processes. Hence, cases such as *RyanAir* would be partly concerned with the question whether the taxing of the airport runway was connected to a wider regulatory framework or legislative context, which implemented, for example, some normative choices with regard to the protection of the environment and whether the measure in question could be perceived as genuine and coherent in light of those wider objectives.

E. Mutual Responsiveness in the Application of the *Altmark* Framework

The problems that a strict application of *Altmark* can bring forth were illustrated in the *BUPA* case concerning health insurance in Ireland.[161] Health insurance in Ireland was closed to competition between 1957 and 1996 and the Voluntary Health Insurance Board (VHI) was the only operator until a liberalisation process commenced between 1994 and 1996. The first competitor to VHI was London-based BUPA, which entered the market on 1 January 1997 as VHI's main competitor. BUPA was significantly hampered in its competitive actions by the provisions that liberalised the sector, which provided for the establishment of a so-called risk equalisation system (RES). The RES is a mechanism that required a contribution to a general fund from insurers that had a risk profile below the average market risk profile. The general fund would then make a corresponding payment to insurers with a risk profile higher than the average. In practice, the application of the RES would lead to funds being transferred from BUPA to VHI. As incumbent the risk profile of VHI was significantly higher than any other provider. This system was notified as state aid to the Commission. The Commission made a decision not to raise objections to the establishment of the RES.

160 See, inter alia, Case C-318/05 *Commission v Germany* [2007] ECR I-6957, para 68.

161 Case T-289/03 *BUPA and Others v Commission* [2008] ECR II-00081.

Rather creatively, the RES was considered as compensation for the obligations associated with a SGEI, namely obligations aimed at ensuring that all persons living in Ireland would receive a minimum level of healthcare services at the same price, independently of their state of health, age or sex. BUPA appealed against the decision of the Commission and based its appeal mainly on the non-fulfilment of the *Altmark* criteria. On first sight this seemed a strong case for the applicants. The PMI obligations were not assigned to the recipient undertaking; the parameters on the basis of which the compensation was to be calculated were not established in advance in an objective and transparent manner since the Health Insurance Authority in Ireland had some latitude in determining the risk differential; the compensation was not based on the costs incurred in the discharge of the public service obligations; and the costs incurred by VHI in complying with the PMI obligations were never compared to those which would have been incurred by the 'efficient operator'.[162]

However, the GC decided to apply the *Altmark* criteria in a flexible manner. It held, first, that the attribution of an SGEI mission may also consist in an obligation imposed on a large number of, or indeed on all, the operators active on the same market[163] and that the discretion in calculating the RES payments would not in itself be incompatible with the existence of objective and transparent parameters within the meaning of the second *Altmark* condition.

> the Member State has a wide discretion not only when defining an SGEI mission *but also when determining the compensation for the costs*, which calls for an assessment of complex economic facts.[164] (emphasis added)

With regard to the third *Altmark* condition, which requires that it be possible to determine the costs occasioned by the performance of an SGEI obligation, the Court considered

> that the quantification of the additional costs by means of a comparison between the actual risk profile of a PMI insurer and an average market risk profile in light of the amounts paid by all PMI insurers subject to the RES is consistent *with the purpose and the spirit of the third Altmark condition in so far as the compensation is calculated on the basis of elements which are specific, clearly identifiable and capable of being controlled.*[165] (emphasis added)

The judgment of the GC suggested that the *Altmark* criteria are to be applied more as guidelines than as strict criteria to be applied to the letter in each individual case.[166] Consequently, the *Altmark* test could be modified and respond

[162] ibid, para 123.
[163] ibid, para 179.
[164] ibid, para 214.
[165] ibid, para 237.
[166] A Bartosch, 'The Ruling in BUPA—Clarification or Modification of Altmark?' (2008) 2 *European State Aid Law Quarterly* 211. Also A Biondi, '*BUPA* v Commission' (2008) 7 *European State Aid Law Quarterly* 408.

to accommodate regulatory idiosyncrasies such as the RES. Importantly, the efficiency requirement as laid down by the fourth *Altmark* condition would not apply if there was *no* danger that costs resulting from inefficiency would have to be paid for by those liable to finance the scheme in question.[167] The *BUPA* judgment was welcomed as a demonstration that state aid law was capable of recognising social concerns mediated through national measures and as 'a potentially significant step towards reworking the European model of competition to include elements of solidarity'.[168] This reading of the *BUPA* case was later explicitly confirmed by the GC in the *Belgium hospitals case (CBI)*:

> It should be pointed out that, although the conditions stated in the Altmark judgment and in the SGEI package concern all sectors of the economy without distinction, their application must take into account the specific nature of the sector in question. [...] The General Court has held, inter alia, that, in the light of the particular nature of the SGEI mission in certain sectors, *it was appropriate to show flexibility with regard to the application of the Altmark judgment*, by referring to the spirit and the purpose of the conditions stated therein which prevailed when they were laid down, in a manner adapted to the particular facts of the present case. (emphases added)[169]

Similar to *BUPA*, the Court in *Chronopost* confirmed the implicit rationale at work in the former case.[170] Implicit in *BUPA* is that it is not always possible, in light of regulatory particularities, to, for example, apply an efficient comparator test. This was confirmed in the *Chronopost*, case which concerned the provision of logistical and commercial assistance by the French monopoly postal service La Poste to its subsidiary (Chronopost), which was operating on a competitive market for express delivery services. A competitor complained that these services provided the Chronopost subsidiary with an advantage. The Commission denied this and found that the services from La Poste were provided under normal business conditions. The GC partially annulled that decision because it found that the Commission should have verified whether the payments that were received by La Poste would be comparable to those demanded by a private undertaking that was not operating in a reserved sector.[171] The Court disagreed with this finding and considered that since La Poste was entrusted with the provision of a universal postal service, it required substantial infrastructure and resources enabling it to provide that service to all users, including sparsely populated areas.

> Because of the characteristics of the service which the La Poste network must be able to ensure, *the creation and maintenance of that network are not in line with a purely commercial approach*. [...] a network such as that available to SFMI-Chronopost is clearly not

[167] ibid.

[168] M Ross, 'A Healthy Approach to Services of General Economic Interest? The BUPA Judgment in the CJEU of First Instance' (2009) 34 *European Law Review* 127.

[169] Case T-137/10 *Belgium hospitals case (CBI)* [2012] np, paras 85, 86.

[170] Case C-341-342/06p *La Poste v UFEX and Others* [2008] ECR I-04777.

[171] ibid, para 116.

> a market network. Therefore that network would never have been created by a private undertaking. (emphases added)[172]

The situation of La Poste was therefore not comparable with that of a private undertaking. Since the provision of logistical and commercial assistance was inseparably linked to the La Poste network it was necessary to determine the normal market price on the basis of available 'objective and verifiable' data without making a comparison with private operators.[173] It is arguably this particular difficulty that has led the GC in *BUPA* to apply a more flexible approach and determine that the efficiency comparator requirement as laid down by the fourth *Altmark* condition would not apply if there was no danger that costs resulting from inefficiency would have to be paid for by those liable to finance the scheme in question.[174] As in the *BUPA* case the Court here acknowledged that the rationale behind the organisation of public services was incomparable with a private operator on the market.

However, no clear rationale has been developed to what extent and when 'the specific nature of the sector' would be able to force a more flexible response in the application of the *Altmark* criteria. On first sight, the effect of the *BUPA* judgment seems, therefore, to be limited to the regulatory idiosyncrasy of the regulatory conditions around the Irish health insurance system. Moreover, the Commission has continued to apply the *Altmark* criteria in increasingly strict fashion.[175] On the basis of the 'Almunia-package' it has been able to steer Member States away from relying on the flexible approach that was discussed above. Importantly, recently, the GC seems to have validated a strict approach based on the Commission's market failure approach in the case of *Zweckverband*,[176] which concerned the financing of the disposal of dead animal carcasses and slaughterhouse waste, which is partly financed by Germany on the basis of annual contributions to the Zweckverband Tierkörperbeseititgung (ZT). The ZT is a public law entity that was founded in 1979. All rural districts and larger urban districts in Rhineland-Palatinate and Saarland and two rural districts in Hessen had become members of the ZT. The ZT was authorised by its members to assume all the rights and obligations incumbent on rural districts and urban districts in their capacity as bodies responsible for the disposal of dead animal carcasses and slaughterhouse waste. The Commission considered that these services could not legitimately be considered as forming part of an SGEI mission. The question arose specifically in relation to the compensation that was provided for the obligation to retain spare operational capacity in case of an epidemic. The Commission considered

172 ibid, para 36.

173 ibid, paras 31–38.

174 Also A Bartosh, 'Clarification or Confusion—How to reconcile the ECJ's rulings in Altmark and Chronopost' (2003) 3 *European State Aid Law Quarterly* 12.

175 See Klasse, 'The Impact of Altmark: The European Commission Case Law Responses' (n 108).

176 Case T-309/12 *Zweckverband* [2014] ECR nyp, paras 45 and 62.

that this was not fundamentally different from other economic activities. The GC agreed:

> Pour autant, le pouvoir de définition des SIEG par l'État membre n'est pas illimité et ne peut être exercé de manière arbitraire aux seules fins de faire échapper un secteur particulier à l'application des règles de concurrence [...]. Pour pouvoir être qualifié de SIEG, le service en cause doit revêtir un intérêt économique général qui présente des caractères spécifiques par rapport à celui que revêtent d'autres activités de la vie économique.[177]

The GC held that the power of Member States to define SGEI is not unlimited and cannot be used arbitrarily in order to evade the application of competition rules. An SGEI exhibits 'special characteristics' in comparison to other economic activities. These special characteristics had to be demonstrated. Interestingly, the GC reasoned, agreeing with the Commission, that the polluter-pays principle as developed under Article 19(2) TFEU applies in general to the disposal of animal by-products and, therefore, that it was primarily the responsibility of producers to see to the disposal of fallen stock and slaughterhouse waste and to bear the costs involved. That is to say that the disposal of dead animals and slaughterhouse waste was to be considered as an intrinsic part of the economic activities of farmers and slaughterhouses. Consequently, the financial burden of that disposal had to be borne by farmers and slaughterhouses as part of the normal economic activities and, hence, inhibited a qualification of these services as an SGEI.

> Il est évident que le risque de survenance d'une épizootie est inhérent à l'élevage d'animaux. En application du principe du pollueur-payeur, il est donc également manifeste que les coûts résultant du maintien d'une réserve de capacités en cas d'épizootie doivent être supportés par les éleveurs et les abattoirs.[178]

There are several interesting aspects to this decision of the GC. First, it allowed the approach of the Commission to test whether the aid addresses a market failure, ie whether the services offered by existing market operators are insufficient to meet the public general interest. This is clearly the way that the Commission would prefer to assess whether a Member State has committed a 'manifest error' to assess the qualification of an SGEI and the GC has endorsed it in this case. Second, the GC established the formative potential of the internal market in the process of embedding economic activities. By insisting that the EU based polluter-pays principle is part of the 'normal operations of economic life' the GC held that this infrastructure of economic activity could no longer be regulated by a Member State on the basis of another organisational principle (such as that the state pays for the risks of an epidemic). Next, the GC confirmed its finding in *BUPA* that Member States have a wide discretion not only with respect to the definition of a public service mandate, but also in determining the compensation cost that was

[177] ibid, para 106.
[178] ibid, para 121.

dependent on an assessment of complex economic facts. However, this should then always be accompanied by procedural guarantees enabling the Commission to verify the existence of objective and transparent parameters and for this reason these parameters must be defined in a way that Member States do not misuse the concept of SGEI.

> C'est d'ailleurs précisément parce que cette détermination n'est soumise qu'à un contrôle restreint des institutions que le deuxième critère de l'arrêt Altmark, point 21 supra, exige que les institutions soient en mesure de vérifier l'existence de paramètres objectifs et transparents, ces paramètres devant être précisés de façon à exclure tout recours abusif de l'État membre à la notion de SIEG.[179]

The GC also acknowledged the interpretation of the fourth *Altmark* condition in *BUPA*. The GC emphasised that the application of the *Altmark* criteria must be flexible and take into account sectoral specificities, in particular, the specificities of discharging public service obligations in individual sectors. The GC specified that this assessment involved establishing that the compensation for keeping the extra storage did not entail the possibility of offsetting any costs that might result from inefficient operations of ZT. Since the compensation payments were not sufficiently distinguishable from the normal operations of ZT, this could not be guaranteed.[180]

The judgment of the GC was appealed but was withdrawn. It would have been interesting to see whether the Court would have validated the few, quite fundamental, choices of the GC. It would certainly not have been the first time that the Court had overruled the GC in this area.[181] In particular, accepting the rationale of market failure to define SGEIs, if validated, would definitely be received as a step towards tightening the grip on national choices concerning the organisation, regulation and financing of local public services. If that were to become the rule it would have to be established that the given activity could not have been performed under 'normal market conditions' and Member States would have to scrutinise their compensatory mechanisms for public services in legal and economic detail. The important question is to what extent this is only a 'nuisance' or to what extent this leads to an actual impediment of legitimate and genuine public services. The Court appears to have built in fragments of responsiveness in its case law that aims to guarantee that this will not happen. However, as indicated before, the Commission pursues a very specific and pervasive agenda, which is based on a strict application of the *Altmark* criteria and there is therefore a risk that the subtler parts of the case law will be ignored in the agenda of the Commission.[182]

[179] ibid, para 148.

[180] ibid, para 115.

[181] As in the *Chronopost* and *British Aggregates* cases.

[182] S Rodrigues, 'The European Commission's Reform Strategy' in Szyszcak and van de Gronden (n 107); M Krajewski, 'Providing Legal Clarity and Securing Policy Space for Public Services through a Legal Framework for Services of General Economic Interest: Squaring the Circle?' (2008) 14 *European Public Law* 377.

IV. A DIALOGUE OF MUTUAL RESPONSIVENESS

A. Introduction

The expedient nature of the MEOP and overly strict efficiency-based proceduralisation threaten social diversity and the development of social objectives through 'normal politics' in various ways. If social objectives pursued by Member States would only be taken into consideration at a stage where justifications are assessed by the Commission,[183] this could lead to instances of incommensurability based on the different contexts within which regulatory objectives on a Member State level are pursued. That is to say, regulatory objectives may pursue objectives or are by nature to be attributed to a particular sphere of accountability. On this basis it can be normatively inappropriate to have them evaluated within the procedural, technocratic state aid framework of the Commission or to enforce a market rationale on the way regulatory objectives are to be pursued. Similarly, an overly strict application of the *Altmark* framework will exclude legitimate regulatory objectives, which are unable or unsuitable to be 'procured' on the basis of adversarial relationships. This is reflected in case law of the Court that concerns instances where the state does not intend to become involved in activities for remuneration 'but carries out its task towards its population in the social, cultural and educational areas'.[184]

The Court has demonstrated responsiveness in the application of the state aid rules by seeking to 'disentangle commercial transactions entered into by Member States from the non-commercial and regulatory objectives that accompany them'.[185] The case law allows for what may be seen as the *inherent justifications* of measures that grant selective economic advantages but are part of general regulatory or legislative schemes, which are themselves incorporating legitimate objectives. This can be seen as an application of a rule of reason approach in the state aid rules.[186] Legitimate and genuinely pursued 'reference frameworks' are able to pull individual measures that form an inherent part of such framework out of the realm of the state aid regime.

Taking a step back from the case law we can see that the framework of analysis that can be derived from the case law of the Court is from the perspective of a dialogue of mutual responsiveness, similar to the free movement rules. The *Dassonville*-like reasoning of the Court in *Steenkolenmijn* captures a wide range of regulatory contexts. This is the starting point of a dialogue in which the regulatory choices of Member States have to be evaluated. The principle of substantive efficiency based on the MEOP should not be applied expediently but incorporate

183 As argued by Biondi and Rubini (n 3) at 89.

184 See, among others, Case C-318/05 *Commission v Germany* [2007] ECR I-6957, para 68.

185 De Cecco (n 1) at 88.

186 See also Bartosch, 'Is there a Need for a Rule of Reason in European State Aid Law?' (n 149) at 729.

responsiveness to allow inefficient outcomes where genuine regulatory objectives are at stake. At the same time, allowing too much flexibility and granting wide margins of discretion in the definition of regulatory objectives may undermine the fundamental role of the state aid rules within the internal market to prevent protectionist measures and discriminatory regulatory choices. Hence, the dialogue of mutual responsiveness within the state aid rules should allow for *genuine* regulatory (as opposed to commercial or protectionist) objectives to be pursued *transparently*, in accordance with *good governance* principles. In this way a dialogue of mutual responsiveness can be established in accordance with the normative requirements of social legitimacy.

B. The Dialogue of Mutual Responsiveness in State Aid

The issue at stake in the *Eventech* case, and especially the opinion of AG Wahl in that case, provides opportunity to further highlight the dialogue of mutual responsiveness in state aid. In the *Eventech* case the Court had to decide whether providing free access to public infrastructure to the exclusive benefit of taxis constituted state aid.[187] In London, both London taxis (the so-called Black Cabs) and private hire vehicles (minicabs) are involved in carrying passengers for payment. However, only the Black Cabs are, on the basis of the regulatory framework, permitted to 'ply for hire' (that is, solicit or wait for passengers without any pre-booking). In contrast, minicabs can only pick up people who have pre-booked their services. Moreover, and central to the case, Black Cabs are allowed to use the bus lanes, but the minicabs are prohibited from doing so, during the hours when bus lane restrictions are operational. Conversely, drivers of Black Cabs are subject to strict standards in relation to their vehicles, their fares and their knowledge of London, whereas those standards do not apply to minicab drivers. The state aid argument that was pursued in this case claimed to see a selective advantage that was granted for the exclusive use of bus lanes by the Black Cabs to the exclusion of others, whereas the non-payment of charges for access to that infrastructure would be considered as a revenue that is forgone. There is a clear analogy available on this point with respect to the legal assessment of the state aid situation in the previously discussed Dutch *Nox case*, where the Court established that when assets are put at the disposal of undertakings free of charge, whereas they could have been sold or put up for auction, state resources are indeed forgone. In his Opinion on the matter AG Wahl was of a different opinion and considered that there are limits to the application of such market rationality in the presence of genuine regulatory objectives:

> the State aid rules do not specifically require that Member States demand payment for access to such infrastructure, but leave it to their discretion whether or not to grant

[187] Case C-518/13 *Eventech* [2015] nyr.

> access free of charge. As an asset in the public domain intended to facilitate transport and mobility for end-users, such infrastructure by its very nature requires that rules be set for its use, including access to it—*most evidently in relation to traffic control and maintaining order. That is a regulatory, rather than a commercial* matter of the kind that does not justify the application of the rules on competition ... including those on State aid.[188] (emphases added)

The AG went on to specify how this distinction between regulation and commercial matters could be evaluated by the Court

> when regulating access to infrastructure, the State must evidently act in a *genuinely* regulatory capacity. That includes regulating comparable situations in the same way so that competition is not distorted. Indeed, where infrastructure is made available to all users on an equal and non-discriminatory basis, that is an indication that no aid has been given to those users. By contrast, if, for example, the State generally requests payment for access to public infrastructure (such as a toll fee for using a public motorway) or other resources in the public domain, but grants various undertakings access free of charge on a discretionary basis, revenue may well be forgone in respect of those undertakings.[189] (emphases added)

The reasoning of the AG shows some interesting analogies with the case law that was discussed in Chapter 2 on free movement, in the context of the good governance model. It was discussed there, for example, that a choice for a monopoly-based policy has to be embedded in a general policy that is aimed at a high level of consumer protection. Moreover, the choice for a monopoly-based system can only be *genuine* if the legislative framework that establishes a monopolist suitably (qualitatively) equips and limits the activities (quantitatively) of the monopolist in a way that genuinely reflects the chosen policy of a high level of consumer protection.[190] This strand of case law of the Court makes clear that the fundamental choice for a system of protection affects the assessment of Member State policy along the consistency yardstick of the Court. The AG in *Eventech* suggests a similar rationale for state aid cases, which can be clearly placed in the context of a dialogue of mutual responsiveness.

Firstly, the AG established the limits of a market rationale by establishing that the requirement to pay for public infrastructure was not required in the context of the exercise of a genuinely regulatory objective, which was fundamentally not a commercial matter. The rules that determine access to public infrastructure were endowed with a certain margin of discretion. Secondly, the AG established an evaluation of that regulatory choice within a good governance evaluation, which would evaluate the broader coherence of the regulatory choice made by the Member State concerned.

The Court largely followed the AG's Opinion. The Court first established that the bus lanes were not constructed for the benefit of any specific undertaking or

[188] Opinion of AG Wahl in Case C-518/13 *Eventech* [2015] nyr, para 29.
[189] ibid, para 32.
[190] See further Ch II, section III.C.

any particular category of undertakings, such as Black Cabs, or the supplier of bus services, and were not allocated to them but constructed as part of the London road network and primarily with a view to facilitating public transportation by bus. The Court held that where the state pursues the realisation of an objective laid down by legislation and grants a right of privileged access to public infrastructure, which is not operated commercially by the public authorities to users of that infrastructure, the state does not necessarily confer an economic advantage for the purposes of Article 107(1) TFEU.[191] Moreover, and importantly the Court held with regard to the identification of the objective that it is

> in principle, a matter *within the prerogative of the competent national public authorities alone* and they must have a *degree of discretion* both as regards whether it is necessary, in order to achieve the regulatory objective pursued, to forgo possible revenue and also as regards how the appropriate criteria for the granting of the right, which must be determined in advance in a transparent and non-discriminatory manner, are to be identified.[192] (emphases added)

The decisive consideration that seems to have inspired the Court towards taking this route was that the access to the public infrastructure is not operated 'commercially' by the public authorities but reflected, in the words of the AG, a *genuine regulatory activity*. In that circumstance the relevant question from a state aid perspective is not whether the state behaviour conforms to the rationality of an investor or a creditor but whether the regulatory action is asymmetric in its effects and thereby provides a selective economic advantage. To be clear, in that situation there is still the potential of a finding of state aid but the evaluative standard is congruent with a social context that is of a genuinely regulatory nature and focuses on the quality of the process that has led to the restriction.[193]

C. The Required *Mutuality* of the Dialogue

The mutuality of the dialogue started in state aid law is perhaps most clearly illustrated in the evaluation of the regulatory context of SGEIs. There the GC has demonstrated a willingness to be responsive and established that Member States have a wide discretion not only with respect to the definition of a public service mandate, but also in determining the compensation cost that was dependent on

[191] Case C-518/13 *Eventech* nyp, para 48.

[192] ibid, para 49.

[193] As a side note: one of the implications of these findings is that there is in fact, as Davies has argued before, a very limited role for Art 106(2) TFEU. Art 106(2) TFEU states that SGEIs are only subject to the internal market rules in so far as this does not obstruct the performance of the SGEI objectives. However, as was established before, a similar rationale basically applies to all genuine regulatory objectives on the basis of the case law of the Court. It is therefore, indeed, questionable if Art 106(2) TFEU reflects more than a pure value statement. See G Davies, 'What Does Article 86 Actually Do?' in M Krajewski, U Neergaard and J van de Gronden (eds), *The Changing Legal Framework for Services of General Interest in Europe* (The Hague, Asser Press, 2009) at 51–69.

an assessment of complex economic facts. However, this freedom is to be accompanied with procedural guarantees enabling the Commission to verify the existence of objective and transparent parameters that allow a review by the European Commission. Therefore, in the area of defining and the financing of SGEIs the model of the Court seems to be based on techniques to assess the coherence and transparency of the regulatory frameworks and measures for the purpose of determining whether they genuinely reflect the intentions of the state.[194] In the previously discussed *Zweckverband* case the GC held that the power of Member States to define SGEI is not unlimited and cannot be used arbitrarily in order to evade the application of competition rules. An SGEI exhibits 'special characteristics' that are not addressed by the market alone. These special characteristics have to be demonstrated and the regulatory framework has to be responsive and be specifically attuned to such objectives in order to benefit from the safe harbour created in *Altmark*. As such and as discussed before, it is clear that this is, more generally, one of the main objectives of the state aid rules: the elimination of any possibility of manipulation of state resources to the benefit of selective undertakings. As noted by Damjanovic, this 'quasi-legislative approach' establishes concrete criteria as to how the Member State's financing system must be organised but they do not oblige Member States to abolish specific state interventions.[195] The criteria that require the welfare services to be provided efficiently require them to be financed in a fair and transparent manner but do not interfere in a substantive way with the Member States' competences.[196]

Although some of the evaluative principles of the Court carry the risk of reducing the role of the state to a prudent private investor and demonstrate a tendency to be applied expediently, the case law of the Court can be clearly interpreted as adopting mechanisms to be responsive to specific Member State context and diversity. The expedient nature of the reasoning of the Court in cases like *Ryanair*, discussed above, where the Court reasons that the fixing of airport fares could also be done by a private operator and, therefore, should be done in accordance with MEOP, is only expedient within a regulatory context that does not pursue regulatory objectives other than financial gain. A margin of discretion is provided to Member States for allowing them to define tasks towards its population in the social, cultural and educational areas, in terms of genuine regulatory activities, provided that these can be considered legitimate in light of the broader EU value system. Advantages that flow forth from such regulatory interventions must either be in accordance with the MEOP or form an integral and inherent part with the general objectives of the regulatory intervention in order not to be qualified as state aid. Regulatory idiosyncrasies and genuine regulatory objectives are not

[194] Also J Baquero Cruz, 'Services of General Interest and EC Law' in G de Búrca (ed), *EU Law and the Welfare State—In Search of Solidarity* (Oxford, Oxford University Press, 2005) at 16.

[195] D Damjanovic, 'The EU Market Rules as Social Market Rules: Why the EU Can Be a Social Market Economy' (2013) 50(6) *Common Market Law Review* 1708.

[196] ibid.

disregarded, provided Member States understand their own regulatory intentions clearly and take an overarching coherent approach in similar regulatory affairs.

Confusion about the application of evaluative principles on social context arises mostly on the basis of ill-designed regulatory frameworks or opaque state actions such as in *EDF*. So, for example, in *Kimberly Clark* the Court held that the contributions of the Fonds national de l'emploi (National Employment Fund) (FNE) in the implementation of social plans was liable to place certain undertakings in a more favourable situation than others, since the FNE enjoyed a *degree of latitude* which enabled it to adjust its intervention in accordance with a number of in-transparent considerations. As AG Jacobs pointed out in that case, the discretion and degree of discretion enjoyed by the FNE in the administration of the aid scheme meant that the FNE contributions were not necessarily available to all undertakings on an equal footing.[197] Therefore, as was discussed in the previous chapters vis-à-vis the competition and free movement rules, problems with the state aid regime often arise due to ill-designed regulatory frameworks within the Member States. As the previous discussion shows, the Court has established some clear principles with respect to how state aid law perceives the relationship between market and non-market concerns on the basis of an idea of mutual responsiveness.

The idea of social legitimacy is therefore clearly present within the adjudicative rationales developed by the Court. The substantive reach of the internal market is reflected in the market-derived standards such as the MEOP, which requires the adoption of an evaluative framework that allows for a diversity (a margin of discretion) and plurality of legitimate possibly inefficient *substantive* outcomes, provided that they are pursued in a transparent, coherent and systematic fashion. Underlying this 'switch' between evaluative frameworks within the state aid rules is the idea of a 'genuine regulatory activity', which is not based on a formalistic idea of traditional state powers but can be shaped in a dynamic fashion by Member States in their fulfilment of tasks towards its population in the social, cultural and educational areas along the yardstick of good governance.

V. CONCLUSION

Similar to the other areas of internal market law, the previous sections demonstrate that the state aid rules are governed by an intermixed application of the principles of substantive efficiency, margins of discretion and procedural unity on the basis of good governance principles. A principle of substantive efficiency is applied on the basis of the MEOP, as a market-derived principle that determines in substantive terms how a Member State should act in certain contexts at the least costs to the Community. A similar idea stands behind the proceduralisation based

[197] Opinion of AG Jacobs in Case C-241/94 *Kimberly Clark* [1996] ECR I-4551.

on efficiency of the financing of SGEIs in the Union.[198] In the application of this principle the Court has articulated clearly that the context has to be established prior to the application of an evaluative principle. Is it a context where the state acts in its capacity as market participant or in its capacity as provider of public tasks towards its population? On this basis the dialogue with the Member States is started.

However, to determine this question the Court has not provided a very clear rationale. The case law suggests that selective advantages that are considered as an inherent part of broader legitimate and genuine regulatory objectives will be excused from the application of the state aid rules. Therefore, margins of discretion are provided to Member States in the definition of regulatory objectives, provided that they are not of a protectionist/discriminatory nature or harmonised at the EU level. Such margins of discretion are combined with requirements of good governance. Selective advantages can only be excused if they are an inherent part of broader regulatory objectives. They have to conform to the broader inherent logic of the reference system, which in itself has to be consistent and coherent in terms of its effects and broader regulatory framework. Moreover, procedural unity on the basis of principles of good governance is clearly advanced in the way Member States are required to set up systems of financing of SGEIs.

The discussion of the state aid regime in this chapter has demonstrated that the area for genuine normative conflicts between the objective of undistorted competition and selective aid measures is limited. In comparison with competition and free movement, the state aid rules clearly have more structural positive integration effects.[199] This is particularly the case with respect to the way national regulatory affairs have to be structured or financed in order to remain within national spheres of accountability and the subjecting of previously unregulated areas of national concern to a common regulatory process.[200] Furthermore, the high degree of proceduralisation of state aid matters have made it a domain of technocracy, highly tuned towards installing common principles and means of evaluation that Member States themselves have to incorporate in the way regulatory and tax schemes are developed. In terms of the internal market's social purpose, the method that is adopted by the Commission is to, as far as possible, install principles within Member States that unify the means of how regulatory objectives take shape. This implies a reduction of potential conflicts between social norms by unifying the means by which such norms take shape. It is therefore important, in view of retaining social diversity, that Member States realise where there exists regulatory space for the formation of genuine regulatory objectives.

[198] E Gromnicka, 'Services of General Economic Interest in the State Aid Regime: Proceduralisation of Political Choices?' (2005) 11 *European Public Law* 429.

[199] A Biondi and M Farley, 'The Relationship between State Aid and the Single Market' in E Szyszcak (ed), *Research Handbook on State Aid* (Cheltenham, Edward Elgar, 2011) 277–92.

[200] See also De Cecco (n 1) at 80.

The chapter discussed how market-derived standards may be potentially expedient and used to evaluate regulatory choices within a metric that risks doing violence to potentially genuine and worthwhile aspects of those objectives. At the same time, the wave of new public management, which installed efficiency principles within Member States' regulatory affairs, has made it more difficult to conceptualise alternative forms of governance outside of the spectrum of cost-benefit analysis. Nevertheless, EU internal market law is not committed to these principles and should allow for the possibility of social diversity. Thus, the social legitimacy of the state aid rules depends on the extent and level of sophistication adopted in legal reasoning that identifies instances of irreconcilability before adopting evaluative principles that are congruent to the conflict that is being adjudicated.

There is a line of case law from the Court that insists that the definition of state aid is an objective exercise and has determined that a measure may not escape the prohibition of state aid on the basis of policy considerations since these come into play once the question as to the existence of a state aid is answered. It would then be for the Commission to evaluate a state measure in light of the policy that it pursues as part of the justifications for state aid. Within this view there is no room for a rule of reason and it would potentially involve questioning as AG Jacobs put it 'the entire social and economic life of a member state'.[201] It is against this background that the inherent justification test, in light of the general objectives of a regulatory scheme or tax can be understood. These are spaces where the Court has attempted to allow for social diversity based on national regulatory autonomy, which is highlighted in the emphasis the Court has placed on distinguishing cases involving state participation in the market and those concerning regulation. In the process of defining a regulatory measure as state aid the Court has shown a responsiveness to explore the limits of the internal market and developed guiding principles for Member States to pursue regulatory objectives which provide selective aid, outside of the realm of the state aid regime. The Court has provided the means for Member States to develop a sort of 'acoustic separation' between the domains of the market and other spheres, thereby allowing the development of different kinds of valuation.

The chapter has developed the argument that if the limits between the market and legitimate regulation are not coherently drawn there is a risk of genuine norm conflict failure, which is to say that the market economy operator principle is applied to govern or foreclose legitimate aims of a regulatory nature that are insufficiently captured or addressed in terms of a market economy operator test. However, it is up to the Member States to create this space themselves. The pursuit of national policy objectives does not necessarily result in a negative outcome from the point of view of state aid, even where the public authority is unable to satisfy the market operator test. Indeed, there is a distinct regulatory space for the genuine pursuit of objectives, provided Member States incorporate clear and transparent objectives that can justify any selective advantages that flow from them.

[201] AG Jacobs in Case C-52-54/97 [1998] ECR I-02629, para 16.

5

Conclusion: Social Legitimacy in the Internal Market on the Basis of a Dialogue of Mutual Responsiveness

I. THE ARGUMENT AS A WHOLE: NORMATIVE CLAIMS AND RESULTS

SOCIAL LEGITIMACY ENCAPSULATES the normative concerns based on the work of Karl Polanyi. Most importantly, from this perspective, a project that promotes market integration amongst a diversity of social systems and more specifically diversity in '*social acquis*' can only endure, with political support, in the presence of a constructive interplay between market and non-market objectives. In order to be sustained in the long run, a trade regime such as the internal market within the European Union depends on the structural institutional design and rationales that embed the normative orientations of societies within those regimes and vice versa. What is required, and provided in this book, is a language that accommodates social conflicts within internal market law. Thus understood, social legitimacy can be traced back to the original compromise of embedded liberalism, which stands at the basis of the internal market infrastructure of the European Union. This outlook has been adopted to approach adjudication in the main pillars of the internal market.

The first chapter developed this normative outlook by studying the work of Karl Polanyi and it was argued that his historical analysis of the societal effects of market dominance is relevant today, primarily owing to his conclusions on the social necessity of a constructive and reciprocal relationship between *global* market integration and the remaining *locality* of the social. The risk of market-dominated integration is that market-based rationales will forcefully reconstruct embedded forms of market-society-state relationships and thus crowd out existing and alternative legitimate social orientations within Member States. Based on the historical insights of Polanyi, the idea of social legitimacy becomes imperative for a political sustainable project that seeks supranational market integration. This has been translated into a normative claim concerning how transnational regimes respond to conflicts between interests of a social nature and trade objectives.

The substantive chapters have adopted this perspective and looked critically at the adjudicative rationales that govern the internal market. The normative outlook based on social legitimacy is shared in the basic set-up of all of the internal market laws. That is to say, the basic embedded liberalism compromise resonates in all areas of internal market law. The primary law confirms the idea that the benefits of a joint commitment to free trade objectives can only be achieved in a sustainable way if combined with a recognition of national public values and societal objectives within those frameworks. However, the studies in the foregoing chapters have all illustrated how, despite this balance, the Court often struggles to adjudicate on the basis of a rationale that can be coherently applied to the question: 'how can the objectives of internal market integration and a commitment to social diversity both be pursued without one *necessarily* trumping the other?' Indeed, the balance between the requirements from the EU internal market for Member States regulatory choices, whilst at the same time respecting the 'fundamental structures' that exist in the Member States, through a recognition of a diversity of regulatory orientations, is one of the structural challenges faced by the internal market project.

I have submitted that within the context of the internal market this question is best addressed with the idea of *mutual responsiveness*, which I consider and discuss in Chapter 1, to be a necessary but underdeveloped element of the constitutional form and the social purpose of the internal market, as envisaged within the EU legitimising theory of transnational effects. The approach suggested on the basis of mutual responsiveness pursues a holistic approach that conceives the market and the social sphere, quite literally, as 'communicating vessels'. Hence, this 'dialogue of mutual responsiveness' is based on the idea that internal market law is foremost a means to start a conversation with Member States on the normative choices of restrictive laws and regulatory schemes, which requires on one side a responsiveness within the application of internal market law to the social context within Member States and, on the other side, a clear understanding and articulation of restrictive objectives that are pursued on a Member State level. The expressive function of internal market law is to unveil these normative conflicts in order to illuminate what is at stake. Questioning and demanding articulation of restrictive regulatory choices within legal frameworks may be an excellent starting point for a dialogue that aims to increase the distinct articulation of regulatory objectives and thereby assists in the identification of embedding organisational principles on the Member State level. The 'dialogue of mutual responsiveness' is therefore based on the idea that internal market law is a means to start an illuminating conversation with Member States on the normative choices of restrictive laws and regulatory choices, which requires on one side a responsiveness within the application of internal market law and, on the other side, a clear understanding and articulation of restrictive objectives that are pursued on a Member State level. That is to say, how responsiveness can be integrated within the legal framework of the internal market and what the proxies and requirements are for the articulation of restrictive regulatory choices.

Thus, it has been argued that market-derived evaluative standards may serve as a tool to tease out discriminatory, disingenuous (protectionist) regulatory choices within Member States but always allow for genuine social objectives to exist in accordance with good governance principles. The rationale adopted to evaluate and resolve conflicts should be instructed by a preliminary stage, which frames the conflict at issue in a way that allows the identification of a clash of normative principles, such as between solidarity and the market. First and foremost, this requires clarity in the framing of potential incommensurable conflicts between principles of organisation in order to instruct the selection of the appropriate adjudicative standard of evaluation. In this way the normative claims of social legitimacy can be accommodated within the internal market, without dismissing the objective of market integration. In this process, a dialogue of mutual responsiveness will establish the substantive scope and reach of the internal market; to what extent the internal market can substantively accommodate social interests, and when objectives become inherently irreconcilable and the dialogue should adapt towards one of procedural unity. Therefore, the struggle that the Court faces in determining this balance should be cherished as a potential source of deliberative and formative potential for both the EU internal market and the Member States. Hence, the term 'dialogue' is purposefully chosen because on the basis of mutual responsiveness, the European adjudicators are able to *speak* to a range of social interests and actors with the help of a coherent model of adjudication. In this way the social legitimacy of judgments of the Court may be improved because the Court will be able to be quite explicit with regard to the normative demands of the internal market.

I have submitted that in the context of adjudication the normative claims of social legitimacy boil down to the issue of valuation in law and the related problems of indeterminacy and incommensurability. Evaluative standards, adopted in adjudicative contexts, may value social realities within a metric that risks doing violence to potentially genuine and worthwhile aspects of objectives that are pursued on a Member State level and, foremost, determinacy in the framing of the economic and social purpose and potential incommensurable conflicts between potentially conflicting aims is needed in order to instruct adjudication. The substantive chapters illustrate that it is specifically *the lack of this clarity*—indeterminacy—that may undermine social legitimacy within the EU internal market. The Member States have an important role in improving this clarity by regulation and organising their affairs in accordance with principles of good governance.

From a comparative perspective the social legitimacy issues across the free movement, competition and state aid rules share some striking commonalities. Firstly, the means of valuation that are implicit within the adjudicative rationales applied by the Court (and GC) are similar even though they take place with regard to different techniques of adjudication (eg proportionality versus categorisation) or with regard to different legal categories (eg undertaking versus public authority). A shared principle of substantive efficiency is pursued on the basis of evaluations that consider the least restrictive (free movement), most efficient (competition) or most profitable (state aid) course of action. The focus in this stage is on substance since the evaluative principle is prescriptive with regard to the chosen course of action on the basis of substantive outcomes. The studies have found shared problems in the way that evaluative standards based on substantive efficiency can value societal realities within a metric that risks doing violence to potentially genuine and worthwhile aspects of social objectives that are pursued on a Member State level. For example, it was found that an evaluative adjudicative method such as strict proportionality applied in free movement adjudication seeks the more efficient or less restrictive state measure, thus potentially excluding a relevant and genuine political compromise. The efficiency-based exemption criteria in competition law may value competition-restrictive sustainability initiatives in terms of the willingness of consumers to pay for a price increase, thus potentially excluding the inherent value of a sustainable environment. The market-based evaluative standards in state aid law may nudge public bodies towards actions that are justified exclusively on the grounds of their commercial self-interest, thus potentially crowding out potential alternative visions regarding the appropriate role of public authorities and the direction that certain policy objectives take. As such, problems of social legitimacy across the different fields of internal market law arise with respect to the unchecked application of the principle of substantive efficiency. It was argued that this is not in alignment with the current values and objectives structure of the EU that points towards the importance of institutionalising diversity.

We should recall that the argument from transnational effects conceptualises the intentions of the EU internal market not necessarily as 'pro trade' but as a means to engage in a dialogue with Member States on how their national systems can and need to be adjusted in order to accommodate the out of nation interests that are to be made part of national processes of governing or governance structures. Somek identified a risk in the terms of the dialogue from transnational effects by highlighting that '[a]nchoring the mitigation of transnational effects in the facilitation of market access modifies the focus of the argument'. Indeed, the focusing on the unchecked and expedient use of the principle of substantive efficiency validates Somek's pressing question: 'what might be done to prevent the argument from transnational effects from slipping into a freewheeling rampage of economic due process?'

Looking through lens of social legitimacy at internal market adjudication in free movement, competition and state aid reveals that the Court has constructed and adopted, albeit incoherently, a mixture of substantive efficiency testing, margins of appreciation and proceduralisation in order to adjudicate internal market conflicts. Therefore, although the chapters have highlighted that there are differences and nuances in the way that social legitimacy problems and solutions arise within the different areas of the internal market, it has also been submitted that they can all be connected on the basis of an interplay of the principles of substantive efficiency, margins of discretion and procedural good governance.

In reconstructing this case law the argument has submitted that the key to social legitimacy, and concomitantly to Somek's question, lies in finding the balance between applying these principles; the substantive reach of the internal market and the 'switch' towards an evaluative framework that allows for a diversity (a margin of discretion) and plurality of legitimate *substantive* outcomes, provided that they are pursued in a transparent, coherent and systematic fashion. The intention of this study has been to consistently reconstruct the European Courts' case law into a coherent model of social legitimacy in which the three evaluative principles of the internal market interact constructively and in congruence with the social context that is being adjudicated. This allows the Court to implement an 'operational rationale' whenever it has to adjudicate a conflict between the objectives of market integration and restrictive domestic (social) interests. All chapters have shown how the terms of substantive efficiency, margins of discretion and good governance provide a common language within a dialogue of mutual responsiveness.

II. SOCIAL LEGITIMACY IN THE INTERNAL MARKET: FREE MOVEMENT, COMPETITION AND STATE AID

A. Social Legitimacy in EU Free Movement Law

With respect to the free movement rules, I discussed in Chapter 2 that the adjudicative model adopted by the Court shows the skeleton of the idea of mutual responsiveness. The starting point of the dialogue in free movement takes place on the basis of an unqualified market access test, which allows the opening of a discussion on an, in theory, unlimited range of Member State rules and regulatory schemes. This was noted by, for example, Spaventa, who in very similar terms describes that

> [t]he broadening of the scope of the Treaty could be seen as a contribution not so much to deregulation but rather to better regulation, through a process of continuous self-reflection and of continuous dialogue between regulators, traders and the Court.[1]

The rationale behind this adjudicative model based on the unlimited scope of the free movement provisions is that the existence of a hierarchical relationship between competing objectives is primarily functional. The conflict is structured only in a prima facie way so that legitimate rights and policies can, from that moment onwards, be established. Within the theory of transnational effects, the prima facie structuring of EU free movement conflicts is in this way a crucial part of the adjudicative model of the Court, allowing it to engage with a range of regulatory contexts and, as explained before, within the constitutional construct of the internal market, to initiate a dialogue with Member States that advances internal market integration. However, to perceive the argument from transnational effects

[1] E Spaventa, 'Leaving "Keck" behind?: The Free Movement of Goods after the Rulings in "Commission v Italy" and "Mickelsson and Roos"' (2009) 34(6) *European Law Review* 914, at 925.

in this way requires an answer to Somek's pressing question, which was cited above. The adjudicative model of the Court can, from a plethora of perspectives, only be perceived as an adequate and acceptable technique if, eventually, conflicts between rights and general public interest are resolved on the basis of responsiveness to context, allowing solutions to be found that respond to all the relevant contextual considerations. Perceived from this angle, responsiveness should be an absolute core aspect and function of proportionality analysis. As was introduced before, the answer to Somek's question, presented in this book, is based on the idea of mutual responsiveness.

However, before expanding on that idea, Chapter 2 highlighted a number of cases that could be used to argue that the Court, indeed, has slipped into a form of analysis that imposes a limited market primacy ruled-balancing framework on restrictive regulatory schemes within Member States. Based on certain lines of case law one may credibly argue that the adjudicative model of the Court in free movement law is functional and under-socialised, threatening the social cohesions, solidarity and identity that a state pursues. The assessment of EU free movement case law in Chapter 2 confirmed this finding by discussing a case law lineage where the valuation of social context was indeed mainly 'purpose' driven and regulatory choices were assessed within a model that can be termed consequentialist, based on utilitarian principles. As such, it was discussed that the substantive efficiency model of proportionality implements a utilitarian approach. In addition to denying an inflexible governing principle (such as the utility principle), incommensurability in the context of the book holds that there cannot be a priority rule in genuine conflicts between organisational principles (that is, no one value always has priority over another). The normative claims of social legitimacy require the recognition of a plurality of legitimate social purposes and, indeed, a liberal society, such as the EU itself claims to be, contains a diversity of social spheres. European adjudicators should therefore make space for different kinds of valuation and although the adjudicative model of the Court in free movement cases carries the inherent risk of 'slipping into a freewheeling rampage of economic due process', Chapter 2 also found that the Court has created different means to evaluate restrictive social context. Based on an ideal types approach Chapter 2 deduced from the case law, in addition to the substantive efficiency standard, evaluative standards based on principles of *margins of discretion* and *good governance*.

One of the key points of the 'good governance'-based case law of the Court is that a system of protection that a Member States installs has to *be embedded by ex ante conditions justifying the Member State choices.* If systems of protection are coherently and systematically part of an existing normative infrastructure that is tailored towards the level or protection that it seeks to protect, these systems of protection are provided with a definite margin of discretion and unlikely to be struck down by EU law. In other words, Member States' systems of protection need to be transparent, systematic and internally coherent but if these conditions are taken into account then the level of protection and the means through which this level of protection is sought remains largely at the discretion of the Member States. Here the dialogue becomes mutual because Member States bear a responsibility to structure their regulatory affairs in a way that the internal market rules can actually be applied in a responsive manner.

Looking through the lens of social legitimacy at EU free movement adjudication tells a mixed story. On the one hand, there is clearly responsiveness, which shows a concern for diversity and respect for local social context. On the other hand, there are plenty of cases where the Court foregoes social context and pushes a normative perception of the way in which social objectives and market integration relate to each other. What is identified in the chapter as lacking is, primarily, a consistent use of the ideal type proportionality models by the Court. In the application of each of these 'ideal type' models, the Court seems to be without a clear rationale as to when a definite margin of discretion is explicitly granted to Member States, when interests are to be considered sensitive and when a focus on procedural context is more appropriate than an evaluation of the necessity of the substantive measures themselves. This incoherence is problematic from the perspective of social legitimacy. On the one hand, because a normative unitary standard of valuation may be pushed that is unresponsive to legitimate social context within a Member State. On the other, through allowing margins of discretion to Member States where regulatory measures could have potentially been implemented in a more Union-friendly way.

I then argued that the key to social legitimacy and, concomitantly, Somek's question, is hidden within the different evaluative principles developed by the Court and what is lacking is a rationale to determine exactly *when* to apply one of the unveiled standards to a specific social context. This choice should find its basis in the identification of the nature of a conflict in terms of normative principles, which *responds* to the potential mixes of different types of normative infrastructures of economies on a Member State level and on this basis the internal market can be positioned within such *legitimate* social purposes. This connects to the first chapter, which developed the idea that the diversity of preferences and social orientations in the EU is the product of specific historical experiences, political contestation, societal learning and continuous political decision-making. In this way the normative fabric of the economic orders within Member States can be seen as their '*social acquis*', which should be recognised within EU law. It was argued previously that the compromise of embedded liberalism depends on a constructive interplay between the objectives of market integration with domestic social objectives. The internal market infrastructure is in this view infused with a strong social purpose and the objective of market integration becomes a tool for the beginning of a societal dialogue. In its ideal form the dialogue in a first stage 'uses' the narrow normative framework of market access to tease out and understand regulatory choices that restrict free trade objectives and in a second stage adopts an evaluative principle that is then congruent with the regulatory context that gave rise to the restriction.

On this point the argument has put forward a test of *inherent irreconcilability*. The choice for an evaluative standard can be instructed by the identification of the nature of conflicting objectives as being inherently irreconcilable. On the basis of a prima facie structuring of a conflict based on the 'narrow' aims of market access, the Court would first assess whether the restrictive aims, which are pursued by Member States, are inherently irreconcilable with substantive efficiency objectives of the internal market (ie the less restrictive measure). *Within the model proposed*, if found to be irreconcilable, the Court would then switch to an assessment of the procedural context of the measures on the basis of good governance principles. As such, within the dialogue of mutual responsiveness, inherently irreconcilable local domestic values will be separated within a rationale of supranational market integration and, vice versa, market integration objectives are pursued on the basis of procedural unity, transparency, consistency and coherence within those local structures. As such, in the EU free movement rules the dialogue of mutual responsiveness takes place on the basis of the three core concepts of substantive efficiency, margins of discretion and good governance. We shall see below that these three concepts indeed connect all areas of internal market law.

B. Social Legitimacy in EU Competition Law

The issue of valuation in law and the related problems of indeterminacy and incommensurability surface in a clearly distinct yet comparable way in the EU competition rules. The issue of valuation of social context is slightly more distinctly present within the application of the competition rules. That is to say, social objectives may, within EU competition law, be more explicitly discussed exclusively in terms of their merits within an efficiency-based evaluation. Similar to the EU free movement rules, evaluative standards within competition law may value social realities within a metric that risks doing violence to potentially genuine and worthwhile aspects of objectives that are pursued on a Member State level. The competition rules have a direct influence on social relations and on the way that societal objectives are pursued collectively by undertakings. For example, undertakings may want themselves to collectively set fair trade minimum standards or a state may want a particular sector to develop a sector-wide solution that induces mutual trust and development of a shared commitment to a societal objective. If such undertakings are (potential) competitors then the agreements amongst the undertakings pursuing such wider societal objectives are likely to restrict competition. Fair trade standards or sustainable energy production are increasingly being used by undertakings to distinguish themselves from each other in the market. A collective or minimum standard may therefore significantly restrict competition. Moreover, most economic theory tells us that commercial entities operate on the basis of incentives and as a rule, undertakings may therefore be presumed to act only in their self-interest. The collective pursuit of proclaimed wider societal objectives should therefore always be met with a healthy level of suspicion.

'We' also do not necessarily want what these undertakings have to offer us in the terms of what *they* perceive as wider social objectives. In other words, '*We Don't Want Mark Zuckerberg's Charity*!', right?[2] This latter issue points towards a democratic legitimacy issue.

However, in the presence of a trend of a retracting and increasingly deferential state, potential genuine intentions should not be all too readily dismissed on this basis alone. Moreover, some countries, such as the Netherlands, are based on a highly consensus-based culture that includes economic sectors and supply chains in their socio-economic policy-making. Hence, particularly the latter, provides an argument that the EU competition rules, in light of their broader constitutional role and commitment to respect regulatory diversity, should be able to accommodate private initiatives that restrict competition. The EU competition rules went through two important developments that influence the ability of EU competition law to accommodate regulatory diversity.

The normative concern, based on social legitimacy, is that evaluative standards may translate societal realities within a metric that risks doing violence to potentially genuine and worthwhile aspects of those objectives. Moreover, an additional point of normative concern of particular relevance for the competition rules is that where an evaluative standard adopts a unitary metric, the balancing of competing values becomes simply a matter of calculation. This is not to say that the calculations will be simple, but that the nature of the problem is transformed into one of quantification. Consequently, in situations where there is a manifest irreconcilability between normative orders, quantification risks losing the expressive value that is inherent in such a normative conflict and the consequent potential for social learning that arises from it. It forgoes the question when competition objectives and non-competition objectives are actually and genuinely irreconcilable. I submitted that the answer to this question matters because it provides instruction as to how evaluative rationales should deal with the interaction between competition and non-competition concerns.

The chapter engaged with some of the important literature on the extent that 'non-competition' interests should and can be integrated within competition law assessments. I discussed that the concept of the non-competition objective has never really been dissected very well within the literature in terms of the potential conflict that exists with the competition interest and that this is where the chapter contributes to the literature specifically. The normative demands of social legitimacy require a mechanism within the competition law assessment to single out the non-competition interest. I submitted an operational rationale to identify potential non-competition interests as objectives that fall outside of concerns that are related with the efficient functioning of markets—it is in this sense residual and defined through a process of opposition *within* the competition law analysis. There is an acceptance of the primacy of competition but merely in terms of a

[2] www.jacobinmag.com/2015/12/facebook-zuckerbergs-charity-gates-philantrophy/.

dialogue, which requires a 'responsive' space for the non-competition interest to be identified as a residual and conflicting objective.

The case studies in the competition chapter have demonstrated that these are not mere theoretical quibbles but manifest in a concrete and tangible way. The case of the Friesian horse, the Energy agreement and the Chicken of Tomorrow all demonstrate, first, the difficulties for competition law to accommodate private-led competition restrictive agreements that pursue wider societal objectives. Both the health of the Friesian horse and the Chicken of Tomorrow can be seen as potentially genuine objectives and as pursuing interests that are irreconcilable with an approach that quantifies value within a calculative framework. Animal welfare is not a number! *However*, was the pedigree not actually concerned with financial gain since an unhealthy horse is simply worth less money? And is sustainable meat not a key factor for both producers and retailers to disassociate themselves from others in the market? In that case we are talking about quantifiable quality issues and something that could perhaps be quantified within the exemption criteria of Article 101(3) TFEU. The Energy agreement brought together civil society actors from all levels of society in the formulation of a 'climate agreement' that was intent on moving towards more sustainable energy sources. Such a society-wide agreement should surely not be derailed by concerns related to the 'efficiency merits' of the closing down of a few coal plants? Isolating that aspect from the rest of the agreement would not do justice to the broader societal aims of the agreement, for which the closing down of the coal plants constituted an inherent part. *However*, was this 'grand societal narrative' perhaps not hijacked by a few energy companies to collectively restrict the output of an outdated energy source, which they would lose in the long term in any case and thereby solve a difficult coordination problem they would have otherwise faced in a situation of full competition?

The case studies demonstrate two important facets of the purported dialogue of mutual responsiveness. On the one hand, there should be a form of responsiveness, a potential accommodation of a genuine non-competition interest that is residual. That is to say, an interest that is not captured or becomes damaged somehow in the strict evaluation on the basis of its efficiency merits alone. Indeed, this approach accepts the primacy of competition but merely to open a conversation and a 'responsive' space for the non-competition interest to be identified as a residual and conflicting objective. There is therefore an implicit understanding that non-competition interests are dynamic because the underlying fabric can develop and evolve. This is reflective of the idea that competition law does not exist in a vacuum but should be able to respond to the current values and aims of society and is as susceptible to change as political thinking and social objectives are generally. Because views and insights shift over a period of time, competition law is infused with the need to move and adapt towards developing notions of what is to be perceived as a non-competition interest. If we accept that effective competition constitutes an important public interest, but only one of the worthwhile interests in society, forming part of a range of other interests that are potentially worth pursuing and in flux, we should ask the question if effective competition and 'broader' societal interests can be aligned harmoniously within an evaluative framework that requires the 'net efficiency result' to be positive. On the other hand, the case studies demonstrate a need for good governance, on the basis of institutional design that *embeds* the concerned objectives within a framework that ensures a form of political oversight. This is in a nutshell the dialogue of mutual responsiveness as perceived within the competition rules.

Fragments of this dialogue of mutual responsiveness can be found in the case law of the Court of Justice, which is more refined than it is often accredited with. From the perspective of social legitimacy the Court of Justice has with the *Albany* and *Poucet Pistre* lines of case law established the requirement for context-specific and responsive valuations of different social spheres and set out the beginnings of a more comprehensive rationale to determine, in a dynamic way, the constructive interplay between competition and non-competition spheres. As was demonstrated in the *AOK Bunderverband* case there is recognition of a potential irreconcilability between normative orders for which the Court of Justice has developed a type of valuation that is specific to the organisation of a sector on the basis of a solidarity principle. *Wouters* has been discussed as an extension of this idea, widening the scope of potential irreconcilable non-competition interests to be transposed to a type of valuation outside of the strict application of the exemption criteria of Article 101(3) TFEU. The emphasis on *mutual* responsiveness is present in all cases, although slightly confused in *Wouters*. It is clear that solidarity or the integrity of the profession of attorneys are interests that originate from the normative choices and institutional design in economies of the Member States. However, the Court is not specific in outlining what is crucial in this design, leaving it rather unclear what the facets of a public law institutional framework would have to look like, to accommodate the pursuit of private initiatives that pursue a non-competitive interest. To complete the dialogue of mutual responsiveness a connection was made to a line of cases where the Court has been quite explicit about these requirements. The *Arduino*, *Cipolla* and *Mauri* cases all concern the design of the public-private framework, which needs to ensure that the aspired goals are, at important points, fed with public legitimacy and provided with affirmative political oversight in order to be excused from the scope of the competition rules.

The case law of the Court of Justice provides a basis for the dialogue of mutual responsiveness and ensures social legitimacy in the application of the competition rules. The Court has developed a responsive model that is capable of identifying objectives that are genuine and inherent to the pursuit of interests, which are irreconcilable with the aims of the competition law framework. This context-specific *in concreto* approach puts emphasis on the expressive value of the interplay of competition and non-competition interests, which requires a specific and concrete articulation of the limits of both competition and genuinely irreconcilable non-competition interests. In this way competition law becomes essentially a tool for societal dialogue, testing old conventions and requiring the renewed articulation of the pursuit of potentially outdated and vested public interests. On the other hand, it avoids the valuation of regulatory systems merely on the basis of their 'efficiency' merits, whilst accommodating a diversity of social spheres that is subject to different means of valuation. This is all part of the responsiveness part of the dialogue. That this is a dialogue requiring *mutual* responsiveness is reflected in the requirements to fulfil a standard of good governance in the organisation of regulatory affairs. As such, the approach suggested in this chapter purports a holistic approach that again conceives the market and the social sphere as 'communicating vessels'. Competition-derived evaluative standards serve as a tool to tease out discriminatory, disingenuous regulatory choices within Member States but allow for genuine social objectives to exist in accordance with good governance principles that focus on the quality and systemacy of a governance process, instead of on the rationality and efficiency of its outcome. As such it can be seen, again, that the dialogue of mutual responsiveness takes place on the basis of the three core concepts of substantive efficiency, margins of discretion and good governance.

C. Social Legitimacy in EU State Aid Law

Social legitimacy concerns in EU state aid law arise on the basis of the normative rationales that Member States are conditioned to implement in their regulatory affairs on the basis of this area of internal market law. The central normative assumption behind the state aid rules is that the role of the state in the market should not lead to competition distortions between undertakings. As such, it is reflective of a joint commitment of the Member States to ensure competitive markets. The Commission has turned the state aid regime into a largely predetermined and proceduralised area of law. As such, the qualification of a regulatory measure as state aid implies a shift towards an arena of control where policy has to fulfil certain pre-determined proxies. It matters whether policy objectives developed by Member States are to be defined within the technocratic domain of the proceduralised world of the state aid rules or whether they are allowed to take shape within 'normal politics' and the democratic arenas of the Member States. The chapter posits that sometimes the political *process* of the pursuit of some regulatory objectives is what matters most. This is reminiscent of the normative concerns that were developed in the first chapter: some non-economic objectives tend to share or require a social and political pact that underlies the objectives that are pursued. That is to say, regulatory objectives may pursue objectives or are by nature to be attributed to a particular sphere of accountability. On this basis it can be normatively inappropriate to have them evaluated within the procedural, technocratic state aid framework of the Commission or to enforce a market rationale on the way regulatory objectives are to be pursued. As such, even if, theoretically speaking, a market or technocratic approach towards something like regulating access to public infrastructure would accommodate the functional features of an objective, there may be something lost in the process of pursuing the objective as part of a genuine political or regulatory process

Hence, the moment of defining a state measure as a state aid counts. It is at this juncture, where a decision is made whether a policy or regulatory framework can be developed *outside* of the state aid rationale or within the standards and justifications that are already prescribed in state aid *control*. The chapter therefore argued that the moment of defining a state aid measure should be responsive to the circumstances and rationales of the specific regulatory context that gave rise to a selective advantage and a distortion of competition. However, the *Dassonville*-like reasoning of the Court in *Steenkolenmijn* captures a wide range of regulatory contexts, on the basis of their effects. Potential social objectives that underlie regulatory choices do, in principle, not matter for the assessment of a measure in terms of state aid. Instead, the chapter demonstrated how market-derived rationales have a tendency to be applied expediently in order to determine whether the effects of a regulatory choice lead to a selective advantage for undertakings.

The Court has established that the application of a market-based evaluation of a governmental intervention should in principle be preceded by an assessment of the 'nature of the measure'. That means that, in principle, it is only if the state is acting to participate on the market that market-based standards should be used to evaluate whether any advantages have been granted. If, instead, the state is acting as a regulator, the 'market rationality' principle is replaced with evaluative standards based on questions whether regulation, asymmetrically, benefits a specific (group of) undertaking(s) or whether a measure involves a state resource. Social legitimacy then depends on whether the chosen evaluative standard is congruent with the underlying social context. It is on this point that some concerns were identified because the Court and the GC sometimes struggle in finding a coherent rationale for this distinction. Specifically, market rationales can become expedient and pervasive because regulatory action is often approached separately, without an explicit analysis of a potentially wider societal context. As such, the setting of charges for the use of public infrastructure (*RyanAir*) becomes a commercial decision and allowing the use of state assets free of charge, whereas they could have been sold or put up for auction, becomes a potential waste of economic resources (*Dutch Nox/Eventech*). In this way regulatory choices may be evaluated within a metric that risks doing violence to potentially genuine and worthwhile, wider, aspects of those objectives. The point here, from the view of the normative expectations that were developed in the first chapter, is the recognition of embedded social context within an economic rationale. Some communal contexts lend themselves easily to economic regulation. The 'instrumental community' context fits within a form of regulation based on an evaluative principle of efficiency. Problems may arise, however, when economic substantive efficiency-oriented governance mechanisms would be installed to regulate social context based on trust, informal values, public-spiritedness and so forth. The balance from the perspective of state aid is difficult because such amorphous elements of state-society-market relations are, from a state aid perspective, perceived as important factors contributing to a lack of transparency and constitutive of relationships, which are likely to end up in granting covert advantages to some undertakings and not to others. The rigidity of the prudent private investor standard *leaving aside all social, regional-policy and sectoral considerations* is, at least partly, based on an idea of administrability and transparency in state aid matters. On the other hand, there is the potential for an inherent reductionist view of the legitimate relationship between the state and the market at play. It is reductionist because the valuation of state action may exclude normative orientations within the infrastructure of economies on a Member State level.

As such, the market-based regulatory standards that state aid law introduces may condition public bodies towards actions that are justified exclusively on the grounds of their commercial self-interest and thereby crowd out potential alternative visions towards the appropriate role of public authorities and the direction that policy objectives take. At the same time, the wave of new public management, which installed efficiency principles within Member States' regulatory affairs has made it more difficult to conceptualise alternative forms of governance outside of the spectrum of cost-benefit analysis. Essentially those processes have obscured the difference between market and non-market approaches in regulatory intervention. Nevertheless, EU internal market law is not committed to these principles and should allow, explicitly, for the *possibility of social diversity*.

Nevertheless, the Court has demonstrated responsiveness in the application of the state aid rules in some lines of case law where it sought to disentangle commercial transactions entered into by Member States from the non-commercial and regulatory objectives that accompany them. The case law allows for what may be seen as the *inherent justifications* of measures that grant selective economic advantages but are part of general regulatory or legislative schemes, which are themselves incorporating legitimate regulatory objectives. Such legitimate and genuinely pursued 'reference frameworks' are able to pull individual measures that form an inherent part of such frameworks out of the realm of the state aid regime.

The chapter reconstructed the case law of the Court within the dialogue of mutual responsiveness in the following way. The substantive reach of the internal market is reflected in the market derived standards such as the MEOP, which requires a 'switch' towards an evaluative framework that allows for a diversity (a margin of discretion) and plurality of legitimate possibly inefficient *substantive* outcomes, provided that they are pursued in a transparent, coherent and systematic fashion, in accordance with requirements of good governance. Underlying this switch in the state aid rules is the idea of a 'genuine regulatory activity', which is not based on a formalistic idea of traditional state powers but can be shaped in a dynamic fashion by the Member States in their fulfilment of tasks towards its population in the social, cultural and educational areas. Thus, the social legitimacy of the state aid rules depends on the extent and level of sophistication adopted in legal reasoning that identifies instances of 'genuine regulatory activity' before adopting evaluative principles that are congruent to the conflict that is being adjudicated.

III. SOME FINAL REMARKS

Clearly, a problem for internal market adjudication which is committed to social diversity within the Union is that plurality may be bought at the price of allowing too much. Internal market adjudication requires coherent approaches to avoid that social diversity turns into a *carte blanche* for communities who prefer their own values at the expense of other Member States. Nevertheless, if we indeed accept the argument that social diversity is a value to which the EU internal market is committed then market-derived utilitarian standards, despite the overarching value of 'administrability', are not appropriate means to adjudicate all types of internal market conflicts, because they simply fail to capture and weigh the true social significance of some restrictive rules. However, it was found with regard to the three areas of the internal market that many restrictive Member State regulations perish within the evaluative frameworks of the Court because Member States themselves do not really understand the functions of their own laws. Such regulatory *indeterminacy* tends not to fulfil consequentialist, purpose-driven evaluative standards. As such, indeterminacy has been identified as a central cause for potential social legitimacy issues in all areas of internal market law and the dialogue of mutual responsiveness serves as a means to improve the articulation of regulatory choices of Member States. In a very real sense the Court calls for better regulation by the Member States. However, better regulation is not necessarily regulation that speaks market talk and the Court has indeed demonstrated that it will respond to genuine regulatory choices and rationales in the pursuit of objectives that are legitimate and serve an important social commitment or normative orientation of a local economy. The point is that responsive adjudication will need something to respond to.

This issue of indeterminacy has some broader structural relevance, not touched upon directly in the book, and this was observed occasionally in the fringes of the discussion of the negative effects of utilitarian purpose-driven standards. The internal market floats as a legal reality above the Member States and, thereby, installs dominant principles of organisation. As soon as there is a restriction, Member States will have to conform to a discourse that recognises and allows *legitimate* objectives to restrict market integration and submerge to a rationality that will determine the suitable means to achieve these objectives. However, in the regulatory vacuum left by Member States, principles of public management and the better, smarter regulation initiatives of the European Commission are likely to become a dominant form of governmentality within the European Union (if they are not already). The fact that there is no immediate autonomous or self-sustainable rationale to support non-market based regulation means that it is much easier and seemingly more transparent to connect regulatory objectives to market-based types of regulation. In this process, the objective becomes either re-defined as a corrective to market processes (as an externality) or is completely translated within a market metric: eg pursuing a sustainable environment through installing self-regulatory trading mechanisms in rights to pollute.

This type of smart regulation is nurtured and promoted by the European Commission. Clearly these 'smart' forms of regulatory design will also quickly fulfil the evaluative standards of the Court. The point of indeterminacy is that social diversity and plurality are not a given and will have to be institutionally 'protected' in order to survive within the purpose-driven rationales of the European Union. Therefore, although there are ways in which the institutional set-up of the EU seems to share Polanyi's concerns for embedding markets in social foundations, the dominant trend of governance in the European Union is clearly to move towards utilitarian types of 'impact assessments' and 'evidence-centred' policy-making. The underlying rationale of these efforts are in close proximity to Polany's observations regarding the choice of design for institutional infrastructures in the process of the industrial revolution:

> the economic system is organized in separate institutions, based on specific motives and conferring a special status, society must be shaped in such a manner as to allow that system to function according to its own laws.

Although we have seen in the studies of the previous chapters that this is not necessarily in all cases dismissive of social objectives, not all societal realities will be equally valued or accommodated within such consequentialist thinking.

As such, the conclusions offered by this book only unveil part of the story. The proposed responsive model of adjudication provides the Court with an adjudicative model through which it can communicate with domestic social objectives/actors in a more constructive manner, explaining what is required from domestic governance in the context of a supranational market integration rationale. As such, the adjudicative rationales of the Court have been reconstructed towards a consistently more responsive model that is able to accommodate Member State diversity *and* promote the objectives of the internal market; an integrated market that is responsive to a Member State's differing sets of social contexts. However, these findings will have to be completed with a more complete account of the effects of internal market legislation, governance and fiscal oversight in order to establish to what extent the respect for social diversity is a part of the values that are actually purported in the internal market.

Despite these shortcomings, the study in this book has demonstrated how the internal market can become *the* platform of a societal dialogue, which the argument of transnational effects had conceived for it, in accordance with the normative claims of social legitimacy. The internal market chapters demonstrate the shared problems and pitfalls that prevent the realisation of this preconceived social purpose for the internal market. I have attempted in this study to allow for the structural inclusion of this social purpose within European legal space by developing a common shared language of substantive efficiency, margins of discretion and good governance, within a dialogue of mutual responsiveness.

Bibliography

Abelshauser, W, 'Ricardo neu gedacht: Komparative institutionelle Vorteile von Wirtschaftskulturen' in W Abelshauser et al (eds), *Kulturen der Weltwirtschaft* (Geschichte und Gesellschaft, Sonderheft, 2012) 24.

Acemogluy, D and Jackson, MO, 'Social Norms and the Enforcement of Laws' NBER Working Paper No 20369 (August 2004) http://nber.org/papers/w20369.

Akman, P, 'Consumer Welfare and Article 102 EC: Practice and Rhetoric' (2009) 32 *World Competition* 71.

—— 'Searching for the Long-Lost Soul of Article 82 EC' (2009) 29 *Oxford Journal of Legal Studies* 267.

Allan TRS, 'Democracy, Legality, and Proportionality' in G Huscroft, BW Miller and G Webber (eds), *Proportionality and the Rule of Law: Rights, Justification, Reasoning* (Cambridge, Cambridge University Press, 2014) 205.

Amato G, *Antitrust and the Bounds of Power* (Oxford, Hart Publishing, 1997).

Andriychuk, O, 'Dialectical Antitrust: An Alternative Insight into the Methodology of the EC Competition Law Analysis in a Period of Economic Downturn' (2010) 31 *European Competition Law Review* 155.

—— 'Rediscovering the Spirit of Competition: On the Normative Value of the Competitive Process' (2010) 6 *European Competition Journal* 575.

Ankersmit L, 'Het einde van de kiloknallers? De grenzen aan zelfregulering van duurzaam vlees onder het kartelverbod' (2011) *Actualiteiten Mededingingsrecht* 149.

—— *Globalization and the Internal Market: Process-based Measures Within the EU Legal Order* (PhD thesis, Vrije Universiteit Amsterdam, 2015).

Apeldoorn, B, van, 'The Contradictions of "Embedded Neoliberalism" and Europe's Multi-level Legitimacy Crisis: The European Project and its Limits' in B Van Apeldoorn, J Drahokoupil and L Horn (eds), *Contradictions and Limits of Neoliberal European Governance: from Lisbon to Lisbon* (London, Palgrave Macmillan, 2008).

Ashiagbor, D, 'Unravelling the Embedded Liberal Bargain: Labour and Social Welfare Law in the Context of EU Market Integration' (2013) 19(3) *European Law Journal* 324.

—— and Kotiswaran, P and Perry-Kessaris, A, (eds), Special Issue: Towards an Economic Sociology of Law (2013) 40 *Journal of Law and Society*.

Azoulai, L, 'The Court of Justice and the Social Market Economy: The Emergence of an Ideal and the Conditions for Its Realization' (2008) 45 *Common Market Law Review* 1335.

—— 'The "Retained Powers" Formula in the Case Law of the European Court of Justice: EU Law as Total Law?' (2011) 4 *European Journal of Legal Studies* 192.

—— 'The European Court of Justice and the Duty to Respect Sensitive National Interests' in B de Witte, E Muir and M Dawson, *Judicial Activism at the European Court of Justice: Causes, Responses and Solutions* (Cheltenham, Edward Elgar Publishing, 2013) 167.

Bacon, K, 'Differential Taxes, State Aids and the Lunn Poly Case' (1999) 20 *European Competition Law Review* 384.

Baquero Cruz, J, *Between Competition and Free Movement: the Economic Constitutional Law of the European Community* (Oxford, Hart Publishing, 2002).

—— 'Services of General Interest and EC Law' in G de Búrca (ed), *EU Law and the Welfare State—In Search of Solidarity* (Oxford, Oxford University Press, 2005) 16.

Barnard, C, 'Viking and Laval: An Introduction' (2007–08) 10 *Cambridge Yearbook of European Legal Studies* 464.

—— 'Social Dumping or Dumping Socialism' (2008) 67 *Current Law Journal* 262.

—— 'Derogations, Justifications, and the Four Freedoms: is State Interest Really Protected?' in C Barnard and O Odudu (eds), *The Outer Limits of European Union Law* (Oxford, Hart Publishing, 2009) 273.

—— and Deakin, S, 'Market Access and Regulatory Competition' in C Barnard and J Scott (eds), *The Law of the Single European Market, Unpacking the Premises* (Oxford, Hart Publishing, 2002).

Bartosch A, 'Clarification or Confusion—How to reconcile the ECJ's Rulings in Altmark and Chronopost' (2003) 3 *European State Aid Law Quarterly* 12.

—— 'The Ruling in BUPA—Clarification or Modification of Altmark?' (2008) 2 *European State Aid Law Quarterly* 211.

—— 'Is there a Need for a Rule of Reason in European State Aid Law? Or how to Arrive at a Coherent Concept of Material Selectivity' (2010) 47 *Common Market Law Review* 729.

Beck Jorgensen, T and Bogh Andersen, L, 'An Aftermath of NPM: Regained Relevance of Public Values and Public Service Motivation' in T Christensen and P Laegreid (eds), *The Ashgate Research Companion to New Public Management* (Farnham, Ashgate, 2011) 335.

Beckert, J, 'The Great Transformation of Embeddedness: Karl Polanyi and the New Economic Sociology' in C Hann and K Hart (eds), *Market and Society: The Great Transformation Today* (New York, Cambridge University Press 2009) 38.

Behrens, P, 'Public Service and the Internal Market' in T Einhorn (ed), *Spontaneous Order, Organization and the Law. Roads to a European Civil Society* (The Hague, Asser Press, 2003) 43.

Bellamy, R, 'The Liberty of the Moderns: Market Freedom and Democracy within the EU' (2012) 1 *Global Constitutionalism* 141.

Beramendi, P, 'Inequality and the Territorial Fragmentation of Solidarity' (2007) 4 *International Organization* 783.

B Bercusson, 'The Trade Union Movement and the European Union: Judgment Day' (2007) 13 *European Law Journal* 279.

Besselink LFM, 'National and Constitutional Identity before and after Lisbon' (2010) 6 *Utrecht Law Review* 36.

Biondi, A, 'Some Reflections on the Notion of "State Resources" in European Community State Aid Law' (2007) 30 *Fordham International Law Journal* 1426.

—— '*BUPA* v Commission' (2008) 7 *European State Aid Law Quarterly* 408.

—— and Farley, M, 'The Relationship between State Aid and the Single Market' in E Szyszcak (ed), *Research Handbook on State Aid* (Cheltenham, Edward Elgar, 2011) 277.

—— and Rubini, L, 'Aims, Effects and Justifications: EC State Aid Law and Its Impact on National Social Policies' in M Dougan, and E Spaventa (eds), *Social Welfare and EU Law* (Oxford, Hart Publishing, 2005) 79.

Blauberger, M, 'With Luxembourg in Mind … the Remaking of Policies in the Face of ECJ Jurisprudence' (2012) 19 *Journal of European Public Policy* 109.

Block, F, 'Karl Polanyi and the Writing of The Great Transformation' (2003) 32 *Theory and Society: Renewal and Critique in Social Theory* 275.

—— and Somers, M, *The Power of Market Fundamentalism: Karl Polanyi's Critique*, (Boston, Harvard University Press, 2014).

Boeger, N, 'Solidarity and EC Competition Law' (2007) 32 *European Law Review* 319.

Bogaert van den, S and Cuyvers, A, 'Money for Nothing: The Case Law of the EU Court of Justice on the Regulation of Gambling' (2011) 48 *Common Market Law Review* 1175.

Bogdandy, A, von and Schill, S, 'Overcoming Absolute Primacy: Respect for National Identity under the Lisbon Treaty' (2011) 48 *Common Market Law Review* 1417.

Bork, RH, *The Antitrust Paradox: A Policy at War with itself* (New York, Basic Books, 1978).

Boston, J, 'Basic NPM Ideas and their Development' in T Christensen and P Laegreid (eds), *The Ashgate Research Companion to New Public Management* (Farnham, Ashgate, 2011).

Boutin, X and Peduzzi, R, 'Searching for "Good Aid": The Role of Evaluation' (2015) 14 *European State Aid Law Quarterly* 250.

Bouwens, B and Dankers, J, 'Competition and Varieties of Coordination' in K Sluyterman (ed), *Varieties of Capitalism and Business History—The Dutch Case* (Abingdon, Routledge, 2015) 105.

Bovens, M, 'New Forms of Accountability and EU-Governance' (2007) 5 *Comparative European Politics* 104.

Buckel, S and Oberndorfer, L, 'Die lange Inkubationszeit des Wettbewerbs der Rechtsordnungen—Eine Genealogie der Rechtsfälle Viking/Laval/Rüffert/Luxemburg aus der Perspektive einer materialistischen Europarechtstheorie' in AF Lescano, F Rödl and C Schmid (eds), *Europäische Gesellschaftsverfassung. Zur Konstitutionalisierung sozialer Demokratie in Europa* (Baden-Baden, Nomos, 2009).

Buendía Sierra, JL, Rivas, P and Manuel, J, 'The Almunia Package: State Aid and Services of General Economic Interest' in E Szyszcak and JW van de Gronden (eds), *Financing Services of General Economic Interest* (The Hague, TMC Asser Press, 2013) 125.

Búrca G, de, 'The Quest for Legitimacy in the European Union' (1994) 59 *Modern Law Review* 349.

—— *EU Law and the Welfare State: in Search of Solidarity* (Oxford, Oxford University Press, 2005).

Buttigie, E, 'Competition Law: Safeguarding the Consumer Interest. A Comparative Analysis of US Antitrust Law and EC Competition Law' in J Drexl, W Kerber, R Podszun (eds), *Competition Policy and the Economic Approach—Foundations and Limitations* (Cheltenham, Edward Elgar, 2010).

Caporaso, J and Tarrow, S, 'Polanyi in Brussels: Supranational Institutions and the Transnational Embedding of Markets' (2009) 63 *International Organization* 593.

Casey, D, 'Disintegration: Environmental Protection and Article 81 EC' (2009) 15 *European Law Journal* 362.

Cecco, F, de, *State Aid and the European Economic Constitution* (Oxford, Hart Publishing, 2013).

Chalmers, D, 'The European Redistributive State and a European Law of Struggle' (2012) 18 *European Law Journal* 667.

—— Davies G and Monti, G, *European Union Law; Cases and Materials*, 2nd edn (Cambridge, Cambridge University Press, 2010).

Christensen, T and Laegreid, P (eds), *The Ashgate Research Companion to New Public Management* (Farnham, Ashgate, 2011).

Clemens, H et al (eds), *Judging Europe's Judges: The Legitimacy of the Case Law of the European Court of Justice* (Oxford, Hart Publishing, 2013).

Cloots, E, *National Identity in EU Law* (Oxford, Oxford University Press, 2015).

Colomo, I, 'Market Failures, Transaction Costs and Article 101(1) TFEU Case Law' (2012) 37 *European Law Review* 54.

Cooter, RD, 'Three Effects of Social Norms on Law: Expression, Deterrence, and Internalization' (2000) 79 *Oregon Law Review* 1.

Copeland, P, 'International Political Economy and European Integration—Applying Karl Polanyi's The Great Transformation' (2009) 40 *IPEG Papers on Global Political Economy* 1.

Coser, L, *The Functions of Social Conflict* (New York, The Free Press, 1956).

Costamagna, F, 'The Internal Market and the Welfare State: Anything New after Lisbon? in M Trybus and L Rubini (eds), *The Treaty of Lisbon and the Future of European Law and Policy* (Cheltenham, Edward Elgar, 2012) 381.

Cotterrell, R, 'Rethinking "Embeddedness": Law, Economy, Community' (2013) 40 *Journal of Law and Society* 49.

Cover, R, 'Foreword: Nomos and Narrative' (1983) 97 *Harvard Law Review* 4.

Craig, P, 'Competence and Member State Autonomy: Causality, Consequence and Legitimacy' in HW Micklitz and B de Witte (eds), *The European Court of Justice and the autonomy of the Member States* (Oxford Legal Studies Research Paper No 57/2009).

—— *The Lisbon Treaty: Law, Politics, and Treaty Reform* (Oxford, Oxford University Press, 2013).

—— and de Burca, G, *EU Law Text, Cases and Materials* (Oxford, Oxford University Press, 2011).

Crane, DA, 'The tempting of Antitrust: Robert Bork and the Goals of Antitrust Policy' (2014) 79 *Antitrust Law Journal* 835.

Craven, R, 'State Aid and Sports Stadiums: EU Sports Policy or Deference to Professional Football' (2014) 9 *European Competition Law Review* 453.

Crocioni, P, 'Can State Aid Policy Become more Economic-Friendly?' (2006)29 *World Competition* 89.

Crouch, C, *Making Capitalism Fit for Society* (Cambridge-Malden MA, Polity Press, 2013) 37.

Dahrendorf, R, *The Modern Social Conflict: An Essay on the Politics of Liberty* (London, Weidenfeld and Nicolson, 1988).

Dale, G, *Karl Polanyi: The Limits of the Market* (Cambridge, Polity Press, 2010).

Damjanovic, D, 'The EU Market Rules as Social Market Rules: Why the EU Can Be a Social Market Economy' (2013) 50(6) *Common Market Law Review* 1685.

Dani, M, 'Rehabilitating Social Conflicts in European Public Law' (2012) 18 *European Law Journal* 621.

Dashwood, A, 'Viking and Laval: Issues of Horizontal Direct Effect' (2007–08) 10 *Cambridge Yearbook of European Legal Studies* 525.

Davies, A, 'One Step Forward, Two Steps Back? Laval and Viking at the ECJ' (2008) 37 *Industrial Law Journal* 126.

Davies, G, Subsidiarity: The Wrong Idea, in the Wrong Place, at the Wrong Time' (2006) 43 *Common Market Law Review* 63.

—— 'What Does Article 86 Actually Do?' in M Krajewski, U Neergaard and J van de Gronden (eds), *The Changing Legal Framework for Services of General Interest in Europe* (The Hague, Asser Press, 2009) 51.

—— 'Understanding Market Access: Exploring the Economic Rationality of Different Conceptions of Free Movement Law' (2010) 11(7–8) *German Law Journal* 671.

—— 'The Court's Jurisprudence on Free Movement of Goods: Pragmatic Presumptions, not Philosophical Principles' (2012) 2 *European Journal of Consumer Law* 25.

—— 'Internal Market Adjudication and the Quality of Life in Europe' (2014) EUI Working Paper 2014/07.

—— 'Democracy and Legitimacy in the Shadow of Purposive Competence' (2015) 21 *European Law Journal* 2.

Dawson, M, *New Governance and the Transformation of European Law* (Cambridge, Cambridge University Press, 2011).

—— and Witte, F, de, 'The EU Legal Framework of Social Inclusion and Social Protection: Between the Lisbon Strategy and the Lisbon Treaty' in B Cantillon et al (eds), *Social Inclusion and Social Protection in the EU: Interactions between Law and Policy* (Cambridge, Intersentia, 2012).

—— and Witte, F de, 'Constitutional Balance in the EU after the Euro-crisis' (2012) 76(5) *Modern Law Review* 817.

Deakin, S, 'Regulatory Competition after Laval' (2007–08) 10 *Cambridge Yearbook of European Legal Studies* 581.

—— 'The Lisbon Treaty, the Viking and Laval Judgments and the Financial Crisis: In Search of New Foundations for Europe's Social Market Economy' in N Bruun, K Lörcher and I Schömann (eds), *The Lisbon Treaty and Social Europe* (Oxford, Hart Publishing, 2012) 19.

Dhondt, N, *Integration of Environmental Protection into other EC Policies: Legal Theory and Practice* (Brussels, Europa Law Publishing, 2003).

Dibben, P and Higgins, P, 'New Public Management: Marketization, Managerialism and Consumerism' in P Dibben, G Wood and I Roper (eds), *Contesting Public Sector Reforms* (London, Palgrave Macmillan, 2004).

Dobbins, T, 'The Case for "Beneficial Constraints": Why Permissive Voluntarism Impedes Workplace Cooperation in Ireland' (2010) 35 *Economic and Industrial Democracy* 497.

Dougan, M and Spaventa, E (eds), *Social Welfare and EU law* (Oxford, Hart Publishing, 2005).

Dukes, R, *The Labour Constitution. The Enduring Idea of Labour Law* (Oxford, Oxford University Press, 2014).

Dunn, W and Miller, D, 'A Critique of New Public Management and the Neo-Weberian State Advancing a Critical theory of Administrative Reform' (2007) 7 *Public Organization Review* 345.

Durkheim, E, *The Division of Labor in Society* (New York, Free Press of Glencoe, 1964).

Dyzenhaus, D, 'Proportionality and Deference in a Culture of Justification' in G Huscroft, BW Miller and G Webber (eds), *Proportionality and the Rule of Law: Rights, Justification, Reasoning* (Cambridge, Cambridge University Press, 2014) 234.

Ebner, A, 'Transnational Markets and the Polanyi Problem' in C Joerges and J Falke (eds), *Globalisation and the Potential of Law in Transnational Markets* (Oxford, Hart Publishing, 2011) 28.

Ehlermann, D, 'The Contribution of EC Competition Policy to the Single Market' (1992) 29 *Common Market Law Review* 257.

Enteman, W, *Managerialism: The Emergence of a New Ideology* (Wisconsin, University of Wisconsin Press, 1993).

Ferrera, M, 'Modest Beginnings, Timid Progresses: What Next for Social Europe?' in B Cantillon et al, *Social Inclusion and Social Protection in the EU: Interactions between Law and Policy* (Cambridge, Intersentia, 2012) 17–39.

Fraser, N, 'Can Society Be Commodities All the Way down? Post-Polanyian Reflections on Capitalist Crisis' (2014) 43 *Economy and Society* 541.

Fuller, L and Winston, K, 'The Forms and Limits of Adjudication' (1978) 92 *Harvard Law Review* 353.

Galligan, DJ, *Law in Modern Society* (Oxford, Oxford University Press, 2010).

Gardbaum, S, 'Proportionality and Democratic Constitutionalism' in G Huscroft, BW Miller, and G Webber (ed.), Proportionality and the Rule of Law: Rights, Justification, Reasoning (Cambridge, Cambridge University Press, 2014).

Gerbrandy, A, 'Competition Law and Private-Sector Sustainability Initiatives' in A Colombi Ciacchi, M Heldeweg, B van der Meulen and A Neerhof (eds), *Law & Governance: Beyond the Public-Private Law Divide*? (The Hague, Eleven International Publishing, 2013) 83.

—— 'Duurzaamheidsbelangen in het mededingingsrecht' (2013) 9 *Nederlands Tijdschrift voor Europees Recht* 326.

—— 'Addressing the Legitimacy Problem for Competition Authorities Taking into Account Non-Economic Values: The Position of the Dutch Competition Authority' (2015) 40 *European Law Review* 770.

Gerner-Beuerle, C, 'Shareholders between the Market and the State: The VW Law and Other Interventions in the Market Economy' (2012) 49 *Common Market Law Review* 97.

Giubboni, S, *Diritti sociali e mercato. La dimensione sociale dell'integrazione europea* (Bologna, Il Mulino, 2003).

—— *Social Rights and Market Freedoms in the European Constitution. A Labour Law Perspective* (Cambridge, Cambridge University Press, 2006).

Glyn, A, *Capitalism Unleashed: Finance, Globalization and Welfare* (Oxford, Oxford University Press, 2007.

Goetschy, J, 'Taking Stock of Social Europe: is there such a Thing as a Community Social Model?', in M Jespen, and AS Pascual (eds), *Unwrapping the European Social Model* (Bristol, Policy Press, 2006) 66.

—— 'The Lisbon Strategy and Social Europe: Two Closely Linked Destinies' in MD Rodrigues (ed), *Europe, Globalization and the Lisbon Agenda* (Cheltenham, Edward Elgar, 2009) 74–90.

Granovetter, M, 'Economic Action and Social Structure: the Problem of Embeddedness' (1985) 91 *American Journal of Sociology* 481.

Gromnicka, E, 'Services of General Economic Interest in the State Aid Regime: Proceduralisation of Political Choices?' (2005) 11 *European Public Law* 429.

Gryse, C, de, 'Historical and Institutional Background to the Cross-industry Social Dialogue' in AD Dufresne and P Pochet (eds), *The European Sectoral Social Dialogue* (Brussels, PIE 2006) 31.

Hall, PA, 'Varieties of Capitalism and the Euro Crisis' (2014) 37 *West European Politics* 1223.

—— and Soskice, DW, *Varieties of Capitalism: The Institutional Foundations of Comparative Advantage* (Oxford, Oxford University Press, 2001).

Hancher, L, "Towards a New Definition of a State Aid under European Law—Is there a New Concept of State Aid Emerging' (2003) *European State Aid Law Quarterly* 365.

Hart, HLA, *The Concept of Law* (Oxford, Clarendon Press, 1961).

Hassel, A, 'Adjustments in the Eurozone: Varieties of Capitalism and the Crisis in Southern Europe' LEQS Paper No 76/2014.

—— 'The German Model in Transition' in B Unger (ed), *The German Model* (Düsseldorf, Hans-Böckler-Stiftung, 2015) 105–34.

Hay, JR, and Shleifer, A, 'Private Enforcement of Public Laws: A Theory of Legal Reform' (1998) 88 *American Economic Review* 398.

—— Shleifer, A and Vishny, RW, 'Toward a Theory of Legal Reform' (1996) 40 *European Economic Review* 559.

Hees, S, van, *A Sustainable Competition Policy for Europe. A Research on how the European Cartel Rules Can Make a Stronger Contribution to Europe's Sustainable Development Goals* (Utrecht, Utrecht University, 2013).

Hemerijck, A, 'The Self-Transformation of the European Social Model(s)' in G Esping Andersen (ed), *Why we Need a Welfare State* (Oxford, Oxford University Press, 2002) 178.

Hervey TK, 'Social Solidarity: a Buttress against Internal Market Law' in J Shaw (ed), *Social Law and Policy in an Evolving European Union* (Oxford, Hart Publishing, 2000) 31–47.

—— 'If only it were so Simple: Public Health Services and EU Law' in M Cremona (ed), *Market Integration and Public Services in the European Union* (Oxford, Oxford University Press, 2011) 179–250.

Hirschmann, AO, 'Social Conflicts as Pillars of Democratic Market Society' (1994) 22 *Political Theory* 206.

Hix, S and Follesdal, A, 'Why There Is a Democratic Deficit in the EU: A Response to Majone and Moravscik' (2006) 44 *Common Market Studies* 533.

Hofmann, H and Pantazatou, K, 'The Transformation of the European Economic Constitution' University of Luxembourg Law Working Paper 2015-01.

Hohfeld, WN, 'Some Fundamental Legal Conceptions as Applied in Judicial Reasoning' (1913) 23 *Yale Law Journal* 16.

Holmes, C, 'Problems and Opportunities in Polanyian Analysis Today' (2012) 41 *Economy and Society Economy* 468.

Hooghe, L and Marks, G, 'The Making of a Polity: The Struggle over European Integration' in H Kitschelt et al (eds), *Continuity and Change in Contemporary Capitalism* (Cambridge, Cambridge University Press, 1999) 70–97.

Höpner, M and Schäfer, A, 'A New Phase of European Integration: Organized Capitalisms' (2010) 33 *West European Politics* 344.

—— 'Embeddedness and Regional Integration: Waiting for Polanyi in a Hayekian Setting' (2012) 66 *International Organization* 429.

Hoque, Z and Moll, J, 'Public Sector Reform: Implications for Accounting, Accountability and Performance of State-Owned Entities—An Australian Perspective' (2001) 14 *International Journal of Public Sector Management* 305.

Horne RE, 'Limits to Labels: The Role of Eco-labels in the Assessment of Product Sustainability and Routes to Sustainable Consumption' (2009) 33 *International Journal of Consumer Studies* 175.

Horváth, E, *Mandating Identity: Citizenship, Kinship Laws and Plural Nationality in the European Union* (Alphen aan den Rijn, Kluwer Law International, 2007) 126.

Horwitz, MJ, *The Transformation of American Law, 1870–1960: The Crisis of Legal Orthodoxy* (Oxford, Oxford University Press, 1992) 193.

Jansson, MS and Kalimo, H, 'De Minimis Meets "Market Access": Transformations in the Substance—and the Syntax—of EU Free Movement Law?' (2014) 51 *Common Market Law Review* 523.

Joerges, C, 'A Critique of the Disregard for History in European Constitutional Theory: Are Those that Forget the Past Doomed to Repeat its Mistakes?' Florence, EUI Working Paper LAW No 2005/14.

—— 'What is Left of the European Economic Constitution?' European University Institute, Working Paper Law No 2004/13.
—— 'What is Left of the European Economic Constitution? A Melancholic Eulogy' (2005) 30 *European Law Review* 461.
—— '"Deliberative Political Processes" Revisited: What Have we Learnt About the Legitimacy of Supranational Decision-Making?' (2006) 44 *Journal of Common Market Studies* 779.
—— 'Unity in Diversity as Europe's Vocation and Conflicts Law as Europe's Constitutional Form' in R Nickel and A Greppi (eds), *The Changing Role of Law in the Age of Supra- and Transnational Governance* (Baden-Baden, Nomos, 2014) 125.
—— 'Market Integration and Europeanisation of Private Law' Jean Monnet Project Conference Paper (May 2015), on file with author.
—— 'The European Economic Constitution and its Transformation through the Financial Crisis' ZenTra Working Papers in Transnational Studies No 47/2015.
—— and Neyer, J, 'From Intergovernmental Bargaining to Deliberative Political Processes' (1997) 3 *European Law Journal* 273.
—— and Rödl, F, 'Informal Politics, Formalised Law and the "Social Deficit" of European Integration: Reflections after the Judgments of the ECJ in Viking and Laval' (2009) 15 *European Law Journal* 1.
—— and J Falke (eds), *Karl Polanyi: Globalisation and the Potential of Law in Transnational Markets* (Oxford/Portland OR, Hart Publishing, 2011).
—— and Everson, M, 'Reconfiguring the Politics–Law Relationship in the Integration Project through Conflicts–Law Constitutionalism' (2012) 18 *European Law Journal* 644.
Judt, T, *Postwar: A History of Europe since 1945* (London, Penguin Group Inc, 2006).
Kaupa, C, 'Maybe not Activist Enough? On the Court's Alleged Neoliberal Bias in its Recent Labor Cases' in B de Witte, E Muir and M Dawson, *Judicial Activism at the European Court of Justice: Causes, Responses and Solutions* (Cheltenham, Edward Elgar Publishing, 2013) 56–75.
—— *The Pluralist Character of the European Economic Constitution* (Oxford, Hart Publishing, 2016).
Kieran, F, 'A Separation of Powers Approach to Non-efficiency Goals in EU Competition Law' (2013) 19 *European Public Law* 189.
Kilpatrick, C, 'Laval's Regulatory Conundrum: Collective Standard-Setting and the Court's New Approach to Postal Workers' (2009) 34 *European Law Review* 844.
Kingston, S, 'Integrating Environmental Protection and EU Competition Law: Why Competition Isn't Special' (2010) 6 *European Law Journal* 790.
—— Greening Competition Law and Policy (Boston, Cambridge, 2012).
Kjølbye, L, 'The New Commission Guidelines on the Application of Article 81(3): an Economic Approach to Article 81' (2004) 25 *European Competition Law Review* 566.
Klasse, M, 'The Impact of Altmark: The European Commission Case Law Responses' in E Szyszcak and JW van de Gronden (eds), *Financing Services of General Economic Interest* (The Hague, TMC Asser Press, 2013) 35.
Komninos, AP, 'Non-competition Concerns: Resolution of Conflicts in the Integrated Article 81 EC' (2008) The University of Oxford Centre for Competition Law and Policy Working Paper (L) 08/05.
Konstadinides, T, 'Constitutional Identity as a Shield and as a Sword: The European Legal Order within the Framework of National Constitutional Settlement' (2011) 13 *Cambridge Yearbook of European Legal Studies* 195.

Krajewski, M, 'Providing Legal Clarity and Securing Policy Space for Public Services through a Legal Framework for Services of General Economic Interest: Squaring the Circle?' (2008) 14 *European Public Law* 377.

—— 'Commodifying and Embedding Services of General Interest in Transnational Contexts: The example of healthcare liberalisation in the EU and the WTO' in C Joerges and J Falke (eds), *Karl Polanyi, Globalisation and the Potential of Law in Transnational Markets* (Oxford, Hart Publishing, 2011).

Kriesi, H, *West European Politics in the Age of Globalization* (Cambridge, Cambridge University Press, 2009).

Kumm, M, 'The Idea of Socratic Contestation and the Right to Justification: The Point of Rights-based Proportionality Review' (2010) 4 *Law & Ethics of Human Rights* 157.

Kurcz, B and Vallindas, D, 'Can General measures be ... Selective? Some Thoughts on the Interpretation of a State Aid Definition' (2008) 45 *Common Market Law Review* 159.

Ladeur, KH, '"Conflicts Law as Europe's Constitutional Form" ... and the Conflict of Social Norms as Its Infrastructure' in C Joerges and C Glinski (eds), *European Crisis and the Transformation of Transnational Governance: Authoritarian Managerialism versus Democratic Governance* (Oxford, Hart Publishing, 2013).

Lane, JE, *New Public Management* (Abingdon, Routledge, 2002).

Lang, A, 'Reconstructing Embedded Liberalism: John Gerard Ruggie and Constructivist Approaches to the Study of the International Trade Regime' (2006) 9 *Journal of International Economic Law* 81.

—— 'The Legal Construction of Economic Rationalities?' (2013) 40 *Journal of Law and Society* 155.

Lange, B, Haines, F and Thomas, D (eds), *Regulatory Transformations: Rethinking Economy-Society Interactions* (Oxford, Hart Publishing, 2015).

Lavrijssen, S, 'The Protection of Non-Competition Interests; What Role for Competition Authorities after Lisbon?' (2010) 5 *European Law Review* 635.

Lenaerts, K, 'The Court's Outer and Inner Selves: Exploring the External and Internal Legitimacy of the European Court of Justice' in H Clemens et al (eds), *Judging Europe's Judges: The Legitimacy of the Case Law of the European Court of Justice* (Oxford, Hart Publishing, 2013).

—— and Heremans, T, 'Contours of a European Social Union in the Case-Law of the European Court of Justice' (2006) 2 *European Constitutional Law Review* 101.

Lianos, I, 'Some Reflections on the Question of the Goals of EU Competition Law' (2013) CLES Working Paper Series 3/2013.

—— 'In Memoriam Keck: The Reformation of the EU Law on the Free Movement of Goods' (2015) 2 *European Law Review* 225.

Liebfried, S and Pierson, P, 'Semisovereign Welfare States: Social Policy in a Multitiered Europe' in S Liebfried and P Pierson (eds), *European Social Policy: Between Fragmentation and Integration* (Washington, Brooking Institution, 1995) 43.

Lindsay MJ, 'In Search of Laissez-Faire Constitutionalism' (2010) 3 *Harvard Law Review* 55.

Lindstrom, N, 'Service Liberalization in the Enlarged EU: A Race to the Bottom or the Emergence of Transnational Political Conflict?' (2010) 49 *Journal of Common Market Studies* 1307–27.

Lopez JJP, *The Concept of State Aid under EU Law—From Internal Market to Competition and beyond* (Oxford, Oxford University Press, 2015).

Lovdahl-Gormsen, L, 'The Conflict Between Economic Freedom and Consumer Welfare in the Modernization of Article 82 EC' (2007) 3 *European Competition Journal* 329.

Lugard, P and Hancher, L, 'Honey, I Shrunk the Article! A Critical Assessment of the Commission's Notice on Article 81(3) of the EC Treaty' (2004) 25 *European Competition Law Review* 410.

Lyon-Caen, G, 'L'infiltration du droit du travail par le droit de la concurrence' (1992) *Droit ouvrier* 313.

Macaulay, S. 'Non-Contractual Relations in Business: A Preliminary Study' (1963) 28 *American Sociological Review* 55.

Maduro MP, 'Reforming the Market or the State? Article 30 and the European Constitution: Economic Freedom and Political Rights' (1997) 3 *European Law Journal* 55.

—— *We the Court: the European Court of Justice and the European Economic Constitution* (Oxford, Hart Publishing, 1998).

Majone, G, *Dilemmas of European Integration. The Ambiguities and Pitfalls of Integration by Stealth* (Oxford, Oxford University Press, 2005).

—— 'The Deeper Euro-Crisis or: The Collapse of the EU Political Culture of Total Optimism' EUI Working Paper LAW 2015/10.

Malmberg, J and Sigeman, T, 'Industrial Action and EU Economic Freedoms: The Autonomous Collective Bargaining Model Curtailed by the European Court of Justice' (2008) 45 *Common Market Law Review* 1115.

Marglin, S and Schor, J, *The Golden Age of Capitalism: Reinterpreting the Postwar Experience* (Oxford, Oxford University Press, 1990).

Marks, G, Hooghe, L and Blank, K, 'European Integration since the 1980s: State-Centric versus Multi-Level Governance' (1996) 34 *Journal of Common Market Studies* 343.

Mathisen G, 'Consistency and Coherence as Conditions for Justification of Member State Measures Restricting Free Movement' (2010) 47(4) *Common Market Law Review* 1021.

McCormick, J, *Environmental Policy in the European Union* (Basingstoke, Palgrave, 2001).

McLaren, L, 'Explaining Mass-Level Euroskepticism: Identity, Interests, and Institutional Distrust' (2007) 42 *Acta Politica* 233.

Menendez, A, 'European Citizenship after Martinez Sala and Baumbast: Has European Law Become More Human but Less Social?'w RECON Online Working Paper 2009/05 (Oslo, University of Oslo, ARENA—Centre for European Studies, 2009).

—— 'United they Diverge? From Conflicts to Constitutional Theory? Critical Remarks on Joerges' Theory of Conflicts of Law' RECON WP 2011/6 (Oslo, 2011).

—— 'Which Citizenship? Whose Europe?—The Many Paradoxes of European Citizenship' (2014) 15 *German Law Journal* 907.

Micklitz, HW, 'Social Justice and Access Justice in Private Law' (2011) EUI Working Paper Law 2011/02.

Moller, K, 'Proportionality and Rights Inflation' in G Huscroft, BW Miller, and G Webber (eds), *Proportionality and the Rule of Law: Rights, Justification, Reasoning* (Cambridge, Cambridge University Press, 2014) 155–72.

Monti, G, 'Article 81 EC and Public Policy' (2002) 39 *Common Market Law Review* 1057.

—— *EC Competition Law* (Boston, Cambridge University Press, 2006).

—— 'EU Competition Law from Rome to Lisbon' in C Heide-Jorgensen et al (eds), *Aims and Values in Competition Law* (Copenhagen, DJOF Publishing, 2013).

—— and Mulder, J, 'Escaping the Clutches of EU Competition Law' (2017) 5 *European Law Review* 635.

Monti, M, Commissioner for Competition, European Commission, 'Competition in Professional Services: New Light and New Challenges' for Bundesanwaltskammer Berlin (2003) available at http://europa.eu/rapid/press-release_SPEECH-03-149_en.htm.

Morijn, J, 'Balancing Fundamental Rights and Common Market Freedoms in Union Law: Schmidberger and Omega in the Light of the European Constitution' (2006) 12 *European Law Journal* 15–40.

Mortelmans, K, 'Towards Convergence in the Application of the Rules on Free Movement and Competition?' (2001) 38 *Common Market Law Review* 613.

Mulder, J, 'A New Chapter in the European Court of Justice Gambling Saga: A Stacked Deck?' (2011) 38(3) *Legal Issues of Economic Integration* 243.

—— 'Finding the Public Interest and the Case of the Friesian Horse' 2013 ACLE Conference Paper http://acle.uva.nl/events/competition--regulation-meetings/conference-papers-9th-cr-meeting-2013.html.

—— 'Re-embedding EU Governance Fields: A Research Agenda' in C Joerges and C Glinski (eds), *The European Crisis and the Transformation of Transnational Governance. Authoritarian Managerialism versus Democratic Governance* (Oxford, Hart Publishing, 2014) 181.

—— 'Op het snijvlak van onafhankelijkheid en openheid: wat is de rol van de ACM in een duurzamemaatschappij?' (2014) *SEW* 565–78.

—— 'Een duurzame maatschappij, wat mag dat kosten?' (2015) 1400 *NJB* 1912–20.

—— 'Responsive Adjudication and the Social Legitimacy of the Internal Market' (September 2016) *European Law Journal* 597.

—— Zomer, S, Benning, T and Leenheer, J, 'Economic Assessment ACM, Effects of the Chicken of Tomorrow—Costs and Benefits for Consumers' (October 2014) (accessible at acm.nl).

Müller, T, 'Efficiency Control in State Aid and the Power of Member States to Define SGEIs' (2009) 1 *European State Aid Law Quarterly* 8.

Munck, R, 'Globalization and Contestation: A Polanyian Problematic' (2006) 3 *Globalizations* 175.

Nazzini, R, 'Article 81 EC Between Time Present and Time Past—A Normative Critique of "Restriction of Competition" in EU Law' (2006) 43 *Common Market Law Review* 497.

Neven, D and Verouden, V, 'Towards a more Refined Economic Approach in State Aid Control' in W Mederer, N Pesaresi and M van Hoof (eds), *EU Competition Law* (Deventer, Claeys & Casteels, 2008) 99.

Nicolaides, P, 'Fiscal State Aid in the EU: the Limits of Tax Autonomy' (2004) 27 *World Competition* 319.

Niglia, L, 'Eclipse of the Constitution' (2016) 22 *European Law Journal* 132.

Nihoul, P, '"Freedom of Choice": The Emergence of a Powerful Concept in European Competition Law' (2012) 3 *Concurrences* 55.

Nourse, V and Shaffer, G, 'Varieties of New Legal Realism: Can a New World Order Prompt a New Legal Theory?' (2009) 95 *Cornell Law Review* 65.

Novitz, T, 'A Human Rights Analysis of the Viking and Laval Judgments' (2007–08) 10 *Cambridge Yearbook of European Legal Studies* 541.

Odudu, O, 'Interpreting Article 81(1): Object as Subjective Intention' (2001) 26 *European Law Review* 60.

—— *The Boundaries of EC Competition Law: The Scope of Article 81* (Oxford, Oxford University Press, 2006).

—— 'The Wider Concerns of Competition Law' (2010) 30 *Oxford Journal of Legal Studies* 599.

OECD, *Public Administration after 'New Public Management': Value for Money in Government, vol 1* (Paris, OECD Publishing, 2010).

Oliver, P, *Free Movement of Goods in the European Community: under Articles 28 to 30 of the EC Treaty* (London, Sweet & Maxwell, 2003).

—— 'Of Trailers and Jet Skis: Is the Case Law on Article 34 TFEU Hurtling in a New Direction?' (2011) 33 *Fordham International Law Journal* 1469.

Osborne, D and Gaebler, T, "Reinventing Government: how the Entrepreneurial Spirit is Transforming the Public Sector' (New York, Addison Wesley Publishing Company, 1992).

Pallemaerts, M, *The New Climate Policies of the European Union: Internal Legislation and Climate Diplomacy* (Brussels, Vubpress, 2010).

Paulus, AL, 'Commentary to Andreas Fischer-Lescano and Gunther Teubner: The Legitimacy of International Law and the Role of the State' (2005) 23 *Michigan Journal of International Law* 1047.

Picciotto, S, 'Liberalization and Democratization: The Forum and the Hearth in the Era of Cosmopolitan Post-Industrial Capitalism' (2000) 63 *Law and Contemporary Problems* 157.

Pijnacker-Hordijk, H, 'Beoordeling van duurzaamheidsinitiatieven onder het mededingingsrecht' (2013) 6 *Markt & Mededinging* 15.

Piris, JC, *The Lisbon Treaty: A Legal and Political Analysis* (Cambridge, Cambridge University Press, 2010).

Polanyi, K, *The Great Transformation: The Political and Economic Origins of our Time*, 2nd edn (Boston MA, The Beacon Press, [1944] 2001).

Posner, R, *Economic Analysis of Law* (Boston, Little, Brown, 1972).

—— 'Social Norms and the Law: An Economic Approach' (1997) 87 *The American Economic Review* 365.

Prechal, S, 'Free Movement and Procedural Requirements: Proportionality Reconsidered' (2008) 3 *Legal Issues of Economic Integration* 201.

Prosser, T, *The Limits of Competition Law* (Oxford, Oxford University Press, 2005).

—— 'Competition Law and Public Services: From Single Market to Citizenship Rights' (2005) 11 *European Public Law* 543.

Putnam, H, 'Meaning and Reference' (1973) 70 *The Journal of Philosophy* 699.

Quigley, C, 'General Taxation and State Aid' in A Biondi, P Eeckhout and J Flynn (eds), *The Law of State Aid in the European Union* (Oxford, Oxford University Press, 2004) 207.

—— *European State Aid Law and Policy* (Oxford, Hart Publishing, 2015).

Rawi, A and Ruggie, JG, 'The Principles of Embedded Liberalism: Social Legitimacy and Global Capitalism' in D Moss and J Cisternino (eds), *New Perspectives on Regulation* (Cambridge, Cambridge University Press, 2009) 151–62.

Regan, M, 'Public Infrastructure Procurement: A Comparative Analysis of Adversarial and Non-adversarial Contracting Arrangements' (2012) *Public Infrastructure Bulletin* 3.

Reynolds, S, 'Housing Policy as a Restriction of Free Movement and MSs Discretion to Design Programmes of Social Protection: Libert' (2015) 52 *Common Market Law Review* 259.

Rodrigues, S, 'The European Commission's Reform Strategy' in E Szyszcak and JW van de Gronden (eds), *Financing Services of General Economic Interest* (The Hague, TMC Asser Press, 2013).

Rodrik, D, *The Globalization Paradox* (London/New York, WW Norton, 2011).

Rompuy, B, van, *Economic Efficiency: The Sole Concern of Modern Antitrust Policy? Non-Efficiency Considerations under Article 101 TFEU* (Alphen aan den Rijn, Kluwer, 2012).

Rose, NS, *Governing the Present: Administering Economic, Social and Personal Life* (Cambridge, Polity, 2008).
Ross, M, 'State Aids: Maturing into a Constitutional Problem' (1995) *Yearbook of European Law* 79.
—— 'State Aid and National Courts: Definitions and Other Problems—a Case of Premature Emancipation?' (2000) 37 *Common Market Law Review* 401.
—— 'Article 16 EC and Services of General Economic Interest: from Derogation to Obligation' (2000) 25 *European Law Review* 22.
—— 'Decentralization, Effectiveness, and Modernization: Contradiction in Terms?' in A Biondi, P Eeckhout and J Flynn (eds), *The Law of State Aid in the European Union* (Oxford, Oxford University Press, 2004).
—— 'Promoting Solidarity: From Public Services to a European Model of Competition?' (2007) 44 *Common Market Law Review* 1057.
—— 'A Healthy Approach to Services of General Economic Interest? The BUPA Judgment in the CJEU of First Instance' (2009) 34 *European Law Review* 127.
Ruggie, JG, 'International Regimes, Transactions and Change: Embedded Liberalism in the Postwar Economic Order, International Organization' (1982) 36(2) *International Regimes* 379.
—— 'Multilateralism: The Anatomy of an Institution' (1992) 46(3) *International Organization* 561.
—— 'Taking Embedded Liberalism Global: The Corporate Connection', Institute for International Law and Justice Working Paper 2003/2, New York University School of Law.
Rusche, TM, 'The Almunia Package' in E Szyszcak and JW van de Gronden (eds), *Financing Services of General Economic Interest* (The Hague, TMC Asser Press, 2013) 108.
Sabel, CF and Zeitlin, J, *Experimentalist Governance in the European Union towards a New Architecture* (Oxford, Oxford University Press, 2010).
Sandel, M, *What Money Can't Buy* (New York, Farrar, Straus and Giroux, 2012).
Sangiovanni, A, 'Solidarity in the European Union' (2013) 196 *Oxford Journal of Legal Studies* 1.
Sassen, S, 'On Concentration and Centrality in the Global City' in P Knox, L Taylor and J Peter (eds), *World Cities in a World-System* (Cambridge, Cambridge University Press, 1995) 63–75.
Sauter, W, 'The Economic Constitution of the European Union' (1998) 4 *Columbia Journal of European Law* 27.
—— and Schepel, H, *State and Market in European Union Law: the Public and Private Spheres of the Internal Market before the EU Courts* (Cambridge, Cambridge University Press, 2009).
Savevska, M, 'Polanyian Reading of the Socio-Economic Transformations of the European Union' (2014) 22 *Journal of Contemporary European Studies* 395.
Scharffs, BG, 'Adjudication and the Problems of Incommensurability' (2001) 42 *William and Mary Law Review* 1367.
Scharpf, FW, 'Negative and Positive Integration in the Political Economy of European Welfare States' in G Marks, FW Scharpf, P Schmitter and W Streeck (eds), *Governance in the European Union* (London Sage Publications, 1996) 15.
—— 'The European Social Model: Coping with Challenges of Diversity' (2002) 40 *Journal of Common Market Studies* 645.

—— 'The Asymmetry of European Integration, or why the EU Cannot be a "Social Market Economy"' (2009) 8 *Socio-Economic Review* 211.
—— 'Legitimacy in the Multilevel European Polity' (2009) 1 *European Political Science Review* 173.
—— 'After the Crash: A Perspective on Multilevel European Democracy' (2015) 21 *European Law Journal* 384.
Schepel H, 'Delegation of Regulatory Powers to Private Parties under EC Competition Law: Towards a Procedural Public Interest Test' (2002) 39 *Common Market Law Review* 31.
—— *The Constitution of Private Governance: Product Standards in the Regulation of Integrating Markets* (Oxford, Hart Publishing, 2005).
—— 'Constitutionalising the Market, Marketising the Constitution, and to Tell the Difference: On the Horizontal Application of the Free Movement Provisions in EU Law' (2012) 18 *European Law Journal* 177–200.
—— 'Rules of Recognition: A Constructivist Approach to Transnational Private Regulation' in PF Kjaer, P Jurčys and R Yatsunami (eds), *Regulatory Hybridization in the Transnational Sphere* (Leiden, Martinus Nijhoff Publishers, 2013) 193.
Sciarra, S, 'Viking and Laval: Collective Labour Rights and Market Freedoms in the Enlarged EU' (2007–08) 10 *Cambridge Yearbook of European Legal Studies* 563.
Scott J, 'Mandatory or Imperative Requirements in the EU and the WTO' in C Barnard and J Scott, *The Law of the Single European Market: Unpacking the Premises* (Oxford, Hart Publishing, 2002) 269.
—— and Marshall, G, *A Dictionary of Sociology* (Oxford, Oxford University Press, 2009).
Schiek, D, *Economic and Social Integration: the Challenge for EU Constitutional Law* (Cheltenham, Edward Elgar, 2012).
—— 'The EU Constitution of Social Governance in an Economic Crisis in Defence of a Transnational Dimension to Social Europe' (2013) 2 *Maastricht Journal of Comparative and European Law* 185.
—— 'The EU's Socio-economic Model(s) and the Crisi(e)s—any Perspectives?' in D Schiek (ed), *The EU Economic and Social Model in the Global Crisis* (Farnham, Ashgate, 2013).
Schleifer, P, 'Creating Legitimacy for Private Rules: Explaining the Choice of Legitimation Strategies in Transnational NON-State Governance' EUI Working Paper 2015 RSCAS 2015/62.
Schmidt, V, 'Democracy and Legitimacy in the European Union Revisited: Input, Output and "Throughput"' (2013) 61 *Political Studies* 2.
Shaw, J, *Social Law and Policy in an Evolving European Union* (Oxford, Hart Publishing, 2000).
Shuibhne NN, 'Margins of Appreciation: National Values, Fundamental Rights and EC Free Movement Law' (2009) 32 *European Law Review* 230–56.
—— *The Coherence of EU Free Movement Law* (Oxford, Oxford University Press, 2013).
—— and Maci, M, 'Proving Public Interest: The Growing Impact of Evidence in Free Movement Case Law' (2010) 50(4) *Common Market Law Review* 965–1005.
Simmel, G, 'The Sociology of Conflict. I' (1904) 9 *American Journal of Sociology* 491.
Smith, A, *An Inquiry into the Nature and Causes of the Wealth of Nations* (London, George Routledge & Sons, 1776; reprint, 1893).
Snell, J, 'The Notion of Market Access: A Concept or a Slogan?' (2010) 47(2) *Common Market Law Review* 437.

—— 'Varieties of Capitalism and the Limits of European Economic Integration' (2011) 13 *Cambridge Yearbook of European Legal Studies* 415.

Somek, A, *Individualism: An Essay on the Authority of the European Union* (Oxford, Oxford University Press, 2008).

—— 'The Argument from Transnational Effects I: Representing Outsiders through Freedom of Movement' (2010) 16 *European Law Journal* 320.

—— *Engineering Equality: An Essay on European Anti-Discrimination Law* (Oxford, Oxford University Press, 2011).

—— 'The Social Question in a Transnational Context' LSE 'Europe in Question' Discussion Paper series, June 2011.

Spaventa, E, 'From Gebhard to Carpenter: Towards a (non-)economic European Constitution' (2004) 41 *Common Market Law Review* 743–73.

—— 'Leaving "Keck" behind?: The Free Movement of Goods after the Rulings in "Commission v Italy" and "Mickelsson and Roos"' (2009) 34(6) *European Law Review* 914.

Sternberg, E, 'Justifying Public Intervention without Market Externalities: Karl Polanyi's Theory of Planning in Capitalism' (1993) 53 *Public Administration Review* 100.

Streeck W, 'Beneficial Constraints: On the Economic Limits of Rational Voluntarism' in J Rogers Hollingsworth and R Boyer (eds), *Contemporary Capitalism: The Embeddedness of Institutions* (Cambridge, Cambridge University Press, 1997) 197–218.

—— 'Educating Capitalists: A Rejoinder to Wright and Tsakalotos' (2010) 2 *Socio-Economic Review* 425.

—— 'E Pluribus Unum? Varieties and Commonalities of Capitalism' (2010) Cologne: MPIfG Discussion Paper 10/12.

—— 'The Crises of Democratic Capitalism' (2011) 71 *New Left Review* 26.

—— 'Democratic Capitalism and its Contradictions' in A Schäfer and W Streeck (eds), *Politics in the Age of Austerity* (Cambridge, Polity Press, 2013).

Streit M and Mussler W, 'The Economic Constitution of the European Community: From Rome to Maastricht' (1994) 5 *Constitutional Political Economy* 319.

Sunstein, CR, 'Incommensurability and Valuation in Law' (1994) 92 *Michigan Law Review* 779.

Syrpis, P, 'Reconciling Economic Freedoms and Social Rights—The Potential of *Commission v Germany* (Case C-271/08, Judgment of 15 July 2010) (2011) 40 *Industrial Law Journal* 222.

—— and Novitz, T, 'Economic and Social Rights in Conflict: Political and Judicial Approaches to their Reconciliation' (2008) 33 *European Law Review* 411.

Szyszczak, E, 'Public Services in Competition Markets' (2001) 21 *Yearbook of European Law* 35.

—— *The Regulation of the State in Competitive Markets in the EU* (Oxford, Hart Publishing, 2007).

Terry LS, 'The European Commission Project Regarding Competition in Professional Services' (2009) 29 *Northwestern Journal of International Law & Business* 1.

Teubner, G, *Transnational Economic Constitutionalism in the Varieties of Capitalism* (Ms, Frankfurt, 2015).

—— and Fischer-Lescano, A, 'Regime-collisions: The Vain Search for Legal Unity in the Fragmentation of Global Law' (2004) 25 *Michigan Journal of International Law* 999.

—— 'Reply to Andreas L. Paulus Consensus as Fiction of Global Law' (2003) 25 *Michigan Journal of International Law* 1059.

Tholoniat, L, 'The Career of the Open Method of Coordination: Lessons from a "Soft" EU Instrument' (2010) 33 *West European Politics* 93.

Toth, F, 'Healthcare Policies over the Last 20 Years: Reforms and Counter-Reforms' (2010) 95 *Health Policy* 82.

Townley, C, *Article 81 EC and Public Policy* (Oxford, Hart Publishing, 2009).

Tsakalotos, E, 'Market Constraints, Economic Performance and Political Power: Modernizers versus Leftists' (2004) 2 *Socio-Economic Review* 415.

Tulio, M, Zanin, F and Migueles, CP, 'Trust as an Element of Informal Coordination and its Relationship with Organizational Performance' (2013) 14 *EconomiA* 77.

Tuori, K and Tuori, K, *The Eurozone Crisis* (Cambridge, Cambridge University Press, 2014).

Vedder, H, *Competition Law and Environmental Protection in Europe: Towards Sustainability?* (Brussels, Europa Law Publishing, 2003).

Verouden, V, 'EU State Aid Control: The Quest for Effectiveness' (2015) 14 *European State Aid Law Quarterly* 459.

Vossestein, J, annotation of Wouters in (2002) 39 *Common Market Law Review* 841.

Watson, P, *EU Social and Employment Law* (Oxford, Oxford University Press, 2009).

Weatherhill, S, 'The Court's Case Law on the Internal Market: "A Circumloquacious Statement of the Result, Rather than a Reason for Arriving at It"?' in H Clemens et al, *Judging Europe's Judges: The Legitimacy of the Case Law of the European Court of Justice* (Oxford, Hart Publishing, 2013) 104.

—— 'Viking and Laval: the EU Internal Market Perspective' in M Freedland and J Prassl (eds), *Viking, Laval and Beyond* (Oxford, Hart Publishing, 2014) 32.

Weiler, JHH, 'The Transformation of Europe' (1991) 100 *Yale Law Journal* 2403.

—— 'Fin-De-Siècle: Do the New Clothes Have an Emperor?' in JHH Weiler, *The Constitution of Europe: 'Do the New Clothes Have an Emperor?' And other Essays on European Integration* (Cambridge, Cambridge University Press, 1999) 238.

—— 'Fundamental Rights and Fundamental Boundaries' in JHH Weiler, The Constitution of Europe: 'Do the New Clothes Have an Emperor' and other Essays on European Integration, (Cambridge, Cambridge University Press, 1999) 102–29.

—— 'The Constitution of the Common Market Place: Text and Context in the Evolution of the Free Movement of Goods' in P Craig and G De Burca (eds), *The Evolution of EU Law* (Oxford, Oxford University Press 1999) 372.

—— 'In the Face of Crisis: Input Legitimacy, Output Legitimacy and the Political Messianism of European Integration' (2012) 34 *Journal of European Integration* 826.

—— 'Van Gend en Loos: The Individual as Subject and Object and the Dilemma of European Legitimacy' (2014) 12 *International Journal of Constitutional Law* 94.

—— and Lockhart, NJS, '"Taking Rights Seriously" Seriously: The European Court of Justice and its Fundamental Rights Jurisprudence' (1995) 32 *Common Market Law Review* 593.

Wendt, I, *EU Competition Law and Liberal Professions: an Uneasy Relationship?* (Leiden, Brill Academic Publishers, 2012).

Wesseling, R, *The Modernisation of EC Antitrust Law* (Oxford, Hart Publishing, 2000).

Whish, R and Bailey, D, *Competition Law* (Oxford, Oxford University Press, 2012).

Whitman, J, 'Consumerism versus Producerism: A Study in Comparative Law' (2007) 117 *Yale Law Journal* 340.

Wilson, T, 'Infrastructure Financing and State Aid Post Leipzig-Halle' (2014) 1 *European State Aid Law Quarterly* 24.
Winterstein, A, 'Nailing the Jellyfish: Social Security and Competition Law' (1999) 20 *European Competition Law Review* 324.
Witt, AC, 'Public Policy Goals under EU Competition Law: now is the Time to set the House in Order' (2012) 8 *European Competition Journal* 443.
—— *The More Economic Approach to EU Antitrust Law* (Oxford, Hart Publishing, 2016).
Witte, B, de, 'Community Law and National Constitutional Values' (1991) *Legal Issues of European Integration* 1.
—— 'Non-market Values in Internal Market Legislation' in N Shuibhne (ed), *Regulating the Internal Market* (Cheltenham, Edward Elgar, 2006) 63.
Witte, F, de, 'Transnational Solidarity and the Mediation of Conflicts of Justice in Europe' (2012) 18 *European Law Journal* 694.
—— 'Sex, Drugs & EU Law: The Recognition of Moral and Ethical Diversity in EU Law' (2013) 50(6) *Common Market Law Review* 1545.
—— *Justice in the EU: The Emergence of Transnational Solidarity* (Oxford, Oxford University Press, 2015).
Woldendorp, J, *The Polder Model: From Disease to Miracle? Dutch Neo-corporatism 1965–2000* (PhD thesis, Vrije Universiteit Amsterdam, 2005).
Woodruff, D, 'Governing by Panic: The Politics of the Eurozone Crisis' LEQS Paper No 81/2014 (October 2014).
Zimmer, D (ed), *The Goals of Competition Law* (Cheltenham, Edward Elgar, 2012).

Index

accountability:
  competition rules, 145–46, 162, 169
  state aid law, 185, 196, 215, 221, 234–35
adjudication, *see* free movement adjudication
Albany case:
  responsiveness, 147–49
Altmark case, 183, 193–95
  safe harbour, 219
Altmark framework:
  BUPA case, 209–14
  Chronopost case, 211–12
  mutual responsiveness, 209–10
    efficiency requirement, 211
    services of general economic interest, 210–14
  Zweckverband case, 212
Amsterdam Treaty:
  coherence of EU policies, 55–56
  European Employment Strategy, 27
animal welfare, 120, 132–33
  Chicken of Tomorrow case, 131–32, 141–44
    mutual responsiveness, 168–69
  competition rules and, 170, 232
    minimum standards, 141, 143, 166–67
    quantification approach and, 133
Arduino case:
  mutual responsiveness, 160–61
argument from containment, *see* transnational effects

balancing unity and diversity, 1, 7, 8–9, 22, 25, 37–38, 225–27
  competition law, 117–18, 136, 169, 231
    non-competition interests, 124–25, 128
    responsiveness, 146–47
  diagonal conflicts, adjudication of, 8
  free movement adjudication context, 1–2, 56, 71–72, 228
    responsiveness, 56–57, 62, 64, 66, 107, 110–12
  state aid law, 173–74, 176, 205–7, 235–36
beneficial constraints, 28–29
better regulation, 79, 227, 237
BUPA case:
  application of *Altmark*, 209–14

capitalism, varieties of, 31–32, 60
Caporoso, J, 45–46
categorisation:
  proportionality and, 11, 62, 225–26
  state aid, 181
Chicken for Tomorrow case:
  animal welfare, 131–32, 141–44, 168–69
  competition law:
    irreconcilable conflicts, 141–44
    mutual responsiveness, 168–69
Chronopost case, 200–1, 211–12
Cipolla case:
  mutual responsiveness, 161–62
coherence, 55–56
  competition law, 164–65, 219
    good governance and, 12, 217
  free movement of adjudication, 96, 98–99, 229–30
    irreconcilability and, 111
    mutual responsiveness, 110
    proportionality analysis and, 100–1
    Viking case, 107–8
    Volkswagen case, 105
commensurability, *see* incommensurability
competition law, 16–17
  animal welfare, 120, 131–33
  balancing market integration and social interests, 117–18
  CJEU case law, 134–36
    Albany case, 147–49
    Arduino case, 160–61
    Chicken of Tomorrow case, 141–44
    Cipolla case, 161–62
    Energy Agreement for Sustainable Growth case, 138–41
    Friesian Horse case, 136–38
    Mauri case, 162–63
    Poucet and Pistre case, 149–54
    responsiveness, 146–63
    Wouters case, 155–60
  Commission intervention, 144–46
  competition law assessments:
    non-competition interests, 123–26
  efficiency-based exemption criteria, 11, 58, 119–20, 226
  environmental protection, 120, 130
  expressive value of competition law, 126–27
    conflicts between economic and social policies, 127–29
    non-competition considerations, 127–29
  free movement rules and, 115–16

goals, 121–23
human rights, 120–21
incommensuratbility, 126–27
modernisation and economisation, 114, 118–20
national competition authorities, 120
self-assessment, 120
private enforcement, 120–21
quantification, 129–30, 133, 146–47
responsiveness:
Albany case, 147–49
Arduino case, 160–61
Cipolla case, 161–62
Mauri case, 162–63
Poucet and Pistre case, 149–54
Wouters case, 155–60
self-regulation, 113
demand, 114
supply, 113–14
social legitimacy and:
animal health and welfare, 232
balancing competing values, 231
incommensurability, 230
indeterminacy, 230
minimum standards, 230–1
mutual responsiveness, 232–34
non-competition interests, 231–32
sustainability, 232
valuation in law, 230
social sphere and, 116–17
societal dialogue and, 133–34
consistency, 11–12, 55–56, 95, 100–1, 103–5, 107–8, 111, 148–49, 207, 217, 229–30
see also coherence
consumer interests, 98, 123–24, 143
Court of Justice of the EU (CJEU):
calls to balance economic and social objectives, 22
competition law, 134–36
Chicken of Tomorrow case, 141–44
Energy Agreement for Sustainable Growth case, 138–41
Friesian Horse case, 136–38
free movement adjudication, 72–73
cold-calling, 74–75
culture of justification, 78–81
Dassonville formula, 73
football transfers, 74
insurance premiums, 75
Keck approach, 73–74
market-access test, 73–74, 81
mode of reasoning, 71
proportionality principle, 78–81
public interest requirement, 69
qualification to market access, 74–77
subordinate nature of social interests, 69–70
unjustifiable obstacles, 76–77
judicial activism, 2–3
labour standards, 48
Laval case, 48
minimal social rights, interpretation of, 7–8
Polanyian analysis of, 45
meaning of embeddedness, 45–47
non-discrimination v non-restriction, 47–48
proportionality principle, 78–81
development of rights inflation proportionality model, 82–83
function of proportionality, 81–2
stages of proportionality assessment, 81
substantive efficiency model, 84–89
tax-avoidance practices, 48
undermining national social foundations, 46–47
Viking case, 48

Dassonville formula, 73–74, 75, 180, 215–16, 235
democracy:
capitalism and, 37–38
proportionality, function of, 81–82
deregulation of industry, 2, 28, 69, 70
diagonal conflicts, 8–9, 71, 102–3
solidarity, 103
substantive efficiency, 85–86
substantive proportionality, 32
direct effect, 29, 47, 205

efficiency-based exemption criteria, 11, 58, 119–20, 226
embedded liberalism, 9–10, 13, 38, 45–46, 49, 109, 115, 223–24, 229
Ruggie, 5, 21–22
transnational effects argument, 90, 102
see also social embeddedness of market liberalisation
embeddedness, 34–35, 39, 191
double-movement, 36, 39, 40–42
Polanyi, 35–39, 42–49
social embeddedness of market liberalisation, 5, 46, 49
Energy Agreement for Sustainable Growth case:
irreconcilable conflicts, 138–41
mutual responsiveness, 167–68
enforcement of laws:
competition rules, 30, 157
state aid law, 173, 175
environmental policies, 11, 27–28, 58, 117, 129–30, 226, 237
animal welfare, 132
electricity consumption,127–28
Energy Agreement for Sustainable Growth case, 138–41
mutual responsiveness, 167–68
road transport, 85–86, 89

state aid rules, 204, 205–9
town and country planning, 98
environmental protection, 55–56, 120, 148–49, 158–59
Euro-scepticism, 2–3
Europe 2020 Agenda, 27–28, 175
European Economic Community:
social competences, 5–6
European Employment Strategy, 27
European Union:
limited social competences, 22
structural institutional incapacity, 1–3
evaluative adjudication:
competition law, *see* competition law
efficiency-based exemption criteria, *see* competition law
free movement adjudication, *see* free movement adjudication
market-based evaluative standards, *see* state aid law
state aid law, *see* state aid law
strict proportionality, *see* free movement adjudication

free movement adjudication, 9–10, 16, 66–68, 109–10
EU organisational principles, 68–69
diagonal conflicts, 71–72
efficiency considerations, 70–71
public interest requirements, 69
valuation biases, 70–72
evaluation of social spheres, 32–33, 58–63
evaluative adjudicative method:
strict proportionality, 11, 32, 58, 62, 126–27, 226
function of proportionality, 81–82
housing policy, 32–33
incommensurability, 225
inconsistent/incoherent application, 100–1
indeterminacy, 225
margin of discretion/appreciation model, 89–91
mutual responsiveness, 102–3, 110–12
good governance, 91–100
margins of discretion, 89–91
Omega case, 105–6
substantive efficiency, 84–89
Viking case, 106–9
Volkswagen case, 103–5
procedural good governance model, 91–100
proportionality:
assessment, 81
evaluative adjudicative method, 11, 32, 58, 62, 126–27, 226
function of proportionality, 81–82
proportionality analysis, 228, 229
rights inflation proportionality model, 72–81, 82–83
strict proportionality, 11, 32, 58, 62, 126–27, 226
substantive proportionality, 32–33
responsiveness and, 62–63
mutual responsiveness, 64–65
rights inflation proportionality model, 72–81, 82–83
social legitimacy, 57–58, 63–65, 226–27
consequentialist evaluations, 229
efficiency-based exemption criteria, 58
embedded liberalism, 229
evaluation of regulatory intervention, 58–63, 226
good governance, 228–29
incoherence, 229
incommensurability, 228
inherent irreconcilability test, 230
internal market infrastructure, 229
margins of discretion, 228
market-based evaluative standards, 58, 226
mutual responsiveness, 228, 229
proportionality analysis, 228, 229
strict proportionality, 11, 32, 58, 62, 126–27, 226
transnational effects argument, 227–28
strict proportionality, 11, 32, 58, 62, 126–27, 226
substantive efficiency model, 11–12, 14–15, 84–89, 90, 100, 103, 104–5, 202–3, 215–16, 220–21, 225–27, 230, 238
economic substantive efficiency-orientated governance mechanisms, 41, 196, 235–36
substantive proportionality, 32–33
valuation in adjudication, 70–71, 225
Friesian Horse case:
irreconcilable conflicts, 136–38
mutual responsiveness, 165–67

globalisation, 6–7
good governance, *see* procedural good governance model
Granovetter, M, 46

health and safety and work, 26–27
healthcare markets, 8
Höpner, M, 3, 46–48, 59–60
human rights, 120–21

incommensurability, 60–2, 64, 225
competition law, 118, 126–27, 230
free movement adjudication, 83, 228
substantive efficiency model, 87–88, 106
mutual responsiveness dialogue, 60–62, 215
state aid law, 179–80
mutual responsiveness, 215
indeterminacy, 15, 58, 225, 237–38
competition law, 118, 126–33, 230

internal market adjudication, 13–15
  social legitimacy and, 57–63
internal market rules:
  interpretation by EU institutions, 6–7

Joerges, C:
  transnational effects argument:
    legitimacy of social deficit, 49–51
judicial activism, 2–3

Keck approach, 73–74, 76
Keynes, JM, 21

labour law (national), 5–6, 45–46
Laval case, 47–48, 69, 97–98, 108
legality, 74–75, 84, 176
legitimacy of governance:
  input legitimacy, 19
  output legitimacy, 12
  social legitimacy, *see* social legitimacy
  throughout legitimacy, 12
liberalisation, 3–4, 5, 28, 31, 47–48, 134, 160–61, 185, 188
Lisbon Treaty:
  abolition of trade barriers, 55
    balancing social objectives, 55
  competition law, 122–23
  consistency requirement, 55–56
  new Europe 2020 Agenda, 27–28
  Open Method of Coordination, 27
  responsiveness obligation, 54–57
  sustainable development, 148–49

Maastricht Treaty:
  Social Protocol of the Maastricht Treaty, 26–27
Maduro, M:
  transnational effects argument:
    legitimacy of social deficit, 51–53
margin of appreciation, *see* margin of discretion
margin of discretion, 12, 226–27
  freedom of movement, 88, 89–91, 93, 99, 100–1, 106, 108, 110, 228–29
  state aid law, 192–93, 202–3, 217, 219–20, 236
market access test, 16, 51, 66–67, 69, 70–71, 73–81, 82–83, 227
market-based evaluative standards, 11, 58, 181–82, 224–25, 226
  market economy operator principle, 182–84
  substantive efficiency model and, 202–3
Mauri case:
  mutual responsiveness, 162–63
minimum standards:
  animal welfare, 141–43, 168–69
  competition law, 120, 141–43, 168–69, 230
  fair trade, 27
  labour conditions, 120

mutual responsiveness, 12, 224
  competition law, 163–65, 169–70
    Chicken of Tomorrow case, 168–69
    Energy Agreement for Sustainable Growth case, 167–68
    Friesian Horse case, 165–67
  free movement adjudication, 102–3
    good governance, 91–100
    margins of discretion, 89–91
    Omega case, 105–6
    substantive efficiency, 84–89
    Viking case, 106–9
    Volkswagen case, 103–5
  social legitimacy through, 32–34
  state aid law, 171–72, 197
    Altmark framework, 209–14
    BUPA case, 209–11
    Chronopost case, 211–12
    Eventech case, 216–18
    Nox case, 216–17
    public powers of the state, 197–98
    required mutuality, 218–20
    Ryanair case, 198
    state as a private investor, 198–200
    Zweckverband case, 212–14

neoclassical economic theology, 4, 46
neoliberalism, 4, 111
New Public Management, 28–29, 185–86, 222, 236
Nice Treaty, 27
non-competition interests, 16–17
  competition law, 118, 133–36, 152–54, 163–64, 166–67
    Albany case, 147–48, 149
    collective negotiations, 170
    competition law assessments, 123–26, 127–33
    irreconcilability with competition interests, 231–32, 233
    non-competition-based public objectives, 169
    residual non-competitive interests, 169, 232
    solidarity, 170
    Wouters case, 157–59, 233
  see also environmental policy; environmental protection; consumer protection
non-contractual relations, 190
non-efficiency interests, *see* non-competition interests

Omega case:
  mutual responsiveness, 105–6
Open Method of Coordination, 27

Polanyi, K, 15, 223
  contemporary relevance, 38–39

embedded and disembedded socio-economic orders, 20–1
Great Transformation: The Political and Economic Origins of Our Time (The), 20, 35–38
Keynsian influence, 21
self-regulating markets, 35–36
capitalism and democracy, 37–38
commodification, 39
double-movement, 36, 39
embeddedness, 39
see also embeddedness
social legitimacy and, 34–35, 63
Polder model, 135
Poucet and Pistre case:
responsiveness, 149–54
privatisation and public sector, 2, 28, 185, 188
procedural good governance model, 226
freedom of movement:
collective action, 97
dental clinics, 91–92
football transfer fees, 91
games of change and gambling, 92–95, 99–100
judicial review, 96–97
monopolies, 95–98
planning of out-of-town retail outlets, 98
proportionality principle, 11
freedom of movement, 78–81
development of rights inflation proportionality model, 82–83
function of proportionality, 81–2
margin of discretion model, 89–91
procedural good governance model, 91–100
stages of proportionality assessment, 81
substantive efficiency model, 84–89
rights inflation proportionality model, 72–81, 82–83
strict proportionality, 11, 32, 58, 62, 126–27, 226
public interest, 22, 36–37, 69, 79–80, 82–83, 92, 94–95, 97, 105, 121, 124–25, 146, 150, 152–53, 162, 163–64, 228, 232–33
Friesian Horse case, 136, 166–67
background, 136–37
restriction of competition argument, 137–38
new public management tools and, 185–86
Wouters case, 155, 158–59, 160
public policy, 21–22, 28, 78–79
limiting competition, 115, 125, 128–29

reconciling social diversity and integration objectives, *see* balancing unity and diversity
responsiveness:
commodification, 44
competition law:
Albany case, 147–49
Arduino case, 160–61
Cipolla case, 161–62
Mauri case, 162–63
Poucet and Pistre case, 149–54
Wouters case, 155–60
double-movement and, 43–44
EU constitutional obligations, 54–57
integration into legal framework of internal market, 62
mutual responsiveness, 44–45
Polanyi's influence, 42–45
privilege and exclusion, 44
social deficit and, 43
state aid, 195–97
see also mutual responsiveness
rights inflation proportionality model, 72–81
Rome Treaty, 5, 26
Ruggie, JG:
embedded liberalism, 21

Schäfer, A, 46–47, 59–60
services of general economic interest (SGEI), 185, 192–95, 210–14, 218–21
services of general interest, *see* services of general economic interest
shareholders:
shareholder primacy, 103–4
state as a, 185, 199–200
smart regulation, 178, 237–38
social cohesion, 27–28, 33, 55, 58, 60, 87, 148–49, 190–91, 196, 228
social deficit, 3–5, 43
transnational effect and, 49–57
Social Dialogue, 27
social diversity, 1, 12, 14, 25
responsiveness and, 32–34
varieties of capitalism, 31–32, 60
value of, 31–32
social embeddedness of market liberalisation, 5–6, 13–14, 21–22
social exclusion, 27
social inclusion as an employment objective, 27–28
social legitimacy, 19–20
Giubbobian approach, 22
mutual responsiveness approach, 32–34
normative meaning, 20–21
Polanyian approach, 21
Ruggian approach, 21
see also competition law; free movement adjudication; state aid law
social spheres of the internal market, 23–24
negative influences on social spheres, 25–26, 29–31
objectives of internal market regime:
irreconcilability, 32
positive influence on social spheres, 25–29
social norms and the law, 24–25

socio-economic diversity:
  varieties of capitalism, 31–32, 60
  see also social diversity
solidarity, 6–7, 23, 46, 55–56, 60, 67, 103, 108, 131, 170, 190–91, 211, 224–25, 228, 233
  case law, 148–49, 151–54, 155–56, 158
Somek, A:
  economic due process test, 70, 77
  transnational effects argument, 15, 53–54, 61, 226–28, 229
state aid law, 17, 220–22
  block exemption regulations, 173
  competition distortions and, 173–74
  good governance model, 208–9
    Aggregates Levy, 206–7
    energy tax rebates, 205–6
    environmental protection, 204–8
    selective advantages as inherent features of regulatory schemes, 203–4
    social contributions of manual workers, 204–5
    unfair dismissals, 203
  market-based evaluative standards, 11, 58, 181–82, 226
    market economy operator principle, 182–84
    substantive efficiency model and, 202–3
  market economy operator principle, 182–84
    airport charges, 186
    Altmark case, 193–94
    crowding out effects, 188–92
    favourable conditions for repayment of state aid, 184–86
    services of general economic interest, 192–95
    state control over assets, 187–88
  margin of discretion, 220–21
  market specific state aid cases, 200–2
  mutual responsiveness, 171–72
    Altmark framework, 209–14
    BUPA case, 209–11
    Chronopost case, 211–12
    Eventech case, 216–18
    Nox case, 216–17
    public powers of the state, 197–98
    required mutuality, 218–20
    Ryanair case, 198
    state as a private investor, 198–200
    Zweckverband case, 212–14
  proceduralisation of rules, 220–21
    conflicts, 176–77
    EU Commission's 2005 State Aid Action Plan, 175
    General Block Exemption Regulation, 176
    incommensurability between evaluative standards, 179–80
    market failure, 177
    State Aid Modernisation initiative, 175–76
    TFEU, 174–75
  public procurement procedures, 193–95
  social legitimacy and, 234–35
    good governance, 236
    margin of discretion, 236
    market-based evaluations, 235–36
    mutual responsiveness, 236
    responsiveness, 236
  social objectives, impact on, 172–73
  substantive efficiency, 220
  valuation in state aid, 180
    nature of the measure, 180–81
substantive efficiency, 11, 225–26
  commensurability and, 87–88
  evaluative standards, *see* evaluative standards of substantive efficiency
  freedom of movement:
    beer purity measures, 84–85
    CJEU margin of discretion, 88–89
    minimum alcohol pricing, 87–88
    road transport restrictions, 85
    social hosing regulation, 86–87
  strict proportionality, 11, 22, 32, 58, 62, 126–27, 226
supremacy of EU law, 6–7, 8, 71, 86
supremacy of free market objectives, 2, 3–4
sustainability:
  Energy Agreement for Sustainable Growth case, 138–39
    valuation of social interests, 139–41

Tarrow, A, 45–46
trade interest bias:
  deregulation of the social, 2
  privatisation and public sector, 2
  scepticisms towards EU, 2
transnational effects argument, 10–11, 61–62, 64, 79, 171, 224, 226, 227–28
  embedded liberalism, 102
  good governance and, 170
  internalisation of transnational effects, 88, 90
  legitimacy of social deficit:
    Joerges, 49–51
    Maduro, 51–53
    responsiveness obligation, 54–57
    Somek, 53–54, 61
Treaty of Amsterdam, *see* Amsterdam Treaty
Treaty of Lisbon, *see* Lisbon Treaty
Treaty of Maastricht, *see* Maastricht Treaty
Treaty of Nice, *see* Nice Treaty
Treaty of Rome, *see* Rome Treaty
Treaty on European Union (TEU), 56
  balancing internal market objectives and social objectives, 56–57, 63

Treaty on the Functioning of the European Union (TFEU), *see* Lisbon Treaty

valuation in law, 225
  competition law, 118–45
  free movement adjudication, 68–83
  state aid law, 172–95
Viking case, 48, 69, 106–9

Volkswagen case:
  mutual responsiveness, 103–5

Wouters case:
  responsiveness, 155–60, 233

Zweckverband case:
  mutual responsiveness, 212